KING ARTHUR

ARTHURIAN CHARACTERS AND THEMES
VOLUME I
GARLAND REFERENCE LIBRARY OF THE HUMANITIES
VOLUME 1915

ARTHURIAN CHARACTERS AND THEMES

NORRIS J. LACY, *Series Editor*

KING ARTHUR
A Casebook
edited by Edward Donald Kennedy

TRISTAN AND ISOLDE
A Casebook
edited by Joan Tasker Grimbert

LANCELOT AND GUINEVERE
A Casebook
edited by Lori J. Walters

ARTHURIAN WOMEN
A Casebook
edited by Thelma S. Fenster

King Arthur
A Casebook

EDITED WITH AN INTRODUCTION BY
EDWARD DONALD KENNEDY

GARLAND PUBLISHING, INC.
NEW YORK AND LONDON
1996

Library of Congress Cataloging-in-Publication Data

King Arthur / edited by Edward Donald Kennedy.
        p.   cm. — (Arthurian characters and themes ; vol. 1)
(Garland reference library of the humanities ; vol. 1915)
    Includes bibliographical references.
    ISBN 0-8153-0495-1 (alk. paper)
    1. Arthur, King—Legends. 2. Arthurian romances—History and criti-
cism. 3. Kings and rulers in literature.   I. Kennedy, Edward Donald.
II. Series. III. Series: Garland reference library of the humanities ; vol.
1915.
PN686.A7K56   1996
809'.93351—dc20   95-36358
                                                                          CIP

Cover illustration: From the 1488 *Lancelot du Lac* (detail) published by
Jean Dupre. Reprinted courtesy of the Newberry Library, Chicago.

Printed on acid-free, 250-year-life paper
Manufactured in the United States of America

For Pat and Stephen

Contents

SERIES EDITOR'S PREFACE

This is volume 1 of Arthurian Characters and Themes, a new series of casebooks from Garland Publishing. The series includes volumes devoted to the best-known characters from Arthurian legend: Tristan and Isolde, Arthur, Lancelot and Guenevere, Merlin, Gawain, and Perceval. One is also devoted to Arthurian women in general, and one to the Grail. Others may be added.

Each volume offers an extended introductory survey and a bibliography and presents some twenty major essays on its subject. Several of the essays in each volume are newly commissioned for the series; the others are reprinted from their original sources. The previously published contributions date for the most part from the past fifteen years, although a few older, "classic" essays are included in several of the volumes, the criterion being the continuing importance of the study. All contributions are presented in English, and each volume includes essays that are translated here for the first time.

Heaviest emphasis remains on the development of the legend and its characters during the Middle Ages, but appropriate attention has been given also to modern, even very recent, treatments. Similarly, the central focus is on literature, but without excluding important discussions of visual, musical, and filmic arts. Thus, a number of the volumes are intently interdisciplinary in focus.

The proliferation of scholarly studies of Arthurian material is daunting. When the *Bibliographical Bulletin of the Arthurian Society* began publishing annual bibliographies, the first volume (1949) included 226 items (books, articles, and reviews). That number has increased regularly until, in the most recent volumes, some 700 items are listed per year. This increase shows no sign of abating. Furthermore, the major contributions to Arthurian scholarship are often dispersed widely through books and journals published through North America, Europe, and elsewhere.

As a result, it is extraordinarily difficult even for the professional medievalist to keep abreast of Arthurian scholarship, and it would be very nearly impossible for the non-scholar with serious Arthurian interests to select and locate a score of the major scholarly contributions devoted to a particular character or theme. These difficulties clearly dramatize the value of this series, but they also remain an insistent reminder that even the most informed selection of fifteen or twenty major essays requires us to omit many dozens of studies that may be equally instructive and engaging. Editors have attempted to remedy this situation insofar as possible by providing introductions that present other writers and texts, as well as bibliographies that document a good many important studies that could find no room in these volumes. In addition, many of the contributions that are included here will provide discussions of, or references to, other treatments that will be of interest to readers.

This volume, edited by Edward Donald Kennedy, includes a detailed introduction surveying the development of the figure and function of Arthur. Following that introduction and a thorough bibliography, the editor offers fifteen essays varying from broad surveys to studies of Hartmann von Aue, the French Vulgate Cycle, Malory, Polydore Vergil, Tennyson, T.H. White, and others.

The contributions by Professors Parins, McDonald, Mancoff, and Thompson are original essays prepared for this volume; the others have been previously published. (In the introduction and bibliography, an asterisk beside a title or an author's name identifies studies that are included in this book.) Six of the essays, as indicated in the headnotes preceding them, were originally published in French or German, and they have been translated into English for the first time. The headnotes also document the original place of publication for articles reprinted here.

Because permissions from copyright holders sometimes prohibited us from modifying the texts in any way, the decision was made to present all of them in their original form, with changes generally limited to the correction of obvious typographical errors. However, in some cases authors have, with permission, chosen to update, expand, or rework their contributions.

The necessity to reproduce many essays in the exact form of their original publication inevitably produces some inconsistencies. Most essays use documentary notes, but one includes a list of works cited and inserts parenthetical references to those works. In addition, style, usage, and even spelling (British versus American) may vary as well. Offsetting these inconsistencies is the advantage of having in one's hand a substantial selection of the finest available studies, new as well as previously published, of Arthurian characters and themes.

Herewith, then, a series of contributions to our understanding of one of the most famous figures in legend and literature.

Such a volume could not be produced without the generosity of museum officials and editors of presses and journals, who kindly gave permission for us to reproduce illustrations and articles. We are pleased to express our gratitude to all of them. Credits accompany essays and plates.

Norris J. Lacy

Introduction

King Arthur is probably the best-known character from medieval literature. Most readers of English are familiar with some of the stories about him: the boy Arthur pulls the sword from the stone and is proclaimed king; with the help of Merlin he establishes the Round Table, which becomes associated with the ideals of chivalry; his incestuous union with his half-sister results in the conception of Mordred, the son/nephew who will betray his father/uncle Arthur; the love of Arthur's wife Guinevere for his preeminent knight, Lancelot, leads to a civil war that ultimately destroys his kingdom; Arthur kills the usurper Mordred in combat; the wounded Arthur is taken to the Isle of Avalon, from which, according to some accounts, he will one day return. He is *rex quondam rexque futurus*, the once and future king.

Many of those familiar with stories about King Arthur know them not through medieval versions but through modern retellings for children; nineteenth- and twentieth-century poems and novels such as those of Tennyson, Mark Twain, T.H. White, Mary Stewart, Donald Barthelme, or Marion Zimmer Bradley; or films like *Monty Python and the Holy Grail* and John Boorman's *Excalibur*. New versions of the story of King Arthur appear in some form almost every year. Legends associated with him probably rank with the Bible and Greek and Roman mythology as popular sources for literature, music, art, and film. In the early 1960s T.H. White's *The Once and Future King* became the basis for the Broadway musical *Camelot*, the title song from which, with its suggestions of an ideal society, provided a theme for John F. Kennedy's campaign. Over thirty years later the July 5, 1993, issue of *Time* carried a review of its revival, with Robert Goulet, the original Lancelot, now playing King Arthur. John Steinbeck, who as a child was fascinated with Malory's *Morte Darthur*, attempted to rewrite it in modern American English, but gave up and left an incomplete manuscript that was published after his death as *The Acts of King Arthur and His*

Noble Knights (1976). In the summer of 1990 a seven-hour dramatization of Malory's book had a brief run at London's Lyric-Hammersmith theater. The list goes on and on. Over 1,200 nineteenth- and twentieth-century works of literature, film, and art have been influenced by the Arthurian legends; and more are on the way: at the beginning of 1993 Hollywood had plans for at least ten film projects concerning King Arthur.[1]

Although most modern Arthurian works were produced in Britain and the United States,[2] in the Middle Ages writing about King Arthur and his knights was much more of an international phenomenon, with medieval Arthurian stories found in most European languages, including Latin, French, Italian, Spanish, Portuguese, Welsh, Serbo-Russian, German, Dutch, Swedish, Danish, Norwegian, and Icelandic. From Italy there are also medieval versions with most of the Christian references omitted, written in Hebrew and Yiddish for Jewish audiences.[3] The fascination of writers from so many countries with King Arthur is not, however, due to any uniform conception of his character. Although Arthur usually enjoys a popular reputation as a great king, the ways in which authors, both medieval and modern, present him vary widely. Few have chosen to portray Arthur as a villain[4] (for then there would be no reason for noble knights to associate with him); he often, however, falls short of the ideal king, and many writers assumed considerable freedom in presenting him as they rewrote the Arthurian stories. In both medieval and modern literature there are many King Arthurs.[5]

ARTHUR IN HISTORY AND THE CHRONICLES

Whether King Arthur and the stories about him have any basis in history has been a topic debated by scholars through much of the nineteenth and twentieth centuries; and while some argue vigorously for Arthur's existence, if not as a king, at least as a fifth- or sixth-century military leader who led British (i.e., the later Welsh) forces against the invading Angles and Saxons, others are more cautious and would agree with Kenneth Hurlstone Jackson that "nothing is certain about the historical Arthur, not even his existence."[6]

Although there were also some skeptics in the Middle Ages, most people in England at that time seem to have believed in a hero named Arthur. Legends about him circulated orally for centuries, particularly among the defeated British, who had fond and exaggerated memories of his triumphs. The elegy *Gododdin*, written about 600, includes a brief reference to Arthur: it says of one hero that although he had killed his enemies, he "was not Arthur." If this reference is not, as some suspect, a later interpolation,[7] it indicates that: 1) by the early seventh century Arthur had become a figure to whom other heroes could be compared; and 2) he was so well known that no explanation of his identity was necessary. Occurrences of his name found in several Welsh Triads, or summaries of groups of three stories told by Welsh bards, offer further evidence of oral circulation of the stories, and his appearance as a character in early Welsh works such as *The Spoils of Annwfn* and *Culhwch and Olwen* indicates his reputation as a robust and vigorous, but far from courtly, leader to whom many warriors were attracted.[8]

Of more significance to the later development of the legend, however, are references to Arthur in chronicles. The *Historia Brittonum* ("History of the British," ca. 829–830), traditionally attributed to a chronicler named Nennius,[9] describes Arthur not as a king but as a *dux bellorum* ("leader in battles") and lists twelve great victories. At the last of these, the Battle of Mount Badon, Arthur is said to have slain 960 men—a statement that indicates that whatever historical basis existed for Arthur, by this time he had developed into a medieval Superman. Another reference to the Battle of Badon appears in the entry under the year 518 in the *Annales Cambriae* ("Annals of Wales," ca. 950), a work that also refers to the Battle of Camlann in 539 where Arthur and "Medraut" were killed.[10] The twelfth-century historian William of Malmesbury refers briefly in the first book of his *De Rebus Gestis Regum Anglorum* ("Deeds of the Kings of the English," ca. 1125) to the distinguished service of the warlike Arthur (*eximia bellicosi Arturis opera*), whose reputation, William thought, should be based on "truthful histories" (*veraces . . . historiae*) rather than on fallacious fables (*fallaces . . . fabulae*). Shortly after this, Henry of Huntingdon incorporated into his *Historia Anglorum* ("History of the English," ca. 1129) the Arthurian material from the chronicle attributed to Nennius; Henry of Huntingdon's work, however, indicates a significant change in Arthur's rank, for here he is described as "dux militum et regum Britanniae" ("leader of soldiers and kings of Britain," Chambers, 16–19, 249–51). This change was based upon a popular conception of Arthur as king that developed some time before Henry had written his chronicle: evidence for this is found in the Welsh *Culhwch and Olwen* (ca. 1100), where Arthur is "sovereign prince of this island," and early eleventh-century saints' lives, such as those of Goeznovius and Cadoc, where Arthur is described as a king. Moreover, MS 1097 of the Bibliothèque Municipale of Reims, a manuscript of English origin that includes a list of Anglo-Saxon kings written between the late eleventh and the first half of the twelfth century, lists the names "Artur" and "Wyrtgeorn" (Vortigern) at the head of a list of Anglo-Saxon kings, a context that indicates that these British leaders were also considered kings.[11]

William of Malmesbury's hope that Arthur would be remembered through "truthful histories" seemed to be realized with the appearance of

Geoffrey of Monmouth's *Historia Regum Britanniae* ("History of the Kings of Britain," ca. 1138), supposedly a translation into Latin of "a very ancient book written in the British language" that was unknown to other chroniclers. Although the *Historia* covers what, according to Geoffrey, was the history of Britain from its founding by Brutus, the great-grandson of Aeneas, until the death of Cadwallader, the last British king, in 689, the most fully developed section concerns King Arthur. While some at the time questioned the truth of the *Historia*,[12] it offered to many a convincing account of Arthur's reign and elevated the legends of Arthur to the status of serious history.

According to Geoffrey, Arthur became king at the age of fifteen, defeated his enemies in Britain and Scotland, and married Guinevere, a lady of noble Roman lineage. Included among his knights were his nephews Gawain and Mordred, sons of Arthur's sister Anna and King Loth of Lothian. After conquering Ireland and Iceland, he began to attract knights from distant lands and became so powerful that he was able to conquer Norway, Denmark, and Gaul. By this time Britain surpassed all other kingdoms in its affluence. As Arthur was holding a great plenary court, however, ambassadors arrived from Lucius, procurator of Rome, and demanded that Arthur pay tribute. Arthur responded by declaring war on Rome. After conquering much of the rest of Europe and defeating the Romans, Arthur was ready to march on Rome when he learned that his nephew Mordred, whom he had left in charge of Britain, had usurped the throne and was living in adultery with Guinevere. Arthur returned home; in the ensuing battle Mordred was killed and Arthur was taken to Avalon so that his wounds could be healed.[13]

Many of the characters, episodes, and themes now commonly associated with King Arthur are missing. Merlin, who in later works appears as Arthur's advisor, disappears from the story before Arthur is born. Mordred is simply Arthur's nephew, not a son born of Arthur's incest with his sister. There is no sword in the stone, no Round Table, no Grail Quest, no Lady of the Lake, no Morgan le Fay, and no Lancelot. Although Guinevere commits adultery, it is with Mordred.

What Geoffrey presents is the basic story of the rise and fall of King Arthur, with the destruction of his kingdom resulting from the treachery of Mordred. Although Fortune is not mentioned, the story nevertheless follows the pattern of a Boethian tragedy in which a great hero at the height of his power falls, not because he has committed some sin or has some flaw, but because earthly things are transient and one may lose them at any time through no fault of one's own.

Geoffrey's *Historia* was one of the most influential books written in England in the Middle Ages. According to E.K. Chambers its effect on the legends of Britain was comparable to that of the *Aeneid* on the legends of Rome (Chambers, 20). It firmly established for many readers of later generations the conception of Arthur as a great king and conqueror. Surviving in at least 215 Latin manuscripts, the *Historia* circulated widely in England and on the Continent. It was translated into French verse by Geffrei Gaimar in the 1140s and by Wace in about 1155 and, through Wace's account, into English alliterative verse by Laʒamon sometime between 1188 and 1250.[14] Much of its importance, however, is due not merely to its circulation as an independent work but also to its influence on later chroniclers in England. As Felicity Riddy points out, Geoffrey wrote a Latin chronicle for a fairly select and learned group; but the group influenced by the *Historia* expanded in the later Middle Ages ("Reading for England," esp. 318–29). As chroniclers incorporated Geoffrey's *Historia* into their own Latin, Anglo-Norman, and English chronicles that told the whole history of England, the history not just of the British but also of the Anglo-Saxons and post-conquest English, they transmitted it to an ever-widening audience, and it changed from what was supposedly a work of Latin scholarship for a learned group of readers to one that became known to a much larger group, particularly as vernacular literacy increased in the later Middle Ages.

The later chroniclers sometimes modified Geoffrey's account by summarizing, questioning some points, and adding minor details and occasionally even whole episodes drawn from romances and other sources.[15] But although some chroniclers added romance material and although medieval readers did not make the distinction between history and fiction that modern readers do, for almost 400 years following the appearance of Geoffrey's *Historia* most of the chroniclers seemed to accept it as a reliable account of past events and used it as the basis for the history of the British up to the time of the Anglo-Saxon conquest. By incorporating the *Historia* into their chronicles, they gave it an authenticity that it would never have had if it remained simply a history of the British, as it was in Geoffrey and in the adaptations by Wace and Laʒamon. It was one thing for the late twelfth-century chronicler William of Newburgh to dismiss Geoffrey's book as impudent and shameless lies disguised under the honorable name of history; but when that history of the British was incorporated into a history of all of England, when it was included as the first part of a chronicle that also told of the Anglo-Saxons, the Normans, and the post-conquest English, it became more difficult to dismiss.[16] A fifteenth-century reader of a chronicle that began with the history of the British but that continued, giving the history of England up to his own time, would know that there had been a Henry V and a Richard II, and he would believe that there had also been a William the Conqueror and a King Alfred; and if he believed that those rulers had lived, he could also believe that there had been an Arthur who, like Henry V, had achieved great victories on the Continent. The context in which the later chroniclers placed Geoffrey's work gave it legitimacy as history.

The Arthurian chronicles after Geoffrey, Wace, and Laȝamon have been ignored by historians as being worthless and by scholars of literature as having little merit. There are no modern editions or translations of most of them, and scholars' comments have done little to encourage interest in them.[17] These later chronicles were nevertheless quite popular. Just as modern conceptions of King Arthur are often formed, not by major works such as Tennyson's *Idylls of the King* and Twain's *Connecticut Yankee*, but by more popular works that are ignored in the classroom, the chronicles were major sources of information about Arthur in England in the Middle Ages and did much to shape the conception that people had of him. Most of the English Arthurian romances, including major ones such as *Sir Gawain and the Green Knight*, the alliterative *Morte Arthure*, and the stanzaic *Morte Arthur*, survive in single manuscripts; Malory's *Morte Darthur* is also found in a single manuscript and does not appear to have circulated widely prior to Caxton's edition in 1485. While allusions to some of the other metrical Arthurian romances in works such as Chaucer's *Tale of Sir Thopas* and Malory's *Morte Darthur* suggest a wider circulation for them than their single surviving manuscripts might suggest,[18] manuscripts of the Arthurian chronicles are nevertheless far more numerous.

Although some of these manuscripts are handsome presentation volumes that were preserved because they never circulated beyond the wealthy families for which they were prepared, many are relatively simple manuscripts produced for people of more modest means for the purpose of teaching what was supposedly the history of Britain and England. Julia Crick's comment concerning the many manuscripts of Geoffrey of Monmouth— "Sometimes the popularity enjoyed by histories in the Middle Ages seems almost inversely proportional to the quantity of reliable information which they impart" (*Dissemination*, 1)—is applicable to many of these: the Anglo-Norman chronicle of Pierre de Langtoft is found in twenty-one medieval manuscripts;[19] the English metrical chronicle attributed to Robert of Gloucester, in fourteen medieval manuscripts and two different fifteenth-century translations into prose; the English *Short Metrical Chronicle*, in seven; the later version of the chronicle of John Hardyng, in sixteen; Higden's Latin *Polychronicon*, a work that expressed some doubt about the reliability of Geoffrey's account, in at least 127; Trevisa's English translation of the *Polychronicon*, which argued against Higden's doubts, in eighteen; versions of the early fourteenth-century Anglo-Norman prose *Brut*, in approximately fifty; and its English translation, in at least 173. This latter chronicle, first translated from the French sometime between the middle and end of the fourteenth century, continued to be updated in some versions until after the middle of the fifteenth century. It was the most popular secular work written in English in the Middle Ages, the number of surviving manuscripts being outnumbered only by those of the Wycliffite Bible.[20] Moreover, thirteen printed editions of the prose *Brut* were published between 1480 and 1528 (with anywhere from 200 to 1,500 copies produced for each edition).[21] When to all of these are added the many other Latin, Anglo-Norman, and English Arthurian chronicles that survive in fewer manuscripts,[22] it is easy to see that chronicles would have had a major influence in England in forming the impressions that people had of King Arthur.

Later chroniclers usually retained the major episodes of Geoffrey's *Historia*, but they became even more enthusiastic about Arthur than Geoffrey had been. His victorious battle against the Romans was the greatest battle in the world, except for possibly that of Troy; people would talk of his deeds until Doomsday; Arthur was "peerlesse throughout ye world," the "wysest without pere," the "worthiest," "hardyest," "most coragious," "moste victorious," and "moste bounteous." During his reign each day was more like "an heuenly life, then erthely."[23] Geoffrey had offered basically a secular view of the history of Arthur's reign;[24] the prose *Brut* added to this secular account elements of popular piety: with the support of God, Arthur "brouȝt his lande in pees and reste"; his men went forth "in Goddes name" and God helped them because they were in the right. In its depiction of Arthur as a Christian champion fighting the pagans ("soche a noble Kyng, and so doughty") the prose *Brut* appears to be influenced by the Crusades as well as by medieval concepts of justifiable warfare and the increased sense of nationalism in the fourteenth and fifteenth centuries.[25] The enthusiasm of the chroniclers influenced Arthurian works such as John Lydgate's popular and influential *Fall of Princes*, where Arthur is presented as the "wisest prince & the beste kniht," who was "a briht sonne set amyd the sterris," and Malory's *Morte Darthur*, where Arthur is "the moste kynge and nobelyst knyght of the worlde."[26]

Although the Arthur of the chronicles would have been a British enemy of the English, he came to be accepted by the English as if he had been one of their own leaders, and he was presented as a model for later English kings to follow.[27] Malory describes him as an English king, not a British one.

The conception of him as a king of England is due to a considerable extent to the interest the Norman rulers of England, particularly Henry II, had in having Arthur honored by everyone, not just the Welsh. They were interested in Arthur in part because stories about him had circulated in France, in part because, according to the chronicles, Arthur had established a great civilization on the island that they now possessed, and in part because they wanted to keep Arthur from being associated exclusively with the Welsh, for then he could become a symbol of nationalism that could help stir the Welsh to rebellion.[28]

The belief that Arthur had ruled a kingdom that had dominion over much of Europe also gave the Arthurian legend political significance in England that it did not have in the other countries of Europe that were interested in the legends. Arthurian chronicles justified Henry II's conquest of Ireland in 1171 and Edward I's control of Wales as well as the claim of Edward and later kings to sovereignty over Scotland. Edward III established a Round Table in order to appear to be following in the footsteps of King Arthur, and Edward IV and Henry VII both strengthened their own claims to the English throne by tracing their lineage back to the Welsh and thus to Brutus and by implication to Arthur. Henry VII named his first son Arthur with the hope of giving England a new King Arthur. Henry VIII alluded to Arthur's conquests to support his independence from Rome. Elizabeth found in Arthur's conquests support for her own imperialist ideas. And as late as the early seventeenth century James I claimed descent from Arthur to help justify the union of Scotland and England under one king. The Arthurian chronicles had also had earlier political repercussions in Scotland when some Scottish chroniclers writing from the fourteenth through the sixteenth centuries maintained, in response to English claims on Scotland, that Arthur had not been a legitimate king and that the true heirs to the British throne had been Mordred and Gawain, the Scottish sons of Arthur's sister Anna and King Loth of Lothian.[29]

That the story of Arthur should have had political implications probably seemed nonsensical in other countries of Europe. In France, for example, although the Arthur of the chronicles was known through Geoffrey of Monmouth's *Historia* and especially through Wace's French verse adaptation of it, most readers would probably not have taken these works seriously as history. The French had their own chronicles, most of which did not include an account of being conquered by the British. In his study of the Arthurian chronicles, Robert Huntington Fletcher cites only three Latin chronicles produced in France during the Middle Ages and early sixteenth century and three French chronicles produced in France in the fifteenth or early sixteenth century that drew extensively upon Geoffrey, and two of the latter were histories of Brittany, where one might expect the readers to have more interest in material that concerned their British ancestry.[30]

Among the few chronicles written in France that tell the Arthurian story are ones that emphasize, like the Anglo-Norman and English prose *Brut*, Arthur's role as a Christian champion fighting the pagans. In one part of the thirteenth-century *Speculum Historiale* ("Mirror of History") of Vincent of Beauvais, Arthur is praised for his great service to the Christian church in France and Britain; his goal in conquering lands had been to spread the Christian faith. In Alain Bouchart's *Grandes Chroniques* ("Great Chronicles," 1514) Arthur is credited with founding the first church of Notre-Dame in Paris out of gratitude to Mary for his conquest of Gaul. In parts of Brittany Arthur was even considered a saint with a feast day on October 6.[31]

Most chroniclers in Germany and Italy had little interest in the history of Britain, and few included Geoffrey's account of Arthur.[32] Adaptations of the Arthurian story that mix elements from chronicle and romance appear in a few of the chronicles of Spain and Portugal.[33] Perhaps the major continental chronicler to treat it as serious history was the fifteenth-century Fleming Jean de Waurin. His massive chronicle of Britain and England, based to a great extent upon the prose *Brut*, included an enthusiastic account of Arthur as a pious Christian warrior; but Waurin, who fought with the Burgundians and English against the French, was writing for the English, with one of his manuscripts intended for Edward IV.[34] The other Flemish Arthurian chronicle of note is the fourteenth-century *Myreur des Histors* ("Mirror of History") of Jean d'Outremeuse (Jean des Preis), but the *Myreur* is difficult to judge as a serious attempt to write history since it added so much nontraditional material to its Arthurian section, some from romance, some apparently of the author's own invention.[35] One of Jean's departures from chronicle tradition, having Arthur march into Italy and be accepted by the Romans as their emperor before he receives the news of Mordred's rebellion, gave Arthur a more exalted status, and this addition also appears in the fifteenth-century English chronicle of John Hardyng as well as in Malory. For the most part, however, chroniclers on the Continent did not have much interest in King Arthur.

Continental skepticism about the truth of the Arthurian story is reflected in Boccaccio's account of Arthur in his *De Casibus Virorum Illustrium* ("On the Fates of Illustrious Men"). Although Boccaccio's primary source was a chronicle, at the outset he describes Arthur as being known through "the celebrated English fables" and announces that he did "not recognize the evidence of his greatness and his fate as worthy of credence."[36] In the early sixteenth century the Italian Polydore Vergil raised serious questions in his *Anglica Historia* ("English History," 1512–13) about the reliability of Geoffrey's *Historia*, and he dismissed the stories of Arthur's conquests on the Continent as *anilibus fabellis* ("silly little tales"). This chronicle, written for England's Henry VII, outraged many English readers,[37] but similar questions about Arthur's foreign conquests had been raised in England in the twelfth century by Alfred of Beverley and in the fourteenth century by Ranulf Higden, both of whom asked why chroniclers on the Continent did not mention Arthur's conquest of much of Europe.[38]

The conception of Arthur as a great and powerful king that was developed in the English chronicles nevertheless influenced continental conceptions of Arthur; and authors, whether they believed in the story of his conquests or not, often mentioned his name to connote valor. Several French chroniclers who do not tell the Arthurian story mention Arthur as a great figure from the past, although some of them, like Froissart, Jean le Bel, and Chandos Herald, were associated with the English court and were writing for people such as Edward III who had great respect for the Arthur of history.[39] In the romance *Voeux du Paon* ("Vows of the Peacock," ca. 1310) Jacques de Longuyon introduces Arthur, along with the other great conquerors Hector, Alexander, Caesar, Joshua, Judas Maccabeus, David, Charlemagne, and Godfrey of Bouillon, as one of the Nine Worthies who represent the transience of earthly power. His conception of the Worthies inspired writers and artists in England, Scotland, Germany, and Italy as well as France. From these nine great figures others could learn how mutable all things on earth are. Those who used Arthur as a figure representing valor or mutability might believe, like the English printer William Caxton, that he was the "noble kyng and conquerour . . . borne wythin this royame and kyng and emperour of the same"; or they might, like the French author Jacques de Longuyon, add to their accounts of Arthur a skeptical "if his story is true."[40] Arthur, like a figure from Greek or Roman mythology, could represent valor or mutability, but authors who used him in this way did not necessarily believe the stories about him.

MEDIEVAL FRENCH ROMANCE

Chronicles were only one source of early information about King Arthur on the Continent. Oral tradition flourished there as well as in Britain. The legends reached the Continent, probably at first through the Bretons, who began emigrating from Britain between the sixth and eighth centuries to escape the invading Anglo-Saxons, and later through Normans and crusaders, who could have heard the stories from the Welsh as well as the Bretons. By the early twelfth century oral legends circulated at least as far away as Italy, as is evidenced by a scene dated between 1120 and 1140 on the archivolt of the north portal of the Cathedral of Modena in northern Italy that depicts Arthur, Gawain, and Kay attempting to rescue Guinevere.[41]

When Chrétien de Troyes, the earliest of the French Arthurian romance writers, began writing verse romances sometime after the late 1150s, he had access to both oral tales and chronicles. His use of the former is suggested, for example, by his reference at the beginning of his first romance, *Erec et Enide*, to earlier versions of the story that storytellers had told and by his allusions, without introduction, to characters such as Lancelot and Yvain who do not appear in the early chronicles but whose names were apparently familiar to the audience listening to the romance. The chronicle account of Arthur, on the other hand, was a source for some of the material in his second romance, *Cligés*.

Chrétien's five romances mark a major change in the presentation of King Arthur. Instead of being the principal character, he becomes a background figure in works emphasizing individual knights at his court. Even more significant for those interested in King Arthur himself is a change in the presentation of Arthur's character. While in *Cligés* Chrétien was influenced by the conception of Arthur in the chronicles as a vigorous, heroic king, in at least his last three romances (the *Chevalier de la charrete* [*Lancelot*], the *Chevalier au lion* [*Yvain*], and the *Conte du Graal* [*Perceval*]), he presents a weak Arthur, a king who, for example, is unable to protect his wife or the honor of the court and who even cannot stay awake at the table.[42] Scholars differ in their assessments of Arthur's character in *Erec et Enide*; and while some argue that Chrétien presents Arthur positively in his first romance, others believe that he presents him as a weak king in this work as well.[43] In any event, Chrétien for some reason introduced an Arthur who is far less heroic than the king found in the chronicles.

Scholars have suggested various reasons for Chrétien's conception of Arthur. Peter Noble, who argues that Chrétien's conception of Arthur changed after he wrote *Erec* and *Cligés*, believes that he could have developed different views toward a king after he stopped writing for a royal court or that Arthur's character was diminished in order to place more emphasis on other heroes (Noble, 234). The change in Arthur's character could also be due to changing political relations between France and England. Rosemary Morris suggests that the chronicles, which presented Arthur's conquest of Gaul as his most important early achievement, may have been a "political irritant" in France that was to be answered in some French romances with the presentation of a much weaker King Arthur ("Growth of French Nationalism," 121).

Chrétien's romances influenced many later writers of Arthurian romance, not just in France but in other countries. In Germany Wolfram von Eschenbach adapted his *Perceval;* and Hartmann von Aue, his *Erec* and *Yvain;* in Norway and Iceland sagas were based upon *Erec, Yvain,* and *Perceval;* and in England the fourteenth-century metrical romance *Ywain and Gawain* drew upon his *Yvain.* Even when authors did not use Chrétien directly as a source, the structure he introduced for a romance (an initial challenge at Arthur's court, a knight's responding to the challenge, the knight's return to court) became a popular one (as, for example, in *Sir Gawain and the Green Knight* in England). Moreover, after Chrétien, authors of Arthurian romances had two conflicting conceptions of Arthur from which to choose, the great conqueror and central character of the chronicles and the sometimes weak, lethargic minor character of Chrétien's romances. Those reading or listening to an Arthurian romance could usually be expected to have some familiarity with the two traditions and to be able to measure the work against either background.

Thus authors of the French prose Arthurian romances of the thirteenth century could draw upon either chronicle or romance or both in their portrayals of Arthur. The prose *Perceval* (or Didot-*Perceval*) follows the chronicles in presenting a heroic Arthur who conquers Gaul, defeats the Romans, and is overcome in his final battle against Mordred. Two other prose romances from this century draw upon traditions of both the heroic and the weak Arthur. In the *Perlesvaus,* a French romance that might have been written in England at Glastonbury, Arthur is depicted at the beginning as a king who has declined from his former greatness and lost all interest in his knights and his court; after making a pilgrimage to the chapel of St. Augustine, however, and receiving instruction from a hermit, he is once again able to hold court and take up his royal activities as a great king.[44] The prose *Lancelot,* a romance that in its shorter version Elspeth Kennedy has argued dates from the early years of the thirteenth century, presents Lancelot as its hero and focuses on the theme of the making of a young knight's name and the theme of love as an inspiration for chivalry.[45] Although this work describes Arthur as a noble and worthy king and alludes to his past triumphs, he is also presented as an often melancholy ruler who is in many ways inadequate: he has been unable to protect his vassal King Ban (Lancelot's father), receives a stern lecture on his failures as a ruler, is unable to defend his realm from the challenger Galehaut, and is twice duped by women and must be rescued by Lancelot.[46]

Although this shorter prose *Lancelot* apparently circulated as an independent romance, it was incorporated, probably between 1215 and 1230 (or 1235), into a series or cycle of Arthurian romances that scholars often refer to as the Vulgate Cycle. There it became the basis for the first third of a long romance, the Vulgate *Lancelot*.[47] The Vulgate Cycle, as it was originally planned, consisted of three romances, *Lancelot, La Queste del Saint Graal* ("The Quest for the Holy Grail"), and *La Mort le Roi Artu* ("The Death of King Arthur"), apparently written by a team of writers who were following a plan designed by an author whom Jean Frappier describes as the "architect."[48] These three romances present a biography of Lancelot, beginning with his birth; they tell of his great achievements as a knight, his love for Guinevere, and his failure on the Grail Quest; they end with his death after the fall of Arthur's kingdom. Sometime shortly after the completion of the three original Vulgate romances two additional ones were added as introductory romances to the cycle: the *Estoire del Saint Graal* ("The History of the Holy Grail"), which tells of the Grail's being taken to Britain in apostolic times, and the *Merlin*, which tells of Arthur's early conquests prior to the birth of Lancelot.[49]

While the shorter version of the *Lancelot* had exalted the love of Lancelot and Guinevere as an inspiration for chivalric deeds, the Vulgate Cycle shows its disastrous results: the adulterous love of Lancelot and Guinevere leads to Lancelot's failure to achieve the Grail in the *Queste* and to the destruction of Arthur's kingdom in the *Mort Artu*. Thus while the content of the noncyclic *Lancelot* and most of the first third of the Vulgate *Lancelot* are almost identical, the context in which the story is placed in the Vulgate Cycle gives it a different significance.[50]

The portrait of Arthur in the Vulgate Cycle is based upon both romance and chronicle traditions. While Arthur appears as a weak king, for example, in some parts of the Vulgate *Lancelot* that were originally a part of the noncyclic version, he plays a more positive role in some later parts of the Vulgate *Lancelot* that emphasize the sin of Lancelot and Guinevere. The authors of the Vulgate romances, particularly the *Merlin* and the *Mort Artu*, were at times influenced by the heroic conception of Arthur in the chronicles. Jean Frappier found the *Mort Artu*'s Arthur inconsistent: at times pathetic, passive, weak, vengeful, tortured by suspicion; but at others a king who fights bravely, rules with dignity and concern for law and justice (*Étude*, 328–29). Frappier's description could be extended to the portrait of Arthur elsewhere in the cycle. The authors knew both the heroic Arthur of the chronicles and the weak Arthur of, for example, Chrétien's *Charrete*, and they were writing for readers or listeners familiar with both traditions.

Sometime between 1230 and 1240 an anonymous author prepared an adaptation of the Vulgate Cycle now known as the Post-Vulgate *Roman du Graal* ("Romance of the Grail").[51] Although this work, like the Vulgate Cycle, was made up of five parts, it differs both in length and in outlook from the earlier work and attempts to present a shorter, more coherent account of the history of Arthur's kingdom. Apparently with the intention of removing the Vulgate Cycle's emphasis upon Lancelot and focusing instead upon Arthur, it greatly reduces the space devoted to the *Lancelot*.[52] Fanni Bogdanow has described this romance as "the Epic of Arthur" in which the tragedy is caused primarily by mischance. In this work, she observes, Arthur becomes an active ruler with the "importance and dignity of a real hero."[53] The Post-Vulgate *Roman du Graal* attempts to reestablish the reputation of Arthur that the chronicles had created.

The romances of the Vulgate Cycle and the Post-Vulgate *Roman du Graal* would have contributed greatly to the varied conceptions of King Arthur that were available in the Middle Ages. They circulated not only in France but in other countries as well, and parts were rewritten and adapted into English, German, Dutch, Spanish, Portuguese, Italian, and Hebrew in the later Middle Ages. Their popularity is suggested by the 120 surviving manuscripts of the versions of the prose *Lancelot* and by at least thirty-nine, forty-five, and fifty-four manuscripts of the *Queste*, *Mort Artu*, and *Merlin*. Although no complete French manuscript of the Post-Vulgate *Roman du Graal* survives, there are at least thirty-nine French fragments as well as translations into Portuguese and Spanish.[54]

Another work from the thirteenth century, the prose *Tristan*, further contributed to a generally positive picture of Arthur by contrasting him with King Marc of Cornwall, who in this work is the most wicked of all kings.[55] This long romance, which survives in five or six versions in at least eighty-six French manuscripts, was the basis for Spanish, Italian, and Serbo-Russian versions of the *Tristan* story, and much of it was adapted into English in the fifteenth century in Malory's *Morte Darthur*.[56]

MIDDLE ENGLISH ROMANCE

The variety in the characterizations of Arthur that began with Chrétien de Troyes is found in romances written in England as well as the rest of Europe, even though the tradition of the heroic Arthur of the chronicles was much more important there than it was elsewhere. One of the most negative portrayals of Arthur, in fact, occurs in the Anglo-Norman metrical romance *Yder*, probably written in England during the reign of King John (1199–1216).[57] A less heroic Arthur also appears in Welsh literature in the thirteenth-century *Dream of Rhonabwy*, where Arthur is presented as an inactive player of games whose days as a warrior are long past.[58] When English metrical romances began to be written in the late thirteenth century, most were written for people who knew little if any French and who thus would have had little familiarity with the French romances. These English romances generally followed the pattern established by Chrétien and focused upon adventures of individual knights, especially Gawain, rather than upon Arthur, who in these works is often little more than a king who presides over a great court. He can be trivialized as a practical joker (*The Avowynge of King Arthur, Sir Gawan, Sir Kaye, and Sir Bawdewyn*) and also presented as unjust and vengeful (*Sir Launfal*). Romances written in northern England or Scotland (*The Weddynge of Sir Gawen, Golagrus and Gawain, Awntyrs off Arthure at the Terne Wathelyne*) present a bias against Arthur (since Arthur had conquered the North) that is also reflected in some of the Scottish chronicles.[59]

Although Chrétien's romances may not have been widely read in England,[60] many of the French prose romances were available there. The fourteenth-century English chronicler Robert Mannyng refers to them as the "grete bokes" about Arthur that "ffrensche men wryten . . . in prose" that "we . . . here alle rede" (line 383). They are frequently mentioned in book lists and wills, and allusions to them appear in works of poets who wrote for the court, such as Chaucer, Gower, and Lydgate, as well as in the works of alliterative poets of the English Midlands such as the author of the *Parlement of the Thre Ages*, where the account of Arthur as one of the Nine Worthies draws upon the Vulgate Cycle for some of its information, and the authors of major English Arthurian romances such as the alliterative *Morte Arthure* and *Sir Gawain and the Green Knight*.[61]

The influence of the French prose romances on the alliterative *Morte Arthure* is most apparent in the title, the portrayal of Arthur, and in the use of the Wheel of Fortune. Arthur is the major character in this complex romance/epic/tragedy that was written in the Northeast Midlands around the beginning of the fifteenth century (Hamel, 53–58, 62, 74–75). While this work concerning Arthur's Roman campaign is based primarily upon chronicles, its portrait of Arthur as a king who, although heroic, is punished for his sins of pride and excessive desire for conquest is foreign to the English chronicle tradition. The suggestion of punishment could have come from the Vulgate *Mort Artu* as well as from Boccaccio's *De Casibus Virorum Illustrium*.[62] The *Mort Artu* also suggested the dream in which Arthur is cast down from Fortune's wheel.

Sir Gawain and the Green Knight is a sophisticated work that was in all probability written for an aristocratic audience that was bilingual and familiar with French romances.[63] How one is to interpret the boyish, fun-loving Arthur of this work is perplexing. The anonymous author of this work alludes to the chronicles and thus assumes familiarity with this tradition, and he has as his hero Gawain, the most popular knight of English romance; but he also is indebted to French metrical romance for the structure of his work and to French prose romances, particularly the Vulgate *Merlin* and *Lancelot*, for some of its *matière* (Griffith, Rigby). Judging from questions that the author leaves unanswered (such as the reasons for Morgan le Fay's hatred of Guinevere), he appears to have expected his audience to have some familiarity with these French prose romances. Whether Arthur is to be seen here negatively as a frivolous king or positively as a king enjoying his court in the relatively carefree days of his youth is debatable.

Although most English metrical romances did not present Arthur as a major character, prior to Malory the only French prose Arthurian romances that were adapted into English were those that focused on either Joseph of Arimathea and the Grail (from the Vulgate *Estoire*) or Arthur (from the Vulgate *Merlin* and the *Mort Artu*). These three Vulgate romances were all associated with the history of Britain and would have had much the same appeal as the chronicles. The Vulgate *Merlin*, which presents the heroic Arthur of the chronicles, was adapted into English three times, twice in verse and once in a close prose translation; one of the metrical adaptations, *Arthour and Merlin,* survives in several manuscripts and was apparently fairly popular.[64]

The *Mort Artu* was translated into English as a metrical romance known as the stanzaic *Morte Arthur*. Its author apparently did not like the portrayal of Arthur in the French *Mort Artu* as an often weak, vengeful, and jealous king who, in spite of warnings to the contrary, foolishly goes into the last battle against Mordred without waiting for Lancelot's help. The English author also knew the contrasting portrait in the English chronicles and consequently revised the ending to make Arthur less responsible for the final disastrous battle and to make the final catastrophe result from mischance.[65] His conception of Arthur's fall thus has more affinity with that found in the Post-Vulgate *Roman du Graal* than it does with the conception of the fall presented in the Vulgate Cycle.

The only English writer other than Malory to adapt any part of the Vulgate *Lancelot* into English was the later Scottish author of the metrical *Lancelot of the Laik* (ca. 1482–1500). This work is based primarily upon the episode in the first part of the *Lancelot* in which a wise man lectures Arthur on his failures as a king and tells him how to be a good and just ruler;

besides echoing the antagonism toward Arthur found in some of the Scottish chronicles, it was probably intended as a piece of *speculum regis* ("mirror for kings") literature for James III of Scotland.[66]

MALORY AND CAXTON

The one medieval English work that is largely responsible for King Arthur's being a well-known character today is Sir Thomas Malory's *Morte Darthur*. Malory completed his book in 1469–70, before the Scottish *Lancelot of the Laik* was written. His major French sources were the *Merlin* of the Post-Vulgate *Roman du Graal*, the prose *Tristan*, and the Vulgate *Lancelot*, *Queste*, and *Mort Artu*. He also used the French *Perlesvaus*, the alliterative *Morte Arthure*, the stanzaic *Morte Arthur*, and Hardyng's chronicle, and he had read several other English metrical romances. Of the French romances that he used, only the *Mort Artu* had previously been adapted into English (as the stanzaic *Morte Arthur*). Thus, in writing a one-volume compilation of Arthurian stories that began with the conception of Arthur and ended with the death of Arthur and Lancelot, he was an innovator in adapting for readers of English parts of French prose romances that others left untouched.

Although Malory throughout his book consistently refers to Arthur as the "noble kynge" and the "floure of kingis and knyghtes" and uses similar expressions that indicate his admiration for the king, his portrayal of Arthur, based upon works by different English and French authors, has seemed to some an inconsistent blend of strengths and weaknesses. Malory was selective in avoiding some episodes, such as those in the first part of the Vulgate *Lancelot*, that give a negative portrait of Arthur,[67] and he modified the portrayal of Arthur found in sources such as the alliterative *Morte Arthure* and the *Mort Artu* in order to put Arthur in a better light.[68] Nevertheless, Malory at times retains some of the unfavorable material in his sources, and some of Arthur's acts, such as his attempt in the first tale to kill Mordred by drowning all of the children born at the time of Mordred's birth—an episode drawn from the generally pro-Arthur Post-Vulgate *Merlin*—seem inappropriate for the king Malory describes as "moste man of worshyp crystynde." In spite of such acts Malory's own enthusiastic view of Arthur as a king characterized by "grete goodnes," "knyghthode," and "noble counceyle" has prevailed with most readers. One critic, after cataloging what he considers to be the many shortcomings of Malory's Arthur, comments with apparent amazement, "Malory, somehow, succeeded in creating the impression of Arthur as an ideal king. . . . And this is exactly how many of the authors, inspired by Malory, were to portray the king" (Korrel, 267).

Malory's plan to produce a book based upon several romances was not unique to the late fifteenth century. His contemporaries Michot Gonnot and Ulrich Fuetrer were writing similar compilations in French and German; and his work might have remained as unfamiliar to modern readers as those of Gonnot and Fuetrer since it survives in a single manuscript that was discovered only in the twentieth century.[69] It became known earlier only because England's first printer, William Caxton, published an edition of it in 1485.

The only book that Caxton published that is better known than *Morte Darthur* is the *Canterbury Tales*. The publication of the edition of Malory, however, was probably a financial risk for Caxton: it was not a well-known work like some of his other editions, such as the *Canterbury Tales* and Gower's *Confessio Amantis;*[70] it was written in prison by an enemy of the former king, Edward IV; it was based upon adaptations of French romances, most of which had not been previously adapted into English and would therefore have been unknown to those who could read only English; and it presented an account of Arthur quite different from that found in the popular chronicles. In fact, before publishing *Morte Darthur*, Caxton published the most popular chronicles in England: two editions of the English prose *Brut* in 1480 and 1482 (*The Chronicles of England*) and an edition of John Trevisa's translation of Higden's *Polychronicon* in 1482, books that, although unknown to most readers today, would, unlike Malory's work, have been certain of success.

Caxton wrote a preface to *Morte Darthur* that was intended to help sell the book. It reveals much about the status of the legend of King Arthur in England at the end of the Middle Ages. Caxton justifies the need for the book since many of the Arthurian stories were not available in English. His remarks also indicate the respect that some people in England had for Arthur, the "moost renomed Crysten kyng, . . . whyche ought moost to be remembred emonge us Englysshemen tofore al other Crysten kynges" (*Works,* cxlii). Caxton mentions, however, that some doubted there ever had been a King Arthur and believed that books about him were "but fayned and fables"; and he therefore cites evidence of Arthur's existence such as the accounts in the chronicles of Geoffrey of Monmouth and the *Polychronicon*. And perhaps because Caxton knew he was publishing a book for readers who would be familiar with the quite different account of Arthur in his own earlier editions of chronicles, he admits that many of the adventures in Malory's book may not be true and emphasizes instead its didactic value: the reader can find in the book "noble chyvalrye, curtosye, humanyté, frendlynesse, hardynesse, love, frendshyp, cowardyse, murdre, hate, vertue, and synne" and should "doo after the good and leve the evyl" for "al is wryton for our doctryne" (*Works*, cxliii–cxlvii). Malory's story of Arthur may be different from the familiar chronicles, but it nonetheless offers readers valuable moral exempla.[71]

The Sixteenth, Seventeenth, and Eighteenth Centuries

In spite of any doubts Caxton may have had, Malory's book was a success and was published by other printers five more times between 1498 and 1634. The moral lessons that Caxton believed could be derived from it were not obvious to some. The Puritan Nathaniel Baxter described it as the "infamous legend of K. Arthur," and Roger Ascham denounced it for its "open mans slaughter, and bold Bawdrye" and complained that it was an immoral work that had replaced the Bible at the English court.[72] Nevertheless, along with the chronicles, it remained an important source for the conception that people had of King Arthur in the sixteenth and early seventeenth centuries. Also important in England and France were the many French editions of the prose romances, such as the *Merlin* and *Lancelot*, that indicated continued interest in the Arthurian stories.[73] English belief in the historical truth of the Arthurian chronicles diminished in the course of the sixteenth century, although some antiquarians and many members of the middle class would patriotically continue to believe that Arthur had been king, and imperialistic desire to claim other regions of the world during Elizabeth's reign caused a revival of interest toward the end of the century. Edmund Spenser, for example, cited Arthur's conquest of Ireland as proof of English sovereignty over it, and Elizabeth's astrologer Doctor Dee maintained that Arthur's conquests had extended as far as the Arctic.[74] Spenser also used Arthur as a major figure in his *Faerie Queene* to represent the virtue "magnificence," but for this he drew relatively little from Arthurian tradition.[75] The fact that Arthur appears in nine Arthurian ballads, some of which were based on Malory, suggests popular appeal of the legend (Dean, 114–15). Shakespeare apparently knew some of the Arthurian stories,[76] but the only Arthurian drama of note is Thomas Hughes's tragedy *The Misfortunes of Arthur* (1588). Although this play is derived largely from chronicles, its King Arthur appears to have been modeled upon either Elizabeth or James VI of Scotland.[77] Arthur became increasingly irrelevant as a figure from history.

The author of one survey of Arthurian literature appropriately entitles the chapter on the Arthurian story in England in the seventeenth and eighteenth centuries "The Death of a Legend" (Merriman, 49). This title could, in fact, apply to the Arthurian legend throughout much of Europe at that period. Tastes had changed, and authors lost interest in the Middle Ages.

Michael Drayton's vast poem *Poly-Olbion* (1612–22) laments the attitude of his contemporaries toward Arthur: "Ignorance had broght the world to such a pass / As now, which scarce believes that Arthur ever was" (Kendrick, 103; also Dean, 121–22). Not many shared Drayton's interest in Arthur, and more typical is the attitude found in John Florio's rather free translation of Montaigne's *Essays* (1603): "For of King Arthur, of Lancelot du Lake, of Amadis, of Huon of Bordeaux and such idle time-consuming and wit-besotting trash of books wherein youth doth commonly amuse itself, I was not so much as acquainted with their names." Florio's translation is suitable here since, although Montaigne had mentioned Lancelot, Florio added King Arthur to the list.[78]

Milton had planned to write an epic with Arthur as his hero but abandoned the project; probably the most likely reason for Milton's loss of interest in Arthur is that the legend glorified a strong king, and Milton, as a supporter of Cromwell, had little use for the monarchy (Merriman, 55–60; Brinkley, 126–41). John Dryden and Henry Purcell also saw the political potential of the legend and attempted to use it to advantage in their opera *King Arthur* (1691). This work, in which Arthur is a great king who fights the Saxons, was intended as a tribute to Charles II, who died, however, before it could be performed. It has little relation to earlier Arthurian material and is remembered today chiefly for the parts of Purcell's music that have survived. Sir Richard Blackmore's long-forgotten epics *Prince Arthur* (1695) and *King Arthur* (1697) had, like Dryden and Purcell's opera, little to do with Arthurian tradition: in what Brinkley describes as "a most incongruous melée of Geoffrey's history and *Paradise Lost*," Arthur is presented as an epic hero who fights Satan (Brinkley, 168). In the seventeenth and eighteenth centuries there continued to be readers of Arthurian stories in France, where Arthur was at times presented far more favorably than he had been in some medieval French romances and where adaptations of the stories provided "fairy-tale escapism" in the days before the Revolution (Muir, "King Arthur: Style Louis XVI," 168). In England in the eighteenth century, however, Arthur's most notable appearance in literature is in Henry Fielding's *The Tragedy of Tragedies, the Life and Death of Tom Thumb the Great* (1731); there Arthur is married to a virago Queen Dollallolla ("of whom he stands a little in fear") and, as "a passionate sort of king," is in love with Glumdalca, queen of the giants. Arthur had become the subject for burlesque.

THE NINETEENTH CENTURY

The beginnings of Romanticism in the late eighteenth and early nineteenth centuries brought renewed interest in the Middle Ages; and while on the

Continent there was at this time little interest in Arthur, in England and Scotland the situation was different. Early nineteenth-century scholars such as George Ellis, David Laing, and Joseph Ritson published some of the English metrical romances as well as summaries of some of the major French prose romances. The major impetus for the revival of interest in Arthur, however, came from the rediscovery of Malory's *Morte Darthur*. Three editions of it were published in 1816 and 1817 (one by Robert Southey), and Sir Walter Scott had planned another. These were the first editions of Malory's work in over 180 years. Altogether twenty-seven complete and abridged editions and adaptations appeared in the nineteenth century; the most popular of the complete editions, the Globe (1868), had by 1917 been reprinted at least twenty times. *Morte Darthur* has remained in print throughout the twentieth century.[79]

The publication of nineteenth-century editions of *Morte Darthur* occurred when many in England believed that medieval chivalry could be a guide to the conduct of a gentleman and when many looked with admiration to the Middle Ages as a time of harmony and order.[80] The emphasis in *Morte Darthur* upon what Malory called the "High Order of Knighthood" and its nostalgia for a nobler past made it well suited for the period. Although some disliked the book for having "the morality of the French novel" and criticized Malory's Arthur for being "what a Norman knight, a Keltic chieftain, would certainly have been, a gratifier of his own lust," and although editions were frequently bowdlerized to omit "such phrases or passages as are not in accordance with modern manners,"[81] many who read it were, to say the least, enthusiastic. It was, Dante Gabriel Rossetti reportedly said, one of the two greatest books ever written, the other being the Bible. William Morris and Edward-Burne Jones supposedly looked upon the book with such reverence that they were almost too shy even to mention it.[82] *Morte Darthur* offered nineteenth-century writers a new source for their work; and like their medieval predecessors, they began to rewrite the stories about Arthur and his knights. To some, such as Morris and Swinburne, the Arthurian legends depicted a simpler and more beautiful world from the remote past; to others, such as Tennyson (and Mark Twain in the United States), they were a way to convey to readers the authors' concerns about the present (materialism, sensuality, cynicism, misplaced idealism) through stories set in the Middle Ages. The Arthurian legends also became a major source of inspiration for artists such as Rossetti, Morris, Burne-Jones, Holman Hunt, Waterhouse, Dyce, Sandys, and Archer.[83]

Much of the credit for the modern popularity of stories about Arthur and modern conceptions of Arthur is due to the great success of Tennyson's

Idylls of the King. Tennyson spent over forty years developing his plan for the *Idylls*, with the first fragment, *Morte d'Arthur*, appearing in 1842 and the final version of the *Idylls* published in 1885. In this work he created an Arthur who, as Richard Barber writes, "appears as little short of perfect: warrior, statesman, the uniting force of the Round Table," with every knight "Stamp'd with the image of the King" (*King Arthur*, 156). Throughout the *Idylls*, from the beginning when, as a baby, Arthur is said to have been washed up on shore by the ninth wave to his journey to Avilion at the end ("From the great deep to the great deep he goes"[84]), Tennyson's Arthur represents an ideal ruler. He has "power on this dark land to lighten it, / And power on this dead world to make it live" (*The Coming of Arthur*, ll. 92–93). Tennyson re-created Arthur as a Christ-figure ("My God, thou hast forgotten me in my death: / Nay—God my Christ—I pass but shall not die," *The Passing of Arthur*, ll. 27–28), an innovation that seemed to some, such as Swinburne, to conflict with the conception of Arthur in medieval accounts (Buckley, 176). Tennyson, however, would have found justification for this conception in the legends of Arthur's establishing a great order, in the portraits of him as a Christian leader fighting the heathen, and in the hope of many that he would someday return.

Tennyson's Arthur is a practical king who tends to the needs of his kingdom. He understands that it is important for most people to take care of their duties in the world and not pursue the "wandering fires" and misplaced idealism represented by the Grail Quest; for most, such quests amount only to evasion of responsibility. Although some readers have found his Arthur too naive to deal effectively with others and have found him "woodenly imperceptive" in his treatment of Guinevere (see, for example, Buckley, 177), Tennyson intended Arthur as a king who set the standards by which others in the *Idylls*—and in Tennyson's own society—were to be judged. Arthur's initial desire to control the "great tracts of wilderness / Wherein the beast was ever more and more, / But man was less and less" (*The Coming of Arthur*, ll. 10–12) and his final disillusionment when he realizes "all whereon I lean'd in wife and friend / Is traitor to my peace, and all my realm / Reels back into the beast and is no more" (*The Passing of Arthur*, ll. 24–26) were as relevant to the industrialized nineteenth century as to the Middle Ages.

Mark Twain's *A Connecticut Yankee in King Arthur's Court* (1889) is the only other modern Arthurian work written by an author who is considered a major writer in the traditional literary canon. Although Twain originally intended much of the book to be a reaction against and a satire on Tennyson[85] and although much of the book is critical of the English class system, an established church, and the Middle Ages in general, Twain's purpose was similar to Tennyson's in that he used the Arthurian story to comment on modern society, American as well as English. The modern narrator Hank Morgan has a name that associates him with the medieval Morgan le Fay, and Hank's mechanical ingenuity turns out to be ultimately more destructive than the other Morgan's magic. Throughout the book Twain draws implicit, and at times explicit, analogies between the status of medieval English serfs and those of nineteenth-century American slaves and factory workers (see Taylor and Brewer, 172–73).

Although the analogies with contemporary society were made even clearer by Dan Beard's illustrations for the first edition,[86] many reviewers in both the United States and England appear to have missed the relevance of the book to contemporary America. Reviewers in both countries saw it essentially as a criticism of England, and some of the English critics were offended by the irreverence with which Twain had treated the Arthurian legends. One complained that it was "discreditable to Mark Twain that he should have spoiled his reputation for humour by the foolish scurrilities of his burlesque upon Malory" (Parins, *Malory*, 308); another, that the book tried "to deface our moral and literary currency by bruising and soiling the image of King Arthur"; another, that "an attack on the ideals associated with King Arthur is a coarse pandering to that passion for irreverence which is at the basis of a great deal of Yankee wit" (both cited in Taylor and Brewer, 173).

Actually Twain's portrait of Arthur, while not idealized as Tennyson's was, is nevertheless generally positive. Arthur admittedly shows the limitations of one who grew up under a class system: when, disguised as a commoner, he attempts to teach the peasants something about farming ("the onion is but an unwholesome berry when stricken early from the tree . . . plums and other like cereals do be always dug in the unripe state"), his comments illustrate the ignorance and lack of practical knowledge of a sheltered aristocrat; he later exhibits foolish pride when, sold as a slave, he becomes outraged when he learns that he is worth only seven dollars but the Yankee is worth nine (*Yankee*, 439, 455). Yet Twain's Arthur is also a humane and courageous king who cares for his people. In a scene in a peasant's hut, for example, Arthur, with no concern for his own safety, carries a child dying of smallpox to her mother: "Here was heroism at its last and loftiest possibility, its utmost summit; this was challenging death in the open field unarmed, with all the odds against the challenger, no reward set upon the contest, and no admiring world in silks and cloth of gold to gaze and applaud; . . . he was great, now; sublimely great" (*Yankee*, 372). His basic goodness is also emphasized when Hank realizes that Arthur had not suspected the adultery of Lancelot and Guinevere because he has "a heart that isn't capable of thinking evil of a friend" (*Yankee*, 532). King Arthur is, in fact, more favorably presented than the Yankee, who, known as "the Boss," creates orders of bureaucrats as subservient to him as any medieval serf was to his lord and who brutally kills those opposed to him with modern technology that eventually brings about his own downfall. Even with all its satire on the aristocracy, *Connecticut Yankee* leaves the reader with the impression that an American boss could be less admirable than a medieval king.

THE TWENTIETH CENTURY

Works that use Arthurian themes have become increasingly popular in the twentieth century. Considering novels alone, Raymond Thompson observes that while in the first half of the century about fifty Arthurian novels were written, the number was more than doubled between 1950 and 1980 (Thompson, *Return*, 3). In a number of these Arthur has been portrayed unflatteringly as a king unable to control political rivalries, a traitor, a brutal oppressor, a fat weakling controlled by Mordred, a capricious tyrant, an old despot, and an outlaw who has broken his tribe's taboo against incest (see Thompson, *"Conceptions of King Arthur"; Thompson, *Return*; Taylor and Brewer, 302). Most twentieth-century authors, however, treat Arthur as a basically good but flawed ruler. In Thomas Berger's *Arthur Rex* (1978), one of the best of the Arthurian fantasy novels, Arthur is portrayed comically as an innocent, but a very gallant and generous one (Thompson, *Return*, 157–58; Taylor and Brewer, 298–300). In Edwin Arlington Robinson's long poems *Merlin* (1917) and *Lancelot* (1920), which are considered among the finest twentieth-century American versions of the Arthurian story, Arthur is given psychological complexity that he lacked in Malory. He is the "tortured king" haunted by "memories . . . / Of old illusions that were dead for ever,"[87] frightened, unable to handle either the adultery or Mordred's treachery; he is "Like a sick landlord shuffling to the light / For one last look-out on his mortgaged hills"; although "father of the law," he is "weaker than his child, except he slay it" (*Lancelot, Collected Poems*, 37–38; see also Starr, 23–37; Brewer and Taylor, 181–88). Robinson derived from the medieval story an Arthur afflicted with the weaknesses and malaise of twentieth-century man.

T.H. White's *The Once and Future King* (1958), probably the best known of the modern Arthurian novels, presents Arthur as a king torn between his personal love for Lancelot and Guenevere and his sense of justice and law, and as a king tormented by guilt for his incest with his half-sister Morgause, guilt for being responsible for the "embittered" and "unhappy young man" Mordred,[88] guilt for having attempted to destroy Mordred by killing the other children in the kingdom who were born at the time Mordred was, and guilt for having attempted to establish a just kingdom through the use of force: "I am afraid I have sown the whirlwind, and I shall reap the storm" (p. 428).

Arthur changes in the course of the book (the first three parts of which had been published in earlier versions). In the first part, *The Sword in the Stone*, he is the Wart, the boy who is Merlyn's student, not overly bright but eager to learn. Arthur, like Lancelot and Gawain and his brothers in later parts of *The Once and Future King*, illustrates White's belief that the experiences of childhood determine one's character as an adult: in the closing pages of the book the old King Arthur understands that "sisters, mothers, grandmothers: everything was rooted in the past! Actions of any sort in one generation might have incalculable consequences in another" (p. 631). In *The Sword in the Stone* he is fortunate in having in Merlyn a tutor who teaches him to think and to question. As a result of his positive experiences as a child he becomes a good man and a conscientious king. In *The Queen of Air and Darkness* he is a king who wants to change the world into what it ought to be but who, in the act of incest with his sister, commits the sin that will bring about his downfall. In *The Ill-Made Knight* he finds himself incapable of controlling those about him. In *The Candle in the Wind* he tries to avoid trouble by pretending not to notice it; as John K. Crane points out, Camelot falls because the virtuous man is the weaker one (Crane, 74–122, especially 115). Although Arthur realizes at the end that he has failed, he hopes that the future will bring a less violent world: "If people could be persuaded to read and write, not just to eat and make love, there was still a chance that they might come to reason" (p. 639). Arthur is the spokesman for many of White's political views (see Gallix, *"T.H. White and the Legend of King Arthur"), and although the book was published in 1958 with ideas that grew out of the rise of Fascism and Communism in the 1930s, several of its political messages—warnings against extreme nationalism, doctrines of racial superiority, and the belief that might makes right—remain relevant.

A number of twentieth-century works have portrayed Arthur as a Romano-British king or chieftain, a portrayal that reflects the modern interest in the Arthur of history rather than the Arthur of medieval romance. In Rosemary Sutcliff's *Sword at Sunset* (1963) Arthur is a fifth-century king who cares for others and is too kind to destroy his enemies. Mary Stewart's

The Hollow Hills (1973) and *The Last Enchantment* (1979), the novels that complete the trilogy begun by the story of Merlin in *The Crystal Cave* (1970), combine interest in the historical Arthur with the conventions of modern romance by presenting an idealized Arthur in a fifth-century setting based upon the author's extensive research. In *The Wicked Day* (1983), Stewart's fourth Arthurian novel, Arthur, although a good king, is less idealized; in this work the reader sympathizes to some extent with Mordred. Marion Zimmer Bradley's *The Mists of Avalon* (1983), one of the most popular of the novels set in prechivalric times, emphasizes the women who influence Arthur's actions and portrays Arthur as a king who, at least in the opinion of one of the women, is too weak and not ruthless enough to rule (see Thompson, 136). In some of the novels, such as Edward P. Frankland's *The Bear of Britain* (1944), Henry Treece's *The Great Captains* (1956), and Peter Vansittart's *Lancelot* (1978), Arthur is a grim, barbaric leader (see Taylor and Brewer, 290, 302, 309; Thompson, *Return*, 40–43; Starr, 94–99), and the emphasis upon dirt, ugliness, and graphic violence is about as far removed as could be imagined from the "colorful surface" of reality that Auerbach described as an essential feature of romance.[89] Although such works may not appeal to the reader accustomed to the versions of Malory or Tennyson, the authors who present Arthur as a leader in a society uninfluenced by the conventions of chivalry have nevertheless returned to the roots of the Arthurian story, to the noncourtly Arthur depicted in Welsh works like *The Spoils of Annwfn* and *Culhwch and Olwen* or alluded to in the Welsh Triads, the Arthur of the legends that existed prior to Geoffrey of Monmouth and Chrétien de Troyes. As Shakespeare wrote in another story set in ancient Britain, "The wheel is come full circle" (*King Lear*, V.iii.174).

Probably few modern Arthurian works, even those that focus on Arthur as a fifth-century Celtic leader, would have been written without the popularization of the legend begun by Malory's *Morte Darthur*. It is largely through this book that the Arthurian legends lived on in English-speaking countries and achieved a popularity they have not achieved elsewhere. Malory's emphasis upon Arthur as a great and good king, which is deeply indebted to the way Arthur was portrayed in the chronicles, fostered the popular conception of Arthur as the noble, relatively blameless king who appears in the works of many writers, from Tennyson's "ideal manhood closed in real man" to the Arthur portrayed by Mark Twain and T.H. White, the king who wants to learn and who tries to rule well. And the shortcomings of Malory's Arthur also provided suggestions for the more seriously flawed Arthurs found in the works of writers like Edwin Arlington Robinson and Marion Zimmer Bradley. The various and often inconsistent Arthurs of the Middle Ages that Malory incorporated into his book suggested new interpretations to modern writers, just as chronicles and romances did to medieval writers; and in light of the many modern Arthurian works that have so far been produced there is every reason to believe the reinterpretations will continue.

THE CONTENTS OF THIS VOLUME

The essays in this book present some of the varied conceptions of King Arthur that have appeared in the literatures of different nations from the Middle Ages to the present. They also give some impression of the varied, and at times conflicting, ways that modern scholars have interpreted this material. In the first essay Marylyn Jackson Parins examines the attempts of nineteenth- and twentieth-century scholars to find the historical basis for the Arthurian legends. In essays concerned with medieval Arthurian literature, Barbara Sargent-Baur, William McDonald, Elspeth Kennedy, Fanni Bogdanow, and Donald MacRae discuss the Arthur of Geoffrey of Monmouth, Chrétien de Troyes, Hartmann von Aue, and the thirteenth-century French prose romances. Karl Josef Höltgen's essay considers the role of Fortuna in several Arthurian works, particularly English ones; and I contrast Malory's conceptions of King Mark and King Arthur with those of his French sources. Karl Heinz Göller and James Carley, like Marylyn Jackson Parins, consider the Arthur of history: Göller discusses the generally negative view of Arthur found in several of the medieval and Renaissance Scottish chronicles, where Arthur was seen as the embodiment of England's imperialist threat to Scotland; Carley examines the Renaissance debate over whether King Arthur deserved the great reputation that past English chroniclers had given him. Merritt Y. Hughes shows the extent to which the Renaissance poet Edmund Spenser departed from medieval tradition in presenting in the *Faerie Queene* a portrait of Arthur that was influenced by sixteenth-century humanist ideals and based, in part, upon Hercules. Elliot Gilbert and Debra Mancoff present two contrasting views of Arthur in the nineteenth century: to Gilbert, Tennyson's Arthur was the "female king"; to Mancoff, his Arthur was the incarnation of Victorian manhood, and he was thus presented in much of the art of the period. François Gallix discusses the relevance the Arthurian story had for twentieth-century politics in T.H. White's *Once and Future King* and *Book of Merlyn* ; and Raymond Thompson surveys some of the interpretations of Arthur's character in twentieth-century literature, interpretations that draw upon the literature of the past and that attest to the continued fascination with and viability of the Arthurian legends.

The essays by Marylyn Jackson Parins, William McDonald, Debra Mancoff, and Raymond Thompson were written especially for this book. Six of the essays were originally published in French or German. Barbara Sargent-Baur has translated her article from French, and I have translated the articles by Elspeth Kennedy, Fanni Bogdanow, François Gallix, Karl Josef Höltgen, and Karl Heinz Göller from French and German. My article on Malory is considerably shorter than the original version that appeared in *Mediaeval Studies*; I have revised it chiefly by cutting most of the material on political theory but also by taking into account recent scholarship. James Carley has also revised his article, adding particularly to the material in the notes. Some of the other articles include minor revisions: Barbara Sargent-Baur has used the 1993 Keith Busby edition of Chrétien's *Perceval*; François Gallix asked me to add to his notes his edition of the letters of T.H. White and L.J. Potts, which had not been published when the original essay appeared, and I also added a reference to Professor Gallix's bibliography of White. Karl Josef Höltgen made minor changes in the content of his article to reflect changes in his views since the article was originally published in 1957, and I have, with Professor Höltgen's permission, changed the dates of several of the Middle English works to reflect recent scholarship on the dating of these works and have revised the footnotes accordingly. The essays by Donald MacRae, Merritt Y. Hughes, and Elliot Gilbert are reprinted essentially as they were, although I have in all of the essays in this book added translations of foreign quotations and corrected typographical errors that I noticed.

I thank Marylyn Jackson Parins, William McDonald, Debra Mancoff, and Raymond Thompson for writing the original essays that appear here. I also thank the authors of the previously published ones and R. Harsch-Niemeyer of Max Niemeyer Verlag, publisher of *Anglia*; Henry H. Peyton, III, editor of *Interpretations*; and the editors and publishers of *Forum for Modern Language Studies*, *Études anglaises*, *Mediaeval Studies*, *Moyen Age*, *PMLA*, and *Romania* for permission to publish essays that originally appeared in these journals. I am especially grateful to Fanni Bogdanow, François Gallix, Karl Heinz Göller, Karl Josef Höltgen, and Elspeth Kennedy for their corrections to and suggestions for my translations of their essays; I appreciate their interest in this project and their gracious cooperation. My wife, Patricia S. Kennedy, read the Introduction and offered suggestions, and Valerie Moses helped read proofs and found a number of errors I had missed. I am indebted to the following colleagues at the University of North Carolina at Chapel Hill for answers to specific questions: Edwin L. Brown and David M. Ganz of the Classics Department; E. Jane Burns of Women's

Studies; Dino S. Cervigni of Romance Languages; Siegfried Mews of Germanic Languages; and Nancy R. Frazier of the Rare Book Collection of Wilson Library. Finally I thank Norris J. Lacy for the support and advice that he has given as editor of this series.

NOTES

1. Works that are cited in full in the bibliography that follows this introduction will appear in abbreviated form either in the notes or in parenthesis within the text. For lists of nineteenth-century Arthurian works in English see Simpson, *Camelot Regained*, 255–61; Eggers, 215–52; for twentieth-century literature and film see the bibliographies by Wildman; Coghlan, Takamiya, and Barber; and Smith. For art see the lists by Poulson and Simpson, "Arthurian Legend in Fine and Applied Art." The announcement about the Arthurian projects in Hollywood appeared in the January 16, 1993 issue of *USA Weekend* and in other newspapers. For a general discussion of modern Arthurian literature in English see the entry by Raymond H. Thompson in *New Arthurian Encyclopedia*, 136–44.

2. Compared with English-speaking countries, there were relatively few nineteenth- and twentieth-century writers in France who were attracted to the Arthurian legends. In Germany until fairly recently most Arthurian adaptations were derived from Gottfried von Strassburg and Wolfram von Eschenbach; since the 1970s translations of modern British and American works have become popular. See Norris J. Lacy, "French Arthurian Literature (Modern)" and Richard W. Kimpel, "German Arthurian Literature (Modern)," *New Arthurian Encyclopedia*, 162–66, 188–94.

3. On Arthurian literature in various countries of Europe see the relevant articles in *New Arthurian Encyclopedia*; Loomis, *Arthurian Literature in the Middle Ages* (Oxford: Clarendon Press, 1959), hereafter *ALMA*; and Lagorio and Day. Also see *King Artus: A Hebrew Arthurian Romance of 1279*, ed. Curt Leviant (New York: KTAV Publishing House, 1969). For the Serbo-Russian version of the prose *Tristan* see *The Tristan Legend: Texts from Northern and Eastern Europe in Modern English Translation*, ed. Joyce Hill, Leeds Medieval Studies 2 (Leeds: University of Leeds Graduate Centre for Medieval Studies, 1977), pp. 47–143.

4. For exceptions see Schmolke-Hasselmann, "Arthur as Villain" and Thompson, *"Conceptions of King Arthur."* (Here and throughout the introduction and bibliography, an asterisk identifies studies that are included in this volume.)

5. See John Steinbeck's comments, cited in the opening paragraph of the essay in this book by Bogdanow, "The Evolution of the Theme of the Fall of Arthur's Kingdom."

6. Kenneth Hurlstone Jackson, "The Arthur of History," Loomis, *ALMA*, 10; similarly Thomas Charles-Edwards, "The Arthur of History," Bromwich, *Arthur of the Welsh*, 29. For a discussion of scholars' attempts to find the Arthur of history see Parins, *"Looking for Arthur."*

7. Some believe that the allusion to Arthur could have been added to *Gododdin* as late as the ninth or tenth century. See Charles-Edwards, 15.

8. See Patrick K. Ford, "Welsh Arthurian Literature," *New Arthurian Encyclopedia*, 507–09; Patrick Sims-Williams, "The Early Welsh Arthurian Poems," and Brynley F. Roberts, *"Culhwch ac Olwen*, The Triads, Saints' Lives," both in Bromwich, *Arthur of the Welsh*, 33–71, 73–95.

9. See, however, the following articles by David N. Dumville, "The Historical Value of the *Historia Brittonum*," *Arthurian Literature*, 6 (1986), 1–26; "'Nennius' and the *Historia Brittonum*," *Studia Celtica*, 10/11 (1975–76), 78–95; "Sub-Roman Britain: History and Legend," *History*, 62 (1977), 173–91.

10. Chambers, 1–16, 238–41.

11. See Idris Llewelyn Foster, "*Culhwch and Olwen* and *Rhonabwy's Dream*," Loomis, *ALMA*, 33; Roberts, "*Culhwch ac Olwen*," Bromwich, *Arthur of the Welsh*, 73–95; for saints' lives see also Chambers, 241–49, C. Grant Loomis, and Rider; for the Reims manuscript see Helmut Gneuss, "Eine Angelsächsische Königsliste," *Scire litteras: Forschungen zum mittelalterlichen Geistesleben*, ed. Sigrid Krämer and Michael Bernhard (Munich: Bayerischen Akademie der Wissenschaften, 1988), pp. 201–9. Although the article describes the manuscript as belonging to the first half of the twelfth century, Professor Gneuss informed me that it could have been written as early as the late eleventh.

12. Writers critical of Geoffrey included Giraldus Cambrensis, Alfred of Beverley, and William of Newburgh in the twelfth century, Ranulf Higden in the fourteenth, Abbot John Whethamstede and Thomas Rudborne in the fifteenth, and Polydore Vergil in the sixteenth. See Kendrick, 12–14; Keeler, 29–85; and Carley, * "Polydore Vergil and John Leland."

13. See Geoffrey of Monmouth, *The History of the Kings of Britain*, trans. Lewis Thorpe (Harmondsworth: Penguin, 1966).

14. For a recent list of the manuscripts see Julia Crick, *The Historia Regum Britannie of Geoffrey of Monmouth: III: A Summary Catalogue of the Manuscripts* (Cambridge: Brewer, 1989) or *IV: Dissemination and Reception in the Later Middle Ages* (Cambridge: Brewer, 1991), pp. xi–xvi. For the date of Geffrei Gaimar's *L'Estoire des Engleis* and of Wace's *Roman de Brut* see Charles Foulon, "Wace," in Loomis, *ALMA*, 94–95; for suggestions concerning the date of Laȝamon's *Brut* see E.G. Stanley, "The Date of Laȝamon's *Brut*," *Notes and Queries*, 213 (1968), 85–88, and Françoise Le Saux, *Laȝamon's Brut: The Poem and Its Sources* (Cambridge: Brewer, 1989), pp. 1–13.

15. In *Arthurian Material in the Chronicles* Fletcher discusses material from romances that various chroniclers incorporated into their works. Also see my "John Hardyng and the Holy Grail," *Arthurian Literature*, 8 (1989), 185–206; Felicity Riddy, "Glastonbury, Joseph of Arimathea and the Grail in John Hardyng's Chronicle," *The Archaeology and History of Glastonbury Abbey*, ed. Lesley Abrams and James P. Carley (Woodbridge: Boydell and Brewer, 1991), pp. 317–31. In "Generic Intertextuality in the *Lancelot en Prose*," the opening plenary lecture of the XVIIth International Arthurian Congress in Bonn (July 23, 1993), Elspeth Kennedy also discussed the interplay between romance and chronicle.

16. See Fletcher, especially 178–92; Keeler, especially 86–88. Evidence that medieval readers considered chronicles to be generally true can be found in the doubts that a few English writers expressed about Geoffrey's account. Thus, when William of Newburgh complained that Geoffrey disguised under the honorable name of history the fables about Arthur, he indicated that he had serious reservations about Geoffrey's book and that he expected a chronicle to be a fairly reliable account of past events. Moreover, when John Hardyng incorporated the account of Galahad and the Grail into his chronicle, he did it for political propaganda, and he apparently expected his readers to accept it as true. See Nancy F. Partner's discussion of William of Newburgh in *Serious Entertainments: The Writing of History in Twelfth-Century England* (Chicago: University of Chicago Press, 1977), pp. 51–140, especially pp. 62–65; my "Hardyng and the Holy Grail," cited n. 15 above; R.F. Treharne, *The Glastonbury Legends* (London: Cresset, 1967), pp. 75–81; also Kendrick, 12–13; Chambers, 106–8.

17. William Aldis Wright, in the preface to his edition of the metrical chronicle attributed to Robert of Gloucester, wrote: "As literature, it is as worthless as twelve thousand lines of verse without one spark of poetry can be" (*The Metrical Chronicle of Robert of Gloucester*, Rolls Series 86, 2 vols. [London: Eyre and Spottiswoode, 1887], p. xl); Thomas Warton described Hardyng's chronicle as being "almost beneath criticism" (*History of English Poetry*, 4 vols. [London, 1774–90]; ed. W. Carew Hazlitt [London, 1871], 3.124), and Eleanor Prescott Hammond described his verse as "dog-

gerel stupidity" with "no literary merit whatever" (*English Verse Between Chaucer and Surrey* [Durham: Duke University Press, 1927; rpt. New York: Octagon, 1965], p. 233).

18. For the metrical romances cited by Chaucer see the notes to *Sir Thopas* in *The Riverside Chaucer*, 3rd ed., gen. ed. Larry D. Benson (Boston: Houghton Mifflin, 1987), pp. 917–23; for Malory's knowledge of metrical romances see my "Malory and His English Sources," *Aspects of Malory*, ed. Toshiyuki Takamiya and Derek Brewer (Cambridge: Brewer, 1981), pp. 27–55. Most of the references to lost Arthurian romances that R.M. Wilson cites in *The Lost Literature of Medieval England* (London: Methuen, 1952), pp. 114–20, are to French works.

19. See Jean Claude Thiolier's edition, Pierre de Langtoft, *Le Règne d'Édouard Ier*, C.E.L.I.M.A. (Université de Paris XII: Créteil, 1989), pp. 35–142.

20. For manuscripts of the Middle English chronicles see my *Chronicles and Other Historical Writing*. Since the publication of my book in 1989, at least one more English *Brut* manuscript has been found: MS. Brogyntyn 8 (Porkington), ff.1a-18b, on deposit at the National Library of Wales; I am indebted to Felicity Riddy for this information. For the Higden manuscripts see John Taylor, *The Universal Chronicle of Ranulf Higden* (Oxford, 1966), pp. 152–59.

21. See Philip Gaskell, *A New Introduction to Bibliography* (Oxford: Oxford University Press, 1972), pp. 160–61, for the number of copies of editions usually produced by fifteenth- and sixteenth-century printers. I am indebted to Nancy Frazier of the Rare Book Collection of Wilson Library, the University of North Carolina at Chapel Hill, for this reference.

22. Examples include Robert Mannyng's metrical *Story of England*, the fifteen manuscripts that represent anonymous Latin *Brut* chronicles (see my *Chronicles and Other Historical Writing*, especially pp. 2625–28, pp. 2638–40), or any of the other twenty-nine Latin chronicles that Keeler shows drew upon Geoffrey even if only for minor details.

23. Robert of Gloucester, *Metrical Chronicle*, ll. 4491–92; *The Story of England of Robert Mannyng of Brunne*, ed. F.J. Furnivall, Rolls Series 87, 2 vols. (London: Eyre & Spottiswoode, 1887), Vol. 1, ll. 10,613–14; *The Chronicle of John Hardyng*, ed. Henry Ellis (London: Woodfall, 1812), pp. 121, 126, 148.

24. See Robert W. Hanning, *The Vision of History in Early Britain: From Gildas to Geoffrey of Monmouth* (New York: Columbia University Press, 1966), pp. 121–72. The concept of God punishing a people, however, enters into the post-Arthurian section of Geoffrey. See Bogdanow, *"Fall of Arthur's Kingdom."

25. See *The Brut or The Chronicles of England*, ed. Friedrich W.D. Brie, Pt. 1, Early English Text Society 131 (1906; rpt. 1960), pp. 69–91, especially pp. 77, 86, 91.

26. *Lydgate's Fall of Princes*, ed. Henry Bergen, Pt. 3, Early English Text Society Extra Series 123 (1924; rpt. 1967), Bk. VIII, ll. 2667, 2795; *The Works of Sir Thomas Malory*, ed. Eugène Vinaver, 3rd. ed. rev. P.J.C. Field (Oxford: Clarendon, 1990), p. 1229.

27. Pierre de Langtoft repeatedly mentions Arthur as a successful ruler and praised Edward I as the most glorious king since Arthur. Froissart expressed similar sentiments about Edward III. See R. Stepsis, "Pierre de Langtoft's Chronicle: An Essay in Medieval Historiography," *Medievalia et Humanistica*, n.s. 3 (1972), 59–60; Loomis, "Edward I, Arthurian Enthusiast," 126; on Froissart see W.M. Ormond, *The Reign of Edward III* (New Haven: Yale University Press, 1990), p. 38. In "The Arthurian References in Pierre de Langtoft's *Chronicle*," a paper read at the XVIIth International Congress of the Arthurian Society in Bonn on July 27, 1993, Thea Summerfield argued against Loomis's assumption that the Arthurian allusions were always intended to flatter Edward I and noted that some of the allusions are not flattering and that other allusions to Arthur appear in parts of the chronicle not devoted to Edward I. This is forthcoming in *The Arthurian Yearbook*, 4 (1995).

28. See Antonia Gransden, "The Growth of the Glastonbury Traditions and Legends in the Twelfth Century," *Journal of Ecclesiastical History*, 27 (1976), 354–56; also Chambers, 123–24.

29. Walter Ullmann, "On the Influence of Geoffrey of Monmouth in English History," *Speculum Historiale*, ed. Clemens Bauer, Laetitia Boehm, and Max Müller (Freiburg/Munich: Karl Alber, 1965), pp. 257–76; Loomis, "Edward I, Arthurian Enthusiast"; Kendrick, especially 34–44, 78–133; Merriman, 36, 49–50; Göller, * "Scottish Chronicles"; Alexander, "Late Medieval Scottish Attitudes"; Kipling, *Triumph of Honour*, 14–15, 83–91. Sidney Anglo ("The *British History* in Early Tudor Propaganda," *Bulletin of the John Rylands Library*, 44 [1961–62], 17–48), discusses Edward IV's interest in the legend and points out that there was some decline in interest in the Arthurian legend after the early years of the reign of Henry VII. There was, however, a revival of interest during the reign of Elizabeth. See the discussion of the Arthurian legend in the sixteenth century, p. xxxi of this Introduction..

30. Fletcher, 171–78, 230–35; also see Albert Gier, "L'histoire du roi Arthur dans les *Chroniques des Bretons* de Pierre le Baud," *Travaux de linguistique et de littérature*, 22 (1984), 275–87. Gier suggests a fifteenth-century date for Pierre le Baud's chronicle, instead of the sixteenth-century date given by Fletcher.

31. Göller, "Arthurs Aufstieg zum Heiligen." Göller points out that the Arthurian section of the *Speculum Historiale* may not have been written by Vincent of Beauvais but may have been added by someone else.

32. See Fletcher, 237–40, for chroniclers in Italy and Germany that use the Arthurian story. Also Gardner, *Arthurian Legend in Italian Literature*, 6–7 and *passim*, discusses allusions to Arthur derived from Geoffrey that appear in Italian works.

33. See Entwistle, 29–47; María Rosa Lida de Malkiel, "Arthurian Literature in Spain and Portugal," Loomis, *ALMA*, pp. 406–07; Harvey L. Sharrer, ed., *The Legendary History of Britain in Lope García de Salazar's Libro de las bienandanzas e fortunas* (Philadelphia: University of Pennsylvania Press, 1979), pp. 12–21; Sharrer, "Spanish and Portuguese Arthurian Literature," *New Arthurian Encyclopedia*, 425–28; Diego Catalan Menéndez-Pidal, *De Alfonso X al conde de Barcelos* (Madrid: Editorial Gredos, 1962), pp. 360–408; Kirkland C. Jones, "The Relationship Between the Versions of Arthur's Last Battle as They Appear in Malory and in the *Libro de las Generaciones*," *Bibliographical Bulletin of the International Arthurian Society*, 26 (1974), 197–205.

34. On Jean de Waurin see Fletcher, 225–30; Antonia Gransden, *Historical Writing in England II: c. 1307 to the Early Sixteenth Century* (Ithaca: Cornell University Press, 1982), pp. 288–93.

35. See Fletcher, 222–24; Omer Jodogne, "Le règne d'Arthur conté par Jean d'Outremeuse," *Romance Philology*, 9 (1955–56), 144–56. His additions include the introduction of the romance character Lancelot into the chronicle, but in an unchivalric light. Lancelot kills Guinevere because of her love for Mordred and then locks Mordred up with her corpse, which the starving Mordred eats.

36. Boccaccio,*The Fates of Illustrious Men*, trans. Louis Brewer Hall (New York: Ungar, 1965), pp. 214–15. For the Latin text see *De casibus illustrium virorum* [sic], facsimile of edition of Paris, 1520, ed. Louis Brewer Hall (Gainesville: Scholars Facsimiles & Reprints, 1962), p. 204. For a study of Boccaccio's account of Arthur see Delcorno Branca, "De Arturo Britonum Rege."

37. See Carley, * "Polydore Vergil and John Leland."

38. See Kendrick, 12–13; Dean, 18–19; Housman, 209–17.

39. Tyson, 237–57, especially 255.

40. See, in addition to Tyson, Karl Josef Höltgen, "Die 'Nine Worthies,'" *Anglia*, 77 (1959), 279–309, especially 288 for the quote from Jacques de Longuyon; Horst Schroeder, *Der Topos der Nine Worthies in Literatur und bildender Kunst* (Göttingen: Vandenhoeck & Ruprecht, 1971). Caxton's statement can be found in Malory, *Works*, cxliv. Examples of allusions to Arthur as one of the Worthies can be

found in France in the works of Machaut and Deschamps, in Scotland in Barbour's *Bruce* and in the *Alexander Buik*, and in England in the French and English works of Gower, in the *Parlement of the Thre Ages*, and the alliterative *Morte Arthure*, as well as in Caxton's preface to Malory's *Morte Darthur*. For the use of this device in the English alliterative *Morte Arthure* see Höltgen, *"King Arthur and Fortuna."

41. See J.E. Caerwyn Williams, "Brittany and the Arthurian Legend," and Rachel Bromwich, "First Transmission to England and France," both in *The Arthur of the Welsh*, 249–72, 273–98. Also see Roger Sherman Loomis, "The Oral Diffusion of the Arthurian Legend," *ALMA*, 52–63.

42. See, for example, the essay by Sargent-Baur in this book; also Peters, *Shadow King*, 170–75; Noble, "Chrétien's Arthur."

43. For the belief that Chrétien's depiction of Arthur in his first romance, *Erec*, is less than positive see Tom Artin, *The Allegory of Adventure: Reading Chrétien's "Erec" and "Yvain"* (Lewisburg: Bucknell University Press, 1974), p. 64; and Donald Maddox, *The Arthurian Romances of Chrétien de Troyes: Once and Future Fictions* (Cambridge: Cambridge University Press, 1991), pp. 13–34.

44. See Bogdanow, *"Fall of Arthur's Kingdom"; also Peters, 175–81.

45. Elspeth Kennedy, ed., *Lancelot do Lac*, 2 vols. (Oxford: Clarendon, 1980), vol. 2, p. 44; also see her *Lancelot and the Grail*, 10–78.

46. See Elspeth Kennedy, *"King Arthur in the Prose *Lancelot.*" Also her articles "King Arthur in the First Part of the Prose *Lancelot*" and "Social and Political Ideas in the French Prose *Lancelot*" and her *Lancelot and the Grail*, 79–110.

47. The Vulgate *Lancelot* consists of eight volumes of text (and one volume of notes) in the Alexandre Micha edition (Paris, 1978–83). Micha believes that what Elspeth Kennedy refers to as the non-cyclic *Lancelot* is an abbreviated version of the first third of the Vulgate *Lancelot* and was not, as Kennedy maintains, an earlier independent romance. See his *Essais sur le cycle du Lancelot-Graal* (Geneva: Droz, 1987), pp. 31–83.

48. Frappier, "The Vulgate Cycle," Loomis, *ALMA*, 295–318, especially 316; also his *Étude sur La Mort le Roi Artu*, 3rd ed. (Geneva: Droz, 1972), pp. 122–46; and E. Jane Burns, "Vulgate Cycle," *New Arthurian Encyclopedia*, 496–99.

49. These were based upon verse romances written by Robert de Boron in the late twelfth century. See, in addition to the Frappier article cited in note 48, Pierre le Gentil, "The Work of Robert de Boron and the Didot *Perceval*," and Alexandre Micha, "The Vulgate *Merlin*," in Loomis, *ALMA*, 251–62, 319–24; Richard O'Gorman, "Robert de Boron," *New Arthurian Encyclopedia*, 385–86. For a translation of the Vulgate Cycle see *Lancelot-Grail: The Old French Arthurian Vulgate and Post-Vulgate in Translation*, ed. Norris J. Lacy, 5 vols. (New York: Garland, 1993– ; vol. 5 forthcoming). For an edition and translation of the prose adaptation of Robert de Boron's romances prior to the Vulgate romances see Robert de Boron, *The Grail Trilogy: Joseph, Merlin, and Perceval*, ed. George T. Diller, 2 vols. (Garland, forthcoming).

50. See Elspeth Kennedy, *Lancelot and the Grail*, especially 310–13.

51. The basic study of this romance is Fanni Bogdanow, *The Romance of the Grail*, listed in the bibliography following this introduction.

52. For the Lancelot section of this romance see *La Folie Lancelot*, ed. Fanni Bogdanow (Tübingen: Niemeyer, 1965).

53. Bogdanow borrows this phrase from Eugène Vinaver's description of Malory's Arthur in *Malory* (Oxford: Clarendon, 1929; rpt. 1970), p. 91, but believes that it is also applicable to the Arthur of the Post-Vulgate *Roman*. See Bogdanow, *Romance*, 200.

54. The most recent listing of the Lancelot manuscripts is in P.J.C. Field, "Malory and the French Prose *Lancelot*," *Bulletin of the John Rylands University Library of Manchester*, 75 (1993), 100–02; I based the number of manuscripts of the *Queste*, *Mort Artu*, and *Merlin* on those listed in the following editions: *La Queste del Saint Graal*, ed. Albert Pauphilet (Paris: Champion, 1972), pp. iii–v; *La Mort le*

Roi Artu, ed. Jean Frappier, 3rd ed. (Geneva: Droz, 1964), pp. xxx–xxxiii; *Merlin*, ed. Alexandre Micha (Paris and Geneva: Droz, 1980), pp. xiv–xix; for the manuscripts of the Post-Vulgate *Roman* see Fanni Bogdanow, ed., *La Version Post-Vulgate de la Queste del Saint Graal*, Société des Anciens Textes Français, Vols. I, II, IV.1 (Paris: Picard, 1991), Vol. I, pp. 1–26; Bogdanow, *Romance*, 271–89.

55. See Emmanuèle Baumgartner, *Le "Tristan en prose": Essai d'interprétation d'un roman médiéval* (Geneva: Droz, 1975), pp. 229–30.

56. For the number of French manuscripts see Baumgartner, 17–28, supplemented by P.J.C. Field, "The French Prose *Tristan*: A Note on Some Manuscripts, a List of Printed Texts, and Two Correlations with Malory's *Morte Darthur*," *Bibliographical Bulletin of the International Arthurian Society*, 41 (1989), 269–87; for the Serbo-Russian version see *Tristan Legend*, ed. Hill, cited n. 3 above.

57. *The Romance of Yder*, ed. and trans. Alison Adams (Cambridge: Brewer, 1983), p.13; also Schmolke-Hasselmann, "Arthur as Villain."

58. See Ceridwen Lloyd-Morgan, "*Breuddwyd Rhonabwy* and Later Arthurian Literature," in Bromwich, *Arthur of the Welsh*, 183–208, especially 185–86.

59. See Helaine Newstead's commentary on the Middle English Arthurian romances in *A Manual of the Writings in Middle English*, vol. 1, 38–79. On the Scottish attitude toward Arthur see Schmolke-Hasselmann, *Arthurische Versroman*, 242; Alexander, "Late Medieval Scottish Attitudes"; Göller, *"Scottish Chronicles."

60. Not many medieval English writers appear to have been familiar with Chrétien's work. The only one of his romances that was adapted into English was *Yvain* (as the metrical romance *Yvain and Gawain*). The English *Perceval of Galles* may not have any direct relation to Chrétien's romance. The late fifteenth-century Scottish work *Golagrus and Gawain* is derived from the anonymous First Continuation of Chrétien's *Perceval*. The evidence that scholars have cited to show Chaucer's familiarity with Chrétien's work can be explained by his having read the Vulgate *Lancelot*. (See my "Gower, Chaucer, and French Prose Arthurian Romance," *Mediaevalia*, 16 [1993], 55–90.) P.J.C. Field suggests that Malory may have been influenced by Chrétien's *Yvain* ("Malory and Chrétien de Troyes," *Reading Medieval Studies*, 17 [1991], 19–30.)

61. On Mannyng's allusions to the French books see Lesley Johnson, "Robert Mannyng's History of Arthurian Literature," *Church and Chronicle in the Middle Ages: Essays Presented to John Taylor*, ed. Ian Wood and G.A. Loud (London: Hambledon, 1991), pp. 129–47. On book lists and wills see my "Gower, Chaucer, and French Prose Arthurian Romance," 79–80, n. 3; Wilson, *Lost Literature*, 117–18; Riddy, "Reading for England," 326–29; for allusions in Middle English works see my "Gower, Chaucer, and French Prose Arthurian Romance"; Mary Hamel, ed., *Morte Arthure* (New York: Garland, 1984), pp. 52–53; Richard R. Griffith, "Bertilak's Lady: The French Background of *Sir Gawain and the Green Knight*," *Machaut's World: Science and Art in the Fourteenth Century*, ed. Madeleine Pelner Cosman and Bruce Chandler (New York: New York Academy of Sciences, 1978), pp. 249–66; Marjory Rigby, "'Sir Gawain and the Green Knight' and the Vulgate 'Lancelot,'" *Modern Language Review*, 78 (1983), 257–66. The author of *The Parlement of the Thre Ages* (ed. M.Y. Offord, Early English Text Society 246 [1959]) mentions "Sir Galaad þe gode þat the gree [Grail] wan" (l. 473).

62. See Höltgen's *"King Arthur and Fortuna"; in "Generic Intertextuality in the English Alliterative *Morte Arthure*: The Italian and Scottish Connection," a paper read at the International Congress of the Arthurian Society in Bonn, July 29, 1993, I argued for the possibility of the author's knowing Boccaccio's account of Arthur. The part of this paper that concerns Boccaccio will appear in *The Arthurian Yearbook*, 4 (1995).

63. See Rosalind Field, "The Anglo-Norman Background to Alliterative Romance," *Middle English Alliterative Poetry and Its Literary Background*, ed. David A. Lawton (Cambridge: Brewer, 1982), pp. 54–69.

64. Newstead, *Manual*, 46–49, 51–53, 72–75; on the English *Prose Merlin* see

also Carol M. Meale, "The Manuscripts and Early Audience of the Middle English *Prose Merlin*," and Karen Stern, "The Middle English *Prose Merlin*," both in *The Changing Face of Arthurian Romance*, ed. Alison Adams, Armel H. Diverres, Karen Stern, and Kenneth Varty (Woodbridge: Boydell and Brewer, 1986), pp. 92–111, 112–22.

65. See my "The Stanzaic *Morte Arthur*: The Adaptation of a French Romance for an English Audience," *Culture and the King: The Social Implications of the Arthurian Legend*, ed. James Carley and Martin B. Shichtman (Albany: State University of New York Press, 1994), pp. 91–112.

66. See Bertram Vogel, "Secular Politics and the Date of *Lancelot of the Laik*," *Studies in Philology*, 40 (1943), 1–13.

67. See my "Malory's 'Noble Tale of Sir Launcelot du Lake,' the Vulgate *Lancelot*, and the Post-Vulgate *Roman du Graal*," *Arthurian and Other Studies Presented to Shunichi Noguchi*, ed. Takashi Suzuki and Tsuyoshi Mukai (Cambridge: Brewer, 1993), pp. 107–29.

68. See my "Malory's King Mark and King Arthur" in this book for Malory's changes in the *Mort Artu*; for his adaptation of the alliterative *Morte Arthure* see the dissertation by Helen I. Wroten, "Malory's *Tale of King Arthur and the Emperor Lucius* Compared with Its Source, the Alliterative *Morte Arthure*," Diss. University of Illinois, 1950, University Microfilms Publications, no. 2231 (1950), and Mary E. Dichmann, "'The Tale of King Arthur and the Emperor Lucius': The Rise of Lancelot," *Malory's Originality*, ed. R.M. Lumiansky (Baltimore: Johns Hopkins Press, 1964), pp. 67–90.

69. For the work of Fuetrer and Gonnot see the entries by Francis G. Gentry and Colette-Anne Van Coolput in *New Arthurian Encyclopedia*, 170–71, 206. Gonnot's manuscript has never been published, but it is the subject of a study by Cedric E. Pickford, *L'Évolution du roman arthurien en prose vers la fin du moyen âge d'après le manuscrit 112 du fonds français de la Bibliothèque Nationale* (Paris: Nizet, 1960). For the manuscript of Malory's book see W.F. Oakeshott, "The Finding of the Manuscript," *Essays on Malory*, ed. J.A.W. Bennett (Oxford: Clarendon, 1963), pp. 1–6.

70. See N.F. Blake, "Caxton Prepares His Edition of the *Morte Darthur*," *Journal of Librarianship*, 8 (1976), 274.

71. In stating that "al is wryton for our doctryne," Caxton may also have been intentionally echoing the *Polychronicon* and Higden's view that the importance of history was moral instruction and that everything in it might not be true. On the similar statement in Higden see Bernard Guenée, *Histoire et culture historique dans l'Occident médiéval* (Paris: Aubier Montaigne, 1980), pp. 27–29. On the mixture of fact and fiction in medieval history, see also Joseph M. Levine, "Caxton's Histories: Fact and Fiction at the Close of the Middle Ages," *Humanism and History: Origins of Modern English Historiography* (Ithaca: Cornell University Press, 1987), pp. 19–53.

72. *Malory: The Critical Heritage*, ed. Marylyn Jackson Parins (London: Routledge, 1988), pp. 57, 59. For a general discussion of humanists' attitude toward romance see Robert P. Adams, "Bold Bawdry and Open Manslaughter: The English New Humanist Attack on Medieval Romance," *Huntington Library Quarterly*, 23 (1959–60), 33–48.

73. French printers published seven editions of the Vulgate *Merlin* between 1498 and 1528, eight of a combined *Lancelot, Queste del Saint Graal*, and *Mort Artu* between 1488 and 1591, two of *L'Hystoire du Sainct Greal* (a work combining the Vulgate *L'Estoire del Saint Graal*, the *Perlesvaus*, and parts of the Vulgate *Lancelot* and *Queste*) in 1516 and 1523; two of *Meliadus de Leonnoys* in 1528 and 1532 (i.e., 1533); three of *Gyron le Courtoys* between 1501 and 1519; and eight of the prose *Tristan* between 1489 and 1533, as well as four editions of a modernization of the *Tristan* between 1554 and 1586. See Cedric E. Pickford's introductions to the following Scolar Press facsimile editions: *Merlin 1498* (London, 1975); *Lancelot du Lac 1488*, 2 vols. (London, 1973); *L'Hystoire du Sainct Greal* (London, 1978); *Meliadus de*

Leonnoys 1532 (London, 1980); *Gyron le Courtoys c 1501* (London, 1977); *Tristan 1489* (London, 1976). Also see Pickford, "Fiction and the Reading Public in the Fifteenth Century," *Bulletin of the John Rylands Library*, 45 (1962–63), 423–38, and his "Les éditions imprimées de romans arthuriens en prose antérieures à 1600," *Bibliographical Bulletin of the International Arthurian Society*, 13 (1961), 99–109; and for the influence some of these may have had upon English writers, particularly Spenser see Rosemond Tuve, *Allegorical Imagery: Some Medieval Books and Their Posterity* (Princeton: Princeton University Press, 1966), pp. 335–436.

74. Dean, 19–31; Bennett, *Evolution of "The Faerie Queene,"* 61–79; Kendrick, 37.

75. See Merritt Y. Hughes, *"The Arthurs of the *Faerie Queene.*"

76. See Field, "Shakespeare's King Arthur"; A. Kent Hieatt, "The Passing of Arthur in Malory, Spenser, and Shakespeare: The Avoidance of Closure," in Baswell and Sharpe, *The Passing of Arthur*, 173–92.

77. See Dean, 118–20; William A. Armstrong, "The Topicality of 'The Misfortunes of Arthur,'" *Notes & Queries*, 200 (1955), 371–73, and "Elizabethan Themes in the 'Misfortunes of Arthur,'" *Review of English Studies*, n.s. 7 (1956), 238–49. For a recent edition see *The Misfortunes of Arthur*, ed. Brian Jay Corrigan (New York: Garland, 1992).

78. Quoted by Vinaver, *Rise of Romance*, 70; also in Dean, 108–09. Vinaver cites Montaigne's French quote in n. 2.

79. See Barry Gaines, *Sir Thomas Malory: An Anecdotal Bibliography of Editions, 1485–1985* (New York: AMS, 1990). For his discussion of the Globe edition see pp. 20–24.

80. See Alice Chandler, *A Dream of Order: The Medieval Ideal in Nineteenth-Century English Literature* (Lincoln: University of Nebraska Press, 1970); Mark Girouard, *The Return to Camelot: Chivalry and the English Gentleman* (New Haven: Yale University Press, 1981).

81. Parins, *Malory*, 169, 184, 245. The second quotation is from Edward Strachey's introduction to his 1868 Globe edition of *Morte Darthur*. Also see Yuri Fuwa, "The Globe Edition of Malory as a Bowdlerized Text in the Victorian Age," *Studies in English Literature*, English Number (1984), 3–17.

82. Philip Henderson, *William Morris: His Life, Work, and Friends* (New York: McGraw-Hill, 1967), p. 29.

83. Girouard, 177–218; Mancoff, *The Arthurian Revival*; Whitaker, *Legends of King Arthur in Art*.

84. *The Coming of Arthur*, l. 410; also *The Passing of Arthur*, l. 445, in Tennyson, *Idylls of the King*, ed. J.M. Gray (London: Penguin, 1983). Quotations from *Idylls* are from this edition.

85. See Taylor and Brewer, 171. Dan Beard's illustrations to the first edition present caricatures of Tennyson as Merlin, who in Twain's book is both a fraud and a bore. See the facsimile of this edition: *A Connecticut Yankee in King Arthur's Court*, intro. Hamlin Hill (San Francisco: Chandler, 1963).

86. One of Beard's illustrations depicts Jay Gould as the slavedriver; another juxtaposes a king and a serf, a plantation owner and a slave, and a millionaire and his servant; another shows two pictures of supposedly blind justice, one representing the sixth century, with the scales weighted toward royalty, the other representing the nineteenth century, with the scales weighted toward money (*Yankee*, 465, 363, 473).

87. Edwin Arlington Robinson, *Collected Poems*, vol. 3 (New York: Macmillan, 1927), p. 35.

88. White, *The Once and Future King* (New York: Berkley, 1966), pp. 549–50.

89. Auerbach, *Mimesis*, trans. Willard Trask (Princeton: Princeton University Press, 1953; rpt. New York: Doubleday Anchor, 1957), pp. 107–24, esp. p. 119.

SELECT BIBLIOGRAPHY

GENERAL ARTHURIAN BIBLIOGRAPHIES

Bibliographical Bulletin of the International Arthurian Society/ Bulletin Bibliographique de la Société Internationale Arthurienne, 1 (1949–) [Annual annotated bibliographies of Arthurian scholarship.]

Bruce, James Douglas. "A Select Bibliography of Arthurian Critical Literature." *The Evolution of Arthurian Romance from the Beginnings down to the Year 1300.* 2 vols. 2nd ed. Baltimore: Johns Hopkins University Press, 1928; rpt. Gloucester, Mass.: Peter Smith, 1958, II, 380–412. [Good to 1922.]

Modern Language Quarterly, 1 (1940)–24 (1963). [Annual Arthurian bibliographies; bibliography in Vol. 1 covers 1936–39.]

Palmer, Caroline L., ed. *The Arthurian Bibliography*: III. *1978–1992*. Cambridge: Brewer, 1993.

Parry, John J. *A Bibliography of Critical Arthurian Literature for the Years 1922–29.* New York: Modern Language Association, 1931.

Parry, John J., and Margaret Schlauch. *A Bibliography of Arthurian Critical [sic] Literature for the Years 1930–35.* New York: Modern Language Association, 1936.

Pickford, Cedric E., Rex Last, and Christine R. Barker, eds. *The Arthurian Bibliography*: I. *Author Listing*: II. *Subject Index.* Cambridge: Brewer, 1981–83. [Complete Arthurian bibliography to 1978.]

Reiss, Edmund, Louise Horner Reiss, and Beverly Taylor. *Arthurian Legend and Literature: An Annotated Bibliography.* I: *The Middle Ages.* New York: Garland, 1984. [Select annotated bibliography.]

OTHER BIBLIOGRAPHIES

Brown, Paul A. "The Arthurian Legends: Supplement to Northup and Parry's Annotated Bibliography, with further supplement by John J. Parry." *Journal of English and Germanic Philology*, 49 (1950), 208–16. [Modern Arthurian literature.]

Coghlan, Ronan, Toshiyuki Takamiya, and Richard Barber, "A Supplementary Bibliography of Twentieth-Century Arthurian Literature." *Arthurian Literature*, 3 (1983), 129–36.

Gallix, François. *T.H. White: An Annotated Bibliography.* New York: Garland, 1986.

Jost, Jean E. *Ten Middle English Arthurian Romances: A Reference Guide.* Boston: G.K. Hall, 1986.

Kennedy, Edward Donald. *A Manual of the Writings in Middle English*, gen. ed. Albert E. Hartung. 8: *Chronicles and Other Historical Writing.* New Haven: Connecticut Academy of Arts and Sciences, 1989.

Northup, Clark S., and John J. Parry. "The Arthurian Legends: Modern Retellings of the Old Stories: An Annotated Bibliography." *Journal of English and Germanic Philology*, 43 (1944), 173–221.

Newstead, Helaine. "Arthurian Legends [in Middle English]." *A Manual of the Writings in Middle English*, gen. ed. J. Burke Severs. 1: *The Romances*. New Haven: Connecticut Academy of Arts and Sciences, 1967, pp. 38–79, 224–56.

Poulson, Christine, and Roger Simpson, "Arthurian Legend in Fine and Applied Art of the Nineteenth and Early Twentieth Centuries," *Arthurian Literature*, 9 (1989), 81–142; 11 (1992), 81–96.

Rice, Joanne A. *Middle English Romance: An Annotated Bibliography 1955–1985*. New York: Garland, 1987.

Smith, A.H.W. "Update: A Supplementary Bibliography of Twentieth-Century Arthurian Literature," *Arthurian Literature*, 10 (1990), 135–60; 13(1995), 157–87.

Wildman, Mary. "Twentieth-Century Arthurian Literature: An Annotated Bibliography," *Arthurian Literature*, 2 (1982), 127–62.

Useful Reference Works

Ackerman, Robert W. *An Index of the Arthurian Names in Middle English*. Stanford University Publications, University Series Language and Literature, 10. Stanford: Stanford University Press, 1952; rpt. New York: AMS, 1967.

Loomis, Roger Sherman, ed. *Arthurian Literature in the Middle Ages: A Collaborative History*. Oxford: Clarendon Press, 1959. [Loomis, *ALMA*.]

Lacy, Norris J., and Geoffrey Ashe. *The Arthurian Handbook*. New York: Garland, 1990.

Lacy, Norris J., Geoffrey Ashe, Sandra Ness Ihle, Marianne E. Kalinke, and Raymond H. Thompson, eds. *The New Arthurian Encyclopedia*. New York: Garland, 1991.

West, G.D. *An Index of Proper Names in French Arthurian Prose Romances*. Toronto: University of Toronto Press, 1978.

———. *An Index of Proper Names in French Arthurian Verse Romances 1150–1300*. Toronto: University of Toronto Press, 1969.

Selected Studies Concerning King Arthur

[Articles marked with * appear in this volume.]

Alcock, Leslie. *Arthur's Britain*. Harmondsworth: Penguin, 1971.

———. "Cadbury-Camelot: A Fifteen-Year Perspective." *Proceedings of the British Academy*, 68 (1982), 355–88.

Alexander, Flora, "Late Medieval Scottish Attitudes to the Figure of King Arthur: A Reassessment." *Anglia*, 93 (1975), 17–34.

Allen, Mark. "The Image of Arthur and the Idea of King." *Arthurian Interpretations*, 2.2 (1988), 1–16.

Archibald, Elizabeth. "Arthur and Mordred: Variations on an Incest Theme." *Arthurian Literature*, 8 (1989), 1–27.

Ashe, Geoffrey. "A Certain Very Ancient Book: Traces of an Arthurian Source in Geoffrey of Monmouth's *History*." *Speculum*, 56 (1981), 301–23.

———. *The Discovery of King Arthur*. Garden City, N.J.: Doubleday, 1985.

———. *King Arthur in Fact and Legend*. Camden, N.J.: Nelson, 1971.

Barber, Richard. *King Arthur: Hero and Legend*. Woodbridge, Suffolk: Boydell and Brewer, 1986.

Baswell, Christopher, and William Sharpe, eds. *The Passing of Arthur: New Essays in Arthurian Tradition*. New York: Garland, 1988.

Baumgartner, Emmanuèle. "Arthur et les chevaliers envoisiez." *Romania*, 105 (1984), 312–25.

Bellamy, Elizabeth J. "Reading Desire Backward: Belatedness and Spenser's Arthur." *South Atlantic Quarterly*, 88 (1989), 789–809.

Bennett, Josephine Waters. *The Evolution of "The Faerie Queene."* Chicago: University of Chicago Press, 1942. ["The Reputation of Arthur" (in the sixteenth century), pp. 61–79.]

Bogdanow, Fanni. "The Changing Vision of Arthur's Death." In *Dies Illa: Death in the Middle Ages*, ed. Jane H.M. Taylor. Vinaver Studies in French I. Liverpool: Francis Cairns, 1984, pp. 107–23.

*———. "La chute du royaume d'Arthur: Évolution du thème." *Romania*, 107 (1986), 504–19.

———. *The Romance of the Grail: A Study of the Structure and Genesis of a Thirteenth-Century Arthurian Prose Romance*. Manchester: Manchester University Press, 1966.

Brinkley, Roberta Florence. *Arthurian Legend in the Seventeenth Century*. Baltimore: Johns Hopkins, 1932; rpt. New York: Octagon, 1967.

Brodeur, Arthur G. "Arthur, Dux Bellorum." *University of California Publications in English*, 3.7 (1939), 237–83.

Bromwich, Rachel. "Concepts of Arthur." *Studia Celtica*, 10/11 (1975–76), 163–81.

———. "First Transmission to England and France." In Bromwich, *The Arthur of the Welsh*, pp. 273–98.

Bromwich, Rachel, A.O.H. Jarman, and Brynley F. Roberts, eds. *The Arthur of the Welsh: The Arthurian Legend in Medieval Welsh Literature*. Cardiff: University of Wales Press, 1991.

Bruce, James Douglas. "The Development of the Morte Arthur Theme in Medieval Romance." *Romanic Review*, 4 (1913), 408–71.

———. *The Evolution of Arthurian Romance from the Beginnings down to the Year 1300*. 2 vols. 2nd ed. Baltimore: Johns Hopkins University Press, 1928; rpt. Gloucester, Mass.: Peter Smith, 1958.

Buckley, Jerome H. *Tennyson: The Growth of a Poet*. Cambridge, Mass.: Harvard University Press, 1960; rpt. Boston: Houghton Mifflin, 1965, especially pp. 171–94. [*Idylls of the King*.]

Bullock-Davies, Constance. "The Visual Image of Arthur." *Reading Medieval Studies*, 9 (1983), 98–116.

Carley, James. *Glastonbury Abbey: The Holy House at the Head of the Moors Adventurous*. Woodbridge, Suffolk: Boydell and Brewer, 1988.

*———. "Polydore Vergil and John Leland on King Arthur: The Battle of the Books." *Interpretations*, 15 (1984), 86–100.

Chambers, E.K. *Arthur of Britain*. London: Sidgwick & Jackson, 1927; rpt. Cambridge: Speculum Historiale, 1964.

Charles-Edwards, Thomas. "The Arthur of History." In Bromwich, *Arthur of the Welsh*, pp. 15–32.

Christoph, Siegfried. "Guenevere's Abduction and Arthur's Fame in Hartmann's 'Iwein,'" *Zeitschrift für deutsches Altertum und deutsche Literatur*, 118 (1989), 17–33.

Crane, John Kenny. *T.H. White*. New York: Twayne, 1974.

Critchlow, F.L. "Arthur in Old French Poetry not of the Breton Cycle." *Modern Philology*, 6 (1909), 477–86.

Culler, A. Dwight. *The Poetry of Tennyson*. New Haven: Yale University Press, 1977, pp. 214–41. [*Idylls of the King*.]

Dean, Christopher. *Arthur of England: English Attitudes to King Arthur and the Knights of the Round Table in the Middle Ages and the Renaissance*. Toronto: University of Toronto Press, 1987.

Delcorno Branca, Daniela. *Boccaccio e le storie di re Artù*. Bologna: Il Mulino Ricerca. 1991.

———. "'De Arturo Britonum Rege': Boccaccio fra storiografia e romanzo." *Studi sul Boccaccio*, 19 (1990), 151–90.

Dwyer, Richard A. "Arthur's Stellification in the *Fall of Princes*." *Philological Quarterly*, 57 (1978), 155–71.

Eggers, J. Phillip. *King Arthur's Laureate: A Study of Tennyson's Idylls of the King.* New York: New York University Press, 1971. [Pp. 94–101 cover Victorian reaction to Tennyson's Arthur; pp. 105–37 cover some other nineteenth-century interpretations of the Arthurian legends.]

Entwistle, William J. *The Arthurian Legend in the Literatures of the Spanish Peninsula.* London: Dent, 1925; rpt. New York: Phaeton, 1975.

Field, P.J.C. "Shakespeare's King Arthur." *The Welsh Connection*, ed. William Tydeman. Llandysul: Gomer, 1986, pp. 11–23.

Fletcher, Robert Huntington. *The Arthurian Material in the Chronicles Especially Those of Great Britain and France.* [Harvard] Studies and Notes in Philology and Literature, 10. Boston, 1906. 2nd ed. Roger Sherman Loomis. New York: Burt Franklin, 1966.

Fredeman, William E. "The Last Idyll: Dozing in Avalon" and "Appendix: The Laureate and the King: An Iconographic Survey of Arthurian Subjects in Victorian Art." In Baswell and Sharpe, *The Passing of Arthur*, pp. 264–76, 277–306.

Gallix, François. "T.H. White et la légende du roi Arthur." *Mosaic*, 10.2 (1977), 47–63.

*———. "T.H. White et la légende du roi Arthur: de la fantasie animale au moralisme politique," *Études anglaises*, 34 (1981), 192–203.

Gardner, Edmund G. *The Arthurian Legend in Italian Literature.* London: Dent, 1930; rpt. New York: Octagon, 1971.

Gerould, Gordon Hall. "King Arthur and Politics," *Speculum*, 1 (1926), 33–51; 2 (1927), 448.

Giffin, Mary. "Cadwalder, Arthur, and Brutus in the Wigmore Manuscript." *Speculum*, 16 (1941), 109–20.

*Gilbert, Elliot L. "The Female King: Tennyson's Arthurian Apocalypse." *PMLA*, 98 (1983), 863–78.

Gillies, William. "Arthur in Gaelic Tradition. Part I: Folktales and Ballads." *Cambridge Medieval Celtic Studies*, 2 (1981), 47–72.

———. "Arthur in Gaelic Tradition. Part II: Romances and Learned Lore." *Cambridge Medieval Celtic Studies*, 3 (1982), 41–75.

Goebel, Janet E. "The Hero as Artist: Arthur among the German Romantics." In Lagorio and Day, *King Arthur Through the Ages*, Vol. 2, pp. 3–26.

Göller, Karl Heinz. "Arthurs Aufstieg zum Heiligen: Eine weniger Entwicklungslinie des Herrscherbildes." In *Artusrittertum im späten Mittelalter: Ethos und Ideologie*, ed. Friedrich Wolfzettel. Beiträge zur deutschen Philologie, 57. Giessen: Schmitz, 1984, pp. 87–101.

———. *König Arthur in den englishchen Literatur des späten Mittelalters.* Palaestra, 238. Göttingen: Vandenhoeck & Ruprecht, 1963.

*———. "König Arthur in den schottischen Chroniken." *Anglia*, 80 (1962), 390–404.

Göller, Karl Heinz, and Anke Janssen. "König Arthur in den populären Unterhaltungsliteratur des 17. Jahrhunderts." In *Festgabe für Hans Pinsker zum 70. Geburtstag*, ed. Richild Acobian. Vienna: Verband der wissenschaftlichen Gesellschaften Österreichs, 1979, pp. 78–108.

Goodman, Jennifer R. *The Legend of Arthur in British and American Literature.* Boston: Twayne, 1988.

Goodrich, Norma Lorre. *King Arthur.* New York: Franklin Watts, 1986.

Gray, J.M. "A Study in Idyl [*sic*]: Tennyson's 'The Coming of Arthur.'" *Renaissance and Modern Studies*, 14 (1970), 111–50.

Greenlaw, Edwin. *Studies in Spenser's Historical Allegory.* Baltimore, 1932.

Grubmüller, Klaus. "Der Artusroman und sein König. Beobachtungen zur Artusfigur am Beispiel von Ginovers Entführung." In *Positionen des Romans im späten Mittelalter*, ed. Walter Haug and Burghart Wachinger. Tübingen: Niemeyer, 1991, pp. 1–20.

Gürttler, Karin R. *"Künec Artûs der guote": Das Artusbild der höfischen Epik des 12. und 13. Jahrhunderts*. Studien zur Germanistik, Anglistik und Komparatistik, 52. Bonn: Grundmann, 1976.

*Höltgen, Karl Josef. "König Arthur und Fortuna." *Anglia*, 75 (1957), 35–54.

Hoffman, Donald L. "The Arthurian Tradition in Italy." In Lagorio and Day, *King Arthur Through the Ages*. Vol. 1, pp. 170–88.

Housman, John E. "Higden, Trevisa, Caxton and the Beginnings of Arthurian Criticism." *Review of English Studies*, 23 (1947), 209–17.

*Hughes, M.Y. "The Arthurs of the *Faerie Queen*," *Études anglaises*, 6 (1953), 193–213.

Hume, Anthea. *Edmund Spenser: Protestant Poet*. Cambridge: Cambridge University Press, 1984. [Spenser's use of Arthurian chronicles in *The Faerie Queene*.]

Hyatte, Reginald. "Arthur as Marc's and Tristan's Double in the French *Tristan* Fragments by Béroul and Thomas." In Lagorio and Day, *King Arthur Through the Ages*. Vol. 1, pp. 110–26.

Jackson, Kenneth Hurlstone. "The Arthur of History." In Loomis, *ALMA*, pp. 1–11.

Jarman, A.O.H. "The Delineation of Arthur in Early Welsh Verse." In *An Arthurian Tapestry: Essays in Memory of Lewis Thorpe*. Glasgow: French Department, University of Glasgow, 1981, pp. 1–21.

———. "La tradition galloise d'Arthur," *Marche Romane*, 32 (1982), 43–60.

Jenkins, Elizabeth. *The Mystery of King Arthur*. New York: Coward, McCann and Geoghegan, 1975.

Johanek, Peter. "König Arthur und die Plantagenets. Über den Zusammenhang von Historiographie und höfischer Epik in mittelalterlicher Propaganda." *Frühmittelalterliche Studien*, 21 (1987), 346–89.

Jones, Thomas, "The Early Evolution of the Legend of Arthur," trans. Gerald Morgan. *Nottingham Medieval Studies*, 8 (1964), 3–21.

Jones, W. Lewis. *King Arthur in History and Legend*. Cambridge: Cambridge University Press, 1912.

Kalinke, Marianne E. "Arthurian Literature in Scandinavia." In Lagorio and Day, *King Arthur Through the Ages*. Vol. 1, pp. 127–51.

———. *King Arthur, North-by-Northwest: The "matière de Bretagne" in Old Norse-Icelandic Romances*. Bibliotheca Arnamagnaeana 37. Copenhagen: Reitzel, 1981.

Keeler, Laura. *Geoffrey of Monmouth and the Late Latin Chroniclers 1300–1500*. University of California Publications in English, 17. Berkeley: University of California Press, 1946.

Kellman, Martin. *T.H. White and the Matter of Britain: A Literary Overview*. Lewiston, N.Y.: Mellen, 1988.

Kendrick, T.D. *British Antiquity*. London: Methuen, 1950.

*Kennedy, Edward Donald. "Malory's King Mark and King Arthur." *Mediaeval Studies*, 37 (1975), 190–234.

*Kennedy, Elspeth. "Études sur le *Lancelot en prose*: 2: Le Roi Arthur dans le *Lancelot en prose*." *Romania*, 105 (1984), 46–62.

———. "Feudal Links and the Role of Arthur and His Court." In *Lancelot and the Grail: A Study of the Prose Lancelot*. Oxford: Clarendon Press, 1986.

———. "King Arthur in the First Part of the Prose *Lancelot*." In *Medieval Miscellany Presented to Eugène Vinaver by Pupils, Colleagues and Friends*, ed. F. Whitehead, A.H. Diverres, and F.E. Sutcliffe. Manchester: Manchester University Press, 1965, pp. 186–95.

———. "Social and Political Ideas in the French Prose *Lancelot*." *Medium Ævum*, 26 (1957), 90–106.

Kimpel, Richard W. "King Arthur in Germany: A Once and Future Tradition." In *Courtly Literature: Culture and Context*, ed. Keith Busby and Erik Kooper. Amsterdam and Philadelphia: John Benjamins, 1990, pp. 355–65.

Kipling, Gordon. *The Triumph of Honor: Burgundian Origins of the Elizabethan Renaissance*. The Hague: Leiden University Press, 1977, especially pp. 14–15, 83–91, 112–14, 127–29.

Knight, Stephen. *Arthurian Literature and Society*. New York: St. Martin's, 1983.

Korrel, Peter. *An Arthurian Triangle: A Study of the Origin, Development and Characterization of Arthur, Guinevere and Mordred*. Leiden: Brill, 1984.

Lagorio, Valerie M., and Mildred Leake Day, eds. *King Arthur Through the Ages*. 2 vols. New York: Garland, 1990.

Lewin, Lois J. "The Blameless King? The Conceptual Flaw in Tennyson's Arthur." *Ball State University Forum*, 10.2 (1969), 32–41.

Lindsay, Jack. *Arthur and His Times: Britain in the Dark Ages*. London: Frederick Muller, 1958; rpt. New York: Barnes and Noble, 1966.

Loomis, C. Grant. "King Arthur and the Saints." *Speculum*, 8 (1933), 478–82.

Loomis, Roger Sherman. *The Development of Arthurian Romance*. London: Hutchison, 1963.

———. "Edward I, Arthurian Enthusiast." *Speculum*, 28 (1953), 114–27.

———. "The Legend of Arthur's Survival." In Loomis, *ALMA*, pp. 64–71.

Loomis, Roger Sherman, and Laura Hibbard Loomis. *Arthurian Legends in Medieval Art*. London: Oxford University Press, 1938; rpt. New York: Kraus, 1975.

MacCallum, M.W. *Tennyson's Idylls of the King and Arthurian Story from the XVIth Century*. Glasgow: Maclehose, 1894. [Actually surveys Arthurian literature from its beginnings.]

*MacRae, Donald C. "Appearances and Reality in *La Mort le Roi Artu*." *Forum for Modern Language Studies*, 18 (1982), 266–77.

Malone, Kemp. "The Historicity of Arthur." *Journal of English and Germanic Philology*, 23 (1924), 463–91.

Mancoff, Debra N. *The Arthurian Revival in Victorian Art*. New York: Garland, 1990.

Markale, Jean. *King Arthur: King of Kings*, trans. Christine Hauch. London: Gordon and Cremonesi, 1977; originally published as *Le Roi Arthur et la société celtique*. Paris: Payot, 1976; rpt. 1983.

Matheson, Lister M. "King Arthur and the Medieval English Chronicles." In Lagorio and Day, *King Arthur Through the Ages*, Vol. 1, pp. 248–74.

Maynadier, Howard. *The Arthur of the English Poets*. Boston: Houghton, Mifflin, 1907.

Mead, William Edward, ed. *The Famous Historie of Chinon of England*, by Christopher Middleton. Early English Text Society 165 (1925), pp. xxv–xlvi. [Surveys sixteenth-century Arthurian literature.]

Merriman, James Douglas. *The Flower of Kings: A Study of the Arthurian Legend in England Between 1485 and 1835*. Lawrence: University Press of Kansas, 1973.

Miller, Helen Hill. *The Realms of Arthur*. New York: Scribner's, 1969.

Millican, Charles Bowie. *Spenser and the Table Round: A Study in the Contemporaneous Background for Spenser's Use of the Arthurian Legend*. Harvard Studies in Comparative Literature, VIII. Cambridge, Mass.: Harvard University Press, 1932; rpt. New York: Octagon, 1967.

Morris, John. *The Age of Arthur*. New York: Scribner's, 1973.

Morris, Rosemary. *The Character of King Arthur in Medieval Literature*. Cambridge: Brewer, 1982.

———. "King Arthur and the Growth of French Nationalism." In *France and the British Isles in the Middle Ages and Renaissance: Essays in Memory of Ruth Morgan*, ed. Gillian Jondorf and D.N. Dumville. Woodbridge: Boydell and Brewer, 1991, pp. 115–29.

Muir, Lynette. "King Arthur: Style Louis XVI." *Studies in Eighteenth-Century French*

Literature Presented to Robert Niklaus, ed. J.H. Fox, M.H. Waddicor, and D.A. Watts. Exeter: University of Exeter, 1975, pp. 163–71.

Nitze, W.A. "The Exhumation of King Arthur at Glastonbury." *Speculum*, 9 (1934), 355–61.

Noble, Peter S. "Chrétien's Arthur." *Chrétien de Troyes and the Troubadours*, ed. Peter S. Noble and Linda M. Paterson. Cambridge: St. Catherine's College, 1984, pp. 220–37.

Parry, John J. "The Historical Arthur." *Journal of English and Germanic Philology*, 58 (1959), 365–79.

Peters, Edward. *The Shadow King*: Rex Inutilis *in Medieval Law and Literature 751–1327*. New Haven: Yale University Press, 1970. ["*Rex Inutilis* in the Arthurian Romances," pp. 170–209.]

Reid, Margaret J.C. *The Arthurian Legend: A Comparison of Treatment in Modern and Mediaeval Literature*. Edinburgh: Oliver and Boyd, 1938; rpt. 1960.

Richey, Margaret Fitzgerald. "The German Contribution to the Matter of Britain with Special Reference to the Legend of King Arthur and the Table Round." *Medium Ævum*, 19 (1950), 26–42.

Rider, Jeff. "Arthur and the Saints." In Lagorio and Day, *King Arthur Through the Ages*. Vol. 1, pp. 3–21.

Riddy, Felicity. "Reading for England: Arthurian Literature and National Consciousness." *Bibliographical Bulletin of the International Arthurian Society*, 43 (1991), 314–32.

Ritson, Joseph. *The Life of King Arthur: From Ancient Historians and Authentic Documents*. London: Payne and Foss, 1825.

Robinson, J. Armitage. *Two Glastonbury Legends: King Arthur and Joseph of Arimathea*. Cambridge: Cambridge University Press, 1926.

Rosenberg, John D. *The Fall of Camelot: A Study of Tennyson's Idylls of the King*. Cambridge, Mass.: Belknap Press of Harvard University Press, 1973.

Ryals, Clyde de L. *From the Great Deep: Essays on Idylls of the King*. Athens, OH: Ohio University Press, 1967.

*Sargent-Baur, Barbara N. "Dux bellorum / rex militum / roi fainéant: la transformation d'Arthur au XIIᵉ siècle." *Moyen Age*, 90 (1984), 357–73.

Schmolke-Hasselmann, Beate. *Der arthurische Versroman von Chrestien bis Froissart*. Tübingen: Niemeyer, 1980.

———. "King Arthur as Villain in the Thirteenth-Century Romance *Yder*," *Reading Medieval Studies*, 6 (1980), 31–43.

Simpson, Roger. *Camelot Regained: The Arthurian Revival and Tennyson 1800–1849*. Cambridge: Brewer, 1990.

Solomon, Stanley J. "Tennyson's Paradoxical King." *Victorian Poetry*, 1 (1963), 258–71.

Staines, David. "King Arthur in Victorian Fiction." In *The World of Victorian Fiction*, ed. Jerome H. Buckley. Harvard English Studies 6. Cambridge, Mass.: Harvard University Press, 1975, pp. 267–93.

———. *Tennyson's Camelot: The Idylls of the King and Its Medieval Sources*. Waterloo, Ontario: Wilfrid Laurier University Press, 1982.

Starr, Nathan Comfort. *King Arthur Today: The Arthurian Legend in English and American Literature 1901–1953*. Gainesville: University of Florida Press, 1954.

Stones, M. Alison. "Aspects of Arthur's Death in Medieval Illumination," and "Appendices: An Iconographic Survey of Manuscripts Illustrating Arthur's Death." In Baswell and Sharpe, *The Passing of Arthur*, pp. 52–86, 87–101.

Taylor, Beverly, and Elisabeth Brewer. *The Return of King Arthur: British and American Arthurian Literature since 1800*. Cambridge: Brewer, 1983.

Thompson, Raymond H. *The Return from Avalon: A Study of the Arthurian Legend in Modern Fiction*. Westport, Conn.: Greenwood Press, 1985.

Treharne, R.F. *The Glastonbury Legends: Joseph of Arimathea, the Holy Grail, and King Arthur*. London: Cresset, 1967.

Tyson, Diana B. "King Arthur as a Literary Device in French Vernacular History Writing of the Fourteenth Century." *Bibliographical Bulletin of the International Arthurian Society*, 33 (1981), 237–57.

Van der Ven-Ten Bensel, E. *The Character of King Arthur in English Literature.* Amsterdam: H.J. Paris, 1925.

Vinaver, Eugène. *The Rise of Romance.* Oxford, 1971.

Warnock, Robert G. "The Arthurian Tradition in Hebrew and Yiddish." In Lagorio and Day, *King Arthur Through the Ages*. Vol. 1, pp. 189–208.

Whitaker, Muriel. *The Legends of King Arthur in Art.* Cambridge: Brewer, 1990.

Williams, Mary. "King Arthur in History and Legend." *Folklore*, 73 (1962), 73–88.

Yeats, Frances A. *Shakespeare's Last Plays: A New Approach.* London: Routledge & Kegan Paul, 1975. [Jacobean interest in Arthur, pp. 17–37.]

KING ARTHUR

LOOKING FOR ARTHUR

Marylyn Jackson Parins

No character, eminent in ancient history, has ever been treated with more extravagance, mendacity and injustice, than the renowned Arthur, the illustrious monarch and valiant commander of the Britons. Extolled by some, as greater in power, more victorious in war, more abundant in dominion, more extensive in fame, than either the Roman Julius or the Grecian Alexander; his very existence has, by others, been, positively and absolutely denied.

These words, from Joseph Ritson's *Life of King Arthur*,[1] published posthumously in 1825 but written by 1803, were intended to express both of the extremes as well as a middle ground in the controversy that had swirled about the "historic" Arthur for centuries. In an earlier work, Ritson had said, "That he was a brave warriour, and in all probability, a petty king, is manifest from authentick history";[2] this position can be called the middle ground. The "injustice" that Ritson mentions reflects an often expressed view that the work of Geoffrey of Monmouth had actually damaged the genuine career and accomplishments of the real Arthur by causing an over-reaction; that is, dismissing these accounts as fictions meant, too often, rejecting an Arthurian reality as well.

Today, the middle position has shifted to a less positive view of this historic Arthur, as the very grounds of what constitutes Ritson's "authentick history" have come under closer scrutiny. The problems associated with reconstructing events that took place in the Britain of A.D. 400–600 are formidable, including as they do long-recognized difficulties in interpreting archaeological evidence as well as the nearly complete lack of written records of the period. Nonetheless, modern scholarship too provides evidence of a considerable margin on either side of center. As this essay shows, even through the last thirty years or so, the debate over just what in fifth- and sixth-century Britain accounts for the legends about Arthur has produced a spectrum ranging from a high king or even emperor to no one at all, certainly no one whose existence can be verified.

In discussions of Arthur from early chroniclers onwards, there is a determined attempt to separate the Arthur of history from the creation of legend and fable. Many of these commentators make explicit what is implied in the passage from Ritson and argue against denying the man out of distrust of the obvious fictions. William of Malmesbury, for example, writing around 1125, had called Arthur "a man who is surely worthy of being described in true histories rather than dreamed about in fallacious myths."[3] This attitude is seen too in Holinshed's *Chronicles,* in Gibbon, and in several nineteenth-century historians, beginning with Sharon Turner as the century opened.[4]

Turner argued that although minstrels and the romancers had embellished Arthur's story, still, "when all such fictions are removed, and those incidents only are retained which the sober criticism of history sanctions with its approbation, a fame ample enough to interest the judicious, and to perpetuate his honourable memory, will still continue to claim our belief and applause" (1, 285–86). In his "probable history" of Arthur, Turner makes no outrageous claims for Arthur, noting that Arthur's victory at Badon Hill only checked the progress of Anglo-Saxon settlement, and he adds, "This state of moderate greatness suits the character, in which the Welsh bards exhibit Arthur. They commemorate him; but it is not with that excelling glory, with which he has been surrounded by subsequent traditions" (1, 289–90).

As this passage shows, Turner was familiar with the poetry of early Welsh bards then less well-known to English audiences. Joseph Ritson also knew this material, but because of the late dates of surviving manuscripts he considered the Welsh poems and triads in their references to Arthur to have been tainted by the influence of Geoffrey of Monmouth, whose version of Arthur's "history" he openly derided. Ritson calls Gildas "querulous," doubts that Arthur was buried at Glastonbury, and dismisses the idea that there were two Guineveres, much less the three that the Welsh triads claim (*Life of King Arthur,* pp. xv, 86, 106–9). However, while both Ritson and Turner set out to include only "those incidents . . . which the sober criticism of history sanctions," both find these incidents in Gildas's general picture of the times and in the accounts of Arthur in such sources as Nennius and various saints' lives, and from them they construct biographies of Arthur, his parentage, his birth, and his battles. Both, for example, include Melwas's kidnapping of Guinevere found in Caradoc of Llancarvan's *Life of Gildas.*

As providers of sober historical evidence about Arthur, however, these sources too would be discounted by most modern scholars.

Along with Sharon Turner, his contemporary William Owen-Pughe did much to advance English public awareness of Celtic history and literature; his *Cambrian Biography*, subtitled "Historical Notices of Celebrated Men among the Ancient Britons," appeared in 1803. Owen-Pughe, like Turner and others mentioned above, distinguishes between a historical and a romance Arthur. The historical Arthur commemorated by Welsh bards who were his contemporaries, Owen-Pughe says, was "a chieftain of the Silurian Britons . . . elected by the states of Britain, to sovereign authority," one who "often led the Britons to battle against the Saxons." But the figure who appears in the *Mabinogion* and in *Culhwch and Olwen*, is "altogether another personage," is, in fact, "a mythological character, of times so ancient as to be far beyond the scope of history."[5]

Owen-Pughe, then, saw a carry-over from Celtic myth into Arthurian story; he says, for example, that Melwas, the kidnapper of Guinevere, was a mythological character and links him, in the description that follows, to vegetation deities and the rites celebrating the return of spring (p. 248). Explorations of this sort, though less emphasized in very recent scholarship, have at several times dominated the field of Arthurian studies. But in Owen-Pughe, the line between historic and mythic is not always so clear as in this example. He confidently identifies "Uthyr, commonly surnamed Pendragon," as "the 85th king of Britain, who reigned from the year 500 until 517."[6] The name Uther Pendragon, or "Wonder the Supreme Leader," he believes, is one adopted "to create an enthusiasm for the emergency of the time; but the real name of this hero probably was Meirig ab Tewdrig, who certainly was the father of his illustrious successor, who, on that occasion [i.e., his succession], assumed the mythological name of Arthur, or the Bear exalted" (p. 340). Expanding upon the mythological figure, Owen-Pughe finds in the Welsh stories of Arthur "adventures which must have had a common origin" with those of Hercules and Jason, and he also associates Arthur with Nimrod, the mighty hunter of Genesis.

Owen-Pughe's pursuit of comparative mythology through the Welsh stories of Arthur was expanded upon considerably six years later, in Edward Davies's *The Mythology and Rites of the British Druids*. Davies followed the "Helio-Arkite" theory, which held that all ancient mythology sprang from a single source and that the authentic account—divinely recorded— was to be found in the early books of the Old Testament. Davies perceived Druidic lore hidden in surviving Welsh poems and triads, and in his view these "British mysteries" reflect the Biblical flood and those characters associated with it. Evidence to support this theory he finds in Taliesin's poem "The Spoils of Annwn," Annwn being the Celtic Otherworld; Davies translates the title as "Spoils of the Deep" and calls it "a poem which treats wholly of Diluvian mythology."[7] Thus "Arthur was one of the titles of the deified patriarch Noah. And with this idea, the account which we have of him in the Bards and the Triads, perfectly accord[s]" (p. 187).

The idea of Arthur as a symbol, not a person, was carried even further in Algernon Herbert's *Britannia after the Romans;* its two volumes appeared in 1836 and 1841. Herbert doubts the existence of a historic Arthur; rather, the deeds and attributes attached to the name Arthur represent mainly those of Hercules, the terrestrial Apollo. For Arthur also represents Apollo, the pagan god of light or, here, the sun, and the Round Table represents the Zodiac. However, Herbert does situate this symbolic mass in the Britain of the fifth and sixth centuries; his explanation of this period can be partly summarized as follows:

After the withdrawal of the Romans from Britain, the Celts who were left behind, most notably the Welsh, reverted from Christianity to the practice of pagan Druidism for perhaps a century. The name Arthur is merely the symbol by which was signified the dominance of this Druidic cult and its worship of Hercules/Apollo. The poetry of the sixth-century Welsh bards is replete with Druidic lore deliberately obscured so as not to be intelligible to the non-initiate. Similarly, wishing to obscure the true history of this period of pagan revival, the bards borrowed historic deeds from the exploits of another warrior, gave them Welsh color and locales, and transferred them to the name of Arthur. This warrior was Attila the Hun, many events of whose career, Herbert believes, closely parallel those of the fictitious Arthur. The final battle at Camlann, where "Arthur" was defeated by "Mordred the Pict," is simply a reference to the fall from power of the Druidic cult and the end of its dominance.[8]

Neither Herbert nor Davies attaches any importance to the existence of a real person behind the myth(s). This tendency was deplored by the historian J.A. Giles, among others:

> Whilst we set aside fables as unworthy of serious attention, we are not justified in asserting with some incredulous historians, that no such person as Arthur ever lived and fought; still less may we compromise the claims which history justly makes . . . by considering Arthur as a personification of the sun, and viewing his round table with the twelve Paladins, as a poetical description of the Zodiac with its twelve signs.[9]

And in 1858, D.W. Nash published a devastating attack on both Herbert and Davies, although his objections were not to their mythologizing of Arthur in itself. In *Taliesin: or the Bards and Druids of Britain,* Nash sets out to prove that their claims to have identified survivals of ancient pagan lore rested on wildly erroneous translations of Welsh poems and triads whose texts could not be reliably dated before the twelfth and thirteenth centuries.[10]

Nash quotes with approval the remarks of the historian Sir Francis Palgrave on the difficulties of documenting the history of post-Roman Britain. In *The Rise and Progress of the English Commonwealth* (1831–32), Palgrave had written:

> Our knowledge of the affairs of Britain, previous to the introduction of Christianity among the Anglo-Saxons, is derived from the most obscure and unsatisfactory evidence. . . . The Welsh, in the days of Giraldus, easily accounted for the loss of all memorials of King Arthur, by asserting that Gildas cast his "authentic history" of his renowned prince and his nation into the sea; but the same misfortune appears to have fallen on all the British annals of the next three centuries.

Palgrave concluded that "British history, during this period, is therefore a mere hypothesis."[11] In his earlier *History of the Anglo-Saxons,* Palgrave does refer to Ambrosius Aurelianus and Vortigern as "contending" in 446, and he notices with some skepticism Hengist and Horsa and "their supposed transactions" with Vortigern; however, he moves on to "Progress of the Invaders" and finally to "Conquest of Britain by the Jutes, Angles, and Saxons" without finding it necessary to mention the name Arthur at all.[12]

However, in *Rise and Progress*, where Palgrave so forcefully expressed his dissatisfaction with available documentary evidence, he also said that he could "neither doubt the existence of this Chieftain, nor believe in the achievements which have been ascribed to him."[13] Nash does not say what he thinks about a chieftain, but as to a King Arthur, he states, "it is by no means clear that the Welsh had ever heard of Arthur as a king [before] . . . the twelfth century" (p. 327).

Nash excels at showing how supposed support for the theories of Davies and Herbert rests in part upon inaccurate translation, and where they had found evidence of ancient religious philosophies and cultic practices, Nash found at most "a machinery of necromancers and magic, such as has probably been possessed by all people in all ages, more or less abundantly." Although much Welsh material, as he notes, abounds in "magical and supernatural wonders," there is "no more necessity for seeking a hidden meaning in the tale of Taliesin than in that of Cinderella" (pp. 180–86). In striving to discredit what he viewed as eccentric claims for Welsh poetry, Nash himself seems extreme in his denial of any uniquely Celtic element in surviving Welsh poetry. At the same time, he ignored or downplayed the role of oral tradition in preserving—often in garbled or fragmentary form—remnants of a pre-Christian stratum of belief.

Nash's denial of this aspect of the Welsh poems and stories led Matthew Arnold to conclude that Nash, "in pursuing his work of demolition, too much puts out of sight the positive and constructive performance for which this work of demolition is to clear the ground. . . . Mr. Nash's skepticism seems to me . . . too absolute, too stationary, too much without a future." This remark comes from Arnold's series of lectures, "On the Study of Celtic Literature," later published (1867) under the same title.[14] While Arnold does not discuss the place of a real or a mythological Arthur in all this, he does see both the Helio-Arkites and Nash as representing extremes, and he urges the restoration of balance in the interpretation of the Celtic past to be gleaned from the surviving Welsh texts.

By the mid-1860s, the period of Arnold's lectures, the scope of Arthurian studies had expanded enormously. The process of bringing medieval Arthurian poems and romances out of manuscript and into print had been going on since the late eighteenth century but was accelerated from the 1860s with, among other things, the founding of the Early English Text Society. Literary histories as early as Thomas Warton's *History of English Poetry* had attempted to formulate chronologies that would help to show how romance had evolved, and the nineteenth-century rise of English studies had created increased demand for these literary histories. In addition, use of Arthurian matter as the subject of nineteenth-century literary and artistic production was widespread even early on; and especially after mid-century it appeared in the work of major artists and writers. Obviously these artistic and literary versions of Arthur lie far outside the scope of this essay. But they do convey a point important to this topic: Tennyson, Hunt, Rossetti, Arnold, Morris, and a bit later Burne-Jones and Swinburne were influential figures who drew their material almost exclusively from, and thus helped to popularize, medieval legend, not the history of fifth-century Britain. Similarly, literary historians and editors of Arthurian texts were concerned with literary influences and sources and with placing a particular work within larger literary contexts. Given these sources of inspiration and these concerns, the question of whether or not an actual fifth-century Arthur had existed was not very important.

A representative example of this trend is found in the introductory materials that F.J. Furnivall attached to his editions of several Arthurian poems and romances. Furnivall was assiduous in promoting the publication of medieval texts, even dull ones, Lovelich's *Seynt Graal* being a case in point. Furnivall recognizes the work itself as uninspiring and perhaps for that reason includes a number of essays by various hands in the two-volume edition (1861 and 1863). Almost as an afterthought to his own preface in Volume one, Furnivall refers the reader interested in "the real history of Arthur" to Professor Charles H. Pearson's *The Early and Middle Ages of England* (1861); he does not tell what one would find there.

Actually, Pearson's brief discussion is quite interesting and anticipates later developments in treating the historical figure. Pearson says that the "real merit of Arthur's struggle" was that Arthur's temporary success insured an intermingling of peoples rather than an eradication of the native population, at least in the southwest. (He places Arthur in Somerset.) But, Pearson cautions,

> . . . if we venture to assert Arthur's existence, it is on condition of restricting his dominions. In the narrative of the ninth century, which describes him as lord-paramount of Britain, fighting twelve battles from the south to Scotland, going as a pilgrim to Jerusalem, and wearing the Virgin's image on his shield, he is already passing into the hero of romance. History only knows him as the petty prince of a Devonian principality, whose wife, the Guenever of romance, was carried off by Maelgoun of North Wales, and scarcely recovered by treaty after a year's fighting.[15]

Furnivall himself seems reluctant to have the question resolved. He admits that Pearson's view "will . . . no doubt meet with ultimate acceptance" but adds, "Still, in speaking of Arthur we are dealing with probabilities, not certainties." He does think it "reasonable to suppose that an original of Arthur was once in the flesh," but where and when he lived "it is difficult to say."[16] And, he implies, it doesn't much matter.

Furnivall founded the Early English Text Society in 1864, and no doubt in an attempt to secure wider support for it, emphasized in the early years the publication of "English Romances Relating to Arthur and His Knights."[17] One of the Society's first publications was Furnivall's edition of a fragment of not particularly good fourteenth-century English verse on Arthur. The *Saturday Review*'s comments, while certainly not typical of the nineteenth-century's reception of Arthurian matter,[18] point up the relative lack of interest in the Arthur of history:

Now, as matters of philological study, we are ready to receive texts about King Arthur or about any other subject under heaven; but, in any other point of view, we must confess that we are tired of King Arthur. That is, we wish to hand him over to the Comparative Mythologists. When they have sat upon him for a befitting time, we shall be glad to hear of him again, and to know whether he really is the Sun or not. . . . But we must confess that we do not enter into the apparently prevalent love of everything Arthurian for its own sake.[19]

However, as the reviewer later suggests, the medieval Arthurian *legend* need not be completely rejected. "Lest we should be thought needlessly to depreciate the Arthurian story as such, we will end with Mr. Furnivall's enthusiastic account of it" [i.e., Furnivall's remarks on the splendors to be found in the French *Queste* and in Malory].

The *Saturday Review*'s wish that Arthur be turned over to the comparative mythologists was granted with, one might say, a vengeance, although this time around more scholarly credentials and somewhat more scholarly caution were in evidence than with a Davies or a Herbert. The seminal work of Max Müller had begun appearing in English translations from the 1850s, and by the century's end, Sir James Frazer's *Golden Bough* would also influence Arthurian studies. In these pursuits, Sir John Rhys and Jessie Weston are names prominent in a field too large to detail further. Here too the Arthur of history fades to insignificance, as seen, for example, in the work of George Cox, whose *Introduction to the Science of Comparative Mythology and Folk-lore* was first published in 1881. "The Historical Arthur" is the title of a brief appendix in which Cox expresses grave doubts that there was one.[20] Cox cites what he considers the spurious proofs offered by some historians and the failure to mention Arthur of others. He then quotes the following passage from John Lingard's *History of England,* first published in 1819:[21]

> . . . when the reader has been told that Arthur was a British chieftain, that he fought in many battles, that he was murdered by his nephew and was buried at Glastonbury, where his remains were discovered in the reign of Henry II, he will have learned all that can be ascertained at the present day of that celebrated warrior. (quoted by Cox, p. 368)

"It is very doubtful," Cox comments drily, "whether he can ascertain or learn nearly so much." We have here, he says, "a chieftain with whose life mythology has by universal consent been busy"; thus Arthur's twelve victories as listed by Nennius "provoke comparison" to the obviously non-historical twelve labors of Hercules. And, he concludes:

> The remaining incidents which Dr. Lingard is content that the reader should believe if he likes to do so, are, of course, perfectly possible; but if our knowledge of them be derived solely from the legendary narrative of his exploits, it is worth neither more nor less than the chronology of the events which took place in the House that Jack built. We may learn the truth of these facts, if they be facts, from other sources. . . . From the legend we learn nothing. (Cox 369)

The work of finding in Arthurian romance vestiges of sun gods and lunar goddesses—some more specifically oriented in Celtic tradition than others—continued apace, and as seen in J.A. Giles's response quoted earlier, provoked reactions, one of them from J.D. Bruce in the 1920s. The title of his monumental work, *The Evolution of Arthurian Romance,* shows where his emphasis lies, but he does deal briefly, if inconclusively, with the historical question. Bruce characterizes the "evidence on the subject" as "meagre, relatively late, and almost wholly fantastic." He finds though that, since Gildas was concerned more with showing how the Britons' ruin was due to their sins than with presenting historical narrative, "no inference can be drawn" from his silence as to an Arthur. Bruce also says that the sections of Nennius concerning Arthur are among that composite's earliest, dating perhaps "within one hundred and fifty years of the time when he must have lived." Thus, when Nennius says Arthur won the battle at Badon Hill, here noted as a demonstrably historical battle of the early sixth century, Bruce says, ". . . it seems wise to accept this statement as authentic and to recognize in him a man of Roman descent or a Romanized Celt who, in these times of stress, attained the leadership of the British hosts." And here is the Gilesian echo: "There is no need, therefore, of regarding [Arthur] simply as a creature of the popular imagination or of vaporizing him into a hypothetical culture-divinity, as various scholars have done."[22]

One of the various scholars Bruce mentions in his notes is John Rhys, and while it is no overstatement to say that Rhys's major concern was with Arthur as a "Brythonic god" and/or Culture Hero, still, in both his *Studies in the Arthurian Legend* and in his preface to the popular Everyman edition of Malory's *Morte Darthur,* Rhys maintained that a historic Arthur may well, after the departure of the Romans, have filled the Roman office of Count of Britain. This supposition is based on Nennius's line describing the

Arthur who fought against the Saxons *with* the kings of the Britons, but who himself, says Nennius, was *dux bellorum*. Bruce's own treatment of Gildas and Nennius, seen above, is also significant, for the Arthur of history is about to be rescued from both skepticism and neglect.

In the meantime, the relevant documents were becoming more accessible to reexamination and reinterpretation. R.H. Fletcher's *The Arthurian Material in the Chronicles* (1906) provided a detailed chronological discussion of Arthurian material from Gildas through fifteenth- and sixteenth-century chronicles. Fletcher allowed that Nennius's account suggested the existence of a "bold warrior and an energetic general" who "sustained the falling fortunes of his country," but he advised caution: "There is always the possibility that Arthur never existed at all, and that even Nennius's comparatively modest eulogy" was based not on fact but on "the persistent stories of ancient Celtic myth or the patriotic figments of the ardent Celtic imagination."[23] E.K. Chambers's wide-ranging *Arthur of Britain* (1927) is still useful as the source of early Latin texts concerning Arthur. Geoffrey Ashe has lately suggested that although Chambers was himself "noncommittal as to Arthur's reality," he had described the king in terms that offered an open invitation for the "reconstruction" of the historical Arthur.[24]

G.M. Trevelyan's widely-read *History of England* had also been noncommittal on the subject of a real Arthur; he mentions a "half mythical King Arthur" leading Celts against the heathen but notes the lack of "authentic chronicles of the Saxon Conquest. . . . The most important page in our national annals is a blank. The chief names of this missing period of history—Hengist, Vortigern, Cerdic, Arthur—may be those of real or of imaginary men."[25] However, the archaeologist Lloyd Laing has recently noted Trevelyan's contribution to the "fire and sword" interpretation of the fifth-century Anglo-Saxon occupation of Britain. Laing cites Trevelyan's description of Anglo-Saxon warriors "storming the earthwork camps and stone girt cities, burning the towns and villas, slaughtering and driving away the Romanized Britons."[26] Laing sees Trevelyan as a continuator, however, not as an innovator: "For some time it has been fairly clear that the traditional picture of waves of Anglo-Saxon incomers exterminating the Britons (ex-Romans) or driving them into the Celtic West is probably a facile model born of nineteenth-century ideas about imperialism and the processes of culture change" (p. 65). Furthermore, Laing adds,

> The Briton *v.* Saxons image was not helped by the political climate of two world wars. The 1930s produced a spate of propaganda which equated Anglo-Saxons with Germans and which tried to either paint

a picture of them as violent barbarians or as vigorous conquering heroes sweeping away a decadent society, depending on the political affiliations of the writers. . . . An anxiety to redress the balance may have resulted in archaeologists stretching meagre evidence for Romano-British survival to its limits. (p. 66)

Of course what may have occurred in archaeological studies need not have been duplicated in attempts to validate a Romano-British hero who rallied disorganized but brave Celts against the Germanic horde. Certainly Laing does not cite R.G. Collingwood, but Stephen Knight calls Collingwood "the historian who really started the modern historical Arthur industry."[27]

In *Roman Britain and the English Settlements* (1936), Collingwood said, "The historicity of the man can hardly be called in question"; he too sees Arthur as fulfilling the latter-day role of Count of Britain, although the way this role was carried out is admittedly conjectural. Collingwood depicts an Arthur of "good romanized family" (his name had long been recognized as originating in the Roman Artorius), and a man of "sufficient acuteness" and "sufficient practical ability" to devise and implement the mustering up of a "mobile field army," "a band of mail-clad cavalry" modeled on Roman lines. This would account for the fact that the sites of the battles named by Nennius are spread over much of the island. Of Badon, Collingwood says, "That there was such a battle and that it resulted in a British victory of so crushing a nature that for at least forty-four years afterwards the Saxons never took up arms again, is beyond question."[28] Thus he sees behind the legend the probability that in "a country sinking into barbarism, whence Roman ideas had almost vanished," there arose for a time a leader who could at least stand for a fact—that, as he phrased it in an earlier edition, "isolated and crippled as she was, Britain preserved for a time her Roman character and went down fighting."[29]

Collingwood's presentation of an attractive Arthur figure under whose leadership cavalry units successfully harried the incoming Saxons at several places and achieved at least one major victory that temporarily checked their advance was popularized over the next several decades; the novelists who turned to this Arthurian material, unlike most of their literary predecessors, attempted to re-create a convincing Romano-Celtic historical milieu. In the meantime, scholars were sifting the possibilities anew; in 1939, for example, Arthur G. Brodeur, better known for his work on *Beowulf*, published a long article exploring "the historical base for the Arthurian legend."[30] As its title—"Arthur, Dux Bellorum"—suggests, Brodeur re-examines the composite *Historia Brittonum* ascribed to Nennius, along with the *Annales Cambriae;*

based on his view that the "dux bellorum" sentence in Nennius consists of two lines in late Latin hexameter verse, he postulates a lost British-Latin poem for both Nennius's Arthurian references and for the *Annales* entries concerning Arthur (pp. 253–54). While this latter theory has not won acceptance, Brodeur's setting out of the fifth- to sixth-century events in Britain that could account for the entries in Nennius and the *Annales* is typical of several subsequent approaches to the Arthur of history. Brodeur deals with some of the problems of assigning dates to Gildas's narrative of the process of Anglo-Saxon invasion and conquest. He also suggests that some of Arthur's twelve victories—especially those with northern locales—may be "apocryphal" (p. 266). However, he sees no reason to doubt a real military leader defending southern Britain against the Jutes, under Hengist's son, and winning a signal triumph at Badon; this victory, around the year 500, resulted, he too says, in a cessation of conflict in the south for a period of some forty years. Brodeur also notes, as others have done, the fact that the name Arthur appears several times among British males from the late sixth century into the seventh, thus suggesting that a famous bearer of that name did exist. His fame, in Brodeur's view, soon spread beyond the southern Britain of his original activities with the result that by the time of the *Historia Brittonum,* northern victories were also attached to his name. However, the Nennian battle list has been explained in other ways, as will be seen below.

For students of medieval Arthurian romance, the year 1959 was an important publication date—that of the influential collection of essays by several scholars, edited by Roger Sherman Loomis under the title *Arthurian Literature in the Middle Ages.* Discussions of the romance literature were preceded by essays written by Kenneth H. Jackson, A.O.H. Jarman, I.L. Foster, Rachel Bromwich, and Loomis, exploring the Welsh backgrounds of the later legends and romances. Here the prevailing view is that the Welsh poems and triads unquestionably preserve traditions—some of them Arthurian—that pre-date Geoffrey by centuries. Even *Culhwch and Olwen,* whose catalogue of Arthur's retainers may contain later interpolations, was, Foster says, composed not later than 1100; thus, *Culhwch* could not have been influenced by Geoffrey's *Historia,* completed in the late 1130s, but, one may infer, it can therefore help us to see the development of Welsh literary traditions concerning Arthur.

Of these essays, Kenneth H. Jackson's "The Arthur of History" is of particular interest.[31] Jackson finds no evidence of historic value in Geoffrey, in Nennius's "Mirabilia" (the dog's paw print and the grave of Arthur's son), or in saints' lives, but he does offer an ingenious explanation of Gildas's failure to mention Arthur by name as the victor at Badon (p. 3). He mentions the lines from the early Welsh *Gododdin* that suggest an Arthur recognized by the sixth century as a military exemplar, but he notes the possibility of interpolation (p. 3). Jackson discounts both Collingwood's mobile cavalry and Brodeur's Latin-British poem as ways to account for Nennius's battle list. Instead he concurs in the suggestion, first made by H.M. Chadwick and Nora K. Chadwick, that the list of Arthur's victories had its origin in an early Welsh poem listing the battles. Such a poem, dating perhaps from the late sixth to late eighth centuries, might, Jackson says, have attached to Arthur's name other "historical or legendary battles." He adds, though, that "some may come from genuine tradition, especially Badon, the crowning victory" (p. 8). Jackson does not here conflate "genuine tradition" with actual history, but he does add that Nennius "could hardly have *invented* Arthur himself, for Nennius was no Geoffrey; he was not capable of creating a character out of nothing at all" (p. 11). But Jackson's essay does not carry the argument past the bounds of his careful opening statement: "Did King Arthur ever really exist? The only honest answer is, 'We do not know, but he may well have existed.' The nature of the evidence is such that proof is impossible" (p. 1).

Discussions of the sites of Nennius's twelve battles, including those just mentioned, are usually linked with questions of Arthur's original locale—northern Britain, southern Britain, or both. In an essay attached to the EETS prose *Merlin*,[32] J.S. Stuart Glennie had argued at length that Arthur was originally a hero of the north—that is, of southern Scotland and the Border country. Stuart Glennie believed he had found evidence for locating virtually every personage and every event of Arthurian legend and romance in the north, even Perceval and Lancelot. Despite such obvious overzealousness, the north as the earliest Arthurian locale has found reputable support in much more recent work. In 1963, for example, Nora Chadwick, calling the evidence for a historical Arthur "highly unsatisfactory," referred to a "growing body of opinion" that sees in north Britain the origin of early traditions about Arthur as the model of a hero-warrior.[33]

Rachel Bromwich, editor of *Trioedd Ynys Prydein* (the Welsh *Triads of the Island of Britain*), has put forth persuasive arguments supporting "the probability that the earliest traditions of Arthur belonged to the *corpus* of north British material which was preserved and developed in Strathclyde and from thence transmitted to North Wales from at least as early as the ninth century."[34] Bromwich does not insist on Strathclyde as the original locale of Arthur, but rather concurs with K.H. Jackson's view of it as a place where various northern traditions were preserved quite early; in fact, she favors the East Riding of Yorkshire. Stories about other "men of the north"—Urien

Rheged and his son Owain, for example—were relocalized in Wales by the ninth century, according to Bromwich, and she notes the fact that the genuine historicity of Owain and Urien would point to the likelihood of a similar process at work on another "local war leader," Arthur. Thus, to have an Arthur at all, she implies, like Pearson above, we must limit his scope.

In presenting this thesis, Bromwich cites and concurs at several points with similar views advanced by Thomas Jones. In an article first published in Welsh in 1958 and translated in 1964, Jones discusses, among other subjects, the battles associated with Arthur.[35] Like Jackson, Jones says that attempts to identify the twelve battles listed by Nennius can prove nothing about a historical Arthur, since it is extremely unlikely that any one person fought all of them. That leaves the two entries in the *Annales Cambriae*—the references to Arthur leading the Britons to victory at Badon and to his falling at Camlann. (Badon has not been convincingly identified with one particular site, but the battle is usually considered to have been fought in the south, possibly in Wessex.) Jones notes that the Badon entry, with its reference to Arthur's carrying the Cross of Christ on his shoulders, is not typical of the other entries, which, he says, are "short and factual, and free of miraculous and fictional elements" (p. 5). Thus he postulates an interpolation here of "a legendary element of ecclesiastical origin" (p. 9). If then the entry had originally read "Bellum badonis & [*or* in quo] brittones uicotores fuerunt," there is nothing in the *Annales* to connect Arthur with Badon. Camlann, however, Jones considers "the most authentic historical reference to Arthur which remains to us" (p. 6). The Welsh triads, too, connect Arthur with Camlann, in references that are thought to pre-date Geoffrey of Monmouth. Jones and others identify this site as Camboglanna, a fort on Hadrian's Wall,[36] thus strengthening the case for a northern sphere of activity (if the battle itself could be proved historic).

Jones concludes that both the *Annales* and the *Historia Brittonum* show only that "in the tenth century there were traditions of Arthur as a leader and winner of victories against the Saxons." And, he adds, "It is very doubtful whether any of these traditions, apart from that of the battle of Camlann, can be accepted as real history" (p. 11). Jones's essay is entitled "The Early Evolution of the Legend of Arthur," and he goes on to trace, through Welsh poetry and narrative, the growth of the legend, showing how Arthur "attracted to himself more and more sagas and popular legends, which were originally independent of him" (p. 21). Examining the development of this particular literary legend is one aspect of the study of Welsh literary tradition. Rachel Bromwich has stressed the importance of this point:

Owing to the scarcity of the early evidence, and to some extent owing to its apparently contradictory character, it is to be feared that in the last resort one's response will be conditioned by the nature of one's interests—whether these lie primarily in the history of "Dark Age" Britain, in early Welsh literature, or in the twelfth-century French romances with their "Camelot" orientation. ("Concepts," p. 180)

Despite a lack of unanimity on locale, in the 1970s it seemed apparent that the trend was a growing if cautious acceptance of a "real" Arthur or Arthur figure discernable through the various Welsh and British-Latin texts that have been mentioned. This impression would have been deepened by the publication, in that decade, of two works, one by an archaeologist, the other by a historian, both using the name Arthur in their titles.

The archaeologist was Leslie Alcock, whose book *Arthur's Britain* was published in 1971. Alcock used both archaeological and written evidence to attempt to reconstruct the history of the period. He had been involved in the excavations at South Cadbury—popularly equated with Camelot—which did seem to demonstrate the existence of a king's or war leader's rather large military headquarters that had been fortified in the late fifth century. Alcock does not set Arthur in this milieu without preparation, and part of that preparation is his discussion of the relevant documents, a discussion which includes a defense of the authenticity of the Welsh Annal entries, though not the accuracy of the dates themselves.[37] Alcock's last chapter speaks of the "most likely interpretations and the most coherent historical pattern" that can be inferred from the evidence presented in the earlier sections, and here he sums up Arthur's activities and locales (pp. 350 ff.). His Arthur was:

. . . the leader of the combined forces of the small kingdoms into which sub-Roman Britain had dissolved. . . . His major victory, the siege of Mount Badon, was fought against the English about 490. . . . His other battles were widespread and against uncertain enemies. . . . He died about 510 in the battle of Camlann, on which we have no firm information. (pp. 359–60)

Alcock sounds quite like Sharon Turner in a passage near the book's end: "There is no reason to believe that the character of the English settlement was changed in any way by Arthur's victory [at Badon Hill]. . . . in terms of *realpolitik* his achievement is negligible" (p. 364). But he does add that Arthur in his own time "was far from insignificant in military terms. His victories were real enough at the time, they were widespread, and they were celebrated." And celebration, of course, gave rise to legend.

The historian was John Morris, who in 1973 published a history of the British Isles from 350 to 650 under the title *The Age of Arthur*. Morris maintained that Arthur was not only real, he was much more than a local or regional war leader. The following summary from his introduction will make this view clear:

> . . . he was as real as Alfred the Great or William the Conqueror; and his impact upon future ages mattered as much or more so. Enough evidence survives from the hundred years after his death to show that reality was remembered for three generations, before legend engulfed his memory. . . . [38]

The book has as one of its subdivision titles "The Empire of Arthur"; this is followed by smaller units with titles such as "The Peace of Arthur," "The Reign of Arthur," "The Legend of Arthur," "Arthur's Frontier Wars," and "Arthur's Civil Government." For this Arthur was "at once the last Roman emperor in the West and the first medieval king of the country now called England" (p. 141).

This goes a great deal further than Alcock, but both authors were in Geoffrey Ashe's word "savaged" in a 1977 article by David Dumville.[39] Dumville's objections to the positions taken by both Alcock and Morris are numerous but revolve around two points. One is that both, in his view, go too far in assigning to the name Arthur not only a historical role but a role historically important in the events of the late fifth century. Rachel Bromwich had made a similar point in the article cited above where, apparently with Morris in mind, she had posed the question: "May it not be that the snow-ball growth of legend around the name of 'king' Arthur between the ninth and twelfth centuries has influenced unduly the attitude of investigators towards the earliest Arthurian documents, as holding a wider significance for the history of this island than is in fact warranted by them?" ("Concepts," p. 167). Dumville's other main objection is that both writers "have seen fit to assign a great importance to written sources deriving from the Celtic-speaking countries," for as he sees it, "most of the available written 'evidence' is more apparent than real" (p. 173). Space does not permit a detailed account of Dumville's essay or of the recent work in Celtic studies that he draws upon in marshaling his attack. However, some of the assumptions he seeks to demolish will be discussed briefly.

The problem, as mentioned, lies in using the so-called written record, those traditional sources, most already mentioned, for any reconstructed Arthur figure. Most damaging perhaps to the traditional Arthurian case is Dumville's rejection of the value of the *Annales Cambriae,* even in regard to Camlann. These annals in present form, Dumville says, belong to the tenth century, and here Dumville cites the work of the late Kathleen Hughes on these records. Hughes traces these annals in part to a contemporary record kept at St. David's in Wales from the late eighth century onward and says that the annalistic entries for the period before about 790 were "a scholar's exercise compiled well after the events," from Irish and north-British annals of the earlier ninth century.[40] Hughes's research shows that there is virtually no possibility of the Arthur entries being anywhere near contemporary with the events they record as Alcock and others had suggested. Of course, since Hughes does not specifically exclude the possibility, one could argue— as some have—that the tenth-century copies of the ninth-century annals reflect the compiler's use of earlier compilers' uses of earlier compilers. But none of this is verifiable, and Dumville ends by calling Arthur "a man without position or ancestry in pre-Geoffrey Welsh sources" (p. 187).

Dumville cites approvingly the work done on the early evolution of the legend of Arthur by Thomas Jones and the "excellent survey" of the same material by Jackson, both mentioned above. So it is not exploration of the legend that Dumville deplores, but rather insistence on its historical roots from basically legendary evidence, as is evident in his pointed comment: "The fact of the matter is that there is no historical evidence about Arthur; we must reject him from our histories and, above all, from the titles of our books" (p. 188).

This admonition as to Arthurian titles has not proved a firm deterrent in the years since 1977. Dumville's article, however, along with the review of Morris's book by Kirby and Williams and the recent series, "Studies in Celtic History," of which Dumville is general editor, have had considerable effect. Over one hundred years ago, F.J. Furnivall, in obvious relief at not having to deal with the question of a historic (and a Celtic) Arthur, wrote the following lines:

> For the date at which Arthur is first mentioned by any writer, I dare not refer to the Welsh legends. Kelts of strong imagination and faith have a list of a succession of poets at and after this time, with specimens (I believe) of their works that leave on the patriot's mind no doubt as to the existence of their hero. But as Nash . . . and other critics, have made such sad havoc among the Welsh theories, that until the reconstructor called for by Mr. Arnold appears, one must leave the whole matter alone.[41]

Something of the same attitude can be seen in recent responses to this current work in Celtic studies. One example is Peter Salway, who brought out in 1981 for the Oxford History of England series a replacement volume for Collingwood's long standard but now dated work of 1936 mentioned above. Salway includes a section titled "King Arthur?" where he starts by saying that the Arthurian element has "so overshadowed attempts to reconstruct the story of Britain in the second half of the [fifth] century that it demands to be considered." But he goes on to say that, although:

> over recent years there has been a growing movement to believe in the historicity of Arthur . . . so much doubt has now been thrown on the state of knowledge about the Celtic written sources for Arthur [here he cites Dumville's article] that both his connection with the archaeology and his very existence are matters that need to be held in abeyance by historians till the value of the texts is re-examined by those specialists qualified to do so."[42]

J.N.L. Myres had in 1936 provided the *English Settlements* companion to Collingwood's *Roman Britain,* and he had done so without mentioning Arthur. In his 1986 revision of this work as a reprint volume for the same Oxford series, Myres said simply (and rather irritably): "The fact is that there is no contemporary or near contemporary evidence for Arthur playing any decisive part in these events at all [i.e., those reported by Gildas]. No figure on the borderline of history and mythology has wasted more of the historian's time."[43] Leslie Alcock in a 1982 lecture and article conceded that any value attached to his source studies of 1971 "has been largely swept away" by the studies of Dumville, Hughes, and Molly Miller.[44] Although he briefly defends one or two points in the "documents" section of his previous work, Alcock announces his present "position on the historicity of Arthur" to be "one of agnosticism" (p. 356). In a recent publication, another British archaeologist, Lloyd Laing, mentions Dumville as sounding "a suitable note of caution" on the problems of using the available written evidence, particularly to try to date the events of fifth- and sixth-century Britain (Laing, *Celtic Britain,* p. 43).

So many assumptions of earlier work in this area have been thrown into doubt or discredit that these reactions are not surprising. And it was time, no doubt, that assumptions be challenged and "evidence" re-examined.[45] But if traditional ways of looking for a historic Arthur seem to have come to an at least temporary halt, several other less traditional avenues have been explored in recent years. Of these, three will be considered here. John Darrah's *The Real Camelot* (1981) has as its subtitle "Paganism and the

Arthurian Romances." This looks as if Darrah, like Roger Sherman Loomis and numerous others, will be exploring the survival of fragmentary Celtic mythology in Chrétien de Troyes, the Vulgate Cycle, Malory's *Morte Darthur*, and so on; actually, Darrah's "paganism" is much older than the variety brought into Britain by the Celts. The "real Camelot" of the title refers to Stonehenge, seen here as the center of a Bronze Age sacred-king cult whose traditions, orally transmitted for centuries, were taken up by Celtic mythologers and storytellers and thence by French romancers. Thus the floating stones, in even as late a version as Malory's, have their origin in the bringing, mainly by sea, of the bluestones of Stonehenge from the Prescelly Mountains of Wales.[46]

Obviously this earlier paganism, as Darrah notes, has "no bearing on the history of the fifth and sixth centuries A.D. " In any case, his interest lies in the "proto-Arthur" whom he sees as representing "the coalition of deities which took over the pre-existing national cult centre on Salisbury Plain at the beginning of the Bronze Age, a coalition which resulted from the same forces as were responsible for the bluestone move." But Darrah does postulate a "real" battle leader named Arthur (p. 12), one "with a renown sufficient to attract into his train a complete mythology, and to finish up with a pantheon as his attendants" (p. 138).

The Real Camelot is included here because it represents a continuing fascination with the mythological components of Arthurian legend and romance, a fascination already noted in this essay. Geoffrey Ashe's recent work on the Arthur of history takes quite a different direction, being firmly rooted in the possibilities offered by fifth-century Britain and Gaul. Ashe has noted Dumville's objections to tracing a historical figure through the Welsh material as well as the numerous contradictions—in dating, in locale, in battles, in significance—surrounding the Arthur variously reconstructed by those who have pursued him through that material. Instead of asking whether Arthur was a real person, Ashe proposes the question "How did his legend originate, what facts is it rooted in?"[47] This leads to a consideration of what might have inspired Geoffrey's account of Arthur's taking an army to Gaul. Ashe finds the answer in Riothamus, a fifth-century Briton who did in fact take an army to Gaul. Piecing together the career of Riothamus from scattered references in early continental sources, Ashe presents a British king who, after landing in Gaul, advanced towards Burgundy to fight Visigoths. The battle was joined, but, "betrayed by a deputy ruler who treated with barbarian enemies," Riothamus "disappears after a fatal battle with no recorded death. The line of retreat shows him moving in the direction of the actual Avalon [in Burgundy]" (*New Arthurian Encyclopedia*, 20).

The harder part is to link these intriguing parallels to Arthur himself or to Geoffrey's account of him.[48] The Breton *Legend of St. Goeznovius*, as Ashe has noted, did put Arthur in Gaul; this account may have been written by 1019, though the date is not undisputed. The other problem of identifying Arthur with Riothamus also concerns dates. Riothamus's campaign in Gaul is placed in 469–70, and if he (as Arthur) died there, it is impossible to link him to the battle at Badon, which is usually placed around 500 or to the presumably even later Camlann. However, Ashe does not insist that Riothamus is the "*only* original" for the Arthur of Geoffrey or of Badon or Camlann; he admits the possibility that Arthur may, like Merlin, be a composite figure.

Ashe says that *Riothamus,* through its British form Rigotamos, means "supreme king" or "supremely royal" and links this title to that of Vortigern ("overking"), mentioning also Gildas's "essential clue to the British High Kingship," his phrase "*superbus tyrannus.*"[49] Thus, Riothamus may be simply the title given Arthur or Artorius. Here Ashe brings up another interesting connection:

> One possibility is that the name is a sobriquet inspired by an earlier Artorius, the imperial commander Lucius Artorius Castus, who led an expedition from Britain to Gaul to suppress a rebellion. A second commander leading an expedition from Britain to Gaul might have been hailed in panegyric, or commemorated in poetry, as a "second Artorius." (*New Arthurian Encyclopedia,* 20)

This brings us to a third approach to the origin of the Arthur of history. This Lucius Artorius Castus had been suggested as an Arthurian connection as early as 1925 by Kemp Malone.[50] Malone notes that this Artorius had been a centurion in a legion stationed in Pannonia (modern Hungary) and later as praefectus was assigned to the VI Victrix, a legion stationed at York. While he was serving there, he led an expedition to Armorica (Brittany) to put down an insurrection there. Later, leaving Britain and active military duty, he was given a "lucrative civil post" in Dalmatia, which was perhaps his birthplace (p. 372).

Malone tabulates the correspondences to the Arthur of later legend as follows: their names, their roles as defenders of Britain against barbarian invaders, and their leading of armies to Gaul (p. 373). Malone suggests that if a legend had developed about Artorius, later continuators of that legend might simply have substituted the "wild Saxons, the enemies par excellence of the fifth century" as adding contemporary interest to the earlier "wild tribes" of the north. He concludes that if the deeds attributed to the "pseudo-historical Arthur" were really those of Lucius Artorius Castus, then the reason Gildas, Bede, and the Anglo-Saxon *Chronicle* do not mention a sixth-century Arthur is that there wasn't one (p. 374). This view does not of course preclude the possibility, even the likelihood, of various British military leaders opposing the fifth- and sixth-century incursions of Anglo-Saxons, either locally or on a broader basis.

If Malone's identification of Arthur with Lucius Artorius Castus were the end of the matter, this commentary would have been a footnote. But Helmut Nickel, of the Metropolitan Museum of Art, and folklorists C. Scott Littleton and Ann C. Thomas have contributed an intriguing corollary in their discussions of the "Sarmatian connection." According to their accounts,[51] the Sarmatians, Iranian "horse nomads from the Eastern European steppes," had by the second century A.D. moved into Pannonia (see above, L. Artorius Castus's biography). In 175 several thousand of these warriors were hired for the Roman army and some 5,500 of them, accustomed to fighting as "heavy armored cavalry," were posted to Britain, to the VI Victrix commanded by Lucius Artorius Castus. According to Nickel, these Sarmatians wore "segmented helmets and scale body armor; even their horses were protected" ("Dawn," p. 151). In addition, their battle standard was a dragon and they "worshipped as their tribal war god a naked sword set upright in the ground or on a platform" (*New Arthurian Encyclopedia*, 397).

After their twenty years' duty was up, says Nickel, they were not sent home, but settled in Lancashire where a "troop of Sarmatian veterans" was on record as late as 428. Nickel suggests that these veterans and their descendants might well have commemorated their leader, a man familiar with their homeland, possibly turning his name Artorius into a synonym for "the General" (as Caesar became Kaiser and Tsar), and that during the fifth century "this title might have been used by a great British chieftain" ("Dawn," p. 151). And the native traditions of the Sarmatians themselves may have contributed more than a name to the development of the legendary Arthur. These traditions have been traced through the only surviving Sarmatian language speakers, the Ossetes, a people of the Caucasus. Their epic literature preserves accounts of "a legendary tribe of heroes, the Narts," whose main hero, Batradz, "has his life bound up with his magic sword, which has to be thrown into the sea by his last companion, after he is mortally wounded." The one trusted with the disposal of the sword tries to deceive Batradz and save the sword, but he is unable to report what "sign" had been witnessed. Finally the sword is thrown into the water and the sea turns blood-colored and turbulent (Littleton, pp. 515–16). Other heroes of the Narts, Soslan and

Sosryko, collect the flayed beards of their defeated enemies for a fur-trimmed cloak, a clear parallel to King Ryon's mantle (*New Arthurian Encyclopedia*, 397).

The suggestiveness of this line of inquiry is quite fascinating, providing as it does, a possible background to the legends that surrounded a later military leader. As to why or how these exotic imports might have displaced native traditions, they need not have done so to a great extent. Rather, common Indo-European features of both Sarmatian and Celtic tradition may have overlapped and blended, first locally, then (with, perhaps, the passing on of the name) over a broader area. This is of course the most general kind of speculation, but it is in support of an engaging hypothesis that combines many elements of both the historical and the legendary Arthur seen already in these pages.

But none of this is proved in relation to an Arthur of history. And, as seen throughout this essay, almost nothing else about him that is not attributable to legend-making can be asserted with any assurance. This situation has not been changed substantially by the recent publication of *The Arthur of the Welsh,* a collection of essays bringing up to date the early chapters of *Arthurian Literature in the Middle Ages,* in view of work done during the intervening thirty-odd years since *ALMA*'s publication. The introduction to this collection does to some extent counter Dumville's absolute skepticism, reiterating the main lines of "defence" of Arthur's historicity laid down by Kenneth H. Jackson and Thomas Jones and suggesting that later tempering of those views has not entirely vitiated their cumulative worth.[52] In the lead essay, "The Arthur of History," Thomas Charles-Edwards explores the place of the Arthurian chapter of the *Historia Brittonum* in relation to the character and structure of that work.[53] Charles-Edwards expands our view of the *Historia*, maintaining that it is comparable to Bede's combining of ecclesiastical history and history of a people. In this analysis, the Arthurian battles provide a secondary means of linking the earlier period of Germanus, Gwrtheyrn (Vortigern), and Hengest with that of Ida, the English royal genealogies, and the Northern History presented in later chapters (pp. 21–22). He also explores the related questions of the possible sources of the *Historia*'s Arthurian material and their relationship to the *Annales Cambriae* entries concerning Arthur. However, while the essay throws interesting light on Arthur's role in the *Historia Brittonum,* it does not similarly illuminate his role in history. Charles-Edwards concludes by echoing Jackson's *ALMA* essay: "At this state of the inquiry, one can only say that there may well have been an historical Arthur." But, he adds, "the historian can as yet say nothing of value about him" (p. 29).

For the present, then, the question "Did Arthur really exist?" cannot be answered. Therefore, Geoffrey Ashe's rephrasing of the question to be asked is worth repeating: "The question 'Was he a real person?' leads to no certain answer but the question 'How did his legend originate, what facts is it rooted in?' can broaden the scope of the inquiry. . . ." Ascertaining such facts will not be easy, but essays like those of Jones and Jackson have led the way towards this approach, and, as Charles-Edwards notes, "later conceptions of Arthur are likely to interest historians almost as much as they do students of medieval literature." Certainly the fabric of the legend is woven of many strands, and it seems apparent that no one view of its origins that excludes all the others will account for the splendid tapestry to be explored in this book.

NOTES

1. Ritson, *The Life of King Arthur: From Ancient Historians and Authentic Documents* (London: Payne and Foss, 1825), Preface, p. i.

2. Ritson, *Ancient English Metrical Romances*, 3 vols. (London: Bulmer, 1803), Vol. 3, p. 232.

3. Quoted in translation by James J. Wilhelm, "Arthur in the Latin Chronicles," in *The Romance of Arthur* (New York: Garland, 1984), p. 9.

4. Raphael Holinshed, *Chronicles of England, Scotland, and Ireland* (1807 edition), Vol. 1, pp. 574 ff; Edward Gibbon, *The History of the Decline and Fall of the Roman Empire*, new ed. (New York: Harper, 1856), Vol. 3, pp. 622 ff.; Sharon Turner, *History of the Anglo Saxons*, 5th ed. (London: Longman, 1828), Vol. 1, pp. 285–90. Turner's first volume had appeared initially in 1799.

5. Owen-Pughe, *Cambrian Biography* (London: Williams, 1803; rpt. New York: Garland, 1979), p. 15.

6. *Cambrian Biography*, p. 340. A date of 517 is in the view of most recent scholars too late for the beginning of Arthur's activities. Owen–Pughe or his source may have been influenced here by the *Annales Cambriae* (*Annals of Wales*), which put Badon Hill at 518 and had Arthur die in 539. Geoffrey of Monmouth dates Arthur's death at 542.

7. Davies, *The Mythology and Rites of the British Druids* (London: Booth, 1809), p. 188.

8. Herbert, *Brittania after the Romans*, 2 vols. (London: Bohn, 1836, 1841), Vol. 1, pp. 130–32 and passim.

9. J.A. Giles, *History of the Ancient Britons*, 2 vols. (1847), Vol. 1, p. 393. This passage was called to my attention through its use, in a somewhat different context, by Roger Simpson in his detailed and well-argued study, *Camelot Regained: The Arthurian Revival and Tennyson, 1800–1849* (Cambridge: Brewer, 1990), p. 9. Of particular interest for the present subject is his first chapter, "The Historical Arthur," which includes a brief survey of historians' attitudes toward the topic.

10. Nash, *Taliesin: or the Bards and Druids of Britain* (London: John Russell Smith, 1858).

11. Quoted by Nash, pp. 3–4.

12. Palgrave's *History of England*, Vol. 1, "The Anglo-Saxon Period," was published in the Family Library Series in 1831. No additional volumes appear to have been written, and in subsequent editions, the work was issued under the title *History of the Anglo-Saxons*; reference here is to a later edition (London: William Tegg, 1871), pp. 27–40.

13. Palgrave, *Rise and Progress*, Vol. 1, p. 401; quoted by Simpson, 8.

14. "On the Study of Celtic Literature," in *Lectures and Essays in Criticism*, Vol. 3 of *The Complete Prose Works of Matthew Arnold*, ed. Robert H. Super (Ann Arbor: University of Michigan Press, 1973), pp. 388–89.

15. Charles Pearson, *The Early and Middle Ages of England* (1861; rpt. New York: Kennikat, 1971), pp. 56–58.

16. This response appeared following a sketch Pearson had provided for a later edition: "Arthur: A General Introduction to 'Merline' and 'Kinge Arthur's Death,'" in *Bishop Percy's Folio Manuscript*, ed. John W. Hales and F.J. Furnivall, 3 vols. (London: Trubner, 1868), Vol. 1, p. 404.

17. F.J. Furnivall, ed., *Le Morte Arthur*, from Harleian 2252 (London: Macmillan, 1864), p. xxvi, for example, and in other publications as well.

18. Roger Simpson has shown, for example, that contrary to the opinions of some Tennyson scholars, there was very little objection to Tennyson's choice of Arthurian matter as a subject. See *Camelot Regained*, esp. 226 ff.

19. "Early English Texts," *Saturday Review*, November 5, 1864, p. 570.

20. 2nd ed. (London: Kegan Paul, Trench, and Company, 1883; rpt. Detroit: Singing Tree Press, 1968), p. 368.

21. Lingard's *History of England* had been generally well-received; it went through several editions, the sixth appearing in 1855.

22. Bruce, *The Evolution of Arthurian Romance*, 2nd ed., 2 vols. (1928; rpt. Gloucester, MA: Peter Smith, 1958), Vol. 1, pp. 3–9.

23. Fletcher, *The Arthurian Material in the Chronicles*, [Harvard] Studies and Notes in Philology and Literature, 10 (Boston, 1906), 2nd ed. Roger Sherman Loomis (New York: Burt Franklin, 1966), p. 29.

24. Ashe, *The Discovery of King Arthur* (London: Guild Publishing, 1985), pp. 74–75.

25. Trevelyan, *History of England*, 3rd ed. (Garden City: Doubleday Anchor, 1952), p. 53.

26. Lloyd and Jennifer Laing, *Celtic Britain and Ireland, AD 200–800* (New York: St. Martin's, 1990), p. 65. He is quoting from Trevelyan, p. 56.

27. In *Arthurian Literature and Society* (New York: St. Martin's, 1983), p. 209.

28. R.G. Collingwood and J.N.L. Myres, *Roman Britain and the English Settlements* (Oxford: Clarendon, 1936; 2nd ed. 1937), pp. 320–24.

29. Collingwood, *Roman Britain* (London: Oxford University Press, 1923; rev. ed., Oxford: Clarendon, 1932), p. 99. Stephen Knight sees the forces behind the modern quest for a historical and heroic Arthur in a combination of the Great Man approach to history, racism, and the last vestiges of imperialism, all part of a dying empire's attempt to be sustained by its former greatness—much in the way, though he does not say so, that the preserved record of Arthur's victories was said to have helped sustain the pride and spirit of a defeated Celtic population.

30. "Arthur, Dux Bellorum," *University of California Publications in English*, 3 (1939), 237–83.

31. In *Arthurian Literature in the Middle Ages*, ed. Roger Sherman Loomis (Oxford: Clarendon, 1959), pp. 1–11.

32. J.S. Stuart Glennie, "Arthurian Localities: Their Historical Origin, Chief Country, and Fingalian Relations," in *Merlin or the Early History of King Arthur*, ed. Henry B. Wheatley, Early English Text Society 10, 21, 36, 112 (1865, 1866, 1869, 1899), rpt. 2 vols. (New York: Greenwood, 1969), Vol. 1, pp. xxi*–cxxxvii*.

33. Chadwick, *Celtic Britain* (London: Thames and Hudson, 1963), pp. 46–48.

34. Bromwich, "Concepts of Arthur," *Studia Celtica*, X/XI (1975–76), 177. Also *Trioedd Ynys Prydein*, 2nd ed. (Cardiff: University of Wales Press, 1978), p. 274, and elsewhere.

35. "The Early Evolution of the Legend of Arthur," trans. Gerald Morgan,

Nottingham Medieval Studies, 8 (1964), 3–21.

36. Jones, 6. Kenneth Jackson (*ALMA,* 5) calls this identification "by no means impossible."

37. Alcock, *Arthur's Britain* (Harmondsworth: Penguin, 1971; rpt. Pelican Books, 1973); chapters 2 and 3 deal with the texts.

38. John Morris, *The Age of Arthur* (New York: Scribner's, 1973), p. xiii.

39. Dumville, "Sub-Roman Britain: History and Legend," *History,* 62 (1977), 173–92. Ashe's comment is in *The Discovery of King Arthur,* 84. Also see the lengthy review of Morris's book by D.P. Kirby and J.E. Caerwyn Williams, *Studia Celtica,* 10 (1975–76), 454–86, which calls attention to numerous errors of both fact and emphasis.

40. Hughes, "The Welsh Latin Chronicles: *Annales Cambriae* and Related Texts," in *Britain in the Early Middle Ages* (Woodbridge: Boydell, 1980), pp. 68–69. See also this entire article and the following one in this collection of Hughes's work, "The A-Text of *Annales Cambriae.*"

41. Furnivall, in *Bishop Percy's Folio Manuscript,* Vol. 3, p. 407.

42. Salway, *Roman Britain* (Oxford: Oxford University Press, 1981), p. 485.

43. Myres, *The English Settlements* (Oxford: Clarendon, 1986), pp. 15–16.

44. Alcock, "Cadbury–Camelot: A Fifteen Year Perspective," *Proceedings of the British Academy,* 68 (1982), 356.

45. Simply browsing through essays of the last ten years, in Dumville's Studies in Celtic History series or in *Cambridge Medieval Celtic Studies,* one comes upon passage after passage undermining the case that has been built up for tracing a historical Arthur through Welsh poetry and triads, through Gildas's picture of the times, and through archaeological evidence that seemed to show a significant halt to the Saxon advance in a conveniently Arthurian time frame. For example: ". . . although some writers like to suppose that Celtic oral tradition is peculiarly reliable, this is not an opinion shared by experienced Celtic historians," or "It once seemed possible that a forty-four year peace after *Badonicus mons* could be recognized archaeologically as a period in which the area of Anglo-Saxon settlement ceased to expand, or even contracted, but the evidence put forward . . . has been reinterpreted. . . . there seems to be no half century in which Anglo-Saxon settlement ceased to expand somewhere" (Patrick Sims-Williams, "Gildas and the Anglo Saxons," *Cambridge Medieval Celtic Studies,* 6 [1983], 24, 26).

46. Darrah, *The Real Camelot* (London: Thames and Hudson, 1981), pp. 85 ff. and passim.

47. Ashe, "Arthur, Origins of Legend," in *The New Arthurian Encyclopedia,* ed. Norris J. Lacy, et al. (New York: Garland, 1991), p. 19. For corroboration of the summary that follows, see also Ashe's *New Arthurian Encyclopedia* entry under "Riothamus" as well as his more leisurely development of his thesis in *The Discovery of King Arthur.*

48. Ashe has noted that Sharon Turner did actually link Riothamus and Arthur as early as 1799. See *Discovery,* 99–100.

49. In *Discovery,* 204. An interesting subject for exploration would be a study of the implications of translating Gildas's *superbus tyrannus* as "high king" versus translating it "proud tyrant," as do Thomas Jones, Kenneth Jackson, and other Celticists. See Jackson's comments on this issue in "Gildas and the Names of the British Princes," *Cambridge Medieval Celtic Studies,* 3 (1982), 35–40.

50. Malone, "Artorius," *Modern Philology,* 22 (1925), 367–74.

51. Helmut Nickel wrote the *New Arthurian Encyclopedia* entry "Sarmatian Connection," from which I have mainly quoted, but Nickel is often summarizing C. Scott Littleton and Ann C. Thomas, "The Sarmatian Connection: New Light on the Origin of the Arthurian and Holy Grail Legends," *Journal of American Folklore,* 91 (1978), 513–27. Additional references are to Nickel's article "The Dawn of Chivalry," in *From the Lands of the Scythians* (New York Metropolitan Museum of Art / Los

Angeles County Museum of Art, 1975), pp. 150–52. See also Littleton and Linda A. Malcor, *From Scythia to Camelot: A Radical Reassessment of the Legends of King Arthur, the Knights of the Round Table, and the Holy Grail* (New York: Garland, 1994).

52. *The Arthur of the Welsh*, ed. Rachel Bromwich, A.O.H. Jarman, Brynley F. Roberts (Cardiff: University of Wales Press, 1991). The Introduction (pp. 1–14) is attributed to the editors collectively.

53. The *Historia Brittonum* is referred to simply if inaccurately as "Nennius" by many authors cited in this essay.

Dux bellorum / rex militum / roi fainéant

The Transformation of Arthur in the Twelfth Century

Barbara N. Sargent-Baur

When Arthur appears for the first time in a narrative that claims to be historic, it is as *dux bellorum,* a leader in war. Nennius designates him as such and supports this title with his well-known list of twelve battles from which this commander-in-chief emerged victorious.[1] When one turns from this pre-medieval document, which apparently dates from the ninth century, to the fifteenth-century version of the Arthurian story written by Thomas Malory, an account which both sums up and brings to a close the vast body of medieval works about King Arthur and his court, one finds again an Arthur who plays, among other roles, those of warrior and leader of warriors. During the centuries that separate these two authors, however, the character of Arthur underwent a profound change. The change occurred rather abruptly during the twelfth century and at the same time as the works concerning Arthur's life, era, and companions evolved from pseudo-history to the obviously fictional genre of romance. Arthur at this point was shifted to the background and changed from a leading actor at the center of events to a supporting player, almost a decoration, while others moved forward to claim our attention. The old center recedes, and to an astonishing degree.

This change is all the more surprising since the source for the Matter of Britain, at least in most of the learned and artistic statements that have come down to us, is Geoffrey of Monmouth's *Historia Regum Britanniae,* and the Arthurian part of this narrative is very Arthurian indeed. For many of the authors of French romances, beginning with the earliest, Geoffrey's *matière* had passed through the filter of Wace's *Roman de Brut,* as Margaret Pelan has shown.[2] Although the two chroniclers differ in many points of detail, in the Arthurian parts of their respective works Geoffrey and Wace

Originally published as *"Dux bellorum / rex militum / roi fainéant:* la transformation d'Arthur au XIIᵉ siècle," *Moyen Age,* 90 (1984), 357–73; translated by the author.

present one and the same conception. Arthur (promoted henceforth to royal rank) is always in the foreground; he dominates the other characters through the length of the passages devoted to his deeds and speeches and through the ways in which others regard him. Some fear him; some envy and hate him; others admire him so much that their admiration dictates their actions. From the beginning of his reign, at a time when the new king is still a very young man, the social and political movement narrated by Geoffrey and Wace is centripetal. Arthur as they depict him is not only powerful, but also attractive in the strict sense of the word: he is a centralizer. Thanks to his fame, he draws to himself many men who travel to his court; once there, they stay with him for a considerable if unspecified period of time. Here we find established, by the middle of the twelfth century, a motif that will often recur in Arthurian literature.

In the present article I shall discuss Arthur as a recruiter of warriors and then as creator of knights. My inquiry will begin with the chronicles of Geoffrey and Wace and will then move on to the realm of fiction as represented by the romances of the originator of the genre, Chrétien de Troyes.

The givens in Geoffrey's *Historia,* although not abundant, are suggestive. The theme appears as early as the coronation of Uther Pendragon's fifteen-year-old son and heir;[3] even at this age, he is a young man endowed with extraordinary merit (*virtus*) and generosity. This last trait is especially important from the time of his coronation, for it causes him to be generally loved and sought after. A great many warriors (*multitudo militum*) flock to his court attracted by his full and generous hand. That hand grows empty. Arthur consequently decides not to give the Saxons any respite, for he hopes to confer on his followers the Saxon booty. He accordingly sets out for York with the *juventus* (i.e., the warriors that his generosity had won to his cause). These are apparently the ones who constitute his striking force during his early campaigns: first at York, then in the rest of Great Britain, and finally in Ireland and Iceland.

The theme of Arthur having the traits of a powerful and prestigious leader who acts as a magnet to young warriors is presented in a still more striking manner a little further on in Geoffrey's account. After the king's first combats and victories, there occurs the establishment of the *pax arthuriana* of twelve years. That, however, does not result in the dispersal of Arthur's troops; on the contrary,

> Tunc inuitatis probissimis quibusque ex longe positis regnis. cepit familiam suam augmentare. tantamque facetiam in domo sua habere. ita ut emulationem longe manetibus populis ingereret. Vnde

nobilissimus quisque incitatus nichili pendebat se. nisi sese siue in
induendo. siue in arma ferendo. ad modum militum arturi haberet.

("Arthur then began to increase his personal entourage by inviting
very distinguished men from far-distant kingdoms to join it. In this
way he developed such a code of courtliness in his household that he
inspired peoples living far away to imitate him. The result was that
even the man of the noblest birth, once he was roused to rivalry,
thought nothing at all of himself unless he wore his arms and dressed
in the same way as Arthur's knights.")[4]

This passage evidently implies that communication is going in two directions:
the reputation of distinguished men (i.e., warriors) reaches Arthur's ears, and
Arthur's reputation for generosity and prowess spreads to the four corners
of the world. Moreover, Geoffrey shows us a king who actively, during a
period of peace, searches for additional military personnel for the purpose
of consolidation of his power.

After this interval the war begins again, and under the same conditions.
Arthur dreams of world conquest; and he apparently does not lack the resources, including human resources, that can make this dream a reality. What
is striking is that a large contingent of this expeditionary force is made up of
those who have been recently conquered; the *juventus* of the conquered isles
(in the absence of any qualification, one gets the impression that this consists
of all of the youth, or at least of all of the young men) forms the reputedly
invincible army with which Arthur launches his offensive. His forces are soon
increased by recruits from another source, the army of Gaul itself. Most of
the soldiers from that army, won by gifts of the enemy leader, defect and fight
for Arthur. In the later campaigns narrated by Geoffrey there are other additions to the royal forces besides these deserters. Here, however, the increases
are due to the feudal levies raised by Arthur's allies in the British Isles and
abroad (IX, 19); the theme of warriors who willingly offer their services to the
great king is no longer found in this account of Arthur's career.

Wace, who is inclined to treat rather freely all of Geoffrey's text that
he undertakes to translate, makes some significant changes, and these begin
with the opening account of Arthur's life. In Wace's adaptation of the *Historia*
into French verse, the generosity that at an early date characterizes the young
king is more generalized than in Geoffrey's account; the Arthur of Wace is

Forz e hardiz e conqueranz,
Large dunere e despendanz;

E se busuinnus le requist,
S'aidier li pout, ne l'escundist.

("Strong and bold and conquering, a generous giver and spender;
and if a person in need appealed to him, if he could help him he did
not refuse.")[5]

Here, as in Geoffrey's text, Arthur decides, shortly after his accession to the
throne, to fight the Saxons. For this purpose he summons his men and, interestingly enough, searches for mercenaries.

Sa gent sumunt, soldeiers quist,
Mult lur duna, mult lur pramist,
Tant manda gent et tant erra
Que Everwic ultrepassa. (ll. 9039–42)

("He calls up his men, he sought for mercenaries, he gave them and
promised them much; he summoned so many men and traveled so
far that he passed beyond York.")

Having survived his first campaigns, Wace's Arthur (like Geoffrey's) enjoys
a peaceful reign for twelve years, but with these modifications:

Par sei, senz altre enseinement,
Emprist si grant afaitement
E se contint tant noblement,
Tant bel e tant curteisement,
N'esteit parole de curt d'ume,
Neis de l'empereür de Rome.
N'oeït parler de chevalier
Ki alques feïst a preisier,
Ki de sa maisnee ne fust,
Pur ço qu'il aveir le peüst;
Si pur aveir servir vulsist,
Ja pur aveir ne s'en partist. (ll. 9735–46)

("On his own, without any other teaching, he undertook such an elevated mode of life and conducted himself so nobly, so well, and so
courteously that there was no talking about any [other] man's court,
not even of the Roman Emperor's. He did not hear about a knight

worthy of some praise without his being of his [Arthur's] entourage provided that he could obtain him; if he was willing to serve for remuneration, never for [lack of] of remuneration would he depart.")

One notes in passing the *adnominatio* on *aveir*, which changes from the neutral verb meaning "to have, to obtain" to the loaded substantive denoting "riches, gain remuneration"; it is here, unmistakably, a matter of the profit-motive. For Arthur wealth is a lure that he uses; whereas for the warriors, it is an incentive. The latter have still other motives for their acts: personal honor and also the opportunity to learn courtliness:

> N'esteit pas tenuz pur curteis
> . . . .
> Des occident jesqu'a Muntgeu,
> Ki a la curt Artur n'alout
> E ki od lui ne sujurnout,
> E ki n'en aveit vesteüre
> E cunuissance e armeüre
> A la guise que cil teneient
> Ki a la curt Artur serveient.
> De plusurs terres i veneient
> Cil ki pris e enur quereient,
> Tant pur oïr ses curteisies,
> Tant pur veeir ses mananties,
> Tant pur cunuistre ses baruns,
> Tant pur aveir ses riches duns. (ll. 9761, 9766–78)

("No one was considered courtly . . . from the West to Saint Bernard's Pass who did not go to Arthur's court nor stay with him nor wear clothing in the fashion observed by those who served at Arthur's court. To it from many lands came those who sought renown and honor: some to hear of his acts of courtesy, some to see his domains, some to make the acquaintance of his barons, some to have his rich gifts.")

All of this is the amplification of a rather unremarkable sentence in Geoffrey that simply states that the men whom Arthur wanted willingly accepted his invitation. As for Geoffrey's *familia* (company, following, *maisniee*), it becomes in Wace a *curt*. In contrast with Geoffrey, who speaks vaguely of men coming from faraway kingdoms (*ex longe positis regnis*), Wace tells us specifically the places from which the noble barons of the *Reonde Table* come.

No one among those from Scotland, Brittany, France (i.e., from the Ile-de-France), Normandy, Anjou, Flanders, Burgundy, and Lorraine was considered courtly unless he had been taught at Arthur's court.

If we follow this theme from what purports to be historiography to what is obviously and consciously fiction, we find ourselves in familiar territory. The well-populated Arthurian milieu occurs in Chrétien's first romance, *Erec*, and will be in evidence throughout this poet's work. All of his romances offer us, in one form or another, variations on the theme of Arthur's court, whether it be a court well furnished from the outset with exceptional knights or one that attracts men from distant places and for various reasons. (These conditions, of course, are not mutually exclusive.) Depending on the character of a specific romance, the topos may be mainly static or predominantly dynamic. In *Erec* it is static at first. The narrative begins with a picture of the court in which the knights, including Erec, are already there,[6] and the comings and goings of the hero and the heroine take place against this background. As for the number of knights who are at court, Chrétien gives us only a suggestion: each of the 500 *demeiseles* there has a lover ready to fight in order to defend the incomparable beauty of his lady,[7] and yet this implied number of 500 knights does not include, it seems, all of the knights who are individualized here and there.[8] Another hint at a large but vague number appears at the moment when Erec and Enide finally return to Arthur's court; they find there a king who feels very much alone, having only 500 barons of his retinue to keep him company.[9] Erec himself belongs to the Round Table from the beginning of the romance; he leaves it permanently only to go into his own country to accede to the throne of his father. Thus the Table is diminished by one member; nevertheless it is a loss that is soon made up. The celebrations that take place at Erec's wedding, and later at the time of his coronation, account for the promotions of numerous *vaslets* to the rank of knight. As a prelude to the two ceremonies, an *hors-d'oeuvre* before the main course, so to speak, Arthur knights *en masse* first 100 *vaslets* and then some 400 sons of kings and counts. In each of these episodes he provides those whom he has just made knight with war horses, arms, and suits of costly clothes. However, these new recruits to chivalry remain anonymous, and their future relation to Arthur's court is not made clear; this creation of knights is decorative rather than utilitarian. As for the other knights in this first romance of Chrétien, those who are individualized (Gauvain, Lancelot, Tristan, etc.) are members of the Round Table from the beginning of the tale.

The same applies, to a large extent, to two other romances of this poet. In both the *Chevalier au lion* and the *Chevalier de la charrete*, the emphasis is upon a quest, one that draws the hero away from the court almost immediately. Therefore in these two works it is not a matter of imposing numbers of courtiers nor of an increase in these numbers. Arthur in his quality as a king who dubs knights and fosters chivalry does not appear in these romances.

It is from this perspective that one can consider Chrétien's two remaining romances, *Cligés** and the *Conte du Graal*, as being the most Arthurian of the five, notwithstanding the fact that a considerable part of their action takes place at some considerable distance from the royal court and for reasons that have nothing to do with the king. Each of these texts is in its way striking as a full-scale *amplificatio* of the passages in Geoffrey and Wace that have already been examined. This development takes a course that can be represented by the following schema:

1. The reputation of Arthur's magnificence or largesse or prowess or power reaches a young man of good birth.
2. On his own initiative he goes to Arthur's court, either to be made a knight or (if he is one already) to test himself against outstanding members of the Round Table.
3. He succeeds brilliantly (although sometimes in a rather eccentric way) and is at last received into the entourage of the king.

This motif is not only present but is of capital importance in both the second and the last romances of Chrétien. In *Cligés*, in fact, it occurs twice in succession. Alexander, son of the emperor of Greece, wishes to become a knight but disdains the prospect of being dubbed in his native country and is restive at his father's court, having heard of another that, in his opinion, must be better. News of Arthur and of the barons kept in his company, who make the court internationally feared and renowned, has reached Constantinople.

> Oï ot feire menssion
> Del roi Artus qui lors reignoit
> Et des barons que il tenoit
> An sa conpaignie toz jorz,
> Par qu'estoit dotee sa corz
> Et renomee par le monde.

*Professor Sargent-Baur uses the spelling "Cligés" when referring to editions of Chrétien's romance; when referring to the character, however, she uses the alternate spelling "Cligès."

("He had heard mention of King Arthur, who reigned in those days, and of the barons who always accompanied him, making his court feared and renowned throughout the world.")[10]

Dazzled by the reports that he has heard, he obtains through trickery his father's permission to make the long journey to Great Britain. If he is not knighted by Arthur, he says, he will never become a knight. Using every means possible, Alexander manages to leave Greece, neither alone nor poorly but well equipped and with a noble retinue; and after a journey of several weeks the whole company disembarks at Southampton. Once he has arrived at Winchester and has been admitted into the royal presence, Alexander pays the king homage and makes his request: he wishes to serve the king until he is found worthy of being made a knight. Without hesitation, Arthur grants his permission; then the thirteen Greeks (like so many postulants) are admitted to a probationary period. However, unlike postulants, it seems that these *vaslets* do nothing in particular except to accompany Arthur on his expedition into Little Britain (and, in the case of Alexander, to fall in love); however, when news of the disloyalty of the regent crosses the English Channel and preparations are begun for the return to England in order to wage war against the usurper, Arthur without hesitation grants Alexander's wish; he bestows the order of chivalry (along with armor, clothes, and horses) upon the thirteen foreign visitors. The rest of this first part of the romance (which makes up almost a third of the whole) shows Arthur vigorously and successfully waging war on the regent Angret and the other conspirators, a war in which the new Greek knights, and above all Alexander, provide inestimable assistance. Arthur, the king who makes knights and who inspires in them the desire to distinguish themselves, does not stop there: he also lavishly rewards them for their services after the victory is won.

Alexander's experience is so satisfactory that, some years later, realizing that he is about to die, he has but one piece of advice to give to his only son, Cligès: he should go to Arthur's court in order to test his prowess against the British and English, indeed against the elite of that society, including his uncle Gauvain. If he does not do this, he will never realize his own worth with respect to *proesce ne de vertu* (line 2567) ("valour and might" [p. 154]).

Like father, like son. When he has the opportunity, during an expedition into Germany, the young Cligès remembers his father's command, and, instead of returning to Greece, goes to Great Britain. Since he has already been knighted on the shores of the Danube by his uncle Alis (who had seized the throne), his objective in setting out for Britain is not quite the same as his father's; however, like him, Cligès has a vision of the grandeur and the glory of Arthur's court. It is a place where a spirited young man can test and improve himself:

> Qu'an Bretaigne sont li prodome
> Qu'enors et proesce renome,
> Et qui enor vialt gueaignier
> A ces se doit aconpaignier:
> Enor i a, et si gueaigne
> Qui a prodome s'aconpainge. (ll. 4212–17)

("In Britain are to be found the worthy men acclaimed by honour and renown, and whoever wishes to gain honour must join their company, for there is honor and profit in associating with worthy men." [p. 174])

He knows all of that, of course, at second hand; but when he arrives in Britain, his expectations and hopes of distinguishing himself are fully gratified. He participates incognito in a tournament and measures himself against the best knights: first, Sagremor, then Lancelot, then Perceval (in addition to many anonymous knights); and finally he fights to a draw his uncle, the formidable Gauvain. In all of this activity, Arthur is spectator, judge, referee, and eager connoisseur; his enthusiasm and energy are in striking contrast with the incompetence of Alis.[11] The British king takes a lively interest in the knightly exploits of the Greek visitor Cligès, and the latter finds that his stay at Arthur's court fulfills all his wishes; he avails himself of it to win an uninterrupted series of triumphs. Only his love of Fénice (who has become empress in Greece) can make him decide to leave. Later, after the interruption of his idyll with her in Constantinople, Cligès, accompanied by his beloved, returns to his great-uncle Arthur; this time it is as a fugitive and suppliant. He begs the king to give him military aid against his uncle, the usurper Alis. Arthur hears the *plainte et clamor* of Cligès and does not hesitate for a moment:

> Et li rois dit que a navie
> Devant Costantinoble ira
> Et de chevaliers emplira
> Mil nes, et de sergenz trois mile,
> Tex que citez, ne bors, ne vile,
> Ne chastiax, tant soit forz ne hauz,
> Ne porra sosfrir lor assauz. (ll. 6562–68)

("King Arthur said that he would take his fleet to Constantinople. He would fill a thousand ships with knights and three thousand with foot-soldiers, until no citadel, borough, town, or castle, no matter how high or mighty its walls, could withstand their assault." [p. 204])

Arthur does not limit himself to comforting promises; he intends to keep his word since he has the means and the authority to do so. He has prepared and assembled all kinds of vessels, weapons and armor; he has the ships loaded; he sends for "Toz les hauz barons de sa terre" (l. 6572) ("all the high barons of his land" [p. 204]). He does not stop there, for his power extends beyond Great Britain.

> Por ostoier fet aparoil
> Li rois, si grant que le paroil
> N'ot ne Cesar ne Alixandres.
> Tote Eingleterre, et tote Flandres,
> Normandie, France, et Bretaigne,
> Et tot desi qu'as porz d'Espaigne
> A fet semondre et amasser. (ll. 6579–85)

("The king's preparatioMns were on such a grand scale that neither Caesar nor Alexander ever equalled them. All England and all Flanders, Normandy, France, and Brittany, and everyone as far as the Spanish passes, were convened and assembled." [p. 204])

Summoned by the prestigious name of Arthur, a good part of the chivalry of Europe becomes mobilized. Only the sudden and opportune death of the usurper prevents a massive attack by the fleet of Arthur and his allies, ready to sail toward Constantinople.

Arthur plays a dominant role in both parts of this romance. His reputation as the supreme authority on chivalric prowess is international; and he demonstrates, over the course of two generations, that he very much deserves this renown. The result is a common experience shared between the two Greek princes, characters in the romance, and the readers or hearers of this story: on the one hand, the characters themselves successively find that their preconception of Arthur, based on rumors reported in the romance, is corroborated by their personal contacts with him and with his court; on the other hand, the hearers or readers to whom the Arthur of the earlier chronicles is more or less known and who naturally base their expectations on this image, find themselves in familiar territory.

In Chrétien's last romance, which was left unfinished, protagonist and audience again share the same notions, at least at the beginning. The *Conte du Graal* opens with an amply-detailed account of the way in which an uneducated young man learns of Arthur's existence and how he reacts to this information. Encountering for the first time in his life a group of knights in the depths of the Welsh forest, the amazed adolescent is struck with the desire to be like them, to become a knight himself (whatever that means); and he soon realizes that this ambition is not impossible. The leader of these resplendent and iron-clad creatures tells Perceval that he was not born that way but that he has very recently been made a knight. This is a revelation to Perceval: one can *become* a knight, and there is someone named Arthur capable of bringing about this transformation. Arthur, according to the title that the boy immediately confers on him, is the "roi qui les chevaliers fait"[12] ("king who makes knights" [p. 385])—a title that he repeats twice with unimportant variants. This notion of a royal and almost magical power is heightened in the course of the journey to Carduel, where the king is staying, by another detail provided by a charcoal-burner whom Perceval meets by chance: Arthur has just returned from a victorious military expedition. The *vaslet*, completely absorbed by his obsession, cares little about this news; once more, however, the hearer or reader familiar with the matter of Britain feels reassured: the news again indicates that we are dealing with a familiar topic (and in recognizing it we experience a certain feeling of a superiority to this Welsh rustic). Chrétien, however, has set up a surprise for us. When Arthur finally appears in the narrative, he belies our slightly smug expectation at the same time that he destroys Perceval's recent enthusiasm. Seen against the background of this intense preparation, of this announcement of a majestic and heroic figure, the "true" Arthur, as this romance depicts him, is for Perceval (and for the reader) a painful disappointment. The king does not join the action; rather the action (in the form of the Welsh boy, on horse-back and full of spirit) joins him. He remains seated at the table and does not utter a word; seemingly blind and deaf to all that happens around him, he is as if paralyzed. When after his long (and not very courteous) silence, he opens his mouth, it is in order to recount not a military triumph but a personal humiliation; just now, a knight has insulted Arthur and challenged him in his own hall, with himself and all his knights unable to stop him or to punish him.[13] This representation of Arthur clashes with the portrayals found in the first two romances of this poet, not to mention those offered by Geoffrey and Wace. Even within the confines of the *Conte du Graal*, the king's conduct corresponds so little with the earlier description of the king that the hero himself notices the discrepancy. Untutored but by no means stupid, the Welsh adolescent seems to be entirely justified in the judgment that he makes of the person for whose sake he has come so far:

"Par foi, dist li vaslés adonques,
Cis rois ne fist chevalier onques.
Comant porroit chevalier faire,
Quant on n'en puet parole traire?"
(ll. 927–30/925–28)

("By my faith," the boy then said,"this king never made a knight! How could he make knights if you can't get a word out of him?" [p. 392])

Upon close examination this observation is not completely accurate since (as we have seen) Arthur had indeed dubbed the first knight whom Perceval ever met. If it does not apply to past events, however, this judgment will be valid for the future, for in all of the long narration that follows Arthur does *not* make knights.[14] Moreover, he fails in the single knighting requested of him, that of Perceval.[15] At the end of this scene Perceval recovers from his initial disappointment since he has (or so he thinks) received the signs that distinguish a knight from other people. The other characters in the romance who witness this interview with Arthur do not share this notion; they know only too well that Perceval's euphoria is without foundation. Inevitably, the reader/hearer is of their opinion. The young Welshman is not a knight; he will not be one until Gornemant takes him in hand and regularizes the situation. Equivocation shadows even his return to Arthur's court: henceforth, it seems, Arthur considers that Perceval is a knight,[16] although he has no apparent means of knowing that a proper knighting ceremony has taken place; and Perceval is never disabused of his erroneous idea of having received his armor, his precious red armor, from the hand of Arthur.[17]

The texts under consideration show a rapid and profound change in the conception of the figure and function of Arthur. In the course of four or five decades[18] in the twelfth century, the great king, maker and unmaker of lesser monarchs, who dubs, recruits, inspires, and rewards knights, has become strangely diminished. Arthur is not only relegated to the background; he is also depicted as unworthy of his glorious reputation. It is passivity, indeed ineptitude, that characterizes him in the *Conte du Graal*.

It may well be that political and sociological explanations account for this phenomenon, as some scholars have suggested.[19] Suffice it to say here that a major difference in attitude is implied in the development that has been considered in this article. The values propounded, without apparent reservation, by Geoffrey and Wace, the values of royalty with its power and glory, are given still more emphasis in *Cligés* thanks to a double exposition. By contrast, Chrétien's last romance clearly reflects a change in attitude. It looks as if he weighed in the balance the character of Arthur that had been made famous by the two popular chroniclers; and after a period of treating it with great respect, he revised his conception of the king and concluded by presenting a legendary figure who had lost much of his royal dignity and importance.

NOTES

1. For the text, see E.K. Chambers, *Arthur of Britain* (London, 1927), rpt. with supplementary bibliography for *Speculum Historiale*, 1964, pp. 238–39. For the original Latin and an English translation, see Nennius, *British History and the Welsh Annals,* ed. and trans. J. Morris (London, Chichester, and Totowa NJ, 1980), pp. 35 and 76. The date and interpretation of this important text are discussed by L. Alcock in *Arthur's Britain: History and Archeology, A.D. 367–634* (Harmondsworth, 1971), pp. 29–41, 55–71.

2. Pelan, *L'Influence du Brut de Wace sur les romanciers français de son temps* (Paris, 1931; rpt. Geneva, Slatkine, 1974), esp. pp. 147–66. It is evidently necessary also to take account of the Breton storytellers, as well as of other oral and traditional sources.

3. Geoffrey of Monmouth, *Historia Regum Britanniae,* ed. Acton Griscom (London, New York, Toronto: Longmans, 1929), IX, 1.

4. *Ibid.*, IX, 11. The translation is by L. Thorpe (based on this edition), *The History of the Kings of Britain* (Harmondsworth and Baltimore, 1966), p. 222. According to J.S.P. Tatlock, this portrait of Arthur and his influence is not found prior to the *Historia;* see *The Legendary History of Britain: Geoffrey of Monmouth's Historia Regum Britanniae and its Early Vernacular Versions* (Berkeley and Los Angeles, 1950), p. 192.

5. Wace, *Le Roman de Brut,* ed. I. Arnold, SATF (Paris, 1938–40), ll. 9021–24; the translation of this and other passages from Wace's *Brut* are by B.N. Sargent-Baur.

6. A similar detail appears in the story *Culhwch and Olwen* (which is perhaps the first text in Welsh prose in which Arthur appears); but the extraordinary mixture of Arthur's men is far from a chivalric following and in any case is present from the beginning. The new arrival Culhwch goes to his cousin Arthur's court not for the purpose of joining the warriors of this leader but instead to have himself initiated and to obtain Arthur's aid in the quest for his future bride.

7. Chrétien de Troyes, *Erec et Enide,* ed. M. Roques, C.F.M.A. (Paris, 1952), ll. 50 ff.

8. The most obvious exception to this is Erec himself. See the partial roll-call of the knights attendant at the court when Erec returns there with his fiancée (ll. 1662 ff.; the specific names, and the total number, vary from MS. to MS.).

9. "V^c barons de sa meison" (l. 6367). Chrétien may have intended his portrait of the "solitude" of the king to be ironic.

10. Chrétien de Troyes, *Cligés,* ed. A. Micha, C.F.M.A. (Paris, 1957), ll. 66–71. (Translation by William W. Kibler in Chrétien de Troyes, *Arthurian Romances,* Penguin Classics [London, 1991], p. 124. Other translations in this article from *Cligés* and *Conte du Graal* are from this edition; page references will appear within parentheses in the text.—E.D.K.)

11. See L.T. Topsfield, *Chrétien de Troyes: A Study of the Arthurian Romance* (Cambridge, 1981), p. 93.

12. Chrétien de Troyes, *Le Roman de Perceval ou Le Conte du Graal*, ed. K. Busby (Tübingen, 1993), l. 333; cf. l. 494 and ll. 840–41. (The verse-numbering in this edition agrees with that used by Hilka and Roach. I also give the numbers used by F. Lecoy in his 1973–75 C.F.M.A. edition.)

13. Those who know the complete work of Chrétien will recall the passive Arthur of the first part of the *Chevalier de la charrete*, but that passivity is exaggerated here. With regard to this, R.S. Loomis finds a link between the *Graal* and the *Charrete*, pointing to the sorry figure that Arthur cuts in these two romances. He explains it by taking account of the sources that the poet used and by his concerns as a storyteller: "The technique of promoting the hero of a particular romance at the expense of established reputations has combined with a traditional formula to demote Arthur to a humiliating role" (*Arthurian Tradition and Chrétien de Troyes* [New York, 1949], p. 201). W.A. Nitze's statement that except for *Cligés* Chrétien mentions several times Arthur's weaknesses and presents Arthur as a *roi fainéant* needs to be nuanced ("The Character of Gauvain in the Romances of Chrétien de Troyes," *Modern Philology*, 50 [1953], p. 222). P. Haidu astutely observes that in the scene under discussion Arthur comes off worse than Perceval (*Aesthetic Distance in Chrétien de Troyes: Irony and Comedy in Cligés and Perceval* [Geneva, 1968], p. 139). In *Aufbaustil und Weltbild Chrestiens von Troyes im Percevalroman* (Tübingen, 1936; rpt. 1967), p. 150, W. Kellermann notes a change in the depiction of Arthur since the *Chevalier au lion*: "Er erscheint greisenhafter als im *Yvain* (von seiner aktiven Rolle im *Cligés* ganz abgesehen" ("He seems more senile than in *Yvain*, irrespective of his active role in *Cligés*."—trans. E.D.K.) One is puzzled by the observation of E. Köhler that in the courtly romance in general, up to the *Mort Artu*, "Artus ist *nie* König im Sinne eines Herrschers, ist kein wirklicher König; er ist *immer* Symbol eines hingestellten idealen Feudalstaats." ("Arthur is *never* king in the sense of a ruler; he is not a real king; he is *always* the symbol of an ideally represented feudal state."—trans. E.D.K. *Ideal and Wirklichkeit in der höfischen Epik*, 2nd ed. [Tübingen, 1970], p. 22; the italics are the author's). In his study *Irony in the Medieval Romance* (Cambridge, 1979), D.H. Green discusses the evolution of Chrétien with respect to Arthur and his court, but he restricts himself to *Erec* and *Yvain* to support his conclusions concerning the king's loss of authority; see pp. 314–15.

14. The subsequent success of Gauvain, who knights 500 *vaslets* at one time, makes Arthur's failure stand out all the more (ll. 9171/8897 ff.).

15. It is perhaps worth emphasizing that Arthur does not show the least reluctance to knight the boy, although he does not know his identity nor his parentage. Later, when he finally learns Perceval's name, he shows him no hostility. M. Blaess has perhaps exaggerated the implications and the significance of the relationship between Perceval and the clan of the Illes de mer ("Perceval et les 'Illes de mer'," *Mélanges de littérature du moyen âge au XXe siècle offerts à Mlle Jeanne Lods* [Paris, 1978], pp. 69–77).

16. The precise expression that he uses is "vostre chevalerie" (l. 4577/4553; "your deeds of chivalry," p. 437). The queen calls him "chevaliers" (l. 4594/4570; "knight" p. 437).

17. This opinion is expressed in Perceval's message to Arthur, as relayed by an adversary vanquished by the new knight:

"Or m'entendez, fait il, biax sire, / Qu'il m'estoet mon message dire. / Ce poise moi, mais tote voie / Reconnois je que cha m'envoie / .I. chevaliers qui m'a conquis; / De par lui m'estuet rendre pris / A vos, que nel puis amender. / Et qui me volroit demander / Se je sai coment il a non, / Je li respondroie que non, / Mais tels noveles vos en cont / Que ses armes vermeilles sont / Et vos li donastes, ce dit" (ll. 2837–49/2835–47).

("Now listen to me, fair sir, for I must deliver my message: though it is painful to acknowledge, I admit that I have been sent here by a knight who defeated me. I have no choice but to surrender myself prisoner to you on his behalf. And if anyone were to ask me if I knew his name, I would answer no; but I can tell you that his armour is red and he says that you gave it to him." [p. 416])

Concerning the knighting of Perceval, the categories established by J. Flori should be corrected ("Pour une histoire de la chevalerie," *Romania*, 100 [1979], Tables II, III and V, pp. 47, 49 and 53). See my study of knighting ceremonies in Chrétien's romances: "Promotion to Knighthood in the Romances of Chrétien de Troyes," *Romance Philology*, 37 (1983–84), 393–408.

18. A discussion of the often debated chronology of Chrétien's works would not be pertinent here. For a bibliography on this subject, consult D. Kelly, *Chrétien de Troyes: An Analytic Bibliography* (London, 1976), pp. 119–21.

19. For example, E. Köhler (*op. cit.*, Chap. I, "König Artus und sein Reich"). I do not agree with his assertion (p. 6) that there is no fundamental change in the portrait of Arthur in these romances.

King Arthur and the Round Table in the *Erec* and *Iwein* of Hartmann von Aue

William C. McDonald

Erec

In the second half of the twelfth century, when Chrétien de Troyes composed his *Erec et Enide,* two traditions concerning King Arthur were regnant. Tom Artin summarizes: "In one, he is the great *dux bellorum,* the once and future king who is Britain's savior; in the other, he is a fool. In a mosaic dated 1165 in the Cathedral of Otranto, for instance, he is shown riding a goat, the animal of Venus, symbol of lechery, and hardly a dignified mount for a king."[1] Artin emphasizes the second of these traditions, King Arthur as essentially negative exemplum, but does not speak of the first, the ruler as military leader. It is derived to a great extent from Geoffrey of Monmouth's *Historia Regum Britanniae* (ca. 1138), in which King Arthur functions as warrior, restorer, and arbiter. Artin believes, however, that the Arthur in Chrétien's *Erec* is a largely negative figure, a foil "meant to serve as contrast to the ideal of holy kingship . . . which the young knight [Erec], in the course of his adventures, attains. Arthur is the model of what a king should not be" (p. 65). W.T.H. Jackson offers the following description of King Arthur in twelfth-century romance: "Never do we see him carrying out any significant public action. He never fights himself but sometimes arranges opportunities for others to engage in adventure. His function is basically that of an arbitrator of individual prowess. In other words, he is a literary king."[2]

Since Hartmann von Aue derived his *Erec* (ca. 1180) from Chrétien's text, the essential characteristics of his King Arthur would seem to depend heavily on the French model.[3] One might expect, in other words, to find Chrétien's monarch and the world that sustains him in German dress. But matters are not so simple, and source relationships cannot account for the differences in both Hartmann's portrait of the king and his presentation of Erec's relationship to the Round Table. Any reading of the German *Erec* labors of course under the burden of its transmission. Preserved in a single late manuscript, the romance is lacking its prologue and approximately the first one hundred lines of narrative. The missing lines are important for the present inquiry, since they introduce King Arthur to the reader through the episode of the Hunt of the White Stag. Nevertheless, it seems possible to reconstruct the opening of the romance and to argue that Hartmann sought a middle ground between the contrasting traditions concerning King Arthur. His Arthur is neither a battle leader nor a fool for love, but is instead a ruler whose actions convey a devotion to ritual, decorum, and courtly bliss. Even without the opening scene, this *Erec* offers a well-rounded portrait of a king who, although a secondary character, emerges as a striking presence.

Chrétien does not mention King Arthur in his prologue, and there is no reason to believe that Hartmann here deviated from his source. Chrétien's romance begins on Easter Day when King Arthur decides to renew the custom of hunting the white stag. Gawain warns that the contest may needlessly stir up passions at court (ll. 41–58).[4] Arthur, however, rejects Gawain's foreboding, arguing that a ruler cannot retract his word. The king justifies the hunt in the forest of adventure by evoking the great pleasure it will bring to the court.

At roughly the point where Erec has stayed behind with Guinevere and an attendant maiden, Hartmann's *Erec* begins. His King Arthur does not appear for over 1,000 lines, when the reader learns that the king catches the stag with his own hands. Consequently, he is by rights in a position to award the kiss:

> Er (solde) . . . undern megeden allen
> eine küssen . . . ,
> swelhe er wolde.
> dô si ze Karadigân wâren komen,
> dô wolde der künec hân genomen
> sîn reht nâch der gewonheit. (ll. 1109–14)

> ("He could kiss anyone he wished of all the maidens. The king wanted to make use of this right, as was the custom, as soon as they returned to Cardigan.")[5]

Here Hartmann describes an active monarch, capable of winning the prize of the hunt. Moreover, he is a model of courtesy, willing to grant his queen's request that he delay bestowing the kiss until the court learns of Erec's fate. When Iders, the knight defeated in combat by Erec, comes to Cardigan as Erec had demanded, King Arthur thanks God that Erec has been so successful and that his first knightly combat had ended so fortunately (ll. 1260–69). In keeping with his courtly ethos of honoring champions, the king then plans to reward Erec with a splendid reception.

At the arrival of Enite and Erec at court, the time has come to award the kiss, the prize for capturing the white stag. Hartmann's narrator looks first to fair Enite, and then to decisive, just Arthur:

> nû gedûhte ouch den künec zît
> daz er den ritterlîchen strît
> zehant enden wolde . . .
> des hâte er unz an die stunt
> durch die künegîn erbiten.
> nû enwart niht dâ wider gestriten,
> si enwære diu schœniste dâ
> und über die werlt ouch anderswâ. (ll. 1750–65)

("He then thought it time to bring the dispute of the knights to a quick end. . . . At the request of the queen he had waited until this moment, but it was needless to delay longer since Enite was without question the most beautiful woman there, and in the rest of the world as well.")

Through oblique reference here to the dispute of the knights, Hartmann and his narrator signal that the German text recognizes, but does not fully assimilate the motif from the source.

What makes Hartmann's portrait of King Arthur appealing is his reluctance to accept whole Chrétien's characterization, which pivots around the consequences of the Hunt of the White Stag. Chrétien's formally complex narrative allows the hunt to serve as an internal structure of dislocation and threatened dislocation. As such, it is mentioned twice after the opening lines. The second reference occurs after Erec has left the Round Table to avenge the insult to himself and to the Queen. Arthur has returned from the successful hunt to preside over courtly revels. The king interrupts the celebration, however, to announce that he will bestow the kiss. The strife that Gawain had foretold now erupts. He had feared that each man at court would take up arms in defense of a claim from his own beloved (ll. 301–06).

Chrétien's Arthur has thus provoked a situation with possible tragic effects. Arthur's "bullish insistence" to renew the stag hunt, Artin observes, harms the order at court by creating dissension. Proud and foolish, the king is contrasted with Gawain, the courtly and wise. "Arthur appears even more foolish," Artin continues, "when, having had his way against the counsel of Gawain—having slain the stag and brought on rumblings of the trouble he has been warned of—he begs his nephew now to get him out of the jam" (p. 64). The best nobles of the court are called to counsel, but it is Guinevere who extricates the king from trouble by cautioning a delay. She wants to put off the kiss until Erec's return, and King Arthur gives his assent (ll. 335–41).

The third time Chrétien associates Arthur with the hunt for the stag is when Erec and Enite first come to Cardigan. Guinevere argues that Enite by virtue of her beauty should receive the kiss. To settle the matter, Arthur invites opposing views from the assembled knights, but sets aside objections with a declaration of his rights and the duties of a ruler:

> Je sui rois, ne doi pas mantir,
> Ne vilenie consantir,
> Ne fausseté ne desmesure:
> Reison doi garder et droiture.
> Ce apartient a leal roi
> Que il doit maintenir la loi,
> Verité et foi et justise.
> Je ne voudroie an nule guise
> Feire desleauté ne tort,
> Ne plus au foible que au fort.
> N'est droiz que nus de moi se plaingne
> Ne je ne vuel pas que remaingne
> La costume ne li usages,
> Que siaut maintenir mes lignages.
> De ce vos devroit il peser,
> Se je vos voloie alever
> Autres costumes, autres lois,
> Que ne tint mes pere, li rois.
> L'usage Pandragon, mon pere,
> Qui fu droiz rois et anperere,
> Doi je garder et maintenir . . .
> La verité an vuel savoir. (ll. 1793–1820)

("I am king and must not lie or be a party to any baseness, deception or high-handedness. I must safeguard right and reason. It's the business of a true king to uphold the law, truth, good faith and justice. I would not wish in any way to commit disloyalty or wrong any more against the weak than the strong. It is not right that any should have a complaint against me, and I do not wish the traditional custom to lapse which my family habitually observes. You would doubtless be unhappy if I wished to introduce for you customs and laws other than those kept by my father the king. Whatever may become of me, I must safeguard and uphold the practice of my father Pendragon, the just king and emperor. . . . I wish to hear the truth.")

Edward J. Buckbee believes that Arthur's words indicate that the king "wants to be honest, moderate and equitable, maintaining the rule of custom and right, truth, faith and justice. . . . In Arthur's view his function is to maintain established practices and time-honored custom."[6]

To accept this reading, however, would be to overlook the emphasis upon the turmoil caused by the Hunt of the White Stag. The preoccupied King Arthur has shown himself determined to revive a custom the outcome of which is far from certain and which finds a happy end only because of circumstance and the intervention of the queen. Perhaps repelled by the aura of failure at Cardigan and the undercurrent of darkness which this fragile courtly setting conveys, Hartmann excises both of these scenes. By omitting them, he gives more emphasis to his portrayal of Arthur as a charismatic leader, and he is implicitly critical of the tradition on which he was drawing.

Hartmann thus eliminates the scene in which a violent situation threatens to erupt at court after Arthur's promise to bestow the kiss and the scene in which the king, wavering between advisers and the queen, relies upon Guinevere to exercise her authority. Absent, too, is the passage modeled on the so-called Mirror for Princes, *Je sui rois. . .* (see above). In Hartmann's conception, the monarch does not veer between roles and defend himself with self-conscious pronouncements on the virtues of the Christian ruler. Instead, by omitting scenes that present a crisis-ridden court in compromising circumstances, Hartmann depicts a king who relies upon deeds, not words. He turns Arthur's indecisiveness, readiness to make compromises, and excessive reliance on advice into their opposites. The king, conscious of his function as lawgiver, calmly and quickly brings the argument to an end (ll. 1750–2). Hartmann's narrator replaces infirmity of purpose with regal resolution.

The irony is, of course, that the German text offers no *ritterlîchen strît* ("dispute of the knights," l. 1751), unless it appeared at the very opening of the romance. Even if disruption of courtly ceremony because of the bestowal of the kiss was alluded to at the outset in the missing verses, Hartmann has removed the scenes that cast King Arthur as a ruler who is in conflict with a tension-filled court and who relies upon Gawain, his nobles, and the queen. The decisive actions of Hartmann's king therefore have the ironic function of remedying the strife that appears only in the French version.

The effect of this editing in the German text is a defining moment in Arthur's rule. He resolutely makes use of his royal *reht* ("prerogative," l. 1754), quickly settling the dispute and relying on his own powers as arbiter. One result directly concerns Guinevere, for it makes her less prominent. The effect of Hartmann's reducing her role as counselor is to elevate Arthur and to allow the king to emerge as a more self-assured, resolute ruler.

Chrétien's queen sets the scene for the reward of the kiss, telling the king when to bestow the prize and to give it to Enite (ll. 1765–76). Although Hartmann's Guinevere is referred to obliquely, the ceremony is concluded on Arthur's terms. He grants her request to postpone the kiss because of courtesy and because she lays out an affair of honor involving Erec, as well as herself (ll. 1124–29). The almost immediate appearance of Iders, the defeated knight, confirms both that Guinevere's request was just and that Arthur had wisely waited to hear the outcome of Erec's adventures.

The wedding of Erec and Enite also shows that Arthur is a judicious and resolute king. While in Chrétien's romance Erec asks the king's permission to hold the wedding at his court (ll. 1915–19), in Hartmann's version Arthur insists that Erec be married in Cardigan castle after the king has had time to invite a host of princes and dignitaries. The monarch wants a magnificent court festival. King Arthur is here described as *der tugenthafte Artûs* (l. 1890), a favorable but broadly allusive term that connotes chivalric virtues as well as the religious virtue, righteousness. Thomas L. Keller renders this as "the good Arthur" (p. 29), whereas J.W. Thomas has "the courtly Arthur" (p. 52), and Michael Resler chooses "the upright King Arthur."[7] None of the three translations, "courtly," "good" or "upright," does the term justice. Peter H. Oettli's suggestions of "excellent," "powerful," "polite," "kind," and "virtuous" are closer to the mark.[8] With a single epithet, *tugenthaft,* Hartmann thus conveys the viewpoint of the narrator, while encapsulating the portrait of the king. He is a fundamentally good man and ruler who carries out the functions that Chrétien places in his mouth (ll. 1793–1820), but without self-consciously expressing the duties and obligations of kingship.

Arthur is as he does, and in the German *Erec* he is a true master of ceremonies. No warrior, he is instead active behind the scenes, reviving and maintaining courtly custom, organizing pageants, dispensing gifts, and presiding over feasts, tournaments, and festivities, such as the marriage of Erec and Enite. When Erec enters a tournament after his wedding, Arthur intervenes by helping him equip himself (ll. 2324–30). After the tournament, Arthur's men leave the field as victors (ll. 2809–10), with the same pageantry and spectacle witnessed at the beginning of the contest (ll. 2368–77). The portrait is consistent and positive; Arthur sets the rules and ensures that they are upheld, appearing at proper junctures to impose the necessary restrictions.

Although Arthur and the Round Table appear prominently in a society that knows to reward Erec and Enite, Hartmann largely limits the intersection of Cardigan and Destregales (Erec's homeland) to the beginning and end of the romance. The middle section is, as in Chrétien's romance, occupied with the quest of the protagonists. The Arthurian court, to which only intermittent reference is made in the quest episodes, is therefore a framing device. Erec's story, like Iwein's, involves the Round Table, but the quest itself, the fulfillment of the hero's destiny, is solitary. Erec does not need to associate directly with those at court to achieve his destiny. He does, however, accept the social consensus of the Round Table, as shown, for instance, by his concern for honor.

The quest portion of Hartmann's *Erec* is prepared for by the knight's requesting the king's permission to return home after his marriage (ll. 2861–69). Arthur thus gives the hero the freedom he requires, a freedom that initiates a series of events exposing Erec as deeply uxorious. The Round Table now proceeds in counterpoint to Erec's conduct: just as the hero is on a quest, the court itself seems to be in an ever-shifting environment, its movement evoking his own. In symbolic terms, Arthur and his knights pursue Erec, enticing him to return. While on a hunt, the Round Table learns that Erec is in the vicinity. The king sincerely wishes to see Erec and tells Keii and Gawain to bring him to the royal tent. Arthur's words emphasize his joy (l. 4861). Joy is Arthur's characteristic emotion and highest value; the dominant aesthetic is sounded again when Gawain informs Erec that his reintegration into the courtly community would make Arthur the happiest man who ever lived (ll. 4954–55).

The situation and dilemma of King Arthur are starkly presented. Erec has taken joy away from the court; hence the only way for happiness to return to Cardigan is for Erec himself to return. But he does not. The knight frames his refusal in the only language that the Arthurian court can understand. He has rejected pleasure and willingly suffered the grief of exclusion:

swer ze hove wesen sol,
dem gezimet vreude wol
und daz er im sîn reht tuo:
dâ enkan ich nû niht zuo. (ll. 5056–59)

("A man should be happy at court and behave accordingly.
I cannot do that now.")[9]

Erec identifies the Round Table with joy, as is seen later when he brings the defeated knight Mabonagrin and his lady to Cardigan. The hero maintains that Mabonagrin and consort can only be happy with King Arthur (ll. 9826–34). This passage, Hartmann's interpolation, tells the reader that Arthur's world is a world of joy. Happiness reigns there, a ruling emotion (and theory of governance) that can only be shattered by the departure of a favored member of the Round Table.

That Erec elects to renounce this joy and to risk bringing sadness to King Arthur by failing to rejoin him is important to Hartmann's romance. It is a scholarly commonplace that Erec consistently maintains distance from the Arthurian world. His failure to participate in the Hunt of the White Stag is one example—and symptom—of the narrative space between the hero and the court. Chrétien bridges this gap, which Buckbee calls "relative detachment from activities at Arthur's court" (p. 82), by having Erec return to the Round Table at the conclusion of the romance and by the coronation of Erec and Enide by King Arthur. The great king hands Erec the scepter, and the story ends amidst great joy, with the devoted pair at Arthur's court. Hartmann, however, in his most significant departure, has Erec return to the Round Table, only to leave King Arthur again in order to assume the rule of his hereditary domains (ll. 9971–79). There is pointedly no coronation, and the story does not end at Cardigan. Since the narrator claims that God had sent Erec home (l. 10054), the clear implication is that Heaven itself did not want the protagonist to remain with King Arthur. The reader is left to infer that the joy that Erec brings to his homeland is echoed, but set apart from, the joy so important to the Round Table.

Erec's departure from King Arthur, however, does not necessarily mean that the author has completely rejected the Round Table. The Arthurian court has a firm structural and ideological place in the story, as Resler has recognized: "The function of the Arthurian court is to witness both the high-points and the low-points of the hero and thereby to measure and confirm his triumphs and defeats against the standards of a larger (Arthurian) society" (pp. 23–24). Although Erec's destiny calls him home and he thus has an ambivalent relationship with the Round Table, Arthur and his world are indissolubly linked to the hero. Hartmann makes this point by mentioning ties of kinship. King Arthur calls Erec his *lieber neve mîn* ("dear kinsman," l. 9944) near the end of the story. The term in the text, *neve*, may also be rendered as "nephew," as Keller has done (p. 137). As Arthur's nephew, Erec therefore enjoys the same familial status as Gawain. Accordingly, the two knights, related in the same way to King Arthur, appear as the best knights of the Round Table.

Arthur's final words to Erec encapsulate both the breadth of vision and the limitations of the Round Table and thereby suggest that Arthur is questioning the hero's progress toward right conduct. The king says that Erec deserves praise and honor because he has greatly increased the splendor of the court (ll. 9947–48). Thomas's translation "splendor" (p. 144) may conceal the fact that *wünne* (l. 9948) appears in the text. Keller more accurately renders Arthur's words as "increased the *happiness* of [the] court" (p. 137); thus he links the happiness of Arthur's first utterance to the absence of the same in the second. And here, it seems to me, is the crucial point: gladness, courtly joy, is Arthur's preoccupation. He is pleased to shelter the eighty bereaved widows whom Erec brings with him upon his return to court, and Arthur instructs his lords to console the ladies in their sorrow (l. 9922). To honor the compassionate King Arthur, we learn, these ladies turn their hearts and lives to joy *(vreuden,* l. 9956). As a coda to this festival of bliss, Arthur exchanges the widows' clothes for ones more suited for pleasure. What is abundantly clear is that the Round Table fails to contain Erec not only because kingship in his own land calls, but also because he has transcended the sensory pleasure of Cardigan. Hartmann has placed the hero outside the society that lives for tourney, feast, the hunt—and joy. In the end, Hartmann von Aue relativizes the values of the Arthurian society that, although incarnated in a just and compassionate ruler, are not adequate for every exigency.

IWEIN

Susan L. Clark summarizes the problems of interpreting the role of Arthurian society in Hartmann's *Iwein* (ca. 1200):

> *Iwein* begins with an idyllic picture of the Pentecostal festival held at Arthur's court. The narrator assures the reader of the presence of many noble knights and describes them at their courtly occupations, which include dancing, singing, chatting, and bragging. It is truly "ein wunschleben" (l. 44; "all that one could wish"), and yet the picture is marred. . . . The Arthurian court has chinks in its armor; not merely

is the smooth surface of that idealized society about to be disturbed in the verbal fracas that erupts, but also the "wunschleben" for the protagonist is going to come to an end.[10]

Clark goes on to list specific examples of discord and uncourtliness at Karidol, such as the insults to Guinevere by Keii the seneschal.

Karl D. Uitti arrives at a similar conclusion in his analysis of Hartmann's source, the *Yvain* (ca. 1170) of Chrétien de Troyes. Uitti notes the dissonance between Chrétien's initial, laudatory reference to King Arthur and the narrative to follow: "A 'good king of Britain,' Arthur, is he 'who teaches us prowess and courtesy'. . . [Then Chretién] begins his narrative proper: an astounding story . . . of Arthur's incivility and of his Round Table entourage's discourtesy."[11] Uitti argues further that "the realities of Arthur's court—the king's lack of courtesy toward his guests, Keu's sarcasm, Guinevere's unladylike language—do not jibe with that court's reputation for graciousness and nobility. What actually takes place there contrasts with the court's fame" (pp. 210–11).

Clark and Uitti have here set forth the interpretive crux in both the German and the French romances. Can the inconsistency between the benign vision of King Arthur and his court at the outset be reconciled with the ensuing scene of the failure of the Arthurian ideal? The German version, like the French, is open to conflicting interpretations.[12] Hartmann's portrayal of King Arthur and his court is less flattering than in *Erec,* but, as in that earlier work, the poet strives for a balanced characterization. He acknowledges the fame and fundamental goodness of the king and his knights, Gawain particularly. However, he relativizes the status of the Arthurian court—and ideal. In contrast to Chrétien's *Yvain,* of which Uitti has said that the poet "refrains from offering any equally systematic alternative to inadequate Arthurian courtliness" and avoids "moralizing" (p. 211), Hartmann's story does moralize and constructs an alternative to the deficient courtliness at the Round Table.

In this romance King Arthur is a less striking figure than he is in Hartmann's *Erec,* his dominance shaken by the more important roles of other characters. Herta Zutt points out that King Arthur appears less often than in the French model.[13] When he does appear—in only three scenes—he reacts to events, primarily with speech. The three scenes are: 1) the end of the feast of Pentecost; 2) the incident of Guinevere's abduction; and 3) the administration of justice in the judicial dispute of the daughters of the Count of the Black Thorn.

The first of these finds Arthur awakened from his bed, annoyed by the bantering at court. Hartmann's narrator immediately establishes the relationship of ruler to court:

> wander was in weizgot verre
> baz geselle dan herre. (ll. 887–88)

("God knows, he was much more their companion than their lord.")[14]

As *geselle* then, not as *herre,* Arthur sits down among his retainers to hear the tale of Kalogrenant's misfortune at the Magic Fountain. Arthur decides to go with his knights to the fountain. His action, a royal avowal, is in truth a reaction to events; in order to restore the honor of his court, he makes an oath that requires societal obedience.[15] The king's action as reaction is now met with the knights' reaction: all the members of the Round Table except Iwein think it a good and chivalrous thing to do. Just as Arthur's pronouncement in *Erec* on the reinstitution of the Hunt of the White Stag rouses the Round Table, so too his words in *Iwein* on the communal quest for honor set events in motion.

But Arthur's words initiate a startling paradox, because they spur Iwein on to challenge the social order. Fearing that Arthur's oath will deprive him of his chance at knightly honor (l. 913), he is the only dissenter from communal consensus. He realizes that Gawain, the knight of highest status, and not he, will be allowed to avenge Kalogrenant. Iwein has absorbed enough of Arthurian values and protocol to recognize that the presence of king and court at the fountain will thwart his own quest. Iwein's reaction, his decision to disrupt the Arthurian social hierarchy, dictates that he slip away from court secretly, "rehte als ein man," the narrator says, "der êre mit listen/kunde gewinnen und vristen" ("just like a man who could win and maintain honor cunningly," ll. 946–48). Whence this reasoning springs is not clear; Iwein's gestures, however, clearly indicate that he is a willing exile from the Round Table. That the Arthurian court cannot contain the hero will become the defining motif of the romance.

The adventure upon which Iwein embarks ends with the murder of Ascalon, the Lord of the Fountain. Iwein's faults may arise from his immaturity and inexperience, but his actions are fueled by the rituals of a social group, the Round Table. Fearing that Keii will mock him if he does not kill or capture Ascalon, Iwein slays the man, and this after he had set out after him, the narrator says, *âne zuht* ("in unmannerly pursuit," l. 1056). Iwein's haste to find honor and avoid shame is now mirrored in his haste to marry Laudine, widow of Ascalon, so that he can defend the fountain *against* King Arthur and his knights.

The end of the Arthurian festival thus signals a descent into a realm of adventure for which Iwein and the Round Table are unprepared. Arthur responds to events by initiating the action with speech. Guided by the convention of swearing his oath upon his father's soul (l. 895), this benign but only occasionally decisive king determines to uphold the honor of his court. The result is different from what he had intended, however. To his mind acting to end the bickering in his society, he complicates matters and cannot prevent the departure of a favorite knight. Iwein, an erstwhile Arthurian, has become the lord of a rival kingdom, which he guards against the assaults of his former companions.

In the scene in which Arthur and his company learn that the defender of the fountain is in fact Iwein, the king's sensibilities now come fully before the reader. Arthur is first a man of the oath: what he has sworn, he will do, as the references to his pledge show (ll. 2410, 2448). Second, the king is naively inquisitive. He reaches for the bucket, fills it from the fountain, and brings about a horrible storm and the ignominious defeat of Keii at the hands of Iwein, because the monarch had wanted to see for himself if the story was true (ll. 2530–35). Third, his judgment is questionable, for although all realize that the fountain has a strong defender, Arthur permits Keii to have the first joust, the results of which are predictable. Has Arthur sworn a holy oath, even though he suspects that the events motivating his oath are invented truth? The elusiveness of reality is a recurring motif, to be sure. Nevertheless, Arthur's doubts cast his response, his reaction to (purported) action, in a dim light. Finally, Arthur appreciates prowess: after the disgraceful defeat of Keii and the chorus of ridicule it inspires (l. 2645), the king and his knights show great admiration for Iwein. The ruler forgives and forgets, honoring Iwein and Laudine by his acceptance of their hospitality at the castle, which has become a counter-court to Karidol. Implicit in Arthur's recognition of the victor is his approbation of a new setting for the hero, who now has left the Round Table. But the Arthurian court's entrance into an alien realm has its consequence: Gawain, leading knight of the Round Table and Iwein's friend, now persuades the hero to ride off with him to compete in tournaments in order to maintain his honor (l. 2801), a course of action that causes the disruption of Iwein's marriage and then madness.

The abduction of Guinevere is the second scene involving King Arthur. This scene, like the first, centers on the king's reliance on speech, which in turn illuminates his method of governance. The narrator describes the episode as a *vremde maere* ("curious tale," l. 4528). An unnamed knight (Meljaganz) arrives at court, asking for an unspecified open favor.

Arthur places restrictions on the request; he announces that he will grant it only on condition that it is *betelich* ("seemly," l. 4546). When the enraged knight leaves court, the blame that he ascribes to the king for refusing his request serves only to highlight the regal trait that is most characteristic of Arthur:

> man saget von sîner miltekheit,
> ezn wurde rîter nie verseit
> swes er in ie gebæte.
> sîn êre sîn unstæte,
> dem er wol gevalle. (ll. 4561–65)

("Men talk of his generosity as if a knight would receive anything he requested. May the honor of the man be fleeting who praises this king!")

Reacting to the knight's departure and to this man's negative reference to Arthur's honor, the members of the Round Table openly criticize their king for his behavior. Asking whether he has ever denied anything to anyone, they claim that he has acted improperly, indeed counter to his customary practices. The court, trusting in the apparent courtliness of the visitor, urges the king to grant the request. Arthur relents, pledging his solemn word (l. 4584). The knight's desire, Arthur learns, is that he be allowed to take the queen with him. The King's first reaction is intense agitation and rage; next, he blames his advisers for having tricked and betrayed him. But the narrator says:

> nû muose der künec lâzen wâr
> daz er gelobete wider in. (ll. 4608–09)

("The king had no choice but to keep the promise he had made to him.")

Arthur's humiliation is presented differently in the French text, where a nobleman explains that, owing to Kay's complicity, a foreign knight is able to carry off the queen. The king, whom Kay dupes, had placed his wife in Kay's keeping and trust. In the scene King Arthur is censured for his gullibility and failures in judgment, indeed for acting like a madman.[16]

Hartmann links the scene to the earlier episode, the "End of the Feast of Pentecost," both of the scenes revealing the entanglements that oral pronouncements initiate. Both times, according to the German version, King Arthur reacts to events with words that bring about the reverse of their intended effect. In order to uphold the honor of his court and to appease the Round Table, the king swears an oath dictating a specific course of action, which is in reality reaction. This oath, as an index of character, places Arthur in the role of lawgiver; as judge, however, he is guided, bound, and betrayed by words, which restrict his sphere of activity. In both scenes, the result is the exile of a member of the royal family.

The virtues that Arthur embodies therefore hinder, not further, his governance. Liberality, hospitality, and fidelity to the oath cannot prevent courtly turbulence or catastrophe. Hartmann thus suggests that laudable traits in excess, and not reinforced by behavior, turn upon themselves, bringing about the opposite effect. Consequently, the world of merriment, of *fêtes* and festivals, becomes a cheerless place, lacking the courtly joy that the king had tried so hard to maintain (ll. 4620–21). Moreover, the collegiality of the first scene has now extracted a great price. As illusion comes up against reality, Arthur's knights are betrayed in their sense of judgment, and the king has placed excessive trust in collaborative gestures. That Kay is the first to take the field against the abductor of the queen echoes the first scene and thus conveys further information about the powers of discrimination at Karidol. King Arthur, although a good and decent man, appears to uphold morally ambiguous rituals.

The third scene in which King Arthur appears is the "Administration of Justice" (ll. 5625–7721). At the death of the Count of the Black Thorn, his two daughters engage in a dispute over their inheritance. The elder sister tries to intimidate the younger into forsaking her rightful share. The elder wins a champion at Karidol, Gawain, while the younger is unable to find a defender among the knights of the Round Table. Seeking a knight, she must look outside the court; her champion is Iwein. Since her cause is just, the scene implies that justice and courtliness are found only outside Arthurian society.

When confronted by strife, King Arthur proceeds as in the two earlier scenes. He reacts to the situation, issuing pronouncements that rely on tradition for their impact. Just as Arthur's oath in the first scene looks backward to justify current practice, his words in the "Administration of Justice" begin with a bow to legal convention. The king fixes a date for the battle after charges have been brought, thus reacting to events by setting others in motion. He is both judge and spectator, eager to witness the fight (ll. 6898–99).

The social mores of Arthur's court contrast with the solution that the younger sister must find for herself. Reliant on custom and orthodoxy, the Round Table is unwilling or unable to help her, and it cannot be by chance that the maiden relies on God, not King Arthur, to be her refuge and the restorer of justice. As Will Hasty has said, "Iwein ends up representing the just and Gawain the unjust cause."[17] Had the Arthurian deputy Gawain defeated the outsider Iwein, then might would have meant right, and justice would not have prevailed.

In Chrétien's version of the "Administration of Justice," the narrator, claiming that the elder sister's injustice toward her sister was manifest, clearly states that King Arthur well knew that the maiden had wronged her sister (ll. 5913–15) and that he was happy Yvain had come to defend the younger disputant. The king, who had attempted to persuade the elder sister to leave the younger her rightful portion, now permits the combat between Gawain and Yvain only because he realizes that the elder sister wants no part of a reconciliation. After the duel, King Arthur forthrightly declares that he wishes to restore the younger sister's rightful share to her. Chrétien's characterization of an active, wise ruler who is a sympathetic and forceful advocate of the rights of the oppressed contrasts markedly with Hartmann's. The German Arthur is a largely passive onlooker who never openly expresses partisanship for the younger sister in her dispute and declares the injustice of the elder sister's claim only at the conclusion of the duel.

By omitting Chrétien's statements that Arthur wished to do what was right and that he never desired to be unjust, Hartmann sketches a legalist and an advocate of tradition who relies on the law, not a king outraged by usurpation. The German King Arthur arranges for the confession of the elder sister not merely on the grounds that she threw her younger sister off her land and disinherited her, as in Chrétien, but on the basis of a moral failing and sin, *übermuot*, "arrogance," "overweening pride," "haughtiness." Here Hartmann shows himself to be a moralist, as Arthur calls out:

> ". . . wâ ist nû diu maget
> diu ir swester hât versaget
> niuwan durch ir übermuot
> ir erbeteil unt taz guot
> daz in ir vater beiden lie?"
> dô sprach sî gâhes "ich bin hie."
> dô sî sich alsus versprach
> und unrehtes selbe jach,
> des wart Artûs der künec vrô:
> ze geziuge zôch ers alle dô.

er sprach "vrouwe, ir hânt verjehen." (ll. 7655–65)

("Now where is the girl who was so arrogant as to deny her sister her share of the inheritance and the property that her father had left for them both?" "I am here," she said hastily. When she incriminated herself in this way and admitted wrongdoing, the king was pleased, and he called on everyone as witness to it, saying, "My lady, you have confessed.")

This theological dimension, pride as the first sin (l. 5661) and confession of wrongdoing, is now joined to the ritual practice of legalism that characterizes Arthur's rule. The scene turns on the assumption that justice will ultimately prevail because the perpetrator is vainglorious, the further implication being that sin will be punished by heaven, not by a secular ruler, even if he is King Arthur. Hartmann's king is therefore the secular representative and executor of a legal system ultimately controlled by Providence.

In the "Administration of Justice" Arthur thus plays a largely passive role, his stance representing a kind of forbearance that trusts in Providence and in the deeds of others. Throughout, as we have seen, Hartmann's king reacts to circumstance. He initiates action only when forced to, and then his response is formulaic language and ritual. Largely immobilized by events over which he exercises sporadic control, the king takes refuge in norms and practices that sway outcomes because they bear the weight of precedent.

Zutt correctly observes that Hartmann's Arthur places enormous reliance on words and that "das gegebene Wort [hat] für ihn eine unbedingte Verpflichtung" (p. 15; "the given word has an unconditional obligation for him"). But Arthur's commitment to his solemn word cannot have the positive cast that Zutt, for example, would ascribe to it, since his words cannot control his milieu and cannot keep beloved individuals (Iwein, Guinevere) from leaving his court. The pattern of departure from the Round Table, the limitations of which are recognized by Erec and Iwein, is stressed when the latter steals away from the Arthurian world for the second time after the "Administration of Justice" (ll. 7805–07). The hero's future adventures take place outside the walls of Karidol, for he seeks an alternative to the Round Table society.

Hartmann's controversial prologue can be more easily assessed against the backdrop of the story proper. Both Chrétien and Hartmann begin with an encomium to King Arthur, but the two poets differ in their attitude toward the king and toward Arthurian society in relation to their own times. Of Arthur, Chrétien says that he is a good king [li boens rois] whose valor [*proesce*] teaches us to be brave [*preu*] and courteous [*cortois*] (ll. 1–3). Because Chrétien uses multivalent terms, such as *proesce* and *preu,* there is no scholarly consensus as to their precise meaning. For the former, translators have rendered "noble qualities," "Rittertugend," and "prowess"; and for the latter "honorable" and "ritterlich."[18] If there is controversy over translations, it no doubt exists concerning the narrator's attitude toward his story, which contrasts a past world of excellence with a present day of diminished distinction. When Chrétien's narrator speaks of Love's disciples (Staines, 257), he invites identification of these with the knights of the Round Table, whose fealty to Love's order represents model behavior *in illo tempore,* the good old days. Those who loved in bygone days, we hear, were courtly [*cortois*] and valiant [*preu*] and generous [*large*] and honorable [*enorable*] (ll. 22–23).

Hartmann, by contrast, differs on the meaning of the past.[19] The past for him is no substitute for the present day, as when his narrator states:

> ichn wolde dô niht sîn gewesen,
> daz ich nû niht enwære,
> dâ uns noch mit ir mære
> sô rehte wol wesen sol:
> dâ tâten in diu werc vil wol. (ll. 54–58)

> ("I wouldn't want to have lived at that time instead of now, when we can get so much delight from hearing about them, whereas they had only their own deeds to enjoy.")[20]

The passage is striking for its awareness of Arthurian tales as fiction. Hartmann also clearly distinguishes the Arthurian world from his own, both in time and in matters of interest. It is a realm of deeds, providing us with pleasant stories [*mære,* l. 56]. Hartmann, however, does not treat his romance or its message lightly. As in *Erec,* he relates the redemptive story of a knight who loses happiness and must regain it through compassionate service to others, most notably women. Again the protagonist begs forgiveness of his lady, presenting himself as a sinner (l. 8105); and again heaven is invoked at the closing to bless the reconciliation of the married couple outside the confines of the Round Table (ll. 8139–48).

Although Hartmann's prologue is in some ways similar to the French model, it is significantly different. Whereas Chrétien offers a brief catalogue of the virtues of the king and his court, Hartmann's offers a laudatory summons to his audience:

Swer an rehte güete
wendet sîn gemüete,
dem volget sælde und êre.
des gît gewisse lêre
künec Artûs der guote,
der mit rîters muote
nâch lobe kunde strîten.
er hât bî sînen zîten
gelebet alsô schône
daz er der êren krône
dô truoc und noch sîn name treit.
des habent die wârheit
sîne lantliute:
sî jehent er lebe noch hiute:
er hât den lop erworben,
ist im der lîp erstorben,
sô lebet doch iemer sîn name.
er ist lasterlîcher schame
iemer vil gar erwert,
der noch nâch sînem site vert. (ll. 1–20)

("He who dedicates himself to a life of true goodness will be blessed with fortune and fame. A perfect example of this is good King Arthur, who with a knightly spirit, could do battle worthy of praise. In his time he lived so magnificently that he wore a crown of honors just as his name does today. Thus his countrymen are telling the truth when they claim he is still alive today: he won such renown that although he be dead in the flesh his name still lives on. He who follows his example will forever be shielded from the shame of dishonor.")

The German Arthur is an exemplary ruler, so exemplary in fact, that one has the impression of reading a saint's life: "He who follows his example . . ." (l. 20). Hartmann sustains this balancing act between the sacred and the secular by cleverly playing on Chrétien's epithet *li boens rois:* Hartmann adopts it for the "good King Arthur" (l. 5), which is anticipated by the call to all men to dedicate themselves to a life of true goodness. The German term, *güete,* admitting the meanings "kindness," "(good) quality," and "goodness," is so ambivalent in its context that some have interpreted it as a spiritual value.[21] Even as goodness is stressed, so, too, is honor, which, in various formulations, appears no less than five times in the passage. Esteem, in turn, justifies Hartmann's single reference to King Arthur's *rîters muote* ("knightly spirit," l. 6): the battleground of the king is the striving for fame. In sum, Hartmann's narrator indexes Arthur and his court under the categories "good" and "renown." Guided by these qualities, the king and his knights are mentor figures for kindness and reputation.

Strangely absent, however, is Arthur's role as the exemplar of courtesy. Whereas Chrétien asserts that the valor of the king teaches us to be brave and courteous, Hartmann unexpectedly expunges the term and vividly conveys a message through its absence. His Arthur nowhere bears the epithets "courtly" or "courteous" and is not known for his courtesy. Arthurian society itself, the finest knights and the loveliest ladies living a life nothing short of ideal (l. 44), would seem to offer a model of courtliness, but the text confounds the reader's expectations; here again courtesy is prominent by its absence. In its place is the bliss *(vreude,* l. 51) that immediately links this Arthurian panorama to that already seen in *Erec.* By removing courtliness from the equation in the programmatic opening of *Iwein,* Hartmann in my view inaugurates a rhetorical strategy meant to expose the discordance between the attitudes to courtesy advanced by the hero and the Round Table. Inasmuch as the conception, in its mature form, is alien to King Arthur and his court circle, Hartmann offers a critique of the moral authority of Arthurian norms.

The importance of the topic of courtliness, whose omission in the prologue is striking, can be inferred from the frequency with which it occurs. The concordance to the works of Hartmann shows how central "courtesy" and its word-family are in *Iwein: hovereht, hövesch, hövescheit, höveschlîch,* and *hovezuht* all appear, and the vocabulary of courtliness is more pronounced in this work than in any other that he composed.[22] C. Stephen Jaeger has noted that *"hövescheit* [courtliness] and its variants have a wide range of meaning in this romance," extending from fine clothes as a mark of the "courtly gentleman" (l. 2195) to "compassion and refined and humane sense of respect for the feelings of others."[23] The polyvalence of courtesy-terminology in *Iwein,* admitting a multiplicity of readings, suggests Hartmann's intent. He chooses arguably the most emotion-laden semantic complex imaginable and compels the reader to think afresh about refined manners, conviviality, discretion, civility, courtly custom, elegance, and courtliness itself. He examines these from different angles for the purpose of revealing what courtesy is, where it resides, and whether the conventional courtliness of the Round Table promotes the dignity of man.

When one considers Hartmann's text to be based upon a definition of courtliness (with Iwein as the agent of change) and organized around the opposition between the attainment and transgression of courtesy, it is immediately apparent that the Round Table is less endowed with *hövescheit* than are those, including Iwein, who live outside Karidol. The vision of courtliness within the walls of the Arthurian court is circumscribed by a gentlemanly sophistication inadequate to an exterior world that acknowledges and furthers Iwein's progress from concern for honor, victory, and rewards to heightened sensibility as "defender of the downtrodden and oppressed, doing service to ladies in distress. . . ."[24]

Hartmann employs courtliness for didactic reasons, strategically placing the concept outside the sphere of the Round Table, with the aim of underscoring his narrative statement that Arthur's court is neither the goal of the protagonist nor the repository of the values of compassion and humanity, the "new" or heightened courtliness, to which Iwein ultimately subscribes. Thus, although King Arthur incorporates laudable qualities and attracts others through his goodness, honor, and battle spirit, he lacks the courtliness that Iwein wants to have. From Arthur's otherwise perfect example Iwein flees as a voluntary exile. The hero departs not only from the Round Table but from its social customs and ritual acts, and as Iwein progresses from his earlier conception of courtliness to his present state of grace, his conduct clearly reveals the ever-widening gulf between his own values and those of the Arthurian court.

To illustrate the contradictory responses to courtliness in *Iwein*, Hartmann places the initial reference to courtly behavior in the mouth of Keii, who ridicules Kalogrenant before the assembled court:

> . . . her Kâlogrenant,
> uns was ouch ê daz wol erkant
> daz under uns niemen wære
> sô höfsch und als êrbære
> als ir wænet daz ir sît.
> des lâzen wir iu den strît
> vor allen iuwern gesellen. (ll. 113–19)

("Sir Kalogrenant, even before today we knew that no one among us was as courtly and well-bred as you think you are. Thus we shall recognize your supremacy over all your fellow knights.")

The first allusion to courtliness and good-breeding is thus embedded in sarcasm, jealousy, and the battle for esteem, contexts that immediately frustrate the expectations of the reader. The irony is of course heavy. In one of Hartmann's most significant additions to Chrétien's *Yvain,* not only does Keii attempt to reveal a fault in an uncourtly manner, but he attacks the very man who defines Arthurian adventure. Since Kalogrenant exemplifies the standard of manners and morality at Arthur's Court (Thomas, *Iwein,* 25–26) and since Arthur soon realizes that this knight's defeat represents collective defeat, Keii's vulgar oral assault is no less than an attack on the very mores that he, as seneschal, is charged to uphold. The effect of his criticism is therefore self-canceling, exposing the entire court—and himself—to ridicule.

That courtliness can be found in women outside the Arthurian world is a mark of Hartmann's narrative pattern. For example, Gawain speaks of Lunete's *hövescheit,* which brings harmony and worldly honors to the protagonist (ll. 2743–49). A new courtliness emerges when Iwein is ill, the intermediary being a woman who stands apart from the Round Table. The narrator claims that a lady serving the Lady of Narison weeps tears of compassion upon discovering the humiliated Iwein insane and naked in a forest. This reaction he attributes to her courtly and compassionate nature.[25] Compassion arising from courtliness is moreover the motivation for the maiden's modest withdrawal after she has rubbed Iwein with healing ointment:

> . . . sî (erkande) daz wol
> daz schämelîchiu schande
> dem vrumen manne wê tuot,
> und barc sich durch ir höfschen muot. (ll. 3489–92)

> ("She was well aware how unpleasant shameful situations can be
> for an honorable man, and in her courtliness concealed herself.")

Courtliness is thus witnessed beyond the limits of polite society—in a forest—manifesting itself in concern for the feelings of others and for the healing of the weak and oppressed.

Another woman from the outside, the younger daughter of the Count of the Black Thorn, who appeared earlier during the judicial dispute, trusts that the Arthurian court will promote those very qualities of compassion and civility that the reader has witnessed in the forest. But her expectations are dashed along with the expectations of the reader. At Arthur's court there is no one to take up her cause, and Gawain, the greatest of the Arthurian knights, is the champion of the older sister—therefore the advocate of manifest injustice. In order to encounter courtliness, the emissary of the younger sister must enter the province of Iwein, the outsider and neophyte champion of social conscience, who is wandering far from the Round Table. The judicial dispute thus emerges as a defining moment in the collision of the differing concepts of courtliness. Iwein is one in whom refined sensibility, warrior spirit and charity are fused; Gawain, on the other hand, embodies an outmoded brand of *hövescheit* that is as hollow as Kalogrenant's. As Arthur's first knight, Gawain might be expected to give Iwein lessons on conduct, and the text causes the reader to assume that this will be the case. The narrator claims that Sir Gawain was always a man of courtly and proper demeanor (ll. 2698–99), and that he was a man of discretion who displayed his courtly manner (ll. 2714–15). The rhetoric of Arthurian courtliness turns in upon itself, however, for in the very passage describing Gawain as "der höfschste man / der rîters namen ie gewan" ("the most courtly knight that ever lived," ll. 3037–38), we learn that it was Gawain who was Iwein's undoing. Gawain has given the hero bad advice: Iwein is swayed by his friend's appeal to knightly honor, and this leads to his downfall—separation from Laudine, insanity, and loss of identity.

To find himself, Iwein must break the symbiotic relationship between himself and Gawain and must sever his new conception of courtliness from Arthurian society. Iwein's alternative courtliness resides in deeds, not in words; in extra-courtly humanity, not in a social code reliant on accepted conventions; in rectitude, not moral obtuseness; and in internal, not external honor. The Arthurians trust in the appearance of courtliness, as in the scene the "Abduction of Guinevere," where a miscalculation causes social turbulence with potentially disastrous consequences. Hartmann's message is that Arthurian society cannot recognize courtliness. It is unable, because of its own cultural values, to discriminate between polite manners and interior disposition.

The mark of Iwein's progress, it would appear, is his movement toward a new definition of courtliness, one whose horizons extend beyond Arthurian society. The uniqueness of this sphere of courtliness rests in the moral rectitude that we observe as a consequence of a developing social conscience in the hero. Its latent shape emerges when the narrator comments on Iwein's rescue of 300 unfortunate women (l. 6234), in a scene that Hartmann expands over Chrétien's version. Iwein's are the reactions and gestures of compassionate courtliness, and he becomes a forceful advocate of a new, extra-courtly orientation, which is most palpable in his treatment of women in distress. Humanity toward women thus characterizes his emancipatory struggle, and women will recognize him as everything a knight should be (ll. 5912–13).

It is the female emissary of the younger sister, a model of courtesy, who is able to spell out the special form of courtliness that the hero must learn. To Iwein she says:

> sît daz iuch got sô gêret hât
> daz alsô gar ze prîse stât
> vür manegen rîter iuwer lîp,
> sô êret got und diu wîp:
> sô sît ir hövesch unde wîs. (ll. 6051–55)

("Since God has honored you with qualities that rank you higher than most other knights, then you should, in turn, honor God and women. In so doing you would be courteous and wise.")

That Iwein follows the path to kindness, compassion, and justice indicates that the hero can now be described as "courteous." It could be argued, in fact, that the rehabilitation of Iwein is the story of his attainment of, and entitlement to, the epithet *ein hövesch man,* a courtly man. The narrator pointedly confers this epithet on Iwein after he has freed the 300 unfortunate women and rides off with them (l. 6856).

The gracious Iwein of the second half of the romance is certainly not the *hövesch man* (l. 1040) alluded to in the first part, the immature hero who had embarked on a bloody adventure in the hope of avenging Kalogrenant and of avoiding the ridicule of the Arthurian court. His earlier self had sought knightly honor and a misguided chivalry that D.H. Green characterizes as "an offence against ideal courtesy."[26] Iwein needs to transcend his former courtliness, alter his sensibility, and to recognize the inadequacy of the Arthurian world for him. The hero comes to represent an extra-Arthurian courtliness with a profound ethical dimension, based on kindness, compassion, altruism, and justice. Attainment of this new *hövescheit* requires Iwein to discover a self-sufficiency that places him outside Arthur's court.

Notwithstanding the strong moralizing strain in *Iwein,* which is alert to every breach of decorum by the Round Table, it is important to stress that King Arthur and his knights do possess virtue. Hartmann recognizes their achievements, their generous tendencies, and their essential goodness and renown, and he does not permit the flaws in evidence to detract appreciably from the credibility of a court that in *Erec* and *Iwein* is neither decadent nor pernicious. The poet admires King Arthur primarily as a benevolent and colorful ruler who, against the backdrop of a brilliant court, strives after conviviality and good form. Arthur's impulses are noble, as evidenced by his well-intentioned efforts to reclaim the hero for the court.

To be sure, in *Iwein* especially, there is reason to question the values and structure of Arthur's reign—the artificiality of adventure, the grandiloquent rhetoric, the hasty oath, the failure to distinguish between semblance and truth, the prevailing code of honor, and the legalism. All invite scrutiny. It would miss the point, however, to expect Hartmann to approach King Arthur and the Round Table in a spirit of awe. Whatever Arthur's idiosyncrasies, he is a decent person with good intentions. That these go awry is not so much an indictment as it is a realistic portrayal of a human being far removed from the restorer, warrior, and arbiter of the chronicles. On the whole, Hartmann's portrait is less concerned with ennobling the king and his society than with probing the ambiguities and fragility of the conduct of life at Karidol, which he views through the prism of realism, not idealism.

The result is a sophisticated depiction of a complex society, simultaneously embodying opposing positions. Placed in the middle ground, the Arthurian court is neither an emblem of folly nor a repository of courtliness, but rather the locus of rituals that represent one stage in Iwein's career. It is his starting point; and, as an initial phase, Arthurian society can provide him with no absolutes, no definitive guide to pleasing God and mankind. In Hartmann's fictional world, the hero cannot reconcile Arthurian paradigms with his spiritual quest. This echoes the pattern in Wolfram's *Parzival,* which also portrays Arthurian norms as having relative merit only. Erec, Iwein, and Parzival assent for a time to the practices of the Round Table. These prove inadequate to the hero's social progress, however, and cannot sustain him. The symbolic representation of the cultural resistance to, and transcendence of, Arthur's realm is the relocation of the protagonist to a counter-court, be it within Erec's kingdom, Laudine's kingdom, or the Grail kingdom.

NOTES

1. Tom Artin, *The Allegory of Adventure: Reading Chrétien's "Erec" and "Yvain"* (Lewisburg: Bucknell University Press, 1974), p. 65. On Chrétien's treatment of the Arthurian court, see Donald Maddox, *The Arthurian Romances of Chrétien de Troyes: Once and Future Fictions* (Cambridge: Cambridge University Press, 1991). Here I thank William Plail for his advice and help.

2. W.T.H. Jackson, "The Nature of Romance," *Yale French Studies,* 51 (1974), 19.

3. See the introduction to Thomas L. Keller's translation, *Hartmann von Aue, "Erec"* (New York: Garland, 1987), pp. xi–xxxvii. On Hartmann's handling of Arthurian subjects, see Christoph Cormeau and Wilhelm Störmer, *Hartmann von Aue:*

Epoche—Werk—Wirkung (Munich: Beck, 1985), esp. pp. 160–226; Karin R. Gürttler, *Künec Artûs der guote: Das Artusbild der höfischen Epik des 12. und 13. Jahrhunderts* (Bonn: Grundmann, 1976), esp. pp. 13–90; Gürttler, "German Arthurian Literature," in *The New Arthurian Encyclopedia,* ed. Norris J. Lacy (New York: Garland, 1991), pp. 182–88; and Klaus Grubmüller, "Der Artusroman und sein König: Beobachtungen zur Artusfigur am Beispiel von Ginovers Entführung," *Positionen des Romans im späten Mittelalter,* ed. Walter Haug and Burghart Wachinger (Tübingen: Niemeyer, 1991), pp. 1–20.

4. English translations of Chrétien's *Erec* are from *Arthurian Romances,* trans. D.D.R. Owen (London: Dent, 1988). Line numbers and the French originals are from the edition by Ingrid Kasten (Munich: Fink, 1979).

5. Unless otherwise noted, English translations are from Hartmann von Aue, *Erec,* trans. J.W. Thomas (Lincoln: University of Nebraska Press, 1982). The German originals are from the edition by Ludwig Wolff (Tübingen: Niemeyer, 1972).

6. Edward J. Buckbee, *"Erec et Enide," The Romances of Chrétien de Troyes: A Symposium,* ed. Douglas Kelly (Lexington: French Forum, 1985), pp. 80–81.

7. Hartmann von Aue, *Erec,* trans. Michael Resler (Philadelphia: University of Pennsylvania Press, 1987), p. 81.

8. Peter H. Oettli, *A First Dictionary for Students of Middle High German* (Göppingen: Kümmerle, 1986), p. 121.

9. See Horst Wenzel, "Repräsentation und schöner Schein am Hof und in der höfischen Literatur," *Höfische Repräsentation,* ed. Hedda Ragotzky and Horst Wenzel (Tübingen: Niemeyer, 1990), p. 173. On the topic of joy in Hartmann's poetry, see Hans-Werner Eroms, *"Vreude" bei Hartmann von Aue* (Munich: Fink, 1970).

10. Susan L. Clark, *Hartmann von Aue: Landscapes of Mind* (Houston: Rice University Press, 1989), p. 169. On Hartmann's *Iwein,* see Hubertus Fischer, *Ehre, Hof und Abenteuer in Hartmanns "Iwein"* (Munich: Fink, 1983); and Timothy McFarland, "Narrative Structure and the Renewal of the Hero's Identity in *Iwein," Hartmann von Aue, Changing Perspectives. London Hartmann Symposium 1985,* ed. Timothy McFarland and Silvia Ranawake (Göppingen: Kümmerle, 1988), pp. 129–57.

11. Karl D. Uitti, *"Le Chevalier au Lion (Yvain)," The Romances of Chrétien de Troyes: A Symposium,* cited n. 6, pp. 202–03.

12. See Volker Mertens, "Imitatio Arthuri: Zum Prolog von Hartmanns *Iwein," Zeitschrift für deutsches Altertum,* 106 (1977), 350–58; and Hartmann von Aue, *Iwein,* trans. J.W. Thomas (Lincoln: University of Nebraska Press, 1979). Thomas writes: "It is true that its king is cited in the opening lines as proof of the story's theme, but the statement is soon found to be ironic, since subsequent events connect him with neither true kindness nor God's favor, but only with an exaggerated regard for the esteem of men" (p. 21).

13. Herta Zutt, *König Artus, Iwein, Der Löwe: Die Bedeutung des gesprochenen Wortes in Hartmanns "Iwein"* (Tübingen: Niemeyer, 1979), p. 4.

14. All English translations, unless otherwise indicated, are from Hartmann von Aue, *Iwein,* ed. and trans. Patrick M. McConeghy (New York: Garland, 1984). German quotations are from Hartmann von Aue, *Iwein,* ed. Benecke-Lachmann-Wolff, trans. Thomas Cramer, 2nd ed.(Berlin: De Gruyter, 1974).

15. See Robert E. Lewis, *Symbolism in Hartmann's "Iwein"* (Göppingen: Kümmerle, 1975), p. 85.

16. ". . . Li rois fist que fors del san/qant aprés li l'en envoia" (ll. 3710–11). (". . . The king was assuredly mad to send her off with him.") English translations and French line numbers are from Chrétien de Troyes, *The Knight with the Lion, or Yvain (Le Chevalier au Lion),* ed. and trans. William W. Kibler (New York: Garland, 1985). I have also consulted *The Complete Romances of Chrétien de Troyes,* trans. David Staines (Bloomington: Indiana University Press, 1990).

17. Will Hasty, *Adventure as Social Performance: A Study of the German Court*

Epic (Tübingen: Niemeyer, 1990), p. 31.

18. Owen, *Arthurian Romances,* p. 281; Chrestien de Troyes, *Yvain,* trans. Ilse Nolting-Hauff (Munich: Fink, 1983), p. 17; and Uitti, *"Le Chevalier au Lion (Yvain),"* p. 202.

19. On the general topic of the meaning of the past, see Ruth Morse, *Truth and Convention in the Middle Ages: Rhetoric, Representation and Reality* (Cambridge: Cambridge University Press, 1991), pp. 85–124.

20. This translation is from Hartmann von Aue, *Iwein,* trans. J.W. Thomas, p. 55.

21. See McConeghy's note 2, p. 337.

22. *Hartmann von Aue: Lemmatisierte Kondordanz zum Gesamtwerk,* prepared by R.A. Boggs (Nendeln: KTO Press, 1979), Vol. 1, p. 179. See William C. McDonald, "Observations on the Language of Courtesy in the *Iwein* of Hartmann von Aue," *The Ring of Words in Medieval Literature,* ed. Ulrich Goebel and David Lee (Lewiston, NY: Mellen, 1993), pp. 219–56.

23. C. Stephen Jaeger, *The Origins of Courtliness: Civilizing Trends and the Formation of Courtly Ideals, 939–1210* (Philadelphia: University of Pennsylvania Press, 1985), p. 243. See also Peter Ganz, *"höveschl hövescheit* im Mittelhochdeutschen," *Curialitas: Studien zu Grundfragen der höfisch-ritterlichen Kultur,* ed. Josef Fleckenstein (Göttingen: Vandenhoeck and Ruprecht, 1990), pp. 39–54; and Aldo Scaglione, *Knights at Court* (Berkeley: University of California Press, 1991), pp. 162–63.

24. Richard J. Berleth, *The Orphan Stone: The Minnesinger Dream of Reich* (New York: Greenwood, 1990), p. 194. See also Kurt Ruh, *Höfische Epik des deutschen Mittelalters* (Berlin: Schmidt, 1967), Vol. 1, p. 155.

25. Hartmann writes:

> ir höfscheit unde ir güete
> beswârten ir gemüete,
> daz sî von grôzer riuwe
> und durch ir reine triuwe
> vil sêre weinen began,
> daz einem alsô vrumen man
> diu swacheit solde geschehen
> daz er in den schanden wart gesehen. (ll. 3387–94)

Jaeger, *Origins of Courtliness,* p. 244, translates: "The sight of a man of such valor suffering such wretchedness and disgrace so weighed down her courtly and compassionate nature that out of profound sorrow and innocent tenderness she burst into tears." See Th.C. van Stockum, *Hartmann von Ouwes "Iwein": Sein Problem und seine Probleme* (Amsterdam: N.V. Noord-Hollandsche Uitgevers Maatschappij, 1963), pp. 30–32.

26. D.H. Green, *Irony in the Medieval Romance* (Cambridge: Cambridge University Press, 1979), p. 69. See Green's treatment of the Round Table, pp. 312–25.

King Arthur in the Prose Lancelot

Elspeth Kennedy

In every romance about Lancelot King Arthur's position as husband of Queen Guenevere and head of the Round Table is necessarily rather delicate. An examination of his role in the non-cyclic version of the prose *Lancelot*[1] will help to clarify both the treatment of the theme of love in this version of the story of Lancelot and the relation between this particular story and the broader literary tradition. The nature of the theme (the hero who, under the impetus of his love for the queen, makes a name for himself and wins a place at the Round Table) and the interplay with other Arthurian romances determine the various ways in which Arthur is portrayed within the work. The presentation of Arthur's character also reflects some of the preoccupations and aspirations of the aristocracy of the period.[2] The role played by the king begins to change when the non-cyclic romance is transformed into the *Lancelot-Graal* cycle, for the incorporation of the early adventures of Lancelot into a larger structure leads to a reinterpretation and re-writing of the earlier events.

In this article I shall first briefly examine the literary tradition concerning Arthur with which the Prose *Lancelot* interacts. In the Arthurian chronicles Arthur plays an active role: he brings peace to his kingdom while affirming his power and triumphing over the fierce opposition of a number of princes and barons; as leader of the Christian forces, he defends Britain against pagan invaders, and he exercises great influence in Europe. In the romances, his role is distinctly more passive: he presides over the Round Table, the focal point of chivalry, and he is the guardian of the traditions and customs of Logres;[3] but his knights are the ones who take up the adventures. In the works of Chrétien he often appears as a rather vulnerable

Originally published as "Études sur le *Lancelot* en prose: 2: Le Roi Arthur dans le *Lancelot* en prose," *Romania,* 105 (1984), 46–62; translated by Edward Donald Kennedy.

character, although in *Cligés*, a romance that focuses not upon Great Britain but upon the Byzantine court, some passages emphasize his qualities as king and evoke the active Arthurian figure found in Wace. Chrétien's audience, one must remember, was capable of placing each individual romance against the background of an Arthurian world in which the king had a more important role as a warrior king.[4]

In the Prose *Lancelot*, a story in which the love felt by Lancelot for the queen causes him to prove himself as the best of the knights and to win a place at the Round Table, there is also interaction between the tradition of the chronicles and that of the romances. If an author wished to present love as a positive force, he obviously had to avoid completely a triangle opposing the lovers and the king, as in the story of Tristan. The integrity of the Round Table as the symbol of the flower of chivalry had to be preserved. Chrétien had avoided the direct conflict between the knight and the king by using the abduction story in which Meleagant carries off the queen, and Lancelot, and not her husband, frees her. One finds in this echoes of a story of an abduction into the other world. Lancelot's night of love with Guenevere takes place in the land of Gorre, described as "lo reiaume don nus n'eschape" ("the realm from which no one escapes"). This land is separated from the ordinary world in the sense that the queen and the other captives can be freed only by a knight who will have crossed one of two marvelous bridges. There are also in this romance echoes of the story of Tristan, especially in the episode of the blood-stained bed. In the non-cyclic Prose *Lancelot* the only land that remains outside earthly feudal society is that of the Lady of the Lake, where Lancelot is taken after the death of his father, Arthur's vassal. Ban dies when on the way to Arthur's court in order to ask him in person for the aid that he has not been able to obtain through the messages he has sent.

In this version of the Prose *Lancelot* where so much emphasis is given to feudal obligations, Arthur's inability to defend Ban has an especial significance. It makes it possible to present the hero in a favorable light, as the lover of the queen who is the savior of the kingdom and not its potential destroyer. In Arthur's first war against Galehot, it is Lancelot who reverses the course of the battle in favor of the king of Logres. When the war begins again after a truce, it is Lancelot who, after having led Galehot to the threshold of victory, persuades him to surrender to Arthur and to pay him homage. Lancelot later saves Arthur from the Saxons. Finally, he protects the Round Table, which the Queen had brought as a dowry to Arthur and which is threatened by the pretensions of the False Guenevere. Here the love of Lancelot and Guenevere does not threaten the kingdom, as it does in the *Mort Artu* with its echoes of the *Tristan* story. The danger instead comes from Arthur's love affairs. Camille, the young Saxon daughter who possesses magic powers, causes him through a magic spell to love her and lures him into captivity. Then after having escaped Camille, thanks to Lancelot's aid, Arthur becomes the victim of a love potion administered by the False Guenevere and her accomplice. He is so blinded by this potion that he falls in love with the false queen and denies the identity of the true one, whom he condemns to having her head and hands skinned, her body burnt and the ashes scattered to the wind, not, in this adaptation of a theme from the Tristan story, for adultery, but for being an impostor, for criminal treachery *(murtre, traïson)*. Lancelot contests the judgment, overcomes three knights, proves the identity of the queen, and re-establishes harmony in the kingdom. It is Galehot, rather than Arthur, who appears as the third member of the triangle. Guenevere and Galehot both contend for the love and the company of Lancelot. Galehot is the one who makes sacrifices for him, and, after being separated from his friend, finally dies of grief when he hears the false rumor of Lancelot's death. Arthur is the chief beneficiary of the sacrifice that Lancelot persuades Galehot to make.

The emphasis upon Arthur's inability to fulfill his feudal obligations and upon his dependence upon Lancelot, son of his vassal, could make questionable the value of belonging to his *maisnie* and of a place at the Round Table, the reward that crowns the efforts of the young hero and the renown that he had acquired as the best knight of the world. The king must therefore be given a more positive role in the work in order to counterbalance his dependence upon Lancelot. This positive element is provided in various ways. The role of his court within the narrative structure, as well as within the thematic structure of the romance, has two principal facets. First, it fulfills its traditional function as the center of chivalry throughout all Christendom and even beyond; the renown of the Round Table attracts the greatest knights of the world in the Prose *Lancelot* as in the work of Wace, Chrétien de Troyes, and Robert de Boron. The court is also the center of the feudal kingdom of Arthur, upon whom, as long as he is overlord, the responsibility of protecting his vassals will fall. In the chronicles Arthur is an active sovereign with a land to govern, armies to lead, barons to control, and enemies to conquer. In the Prose *Lancelot* particular emphasis is placed upon the king's responsibility toward every vassal who holds land from him and who in exchange provides him with knights to lead his wars. In this respect, the knights of the Round Table are not so much champions of justice in the general sense as they are auxiliaries of the king who see that the rights of the vassals within Arthur's kingdom are respected. Since Arthur's court is a place that attracts knights from all over the world and is at the same time a more limited feudal center, it fulfills its traditional role as a point of departure for adventures and a rallying point for communal enterprises, with the result that the narrative threads set out from the court, diverge, and come together at the court from time to time, for it is there that every reputation must be established. The inspiration which leads Lancelot to accomplish the great feats through which he acquires such a reputation is represented at the court in the person of the Queen. Gawain, Arthur's nephew and recognized leader of the knights of the Round Table, sets out to reveal the identity of the unknown knight; in doing so he provides a point of comparison for Lancelot's exploits and then presents him at court as the greatest of all knights. The fact that the king is perfectly worthy to preside over this court is not only suggested by his exploits during the battles against his traditional enemies, the Saxons, before he was under the spell of Camille, but also by a series of references to events that took place before Lancelot was born and that occurred in Britain at the time that Lancelot was a child.

At the beginning of the Prose *Lancelot*, the reference to the troubled times after the death of Uther and to the wars Arthur conducted against his barons during the first years of his reign and of his marriage to Guenevere put the story back within the general framework of the chronicle tradition, as in the work of Geoffrey of Monmouth and Wace. The reference also links up with the situation described in the *Conte del Graal*, where Perceval's father and other *gentil home* are disinherited.[5]

During the account of the childhood of Lancelot and his cousins there are references to Arthur's inability to avenge Ban and to the wars which have prevented him from doing so.[6] When Claudas visits Britain in disguise, there is another allusion to Arthur's wars against his barons shortly after his marriage to Guenevere (*P.L.* 33.20–23; *L.M.* VIIIa 9). When a *rendu*, a man who has entered a religious order late in life, comes to Arthur's court on behalf of Queen Hélène to reproach him for not having avenged her husband Ban, we are told that the king is holding his court at London because of a truce in his war against Aguisçant and the King from Over the Borders. This emphasis on the wars that Arthur must wage offers justification for his inability to fulfill his duty toward his vassal and also recalls the victories that he won against powerful forces, such as those found in Wace's account. The *rendu* explains Arthur's difficult situation to the widowed queens before going to Arthur's court:

"Et neporqant ge sai bien que tant a eü affeire ça en arrieres li rois
Artus que n'est mie mervoille s'il a ceste chose mise an delai, car il

n'a gaires baron qui ne li ait mené guerre tant que maintes genz ont quidié qu'il remainsist essilliez a la parclose. Et par aventure, de ceste chose n'oï onques nul clamor, si n'an fait pas tant a blasmer." (*P.L.* 53.25–30; *L.M.* Xa 14)

("Nevertheless, I know that King Arthur has had so much to do for so long now that it is no wonder if he has delayed attending to your case. There is scarcely a baron who has not taken up arms against him, to the point where many have believed he would in the end be driven from the court, and it is perhaps for this reason that he has not been hearing any suits. It is hard to blame him for it." [based upon Rosenberg, p. 24])

Arthur justifies himself in similar terms for having failed to avenge the death of Ban:

"Sire preuzdom, fait li rois, certes ge m'acort bien a vos que vos dites raison et droit, mais certes ge n'en oï onques complainte. Il est voirs que ge l'ai pieç'a seü, et neporqant tex hore a esté que se g'en oïsse la conplainte, n'eüsse ge pas pooir de l'amender, car trop ai eü lons tens affeire tel hore que maintes janz ne baoient pas que ge en venisse au desus, ainz disoient par darriere si que maintes foiz l'oï, que en la fin me covendroit terre a guerpir. Mais ce que j'ai mauvaisement fait me covendra amender, qant Dex m'en donra lou pooir. Et bien sachiez que ja si tost n'en vendrei en point que gel cuit si bien amender que nus ne m'en porra blasmer s'a son tort non; car bien conois que gel doi faire come cil qui sui sires liges au roi Ban de Benoyc (et il mes hom) et au roi Bohort de Gaunes. Et Dex me doint prouchiennement lou pooir de l'amender, car mout volentiers l'amenderoie." (*P.L.* 56.30–57.3; *L.M.* Xa 23)

("Worthy man," said the king, "it is true I agree that what you are saying is right and just, but it's also true that I have never heard this plea. In fact, word of the case did reach me a while ago; the time was such, however, that even had I heard the plea, I would not have had the means to redress the wrong. For a long time I had much to do; it fell out that many men did not wish to see me triumph but would often say, and I would often hear them, that in the end I would have to flee from my land. But what I have done wrong I must put right as soon as God gives me the means. You may be sure that, once the time comes when I deem it proper to act, I will; and anyone who accuses me of failing to will be in error. King Ban of Benoic was my liegeman; I well know what I am duty-bound to do as his liege lord, and as liege lord of King Bors of Gaunes as well. May God soon grant me the power to redress this wrong, for I would very gladly do so." [Rosenberg, p. 25])

After Lancelot's first visit to Arthur's court and the beginning of his adventures as knight, Arthur and the members of the Round Table become more involved in the main thread of the narrative. The author, however, continues to introduce allusions to earlier events in the story of Arthur's kingdom which, because they are incomplete, contribute to presenting the story of Lancelot as a part of a greater Arthurian "reality" in terms of time and space, of a world outside the story of Lancelot where the king plays a major role. For example, in the middle of the episode of the Queen's Ford in which Lancelot vanquishes Alybon, who has guarded the ford in the name of the queen without her ordering it, an explanation is given for the origin of the name of the ford: the queen discovered it during the first two years of her marriage when Arthur was waging war against the seven kings (*P.L.* 180.37–181.29; *L.M.* XXIIIa 33). The allusion is mysterious in that the names of the seven kings are never given nor does a reference to this episode appear in surviving Arthurian texts. The active role played by Arthur and Kay in that adventure is in conformity with their role in the tradition of the chronicles and serves to justify their important positions as king and seneschal of the famous land of Logres. In the context of general battles in the Prose *Lancelot,* Arthur and Kay both conduct themselves in the same positive and courageous manner as they did at the time of this incident, which is brought into the story more by way of allusion than as a complete account.

The necessary balance between a positive and a negative portrait of Arthur is also presented by a number of parallels and contrasts associating Claudas, Arthur, and Galehot. The first contrast concerns the pair Claudas/Arthur, and the opposition between the two is centered on *largesce,* a quality which Claudas lacks, as his portrait in the romance shows (*P.L.* 30.10–13; *L.M.* VIIIa 1). Arthur is at first shown as failing in connection with Claudas because he faces so many difficulties at the beginning of his reign that he cannot come to the aid of his vassal Ban; but he is soon presented in a more favorable light at the time of the episode of Claudas's journey to Britain. When Claudas considers his own position as king, he compares himself with Arthur:

"Ge sui mout riches et mout viguereus et dotez de maintes genz, car li rois Artus meesmes ne s'ose mie reveler encontre moi, car ge taig plus a de deus anz deus roiaumes de son fié, que onques plus n'en osa faire. Si sai bien qe mout sui dotez d'autres genz, qant meesmes li rois Artus me crient et dote. Ne ge ne me tandrai pas por si preuz com ge doi estre, se ge ne faz tant qu'il taigne de moi tote sa terre. Si ai an talant que ge lo guerroi sanz demorance; mais por ce qu'il est tenuz a si preudome de totes genz, si voldrai avant savoir s'il a tant de valoir com les genz dient, car il ne m'est pas avis que nus hom puisse estre tres durement loez ne blasmez, que aucune chose n'i ait de verité. Por ce voil avant de son covine aprendre une partie, et s'il est tex que gel doie assaillir de guerre, ge l'an asaudrai prochainement, et se ge voi que ge nel puisse metre au desoz, si lairai a itant ester ma fole emprise." (*P.L.* 31.21–34; *L.M.* VIIIa 4)

("I am a man of great means and energy and am feared by many people. King Arthur himself does not dare stand against me: for more than two years I have held two of his vassals' kingdoms, and he has never dared do anything about it. In fact, I can be sure that I am feared by others if King Arthur himself is afraid of me. But I cannot go on considering myself as bold as I have to be, unless I succeed in making myself his overlord. What I want to do is go to war with him without delay. But since everyone takes him for such a worthy man I want to find out first whether he is as valorous as people say, for it seems to me that no man can receive extreme praise or extreme blame without some of it being true. That is why I want first of all to learn something about him and what he is like; and if he is the sort of man I should go to war against, I will do it very soon; and if I see that I could not defeat him, I'll abandon at this point my folly." [based upon Rosenberg, p. 15])

He hopes to crown his success by attacking Arthur himself and by forcing him to pay homage for his own land; however, because of the great reputation of the king of Logres, he wants first to see if this renown is merited and if he has much chance of success in a war against Arthur. When Claudas goes incognito to Arthur's court, he is very impressed by the qualities in the king:

"En tel maniere fu Claudas en la maison lo roi Artu, des la Miaost jusq'a l'issue de mai, an sanblance d'un estrange soudoier, et esgarda lo contenement lo roi et sa largesce et sa debonaireté et son grant san et sa biauté et sa bonté et sa proesce, si lo vit de totes valors de cuer et de cors si entechié qu'il ne prisoit envers lui rien nul home dont il onqes eüst parole oïe." (*P.L.* 33.29–34; *L. M.* VIIIa 10)

("Claudas remained at King Arthur's court from mid-August to the end of May, disguised as a foreign mercenary. He observed the king's behavior, his generosity and his graciousness, his great intelligence, his handsomeness, his goodness, and his prowess. He saw him so stamped with all the virtues of heart and body that he could hold no other man in such high regard." [based upon Rosenberg, p. 16])

When during the return journey, he asks his squire his opinion of his plan to vanquish Arthur, the latter does not hesitate to describe the king of Britain as the greatest of all sovereigns and the pillar of chivalry. He continues by saying that he would be prepared to renounce his allegiance to Claudas if he attacked Arthur. The qualities of Arthur that he praises most are his *largesce, proesce,* and *debonaireté:*

"M[oi est avis que cil do]it avoir cuer de totes choses passer [qui bee a] vaintre et a metre au desouz lo roi Artu; car ge [ne] cuideroie que Dex eüst fait an lui ce qu'il i a por estre deshonorez ne abaissiez, mais por vaintre tote gent et conquerre les uns par proesce de soi et de sa haute compaignie, et les autres par sa largesce et par sa debonaireté; car ce savons nos bien qu'il est riches de terre a grant mervoille, et il a en sa maison la flor de tote la terriene chevalerie. Il est si biax chevaliers que plus bel ne covient a demander. Il est plains de si grant proesce et de si haute qu'il vaint de totes chevaleries et cels de son ostel et les estranges. Il est si larges et si abandonez que nus n'oseroit penser ce qu'il oseroit despendre. Il est si debonaires et plains de si grant compaignie qu'il ne remaint por les hauz homes qu'il ne face granz joies et granz honors as povres preuz, et done les riches dons et les plaisanz. Ensins fait gaaignier les cuers des riches et des povres, car il enhore les riches come ses compaignons, et les povres por lor proesces et por son pris et s'anor acroistre et vers Dieu et vers lo siegle, [car bien gaaigne pris et honor vers le siegle] et grace et amor de Deu cil qui fait el siegle ce qu'il doit de tel baillie come Dex li avra donee." (*P.L.* 34.13–32; *L. M.* VIIIa 11–12)

("To my mind, the man who yearns to overthrow King Arthur must be a man of unlimited ambition. I think that God made King Arthur what he is, not to be dishonored or humbled, but to hold sway over all people, to win some over through his prowess and that of his knights, and others through his generosity and his graciousness. And we do know that he is extraordinarily rich in land and has at his court the flow of all earthly knighthood. He is the handsomest knight you could imagine. He has such great prowess and is in so high a position that he surpasses all other knights, both those of his court and foreign ones. He is so generous and openhanded that you wouldn't dare imagine what he dares to spend. He is so well-bred and gracious and so outgoing that he shows great hospitality and affection to poor valiant men no less than to the high-born and gives them costly and attractive presents. In that way he wins the hearts of both rich and poor, for he honors the rich as his companions and the poor for their bravery. He does it in order to increase his fame and his honor in the eyes of God and the world, for whoever accomplishes in the world that which God has given him the power to do earns fame and honor in the eyes of the world and grace and love in the eyes of God." [based upon Rosenberg, pp. 16–17])

The squire's description of Arthur explains why Lancelot's winning a seat at the Round Table indeed represents a high point in this romance about the young hero without a name who has become the best knight in the world. However, Arthur's inability to protect Ban and his brother Bors first suggested to Claudas the plan to conquer Great Britain, and two sequences of episodes in the first part of the romance prepare for the more serious criticism and humiliation that Arthur will still have to undergo. The basic model for each sequence is as follows: a widowed queen weeps over the disappearance of her children; she is reassured concerning their safety; Arthur is publicly criticized for his inability to avenge his vassal. In the first of these sequences there are also episodes in which both Arthur and Claudas are accused of conduct unworthy of a king.

In sequence A (*P.L.* 48–60; *L.M.* Xa 1–XIa 10) the widowed queen (Lancelot's mother) laments near the abbey. She is reassured by a *rendu* who tells her that her son is indeed alive. The *rendu* then leaves for Arthur's court where, finding the king seated at the table with all of his knights, he announces the king's failure, a sin of omission rather than one of commission. A maiden sent by the Lady of the Lake arrives at the court of Claudas, where she criticizes him at his table before all of his knights because of the way in which he has treated Bohort's children; she accuses him of lacking *san, debonaireté* and *cortesie*.

In sequence B (*P.L.* 133–38; *L.M.* XIXa 4–XXa 12) the widowed

queen Évaine laments the disappearance of her sons. She is reassured by a
vision that they are safe and sound. Banyn, godson of King Ban, goes to the
court where his presence reminds Arthur of his inability to avenge the death
of Ban and of the disappearance of Ban's son Lancelot. Arthur sits brood-
ing at the table, and when called upon to explain his melancholy, he publicly confesses his failure. This last sequence, along with the repetition later
in the romance of scenes of meditation that present an essentially passive
Arthur, helps to link the account of events prior to Lancelot's departure from
the land of the Lady of the Lake with the last part of the story.[7] It also recalls various episodes of the *Conte del Graal* and its *Continuations,* in which
Arthur is similarly passive.

There is then ambiguity in the contrast between Arthur and Claudas,
ambiguity that is confirmed by what might be called the reverse pairing of
Arthur/Galehot. In this pairing Arthur is the king accused of lacking *largesce*
and of having lost the hearts of his subjects, in contrast to Galehot, who is so
loved by his men that he is able to raise an immense army. Dreams predicting
the loss of Arthur's kingdom prepare for the king's indictment by a *preudomme*
in an episode that echoes to some extent the visit of the *rendu.* But the visit
of the *rendu* takes place at a time of celebration, rather similar to the situation at the time of the visit of the ugly damsel in the *Conte del Graal.* The
visit of the *preudomme* takes place at a time of great anxiety: the king has
just been saved from defeat by a mysterious knight in red arms, but after the
battle, the knight had disappeared, and the king did not know where he had
gone. The parallels between the two scenes are particularly interesting since
the qualities that the *preudomme* accuses Arthur of not having are precisely
those which Claudas lacked and the presence of which had so strongly impressed Claudas and his squire at the time of their visit to Arthur's court. The
preudomme claims that Arthur has not fulfilled his duties as king:

> "Si doiz savoir que nus hom mortex ne te baillast a garder la seignorie
> que tu tiens, mais Dex solement la te bailla por ce que tu l'an feïsses
> bone garde, et tu li as faite si mauvaisse que tu la destruiz qui garder
> la deüsses. Car li droiz do povre ne dou non puissant ne puet venir
> jusqu'a toi, ainz est li riches desleiaus oëz et henorez devant ta face
> por son avoir, et li povres droituriers n'i a loi por sa povreté. Li droit
> des veves et des orphelins est periz en ta seignorie. Et ce demandera
> Dex sor toi mout cruelment, car il meïsmes dit par la boiche Davi son
> prophete qu'il est garde des povres et sostient les orphenins et
> destruira les voies des pecheors. Tel garde fais tu a Deu de son pueple
> don il t'avoit [baillié] la terriene seignorie. Et par ce vandras tu a

[d]estruiement, car Dex destruira les pecheors. Adonc destruira il toi, car tu ies li plus vis pechierres de toz les autres pecheors." (*P.L.* 283.21–33; *L.M.* XLIXa 18)

("And you should know that no mortal man gave you the dominion you hold to take care of, but God alone gave it to you so that you should take good care of it, and you have taken such bad care of it for Him that you, who should take care of it, are destroying it. For the right of the poor and the powerless cannot reach you; instead the faithless rich man is heard and honoured before you because of his wealth, while the righteous poor man has no justice because of his poverty. The right of widows and orphans has perished under your dominion. And God will call you most cruelly to account for this, for He Himself said through the mouth of His prophet David that He is the guardian of the poor and sustains the orphans and will destroy the ways of the sinners. That is how you take care of God's people, over whom He has given you earthly dominion. And that will bring you to destruction, for God will destroy the sinners. Therefore He will destroy you, for you are the vilest of sinners." [Corley, pp. 237–38])

He explains why Arthur's men are abandoning him. He severely condemns the king for not having protected the poor and just from the rich and powerful; he reproaches him for still not having avenged the death of Ban, his loyal vassal, and for having allowed his widow to lose her land and her son, a failure that had at the beginning of the romance suggested to Claudas the plan to vanquish Arthur. The king learns that he has lost the heart of his knights because he has not been generous to those who deserve rewards and has given gifts only to the great barons and not to the lesser nobility:

"Ha! fait li preudom, ce n'est mie mervoille se ti home te faillent, car [puis que li hon se faut, bien li doivent faillir li autre. Et tu ies failliz quant tu messerras contre ton Signor de tel signorie con tu devoies tenir de lui, non pas d'autrui. Pour ce convient que il te faillent, car] ceste demostrance premiere t'a faite Dex, por ce que tu t'aparceüsses qu'il te voloit oster de ta seignorie, por ce qu'il te toloit cels par cui aide tu l'as longuement maintenue. Et neporqant, li un te faillent de lor gré, [et li autre estre lor gré]. Cil te faillent de lor gré] cui tu deüisses faire les granz onors et porter les granz seignories et les granz compaignies: ce sont li bas gentil home de ta terre par cui tu doiz estre maintenuz, car li regnes ne puet estre tenuz se li comuns des genz ne s'i acorde. Cil te sont failli de lor gré. Li autre qui estre lor gré te faillent, ce sont cil de ta maison cui tu as donees les granz richeces, cui tu as faiz seignors de ta maison. Cil te faillent estre lor gré, por ce que Dex lo velt. Einsi, contre la volenté Damedeu ne puet durer nule deffanse." (*P.L.* 285.28–286.5; *L.M.* XLIXa 22)

("Ha!" said the worthy man, "small wonder if your men are failing you, for when a man fails himself, others will certainly fail him. And you failed when you erred against your Lord regarding the dominion that you should have held from Him, and from no one else. For that reason they must fail you, for God has given you this first sign, so that you may realize that He means to remove you from your dominion, because He is taking from you those by whose aid you have long maintained it. Even so, some of them are failing you of their own free will, and the others in spite of themselves. Those are failing you of their own free will to whom you should have done great honour and given noble treatment and good fellowship: that is, the lesser gentry of your land, by whom you should be maintained, for the kingdom cannot be held without the consent of the common people. They have failed you of their own free will. The others, who are failing you in spite of themselves, are the men of your household to whom you have given great riches, whom you have made the lords of your household. They are failing you in spite of themselves because God wishes it. So, no defence can endure against God's will." [Corley, pp. 240–41])

The *preudomme* says:

"Or te pran garde que puet valoir escuz ne auberz n'espee ne force de chevaus; sanz cuer d'ome nule rien ne puet valoir." (*P.L.* 286.11–13; *L.M.* LXIXa 23)

("Now take note of the value of shield and hauberk and sword and the power of the horse; without a man's heart, none of them has any value." [Corley, p. 241])

This statement is comparable to some remarks that Claudas makes when he declares that the conquest of realms is nothing if one has not conquered the hearts of the people:

"Et mout a petit seignorie sus son pueple cil qui les cuers n'en puet avoir." (*P.L.* 81.28–29; *L.M.* XIVa 30)

("And the king who fails to win the love of his people can have no mastery over them." [Rosenberg, p. 35])

The *preudomme* gives Arthur advice on the way to win back the hearts of his people through gifts adapted to the needs of their recipients. His remarks concerning the ways that Arthur could improve his manner of giving should be compared with the praise for Arthur given earlier by the squire of Claudas. The *preudomme* tells Arthur that he can be a splendid and generous king able to win the hearts of his subjects by showing the particular form of generosity appropriate to each rank, by bestowing gifts that are suitable, and by paying attention to the poor as well as the rich of his court:

> "Aprés donras as hauz omes, as rois, as dux, as contes, as hauz bar-
> ons. Et coi? Les riches vaisselementes, les co[i]ntes joiaus, les biaus dras
> de soie, les boens chevaus, et si ne bee mie a els tant doner les riches
> dons come les biaus et les plaissanz, car l'an (f. 91c) ne doit mie doner
> a riche home riches choses, mes plaisanz choses poi riches, car ce est
> uns anuiz de fondre l'une richece sor l'autre. Mais au povre home doit
> l'en doner tex choses qui soient plus boenes que beles, et plus porfitables
> que plaisanz, car povretez n'a mestier que d'amendement, et richece
> n'a mestier que de delit." (*P.L.* 288.18–27; *L.M.* XLIXa 29)

("After that you must give to the men of high estate, to the kings, the dukes, the counts, the noble barons. And what? Rich plate, elegant jewellery, fine silks, good horses; do not aim to give them rich gifts, so much as beautiful and attractive ones, for one should not give a rich man valuable things, but attractive, not very valuable things, for it is a tiresome thing to pile riches on riches. To the poor man, though, one should give things which have more value than beauty, which are more useful than attractive, for poverty needs only betterment, and riches need only pleasure." [Corley, p. 244])

Galesguinanz the Welshman describes Galehot in eulogistic terms, which suggest that he possesses the qualities that the *preudomme* does not find in Arthur; but he also adds that he would rather die than see the defeat of Arthur:

> "Sire, ge ai veü Galehot. Il est bien plus granz demi pié que chevalier
> que l'an saiche, si est li hom del monde plus amez de sa gent et cil

qui plus a conquis de son aage, car il est juenes bachelers. Et dient
cil qui l'ont a acointe que c'est li plus gentis chevaliers et plus
deboenneres do monde et toz li plus larges. Mais por ce, fait il, nel
di ge mie que ge ja cuit ne il ne autres ait desus vos pooir, car ge lo
cuidoie, ja ne m'aïst Dex se ge ne voloie miauz estre morz que vis."
(*P.L.* 264.30–37; *L.M.* XLVIa 3)

("Sire, I have seen Galehot. He is at least six inches taller than any
knight known, and of all the men in the world, he is the most loved
by his people, and the one who has conquered most, for his age, for
he is a young knight. And those who know him say that he is the most
noble and gracious knight in the world, and the most generous. However," he said, "I do not say that because I think that he or anyone
else could ever have power over you, for if I thought that, may God
never be my witness if I should not rather be dead than alive." [Corley,
p. 213])

This remark provides a significant variation on those made by Claudas's squire:

"Et se cist estoit fox et mauvais et de grant coardise plains, ne voi ge
mie encor, ne ne sai l'ome qui au desouz lo poïst metre, tant com il
voudra les prodomes croire qui conversent o lui; car il covandroit a
celui qui lo cuideroit deseriter qu'il fust plus riches hom de lui, et eüst
planté de meilleurs chevaliers en son pooir, ce que ge ne cuit ores mie
que nus ait, et qu'il fus miauz en (f. 13c) [techiez dou roi Artu, qui a
painnes porroit avenir, car ge ne cuidei onques en nul cors de haut
home si hautes teches] ne si be[les come les soes me samblent estr]e.
Por ce ne m'est [il pas avis qu'il poïst estre] par nul hom [deseritez,]
ne Dex nel fist onqes tel por [oblier] enjusque la. Ne Dex ne fist
onques home, tant soit mes charnex amis, ne tant m'ait de granz biens
faiz, s'il lo pooir deseriter et ge l'an pooie garantir, que ge ne l'an
garantisse a mon pooir sanz moi mesfaire, et ençois me mesferoie gié
que ge nel garantisse a mon pooir et aprés an feroie ma penitance."
(*P.L.* 34.32–35.8; *L.M.* VIIIa 13)

("Even if he [King Arthur] were a fool and a bad man and an utter
coward, I still see or know of no one who could conquer him, as long
as he would be willing to believe the counselors who associate with him;
for anyone who wished to overthrow him would have to be a more
powerful man and have great numbers of superior knights under his

command. I do not believe that there is anyone like that, anyone more capable than King Arthur; and there could hardly be, for I have never seen in any other high-born man qualities as noble and as fine as I have found in him. For that reason it does not seem to me that he could be overthrown by any man. God never made him the way He did to that extent just to abandon him. And God never made any man, however closely related to me or however good to me he may be, against whom I would not defend King Arthur with all my might, if he wanted to overthrow him and if I could protect him without failing in my duties. And I would even fail in my duties rather than not defend him to the best of my ability; and I would do my penance afterward." [based upon Rosenberg, p. 17 and Mosès, p. 127])

Galehot and Claudas share the same ambition: both wish to triumph over Arthur. Claudas, however, does not have the superior qualities necessary to accomplish this. In spite of the loyal protestations of Galesguinanz, the way in which Arthur is presented during the war against Galehot makes it clear that the latter would have overcome Arthur if Lancelot had not intervened, while Claudas, not seeing any hope of success, withdrew.

If Arthur appears to Claudas and his squire as Galehot appears to Galesguinanz, with the role reversed for Arthur, there is also another point of comparison between Arthur and Galehot: both have two series of dreams, each announcing a disaster. Arthur's efforts to follow the advice of the *preudomme* and the help that he received from Lancelot save him from the disaster. Galehot cannot escape the catastrophe that threatens him, and it is Lancelot who will unwittingly cause his death. Arthur and Galehot both have disturbing dreams. Arthur's dreams are directed toward the future and help to provide a context for events in the central part of the romance. Galehot's dream is directed toward both past and future events and thus helps to link the last part of the non-cyclic romance to its middle part. The two series of dreams are clearly linked in that Galehot asks Arthur to send him the clerks who interpreted the king's dreams, and both recall for the reader the interpretation of the fall of Vortigern's tower in Wace's *Brut* and Robert de Boron's *Merlin*. It is only in the case of Galehot that the castles collapse and the towers fall down, as was the case for Vortigern's tower, and this collapse of the castles indeed has significance for Galehot, as he himself guesses: "C'est aucune senefiance" (*P.L.* 575.10; *L.M.* I 7, short version). This feeling is confirmed by Arthur's chief clerk, who tells Galehot that the dream is a warning for having wanted to conquer Arthur against divine will:

"Et ce que voz fortereces fondirent si tost com vos meïstes lo pié dedanz vostre terre, fu por ce que Dex voloit que vos aparceüssiez que force estoit et ancontre sa volenté, et qu'il avoit l'orgoil abatu par quoi vos aviez anpris a guerroier lo plus prodome do monde." (*P.L.* 582.29–32; *L.M.* I 21, short version)

("That your castles will collapse as soon as you set foot in your land was because God wanted you to see that violence was also against his will and that he had struck down the pride through which you had undertaken to wage war against the most worthy man in the world." [E.D.K.])

The evocation of Vortigern, who soon after having allied himself with the pagan Saxons, was replaced by the true champion of Christianity, Arthur's father Uther, plays a role in this intricate interlacing of changing positions. Toward the beginning of the work we learn of the ambition of Claudas to conquer Arthur:

"Ge me pensai antan que g'estoie un des plus viguereus hom do monde, et que se ge pooie avoir lo reiaume de Logres, ge seroie li plus dotez rois qui onqes fust et conquerroie tant que ge seroie rois de tot lo monde; si pen(f. 13b)[soie a guerroier lou roi Artu tant que ge lou poïsse metre au desouz]." (*P.L.* 34.4–8; *L.M.* VIIIa 11)

("It occurred to me one day that I was one of the most dynamic men in the world and that, if I could take over the kingdom of Logres, I would be the most formidable king ever and could conquer so much that I would become king of the whole world. It occurred to me that I should go to war against King Arthur and not stop until I had defeated him." [Rosenberg, p. 16])

Toward the end of the work, Galehot reveals the proud and ambitious projects that inspired the construction of his castle, l'Orgueilleuse Angarde:

"Certes, dist Galehoz, voirement diriez vos qu'ele fu fermee de haut cuer, se vos saviez que ge pensoie au jor que ge la fis faire, car j'avoie trente reiaumes conquis et mis en ma seignorie, si dis a moi meïsmes que g'estoie li plus viguerex hom del siegle et li plus redotez et que ge n'oseroie nulle chose anprandre dont ge ne. venisse bien a chief, por ce que toz avoie mes anemis mis au desoz. Si me pansai que ge feroie tant que j'avroie lo reiaume de Logres. Alors si seroie coronez et porteroie corone en cest chastel si richement c'onques nuns rois si richement ne l'i porta, car ge avoie fait trente et une corone, si avoie enpensé que tuit mi roi seroient a ceste feste et que por l'anor de mon coronement porteroit chascuns d'aus corone." (*P.L.* 574.19–30; *L.M.* I 6, short version)

("Certainly," Galehot said, "you would truly say that it [the castle] was built with a proud spirit if you knew what I thought at the time that I had it built, for I had conquered and subjugated thirty realms, and so I told myself that I was the most vigorous and the most feared man in the world and that I would not dare undertake anything that I would not achieve, for I had overcome all my enemies. So I thought that I would continue in this way until I would have the realm of Logres. Then I would be thus crowned and would wear a crown in this castle more splendidly than any king had done before, for I had created thirty-one kings and so had thought that all my kings would be at this festivity and that in honor of my coronation each would wear his crown." [E.D.K.])

At this point, then, the terms used by Galehot echo those of Claudas when he announced his intention to conquer Arthur, a plan that, through prudence, he ultimately abandoned. Galehot has no such inhibitions. He possesses the qualities that make such an undertaking possible, but whatever may have been Arthur's weaknesses as ruler (in comparison with Galehot), it is not God's will that Galehot succeed. Thus Lancelot, intervening to save Arthur's kingdom, acts in conformity with God's will, although his conscious inspiration may be his love for Guenevere. Lancelot loses his father and his land during the conflict between Claudas and Arthur's vassal Ban, whom Arthur is unable to defend or avenge. Arthur keeps his land thanks to Lancelot's intervention and in accordance with divine law. Galehot, a great prince and a great ruler, achieves victory over Arthur with Lancelot's help, but then gives up his supreme ambition at Lancelot's request and finally dies, again because of Lancelot. However, Galehot shows noble resignation when faced with his destiny, and this gives him a tragic grandeur that Arthur does not attain in this text, even if the latter is described by his greatest clerk as "lo plus prodome do monde."

I pointed out at the beginning of this article that it is important in this romance, which has for its central figure Lancelot accomplishing great deeds because of his love for the queen, that Arthur should not be given heroic stature throughout the text. There are alternating contrasts between the three characters Claudas, Arthur, and Galehot, whose relations between one another are to a certain extent determined by their relationship with Lancelot, and these contrasts are suggested by the skillful use of repetitions, contrasts, and parallels in such a way as to give the entire work cohesion. Interestingly, Galehot and Arthur both depend on Lancelot, a poor knight who has no land, for the outcome of the battle. The *preudomme*, in the advice he gives Arthur, emphasizes that if a king wishes to defend his land, he must depend not only on his great barons, but also on the lesser nobility who have smaller fiefs. The successive comparisons between the three rulers, Arthur, Galehot, and Claudas, indicate that even kings must stay within their proper limits, because they cannot preserve their power without help.

This alternation of models, which gives Arthur a number of contrasting traits, must not be interpreted as inconsistency in characterization, as certain critics once seemed to think, but rather as an integral part of the whole complex system of tensions and balances on which the structure of the work is based. This system depends also in part on the interaction between the *Lancelot* and the Arthurian chronicles and romances of the twelfth century; this interplay may take the form of echoes set off by events related in the body of the narrative or of references to some incidents never related in full in the text. The different lights in which Arthur is placed may also, on another level, correspond to some analogous social and political tensions in the society of the time.

In the second version of the Journey to Sorelois and of the episode of the False Guenevere, the situation changes. The second version of these episodes marks the beginning of the preparations for the *Queste du Graal* with Galahad as hero, and the potentially destructive aspect of the love between Lancelot and Guenevere is no longer carefully avoided. In the False Guenevere episode of the cyclic romance, where Guenevere sees in her misfortunes a punishment for the sin committed with Lancelot, the echoes from the Tristan story have a function different from the one that they have in the non-cyclic romance. They prepare for events in the *Mort Artu* which end with the collapse of the Arthurian world. In the *Lancelot-Graal* cycle Arthur's love for Lancelot is still based upon the admiration he has for Lancelot's qualities as a knight and on the recognition of the debt he owes him, but a conflict forces its way between his love and his feelings as husband of Guenevere and king of Logres. Some earlier events, like the famous kiss exchanged between Lancelot and Guenevere, are placed in a new context by means of the pictures that Lancelot paints of these scenes and the use that Morgan makes of his works of art as a weapon against Arthur and Guenevere. The interplay of parallels and contrasts in the presentation of Arthur operates henceforth at the heart of the structure of a cyclic romance that includes the *Queste du Graal* and the *Mort Artu*, and this creates a new network of tensions and balances.

NOTES

1. *Lancelot do Lac: The Non-Cyclic Old French Prose Romance*, ed. E. Kennedy (Oxford, 1980). All citations to *P.L.* refer to this edition, which has as its base manuscript Bibl. Nat., fr. 768. This manuscript presents the non-cyclic version of the romance which ends with the death of Galehot and which does not include the *Queste del Saint Graal* or the *Mort Artu*. The cyclic romance has taken without change the part of the text which tells of the adventures of Lancelot up to his installation as knight of the Round Table, but it contains a new version of the episodes of the Voyage to Sorelois and the False Guenevere. I also give references to the edition of A. Micha, *Lancelot: Roman en prose du XIIIᵉ siècle*, T.L.F. (Geneva: Droz 1978–1983 [*L.M.*]). Volumes 7 and 8 of this edition contain the adventures of Lancelot until his installation as knight of the Round Table; the base manuscript is Brit. Libr., Add. 10293. For the non-cyclic version of the episodes of the Voyage to Sorelois and the False Guenevere in Micha's edition, see Vol. 3, pp. 2–69 (base manuscript, fr. 768). The two versions do not diverge before Lancelot becomes a knight of the Round Table (at the end of Vol. 8 of Micha's edition).

For translation of the quotations from Elspeth Kennedy's edition, I have used where possible the abridged English translation of her edition, *Lancelot of the Lake*, trans. Corin Corley (Oxford: Oxford University Press, 1987), cited as "Corley." I have based translations of most of the quotations that do not appear in Corley upon the translation of the Micha text by Samuel N. Rosenberg in *Lancelot-Grail: The Old French Arthurian Vulgate and Post-Vulgate in Translation*, gen. ed. Norris J. Lacy, Vol. 2, trans. Samuel N. Rosenberg and Carleton W. Carroll (New York: Garland, 1993), cited as "Rosenberg." Since the Micha text does not always correspond to the Kennedy text, I have at times had to make changes in the Rosenberg translation. When I have done so, I have cited the passages as "based upon Rosenberg" instead of as "Rosenberg." For these passages I have also consulted the modern French translation of the first part of Elspeth Kennedy's edition, *Lancelot du Lac*, trans. François Mosès (Paris: Librairie Général Française, 1991). Two of the passages from the Kennedy edition and from Micha's "short version" appear in none of the above translations, and I have translated these myself.—E.D.K.

2. See Elspeth Kennedy, "Social and Political Ideas in the French Prose *Lancelot*," *Medium Ævum*, 26 (1957), 90–106; E. Köhler, *L'Aventure chevaleresque, idéal et réalité dans le roman courtois* (Paris 1974); E. Peters, *The Shadow King: Rex Inutilis in Medieval Law and Literature, 751–1327* (New Haven and London, 1970), pp. 196–209; Y. Robreau, *L'Honneur et la honte: leur expression dans les romans en prose du Lancelot-Graal (XIIᵉ-XIIIᵉ siècles)* (Geneva, 1981).

3. See E. Köhler, "Le rôle de la *coutume* dans les romans de Chrétien de Troyes," *Romania*, 81 (1960), 386–97.

4. See Elspeth Kennedy, "King Arthur in the First Part of the Prose *Lancelot*," *Medieval Miscellany Presented to Eugène Vinaver* (Manchester, 1965), pp. 186–95.

5. *Le Roman de Perceval ou le Conte du Graal*, ed. W. Roach, T.L.F. (Geneva, 1971), ll. 442–49.

6. *P.L.* 2.8–13, 3.17–30; *L.M.* Ia 4, 8.

7. *P.L.* 296–98, 359–61; *L.M.* LIa 1–7, LIVa 1–7; also see Elspeth Kennedy, "Royal Broodings and Lovers' Trances in the First Part of the Prose *Lancelot*," *Mélanges J. Wathelet-Willem, Marche Romane* (Liège, 1978), pp. 301–14.

The Evolution of the Theme of the Fall of Arthur's Kingdom

Fanni Bogdanow

John Steinbeck, in one of his letters published as an appendix to his adaptation of the first part of Thomas Malory's *Morte Darthur,* makes the following observation: "So many scholars have spent so much time trying to establish whether Arthur existed at all that they have lost track of the single truth that he exists over and over again."[1] Steinbeck is by no means criticizing research concerning Arthur's historicity; rather he is reminding us that the figure of Arthur is not unitary, but multiple, that there is not one Arthur, but that there are many. Concerned with re-creating the Arthurian legend for twentieth-century readers, Steinbeck understood that not only Malory, but also each of his predecessors interpreted the role of Arthur according to his own concerns.

Unfortunately, Steinbeck died before he could undertake the last part of his adaptation, the part that would have dealt with the fall of Arthur's kingdom. The first coherent account of the Arthurian tragedy that has come down to us is an integral part of Geoffrey of Monmouth's *History of the Kings of Britain (Historia Regum Britanniae).*[2] From the time of the Church Fathers, medieval writers, like the writers of the Old Testament, had explained calamities that strike people as divine punishment.[3] It is in this way that Gildas, a monk of the sixth century, had interpreted the misfortunes of his country in a work entitled *De Excidio et Conquestu Britanniae.*[4] Gildas, of course, does not mention Arthur, but the events of which he writes took place at the time when, according to other sources, Arthur would have lived. Geoffrey of Monmouth follows Gildas in his interpretation of the desolation that Britain was to suffer. But since for him Arthur's reign is the most glorious period in the history of Britain, Geoffrey transposes into the Post-Arthurian period the theme of the moral decline and the subsequent collapse

Originally published as "La chute du royaume d'Arthur: Évolution du thème," *Romania,* 107 (1986), 504–19; translated by Edward Donald Kennedy.

of the British people envisaged as divine punishment. On the other hand, anxious not to tarnish the reputation of his hero, Geoffrey, without using the symbol of the wheel of Fortune, explains the tragedy which brings to an end Arthur's kingdom by invoking the concept of Fortune, according to which empires fall independent of their merit or lack of merit.[5] Arthur, presented as a just and God-fearing king, had, in the first years of his reign, fought against the Saxon infidels and had subjugated all of Europe with the exception of Rome. The war, which at the end of his career once again forces King Arthur to be absent from his country and has the well-known tragic consequences of Mordred's revolt culminating in Arthur's death, is also interpreted as a just and honorable military operation. Knowing that the Romans would invade Great Britain a second time if he refused to submit to them, Arthur had no choice but to accept the challenge of the Roman emperor. To emphasize the sudden and unjust reversal of Fortune, Arthur hears the news of Mordred's treason at the very moment he reaches the height of his glory.

While later romance writers did not significantly change Geoffrey of Monmouth's sequence of events, they did not always accept his interpretation of them. The anonymous author of the *Didot-Perceval* or prose *Perceval*,[6] a work intended to complete the Arthuriad begun by Robert de Boron, is one of the writers who, in imitation of Geoffrey or of Robert de Boron himself, idealized the Arthurian world. Robert, who wanted to produce an edifying work, a kind of apocryphal Gospel, had thought of the reign of Arthur as the glorious period when the predestined hero, in completing the adventure of the Grail, would redeem the Arthurian world. The author of the prose *Perceval,* who generally respected the intentions of Robert, understood that in this perspective it was necessary to avoid presenting the downfall of Logres as a punishment. Also, in order to enhance Arthur's prestige and to emphasize that this king did not deserve the misfortune about to strike him, he blackened the character of the Roman emperor and at the same time elevated the conflict to the level of a holy war. According to this version, in fact, the Roman emperor allies himself not only with infidels (the King of Spain and the Sultan), but he also marries a pagan, the daughter of the Sultan: "si messerra molt li emperere vers Diu et vers sainte yglise" ("the emperor transgressed greatly against God and Holy Church").[7] King Arthur and his knights, on the other hand, are presented as Christians who fight not only for reasons of political order but also for the defense of Christendom, which the Roman emperor wants "mestre en servitude" ("to enslave").[8] For the same reason, the war against Mordred is also elevated to a struggle between Christians and pagans. While in Geoffrey of

Monmouth Mordred's army is composed not only of pagans but also of Christians, in the Prose *Perceval* his only allies are pagans, the *Saisnes* who had fought with that Hengist who had once waged war against Arthur's father. And in order to better bring out the new significance of this conflict, the author places the final battle in which Mordred will be killed and Arthur fatally wounded not in Cornwall, as in Geoffrey's account, but near Ireland on an island belonging to the son of Hengist, a pagan king who had given asylum to Mordred.[9]

On the other hand, in the Vulgate Cycle,[10] where the account of Arthur's downfall[11] is preceded by the *Queste del Saint Graal*[12] and the story of the love affair of Lancelot and Guenevere, the king of Great Britain is no longer idealized. The authors of the various branches of the Vulgate cycle did not agree, however, on the underlying causes for the downfall of Arthur's kingdom.[13] The author of the *Queste,* deeply influenced by the mystical theology of St. Bernard, wanted, like Gildas and Geoffrey of Monmouth, to warn his contemporaries of the wrath of God if they persisted in sin. Hence he took up again the theme of the moral and religious decline of the people of Britain, which had been suppressed in the Prose *Perceval.* But unlike Geoffrey of Monmouth, he transferred this theme from the post-Arthurian to the Arthurian period. In spite of the arrival of Galaad, neither Arthur nor most of his knights will again find the way to God; consequently, the achievement of the adventure of the Grail will not exalt the Arthurian world as it did in the Prose *Perceval.* On the contrary, with the departure of the chosen knights from the castle of Corbenic, the Grail, the symbol of God and His grace, will abandon the realm of Logres,[14] which henceforth will be destined to destruction as foretold in both the Vulgate *Lancelot*[15] and the *Queste.*[16]

Now in the Vulgate *Mort Artu,* as in earlier accounts, Mordred's revolt will be the immediate cause for the destruction of Arthur's kingdom. The events which precede and lead up to this catastrophe, however, do not enhance Arthur's reputation. In this account the war against the Romans is no longer the principal reason for Arthur's absence from his kingdom; instead the civil strife between Arthur's knights and those of Lancelot's family is the primary reason for Arthur's departure from Britain. The news of the Roman emperor's challenge reaches Arthur only after he pursues Lancelot into his kingdom of Benoic. However, if the discovery of the adulterous love of Lancelot, who had relapsed into sin almost as soon as he had returned from the Grail quest, is the initial cause of this civil strife, the *Mort Artu,* in contrast to the *Queste,* does not attempt to condemn earthly chivalry and show that a religious ideal is preferable to it. Lancelot remains, as he is in the Vulgate *Lancelot,* the real hero. Concerned with both exonerating him and keeping the reader's sympathy for him, the author places almost all responsibility for the civil war, and consequently for the final catastrophe, upon King Arthur and his nephew Gauvain. The war between Arthur's knights and those of Lancelot becomes inevitable only after Lancelot accidentally kills Gaheriet in the combat that occurs as he tries to rescue Guenevere from the stake. In order to suggest that King Arthur had himself contributed in large measure to the situation that had forced Lancelot to go to the Queen's aid, the author presents a scene that recalls a similar incident in the Vulgate *Lancelot*. In the episode of the False Guenevere in the latter work Arthur had wrongly condemned the Queen to a cruel punishment from which only Lancelot's combat against three knights had been able to save her.[17] By analogy, the author of the *Mort Artu* implies that this time Arthur had again been wrong in condemning his wife to death; in fact, this will be confirmed as true when later, as in the Vulgate *Lancelot*, the Pope threatens to place the realm of Logres under an interdict if Arthur does not take his wife back.[18] Similarly, each time that there is an opportunity to end the war against Lancelot, Arthur prolongs it, encouraged and urged on by Gauvain who persists in avenging the death of his brother Gaheriet. On the other hand, in order to present Lancelot still more sympathetically and, as a consequence, to tarnish Arthur's character still further, the author emphasizes that while Arthur has no qualms about pursuing Lancelot, Lancelot is torn by the painful conflict between his love for the Queen and his loyalty for the King.[19]

The messenger charged with telling Arthur of Mordred's treason arrives, as in the earlier accounts, just as Arthur is celebrating his victory over the Romans.[20] But although the author emphasizes the sudden reversal of Fortune by introducing the symbol of the wheel of Fortune, his purpose is no longer to make Arthur seem innocent. It is instead a means of transferring from Lancelot to Arthur the responsibility for the final disaster. Thanks to this symbol, Lancelot's indiscretion, instead of being the major cause for Arthur's fall, is from that moment no more than the impetus necessary to make Fortune's wheel turn; for, as Fortune herself says: "tel sont li orgueil terrien qu'il n'i a nul si haut assiz qu'il ne le coviegne cheoir de la poesté del monde" ("Such is earthly pride that no one is seated so high that he can avoid having to fall from power in the world").[21]

The mystical doctrine of the Grail and that of the wheel of Fortune are incompatible. The Post-Vulgate *Roman du Graal*, which is derived from the Vulgate Cycle, forms a more homogeneous whole, free of the ideological dichotomy of the Vulgate.[22] The work focuses not upon Lancelot, but upon King Arthur and the Grail. Here, for the first time, the account is permeated with tragic irony; for while preserving the theme of the spiritual degeneration of most of Arthur's knights, the Post-Vulgate *Roman* interprets the fall of Logres as divine punishment for the sin of incest that Arthur had once committed. Of course, the Vulgate had already presented Mordred as both the nephew and the son born of Arthur's incestuous union with his sister. On learning of Mordred's treason, Arthur proclaimed that he would get vengeance on his son:

> "Ha! Mordret, or me fez tu connoistre que tu ies li serpenz que ge vi jadis eissir de mon ventre, qui ma terre ardoit et se prenoit a moi. Mes onques peres ne fist autretant de fill comme ge ferai de toi, car ge t'ocirrai a mes deus mains, ce sache touz li siecles, ne ja Dieu ne vueille que tu muires d'autrui meins que des moies."

> ("Ah! Mordred, now you make me realize that you are the serpent I once saw issuing from my stomach, which burnt my lands and attacked me. But never will a father have done to a son what I shall do to you, because I shall kill you with my two hands. May the whole world know this; God forbid that you die at anyone else's hands but mine.")[23]

In the Vulgate Cycle, however, the theme of Mordred's incestuous birth is used primarily, it seems, to reinforce the horror of the final catastrophe and perhaps also to remove still more of the blame from Lancelot. If there is a slight suggestion that Arthur is killed by his son because of his sin, the authors of the various branches of the cycle refrain from developing this theme. The hermit who in the Vulgate *Lancelot* tells Mordred that he will destroy his father and the kingdom of Logres does not reproach Arthur: he is blaming Mordred for the evil that he will do later.[24] Only the Post-Vulgate *Roman* establishes a direct link between Arthur's sin and his death. When, a little after his coronation, Arthur becomes enamored with the wife of King Lot without realizing that she is his sister, the author emphasizes that the son who will be born from their incestuous union will be the instrument of the destruction of Arthur's realm: "puissedi le traist a mort et mist a destruction et a martyre la terre" ("Subsequently he brought about his death and the destruction and devastation of the country").[25] As soon as King Lot's wife has returned home, Arthur has a terrifying vision. Though this vision was undoubtedly inspired by the dream that Arthur was said to have had in the Vulgate *Lancelot*,[26] its purpose is completely different. In the *Lancelot* the vision identifies Mordred as the serpent who will destroy the country; in the Post-Vulgate it serves to place the blame upon Arthur.

Merlin, who reveals to Arthur the meaning of the dream, tells him at the same time of his "grant desloiauté" ("great disloyalty"). He calls him "dyables et anemis Jhesucrist" ("devil and enemy of Jesus Christ"),[27] and from then on Arthur fears divine vengeance.

This does not mean that Arthur's incest was a premeditated sin. For Aristotle, there was no tragedy if a completely wicked man fell from happiness into misery. Such a story could evoke neither pity nor fear. One feels pity for the man who has not deserved his misfortune and whose fall is due not to vice and wickedness but to some flaw.[28] Aware of that, the author of the Post-Vulgate *Roman* closely links the theme of Arthur's guilt to a theme to which the Vulgate paid little attention, that of "aventure et mescheance" ("chance and mischance"). Arthur and his knights are destined to be pursued by *mescheance* not because they have climbed too high, but because they are its chosen victims. From the beginning of Arthur's reign, unfortunate and unanticipated events occur. Pure accidents unleash catastrophes: the Dolorous Stroke, which destroys three realms and inaugurates the adventures of the Grail and which is presented here as a divine punishment, is not a deliberate outrage, but an accident, one of several tragic accidents that take Balain, the "chevalier mescheant" ("unfortunate knight") by surprise. The incest committed by Arthur is likewise an example of this *mescheance* which haunts Logres. Arthur, who had no way of knowing his sister's identity and who, in contrast to the king of the Vulgate *Lancelot*, never neglects his royal duties, could, like Balain, have said: "Ceste male aventure est plus avenue par male meskeanche que par autre chose" ("This evil luck has happened more through evil mischance than through anything else").[29]

However, while Arthur, like Balain, may have involuntarily violated one of God's commandments, his fault is nevertheless similar to a sin that brings down the wrath of God. The author here appears to follow the thought of St. Bernard who, in refuting Abélard's assertion that no sin is committed in ignorance,[30] had reaffirmed the doctrine of the Old Testament. According to this, "When anyone sins without knowing it against one of God's commandments concerning things which must not be done, he will be considered guilty and will be held accountable for his deed" (Leviticus 5:17).

Nothing, in fact, will set aside the judgment against King Arthur. In the beginning, all that he knows is that a child already conceived but not yet born will cause him to die and will destroy the realm of Logres. He wants to find this child in order to avoid the misfortune that threatens him, but a divine vision warns him of the futility of this plan:[31] "Car a Nostre Signeur ne plaist mie" ("For it is not pleasing to our Lord").[32]

The events that culminate in Arthur's fatal battle against Mordred in Salisbury Plain are the same as those in the Vulgate Cycle. But wishing to present Arthur as a tragic hero whose destiny will arouse in us "pity and fear," the Post-Vulgate author, in contrast to the author of the Vulgate *Mort Artu,* tries to direct the reader's sympathy toward Arthur and not Lancelot. The punishment that is destined for the king is able to strike him only because he himself is the innocent victim of a civil war for which he is in no way responsible. While in the Vulgate Cycle, the quarrel between Arthur's knights and Lancelot breaks out only after Arthur's actions have precipitated the death of Gaheriet, in the Post-Vulgate *Roman* the discord has an earlier origin. After his return from the quest for the Grail, Hector had accused Gauvain of having treacherously killed Erec and Palamedes, and it was to avenge themselves on the lineage of King Ban that the closest relatives of King Arthur had denounced Lancelot: "et doivent ceste chose fere entendre au roi pour meitre mortel haine entre le roi Artus et le parenté le roi Ban" ("And they must make the king hear of these things so that there will be mortal hatred between King Arthur and the lineage of King Ban").[33] Moreover, the author of the Post-Vulgate tries to reduce to a minimum the emotional theme of the conflict between love and loyalty. In the account of the siege of Joyous Garde and of Benoic, he suppresses almost all of the details which in the Vulgate had served to exalt Lancelot to the detriment of Arthur. Thus the moving scene in which Lancelot, attacked by Arthur, refuses to defend himself and later puts Arthur back on his horse and saves his life does not appear in the Post-Vulgate *Roman.* And instead of including the Vulgate's remark that King Arthur will continue his war against Lancelot even if the Queen comes back to him, the Post-Vulgate emphasizes Lancelot's less noble traits: the author emphasizes that Lancelot is guilty of treason against King Arthur and that he would never have returned the Queen if he had not feared that the people would then have learned that the gossip about them was true.

On the other hand, in order to reinforce the tragic atmosphere and the feeling of pity for Arthur, the Post-Vulgate throws into relief all the pathos of the situation. We learn the news of Mordred's treason precisely at the moment when Arthur, thanks to his victory against the Romans, has succeeded, as in Geoffrey of Monmouth, in warding off the catastrophe of a new invasion of his country. On the day that Arthur prepares to march from Dover to Salisbury, no vision of the Wheel of Fortune will comfort him or warn him of his destiny. *Mescheance* from that time on again oppresses the country and justifies the final tragedy. In the final battle where all emphasis is upon the conflict between Arthur and Mordred, the king, instead of complaining of his misfortune as in the Vulgate *Mort Artu,* defends himself courageously and inspires confidence in those who surround him. When in the Vulgate he sees Mordred kill Sagremor, he inveighs against God. In the Post-Vulgate *Roman* he regrets the tragic loss of so many good knights who perish as victims of a traitor: "Ah! God, what *mescheance* to see a traitor kill so many good loyal knights!"[34] And instead of fearing Mordred, Arthur pursues him. In their last encounter it is he and not Mordred who strikes the first blow. But the victory costs dearly, and Arthur better than anyone understands the extent of the tragedy. He leaves the field "in great sorrow" and when the Archbishop of Canterbury tries to comfort him, the king of the Post-Vulgate does not content himself with saying "Ah! If I have escaped alive, that means nothing to me, since my life is nearing its end." He adds some words that are still more poignant: "Ah! God, what *mescheance* has befallen this great land through the treason of one man."[35]

According to Aristotle, there can be no tragic flaw without recognition of the flaw.[36] That such recognition increases the sense of pathos is something that the author of the Post-Vulgate understood well. He does not deny Arthur this cruel recognition. When on the evening of the final battle a tragic accident at the Black Chapel costs Lucan, one of the four survivors, his life, Arthur does not place the blame only on Fortune as he does in the Vulgate. He realizes that the calamities that have happened to him are a just retribution for his sin: "Girflet, [he says] I am no longer the King Arthur whom people call the *roi aventureux* because of the good fortune that he enjoyed. The only name that is appropriate for me now is miserable and wretched. Fortune did this; she has become my stepmother and my enemy. And Our Lord, who wants me to spend the little time remaining to me in my life in sorrow and unhappiness, makes me understand that just as once he wanted to raise me without my deserving it, now he has the power to cast me down because of my sin."[37]

Arthur's pathetic death is not the last *mescheance* that strikes the *royaume aventureux*. In Geoffrey of Monmouth's earlier account Mordred's two sons had revolted after the death of their father against the new king of Britain. The author of the Vulgate, concerned up to the end with exalting Lancelot, presents him as the savior of the realm: he returns from Gaunes and in a battle at Winchester kills Mordred's two sons, who had seized the realm. The Post-Vulgate retains this incident, but it eclipses the success of Lancelot and emphasizes the ill-luck of Arthur's realm. Perhaps remembering the series of disasters that in Geoffrey of Monmouth had overwhelmed Great Britain in the period following Arthur's disappearance, the Post-Vulgate author predicts during the early years of Arthur's reign that after his death there will reign "les mauvaiz hoirs de pis en pis" ("evil heirs that are worse and worse"). At that time, the Great Britain that God had exalted so much will lament the worthy men of past times "car alors seront en ceste terre toutes proesces tournees a neant" ("for then in the land all valor will be turned to nothingness").[38] The Post-Vulgate *Roman* does not mention the names of the bad kings who will reign after Arthur, with the exception of one, King Marc of Cornwall. He had been in his youth the faithful vassal of King Arthur,[39] but, as ill-luck would have it, his loyalty had changed into an implacable hatred from the time that he knew that Arthur had given asylum to his wife Yseut and his nephew Tristan. During the Grail Quest Marc had succeeded in taking his wife away from Joyous Garde, but during the lifetime of Arthur and his knights he had not been able to avenge the shame he had suffered at the time of this first invasion of Logres.[40] Thus, after the death of Lancelot, Marc invaded Logres a second time and had not only Camelot destroyed, but also the symbol of Arthur's glory, the Round Table.[41]

This pessimistic vision of the destiny of King Arthur and his realm is, however, not accepted by all of the authors of romances in the Middle Ages. The anonymous author of the *Perlesvaus*,[42] a prose romance of the thirteenth century written after the Vulgate Cycle but probably before the Post-Vulgate *Roman du Graal*,[43] rehabilitates the Arthurian world. Arthur, like most of his knights, is "bien creanz en Dieu" ("very trusting in God"), and, as in the Prose *Perceval*, the end of the Grail Quest, far from being the prelude to the destruction of the realm of Logres, will glorify the Round Table. The author sought an objective quite different from those of the Vulgate *Queste* and the Post-Vulgate *Roman*. He compromises with sin no more than the others, and he strictly condemns lechery. But instead of alerting his contemporaries to the disastrous consequences of sin, he wanted to encourage them to cooperate with the plans of the Lord by going into combat against the enemies of the New Law. It was therefore necessary to present Arthur and his knights as exemplary and to show at the same time the beneficial effects of both the redemption and the Grail Quest, here an image not of an internal quest, but of the crusades, and more precisely of the crusades in the Holy Land. Arthur, who, following the silence of Perlesvaus at the time of his first visit to the Grail Castle, has neglected his royal duties, becomes himself the living example of the efficacy of the Redemption; for, thanks to the eucharistic miracle which he witnesses at the time of his pilgrimage to the chapel of St. Augustine, he recovers "par le plesir de Dieu" ("by the grace of God")[44] the desire to do that which is good. And later, when after the Grail Castle has been recaptured, an act symbolizing in this work the reconquest of Jerusalem, he returns on a pilgrimage to this holy spot, all Logres will benefit from it; for Arthur, thanks to his repentance and his efforts to "edier e essaucier la Nouvelle Loi" ("support and exalt the [New] Law")[45] will have deserved the right to see the Grail and will share its spiritual fruits with his country. The goodness which henceforth reigns in the Arthurian world is symbolized by taking up again the theme of the Wheel of Fortune, but with a different significance: the Demoiselle du Char, who here represents Fortune, bald since Perlesvaus's silence, receives a new head of hair after the retaking of the Grail Castle.[46] This signifies that Arthur's kingdom is redeemed and not destined to be destroyed as in the Vulgate and Post-Vulgate.

That does not mean that there will not be more wars in Arthur's kingdom. But the author takes a position deliberately contrary to that of the Vulgate Cycle and suggests how the internal war between Arthur's knights, and consequently the final catastrophe, could have been avoided. Although in his version Lancelot refuses to repent for his sin of lechery, he nevertheless will always be discreet.[47] Neither Arthur nor Gauvain will ever hear of his love for the queen, who will die before his return to the court. Moreover, Lancelot will not cause, as in the Vulgate Cycle, the death of his best friends; on the contrary, he will reestablish peace and at the same time convert the infidels when, after Arthur's pilgrimage to the Grail Castle, Brian of the Isles, aided by Kay, who has become a traitor, invades the realm of Logres.[48] The situation is obviously parallel to that of the *Mort Artu,* but its outcome is quite different. And that is not all. In the Vulgate, Arthur was as responsible as Lancelot for the destruction of the realm. Lancelot, despite his indiscretion, would have been able to save Logres if Arthur, before confronting Mordred, had followed Gauvain's advice and had become reconciled with Lancelot.[49] In the *Perlesvaus,* on the other hand, where for quite different reasons the king had, at one time, fallen out with Lancelot and had him put in prison, Arthur shows himself to be much more of a conciliator. As soon as his old enemy King Claudas tries to take advantage of Lancelot's imprisonment to wage war against Arthur, the latter, accepting Lucan's advice, becomes reconciled with Lancelot to the advantage of all.[50]

If the author of the *Perlesvaus* advocates a happier future for the realm of Logres, it is because the ideas about civil peace and crusading are closely linked. St. Bernard, while justifying combats against the infidels, had condemned wars among Christian lords since "victory would not be good whenever the cause of the war is not good and the intention of those who wage it is not just."[51] Influenced by St. Bernard's ideas about the crusades, the author of the *Perlesvaus* carried St. Bernard's teachings over to his narrative plan.[52]

Steinbeck wanted to make King Arthur what he chose to call "an understandable character."[53] The concerns of his medieval predecessors were obviously quite different. What dominates their conception of King Arthur and of the destiny of his realm is not the desire to explain the king's actions in "human" or psychological terms, but to use the legend of Arthur to make more vivid their ideological preoccupations.

Notes

This article is the revised and expanded version of a paper that I read at Bouillon in May 1983 at the meeting of the Belgian section of the International Arthurian Society. The paper itself is an adaptation of a lecture that I gave in English at a colloquium dedicated to the memory of Eugène Vinaver (Manchester, March 6, 1983). The earlier version appeared under the title "The Changing Vision of Arthur's Death," in *Dies Illa: Death in the Middle Ages,* ed. Jane H.M. Taylor, Vinaver Studies in French, 1, gen. ed. A.R.W. James and Jane H.M. Taylor (Liverpool, 1983), pp. 107–23.[F.B.]

1. John Steinbeck, *The Acts of King Arthur and His Noble Knights from the Winchester MS of Thomas Malory and Other Sources,* ed. Chase Horton (London, 1976), p. 299.

2. Geoffrey of Monmouth, *Historia Regum Britanniae,* ed. Acton Griscom (London, New York, Toronto: Longmans 1929); E. Faral, *La légende arthurienne* (Paris, 1929), III, pp. 64–303.

3. Cf. E. Gilson, *La Philosophie au Moyen Age* (Paris, 1976), pp. 168–72; Andre Vauchez, *La Spiritualité du Moyen Age* (Paris, 1975), pp. 63–65; A.M. Dubarle, *Le péché original dans l'Écriture* (Paris, 1976), pp. 25–31.

4. Gildas, *The Ruin of Britain and Other Works,* ed. and trans. Michael Winterbottom (London and Chichester, 1978).

5. Jean Frappier, *Étude sur la Mort le Roi Artu* (Paris, 1936), p. 256.

6. *The Didot Perceval according to the Manuscripts of Modena and Paris,* ed. William Roach (Philadelphia, 1941). On the Prose *Perceval en prose,* see F. Bogdanow, *La trilogie de Robert de Boron: le Perceval en prose,* in *Grundriss der romanischen Literaturen des Mittelalters,* ed. Hans Robert Jauss and Eric Köhler (Heidelberg, 1978), IV/1, pp. 513–35.

7. *Didot Perceval,* ed. Roach, MS E, 2386–87; MS D, 1778–79; translation from *The Romance of Perceval in Prose,* trans. Dell Skeels (Seattle: University of Washington Press, 1966), p. 84.

8. *Didot Perceval,* ed. Roach, MS D, 1879.

9. *Didot Perceval,* ed. Roach, MS E, 2629–33.

10. On the Vulgate Cycle, see Jean Frappier, *Grundriss,* IV/1, pp. 536–89.

11. *La Mort le Roi Artu,* ed. Frappier (Paris, 1936); rev. ed. *T.L.F.* 1954. All of my references are from the 1936 edition.

12. *La Queste del Saint Graal,* ed. A. Pauphilet, *C.F.M.A.* (Paris, 1923).

13. The entire Vulgate Cycle, which included the prose *Lancelot,* was published by H.O. Sommer as *The Vulgate Version of Arthurian Romances,* 7 vols. (Washington, 1908–1916). For more recent editions, see *Lancelot: roman en prose du XIIIe siècle,* ed. A. Micha, *T.L.F.,* 8 vols. (Paris, Geneva, 1978–82); *Lancelot do Lac: The Non-Cyclic Old French Prose Lancelot,* ed. Elspeth Kennedy, 2 vols. (Oxford, 1980).

14. *La Queste,* ed. Pauphilet, pp. 271.10–11, 274.28–275.4.

15. See, for example, *Vulgate Version,* IV, 345, 348–49, 369; V, 284–85.

16. *La Queste,* ed. Pauphilet, p. 149.28–29.

17. *Vulgate Version,* IV, 56–66.

18. *Mort Artu,* ed. Frappier, § 93, 117; *Vulgate Version,* IV, 73.

19. See, for example, *Mort Artu,* § 109, p. 115.26–30.

20. *Mort Artu,* § 163.

21. *Mort Artu,* §176, p. 201.2–3; translation from *The Death of King Arthur,* trans. James Cable, Penguin Classics (Harmondsworth, Middlesex, 1971), p. 205.

22. On the Post-Vulgate *Roman du Graal,* see F. Bogdanow, *The Romance of the Grail* (Manchester, 1966). This cycle has not been preserved in its entirety in any French manuscript, but it can be reconstructed from various fragments and from the Spanish and Portuguese translations. It consists of the following parts:

i. A *Estoire del Saint Graal* almost identical with that of the Vulgate (*Vulgate Version I*) and preserved in Portugese (*Livro de Josep Abaramatia,* ed. Henry Hare Carter [Chapel Hill: University of North Carolina Press, 1967]).

ii. A prose version of the *Merlin* of Robert de Boron followed by a continuation which differs from that which is found in the Vulgate Cycle. This Post-Vulgate *Suite,* parts of which are found in MSS Brit. Libr. Add. 38117, Cambridge Add. 7071, B.N. fr. 112, 12599 and Siena (unnumbered fragment), has been published in an edition based upon the London manuscript, *Merlin: roman en prose du XIIIe siècle,* ed. G. Paris and J. Ulrich, *S.A.T.F.,* 2 vols. (Paris, 1886). One part of the continuation of the London manuscript found in MS 112 was edited by H.O. Sommer (*Die Abenteuer Gawains, Ywains und Le Morholts mit den drei Jungfrauen aus der Trilogie [Demanda] des Pseudo-Robert de Borron. Die Fortsetzung des Huth-Merlin nach der allein bekannten HS. Nr. 112 der Pariser National Bibliothek. Beihefte zur Zeitschrift für romanische Philologie,* 47 [Halle, 1913]). Another fragment of the Post-Vulgate *Suite* which provides a continuation to Sommer's text has been published by F. Bogdanow (*La Folie Lancelot: A Hitherto Unidentified Portion of the Suite du Merlin Contained in MSS. B.N. fr. 112 and 12599, Beihefte zur Zeitschrift für romanische Philologie 109* [Tübingen, 1965]). For an edition of the Siena fragment as well as of the *Coup Douloureux* found in the Cambridge MS, see F. Bogdanow, *The Romance of the Grail,* pp. 230–49. The Spanish translation of the *Suite du Merlin* has been published by Adolfo Bonilla y San Martin (*La Demanda del Sancto Grial,* Primera Parte: *El Baladro del Sabio Merlin,* Segunda Parte: *La Demanda del Sancto Grial . . .* [Madrid, 1907]).

iii. A *Queste del Saint Graal* and a *Mort Artu,* both of them revisions of the Vulgate versions. I am preparing a critical edition of the Post-Vulgate *Queste* and *Mort Artu* for the S.A.T.F. that is based upon all of the surviving manuscripts (MSS. Oxford Bodl. Libr. Rawlinson D 874; B.N. fr. 112, 340, 343, 772; Bodmer 105, as a representative of all of the manuscripts of the second version of the *Tristan en prose* which incorporate the Post Vulgate *Queste* (for a list of these manuscripts, see *The Romance of the Grail,* pp. 88–120). The Post-Vulgate *Queste* and *Mort Artu* have both been translated into Spanish and Portuguese (*La Demanda,* ed. Bonilla y San Martin; *A Demanda do Santo Graal,* ed. A. Magne [Rio de Janeiro, 1944]; 2nd rev. ed. [Rio de Janeiro, 1955–70]).

[Since the publication of the French version of this article in 1986, Vols. I, II, and IV.1 of Fanni Bogdanow's edition of the Post-Vulgate *Queste* have been published: *La version Post-Vulgate de la Queste del Saint Graal et de la Mort Artu,* S.A.T.F. (Paris: Picard, 1991). For an account of the manuscripts of the Post-Vulgate *Queste* that have come to light since the publication in 1965 of her *Romance of the Grail,* see *La version Post-Vulgate de la Queste del Saint Graal,* Vol. I, pp. 1–26.—E.D.K.]

23. *Mort Artu,* ed. Frappier, § 164, p. 185.12–17; Cable, p. 192.
24. *Vulgate Version,* V, 284.10–41.
25. *Merlin,* ed. Paris and Ulrich, I, 147–48; translation by E.D.K.
26. *Vulgate Version,* V, 284.25–30.

27. *Merlin*, ed. Paris and Ulrich, I, 154.

28. Aristotle, *La Poétique*. *Texte, traduction, notes*, by Roselyne Dupont-Roc and Jean Lallot (Paris, 1980), Chap. 13, p. 77.

29. *Merlin*, ed. Paris and Ulrich, II, 42; translation by E.D.K.

30. *Patrologia Latina*, 182, 1041–42.

31. *Merlin*, ed. Paris and Ulrich, I, 207–08; translation by E.D.K.

32. *Merlin*, ed. Paris and Ulrich, I, 159.

33. MS B.N., fr. 772, f. 418a–b; translation by E.D.K.

34. "Ay, Deus, camanha ma adança do traedor, matar os bõos cavaleyros e os leaes!" (Vienna, Bibl. Nat., MS 2594, f. 193c; *A Demanda do Santo Graal*, ed. A. Magne [Rio de Janeiro, 1955–1970], § 666).

35. "Ay, dise el rey, se eu escapey vivo, que prol me vem? Ca mĩa vida nom e nada, ca eu bem vejo que sõo chagado aa morte. Ay Deus! que foy fatal vĩr tam maa andança a hũa gram terra, per trayçom d'ũu mao homem" (Vienna, Bibl. Nat., MS 2594, f. 193d; *Demanda*, ed. Magne, § 668).

36. Aristotle, *La Poétique*, chaps. 11 and 16.

37. "Giflet, eu nom sõo rey Artur, o que soyam chamar rey aventuroso polas bõas andanças que avia. Mas quem m'agora chamar per meu direyto nome, chamar-m'a mal aventurado e mizquinho. Esto me ffez ventura, que xi me tornou madrasta e enmiga. E Nosso Senhor, que praz que viva en doo a en tristeza este pouco que ey de viver, a bem mo mostra: que asi como el quis e foy poderoso de me erguer per muy fremossoas aventuras e sen meu merecimento, bem assi e poderoso de me dirribar per aventuras feas e mas, per meu mericimenti e par meu pecado" (Vienna, Bibl. Nat., MS 2594, f. 194b; *Demanda*, ed. Magne, § 672).

38. *Die Abenteuer Gawains, Ywains und Le Morholts*, ed. H.O. Sommer, *Beihefte zur Zeitschrift für romanische Philologie*, 47 (Halle, 1913), p. 63.

39. See *Merlin*, ed. Paris and Ulrich, I, 230.

40. This incident is related in the Post-Vulgate *Queste* (MS B.N., fr. 343, f. 61a–72c).

41. F. Bogdanow, *The Romance of the Grail*, pp. 264–70.

42. *Perlesvaus*, ed. William A. Nitze and T. Atkinson Jenkins (Chicago, 1932; rpr. New York, 1972).

43. On the date of the *Perlesvaus*, see my chapter in *Grundriss* (1984), IV, 2, pp. 43–67.

44. *Perlesvaus*, ed. Nitze, 1.569; translation from *The High Book of the Grail*, trans. Nigel Bryant (Cambridge, 1978), p. 33.

45. *Perlesvaus*, ed. Nitze, 1.348–9; trans. Bryant, p. 26; cf. 1.7221–33; 7864–70.

46. *Perlesvaus*, ed. Nitze, 1.9946–47.

47. Cf. *Perlesvaus*, ed. Nitze, 1.7602–5.

48. *Perlesvaus*, ed. Nitze, l.7107–74, 7634–749.

49. *Mort Artu*, ed. Frappier, §176, pp. 199.26–200.6.

50. *Perlesvaus*, ed. Nitze, l.8554–660, 9429–536.

51. Bernard de Clairvaux, *De Laude novae militiae*, chap. I (*Œuvres complètes de saint Bernard*, trans. Charpentier [Paris, 1866], Vol. 2, p. 390). *Patrologia Latina*, vol. 182, p. 922: "sicut nec bonus judicabitur finis, ubi causa non bona, et intentio non recta praecesserit."

52. On the influence of the ideas of St. Bernard on the *Perlesvaus*, see my chapter in *Grundriss*, IV, 2.

53. Steinbeck, *The Acts of King Arthur*, p. 336.

APPEARANCES AND REALITY IN *LA MORT LE ROI ARTU*

Donald C. MacRae

In his *Etude sur la Mort le Roi Artu,* Jean Frappier has suggested that the
". . . thème de Fortune—du Destin—est sans doute le thème majeur de *La
Mort Artu*" (". . . theme of Fortune—of Destiny—is undoubtedly the major theme of *La Mort Artu*").[1] Elsewhere he restates this conviction when
he refers to the ". . . cercle de fatalité qui pèse sur son [Arthur's] royaume
terrestre" ("circle of fatality that weighs heavily upon his [Arthur's] terrestrial kingdom"). Everything, he insists, gives the impression of tragic inevitability so that at times Fortune even seems to acquire a force all its own:
". . . le destin est comme l'âme du roman; le thème en est traité avec assez
de force et de profondeur pour que la *Mort Artu* . . . puisse faire penser par
endroits aux tragiques grecs ou au drame élisabéthain" ("destiny is, as it
were, the soul of the romance. The theme is treated with enough force and
profundity that the *Mort Artu* reminds one in places of Greek tragedy or
Elizabethan drama").[2] There is no doubt about the importance of fate in
the *Mort Artu,* but to suggest, as Frappier and others have done, that the
role of this one motif is so striking that it dominates all others would seem
to place too great an importance upon its function to the detriment of other
important themes in the story.[3] Indeed, consideration of the work essentially
as a fate-tragedy is to ignore, or at least to play down, certain essential characteristics which contribute not only to the superb psychological portraits
of which the mediaeval author has proved himself a master, but also to the
very structure of the romance itself.

Without denying the slow but inexorable rotation of the Wheel of
Fortune in turning the tide in the affairs of men, Eugène Vinaver, however,
argues convincingly for a much more complex and subtle pattern of cause
and event leading to the final catastrophe. In his discussion on the poetry

Reprinted from *Forum for Modern Language Studies*, 18 (1982), 266–77.

of interlace, he draws attention not just to ". . . one major cause, but [to] . . . several concurrent causes,"⁴ citing in addition to this theme: the withdrawal of divine protection from both Arthur and Lancelot; conflicts arising out of the divided loyalties which Lancelot feels toward Guinevere on the one hand and Arthur and Gauvain on the other, as well as Mordred's incestuous birth. These, he indicates, are a part of the intricate setting, the vast design, without which there can be neither plot nor characterization. This complex fabric provides a ". . . continuous and constantly unfolding panorama stretching as far into the past as into the future—such are the things that hold the reader spell-bound as he progresses through these interwoven 'branches' and themes."⁵ Destiny, he asserts, is inextricably linked with character, and destiny means ". . . the convergence of simultaneously developed themes, now separated, now coming together, varied, yet synchronized, so that every movement of this carefully planned design remains charged with echoes of the past and premonitions of the future."⁶ Vinaver's arguments are eminently reasonable, accounting, as they do, for the complexity and apparent confusion of the many themes of the *Mort Artu* and lifting it above the state of a mere fate-tragedy to which the others would seem to relegate it.

There is, however, one essential theme which Vinaver does not take into account and which plays a major role in the development of character and plot in the *Mort Artu*. I refer to a critical measure of free choice, granted to Arthur in particular, which permeates the story from beginning to end. It is this measure of free choice which lies behind all of Arthur's decisions, influencing and directing his behaviour in the various situations in which he finds himself. If, to the thirteenth-century mind, his fall from grace is unavoidable ". . . as a result of Arthur's rise to excessive heights of success and fame"⁷ the introduction of this theme of free choice clearly provides a tangible and logical foundation for the inevitability of that process. In this fact lies ". . . the convergence of simultaneously developed themes" to which Vinaver has referred. There is absolutely nothing inconsistent in that. However, the role of free choice is not a simple one in the *Mort Artu*. The King's inability or, more frequently, his unwillingness to distinguish between the appearance and the reality of a given situation directly affects his subsequent course of action. Consequently, this clouds his vision and prevents him from choosing wisely and correctly. When one realizes that the decisions which Arthur must make are invariably imposed upon him during a time of crisis in the story, it is relatively easy to understand how the effect of these decisions gradually builds up to the tragic battle on the Salisbury Plain where not only King Arthur but also the entire Kingdom of Logres are destroyed.

This, then, is the essential theme of the romance to which we have referred: confronted by a need to make a decision in a moment of crisis, Arthur is unwilling or unable to see the situation as it really is and invariably chooses the wrong course of action. It is not Fate acting wilfully and arbitrarily, but Arthur himself, who is ultimately responsible for his own demise.

In the opening pages of *La Mort le Roi Artu,* King Arthur is confronted by the insistence of his nephew, Agravain, that his Queen, Guinevere, is involved in an adulterous affair with Lancelot del Lac. Even though the situation is a recurrence of an earlier illicit relationship which Lancelot has vowed to terminate *[Queste del Saint Graal],* Arthur is outwardly struck by disbelief and, at least initially, refuses to pay heed to the accusations. In spite of the fact that Agravain's suspicions are well-founded, the King's angry rejections of this contention as totally without justification would seem to indicate the impossibility of such a relationship. Arthur seems certain that Lancelot could never betray their friendship in so base a way, and yet, in virtually the same breath, he belies this apparent conviction and vacillates: ". . . et certes se il onques le pensa, force d'amors li fist fere, encontre qui sens ne reson ne peut avoir duree" ("and indeed if he ever did, he was compelled by the force of love, which neither common-sense nor reason can resist").[8] Aware of the inherent dangers in Agravain's accusation, Arthur vehemently denies the possibility of such behaviour on Lancelot's part, but in spite of his protestations, he knows there may well be something in his nephew's words. Thus, he immediately leaves himself this opening, but in so doing, he contradicts his own certainty in the matter.

This is but the first hint of many such instances in which the King proves himself at best indecisive and hesitant, at worst weak and pitiful. He is ill at ease in this situation, and his anger that he must do something is clearly evident. Thus when Agravain pursues the matter further and suggests that Arthur have the two lovers closely watched in order to prove the validity of these accusations, Arthur finds himself in a dilemma from which there is no easy escape. Although he has the choice whether or not to act upon Agravain's information, he closes his eyes to the truth of the matter because he is immediately and painfully aware of the consequences for the Kingdom should they prove to be true. Arthur does not want to know the truth and this is why he neither approves nor disapproves of Agravain's plans, for any confrontation with Lancelot del Lac at this particular moment would hardly be in the best interests either of Arthur or of the Kingdom of Logres. The quest for the Holy Grail has just been brought to a conclusion, but only at the cost of the lives of many of Arthur's knights. Indeed, aware of the crisis now facing them, and in a last desperate attempt to bolster the failing morale of a sadly-depleted Round Table, the King has just announced a tournament. Conflict with Lancelot at this time would surely spell disaster to his hopes for a rebirth of his Kingdom. It is abundantly clear to him that the well-being of the Round Table is directly dependent upon the choice he must now make. Consequently Arthur avoids taking the firm course of action necessary to discover the truth for himself, and at the risk of his honour, he is forced to close his eyes to the reality of Agravain's accusations, all the while trying to convince himself that they are not true.

That night there follows a period of deep soul-searching during which the King must wrestle with his problem. Ultimately, his predicament being what it is, he is able to persuade himself that there is no truth to Agravain's contention and therefore no need for action on his part, and yet, in spite of this, his actions in leaving the Queen behind when he goes to the tournament, ". . . por esprouver la mençonge Agravain" (7:12–13; "to put Agravain's accusation to the test" [p. 27]), clearly show that he is deceiving himself in order to avoid coming to terms with reality.

Although this psychological aspect of Arthur's character is important in itself, it has further implications for the structure of the romance. His moments of weakness, his vacillations and self-deception invariably occur in times of crisis during which the necessity for decisive action, the hallmark of the young King Arthur, is of the utmost importance. Here, as elsewhere, Arthur is faced by a freedom of choice between two distinct alternatives: the one centered in reality, the other in the illusion of reality. It is the latter, however, the deception of appearances, assuming the form of deliberate distortion or misinterpretation of the facts and half-truths, which invariably holds sway at these crucial moments in the story and ultimately brings about the final hours of the Round Table on the Salisbury Plain.

If the hatred of Agravain for Lancelot has been the impetus for Arthur's dilemma, his meeting with his sister, Morgan, further complicates the situation. Like Agravain, she, too, is motivated by hatred, but her means of revealing to Arthur the deceit of the two lovers whom she would destroy is even more carefully and deliberately planned. The proof with which she thus confronts him with all the supernatural powers at her disposal is, therefore, all the more difficult for him to ignore. Even the circumstances of the King's arrival at Morgan's castle would seem to suggest something more than mere chance; the subsequent systematic way in which she sets about to convince Arthur to take action against Lancelot and Guinevere would tend to reinforce this assertion. After his stay in Tauroc, Arthur enters the forest in which Morgan once imprisoned Lancelot del Lac. As he does so, he feels unwell and shortly thereafter he and his company have lost their way. The suspicion that the supernatural powers of Morgan are already at work is strengthened by the sound of the horn. Although it is later made clear that the King is tired after a long ride from Tauroc, the fact that no further issue is made of Arthur's illness suggests that it was a transitory state, probably induced by the supernatural powers of Morgan herself and followed up by the sound of the horn and the dazzling display in the castle itself. Clearly Morgan has laid the groundwork for her plan most carefully.

At first she tells him no more than is necessary for her purposes until such time as she is prepared to reveal her identity to him and to allow him to discover the pictures on the wall of the room to which he has been brought. Having once examined these pictures and deciphered them, Arthur is forced to consider the truth of the message they convey. Significantly, he is not yet prepared to accept the reality of the evidence that they present, for once he has recovered from the initial shock of his discovery, he immediately questions their authenticity. The consequences of the situation and the need for a decision, however, are obvious to him; his own honour and the well-being of the Kingdom of Logres are at stake. And so, in the light of Morgan's carefully prepared arguments which corroborate the message of the pictures on the wall, Arthur declares that he sees "toute aparissant" (53.21) ("clearly") and that he is more convinced than ever of the need to act. In spite of the overwhelming evidence before him and in spite of his apparent resolve to take the steps that the situation demands, Arthur still refuses to admit the truth to himself and continues to seek a way out of the unpleasant circumstances which a deliberate decision on his part would bring about. "Et *se* il est einsi . . ." (53:59: the italics are my own; "*If* it is as . . ." [p. 73]). And again:

"Je en ferai tant . . . que *se* li uns ainme l'autre de fole amor, si com vos me dites, que ge les ferai prendre ensemble ains que cis mois soit passez, *se* il avient que Lancelos viegne a court dedens celui terme." (53: 77–81; the italics are my own)

("I shall make sure . . . that *if* one loves the other adulterously as you say, I shall have them caught together before the end of the month, *if* Lancelot should return to court by then." [p. 74])

Putting his crown on the line, he promises punishment to both, *if* they are guilty. It is obvious that Arthur has a choice how he will react: the tragic truth of the matter is that whichever way he moves, he stands to lose. Should he fail to take action to avenge his shame, his own position as King would be jeopardized, his authority a sham and his honour degraded. If, however, Arthur were to move against Lancelot he is certain that the reverberations of his actions would be sufficient to bring about the final destruction of the Round Table as he knows it. This is for him the greatest fear of all.

This latter consideration should not be underestimated. Subtle but repeated references to the glories of the past punctuate the entire text and make obvious the concern of an old man for a world—the only one he has ever lived for—which is slowly but surely crumbling about him. Nowhere is this more clearly stated than in the scene in which Gauvain and Arthur come upon the boat containing the corpse of the maid of Escalot. Gauvain remarks to the King:

> "Par foi . . . se ceste nacele est ausi bele dedenz com dehors, ce seroit merveilles; a poi que ge ne di que les aventures recommencent." (70:21–24)

> ("In faith . . . if that boat is as beautiful inside as it is outside, it would be a marvel; it is almost as if adventures were beginning again." [pp. 92–93])

Both are aware that they are living in the twilight of the Round Table.

When Arthur finally leaves Morgan and returns to Camelot, he is surprised to learn that Lancelot has spent but one day at court. As a result he becomes confused why this should be so if he loves the Queen adulterously. More than willing to accept the situation at face value, Arthur immediately finds in this just cause to doubt the words of both Agravain and Morgan:

> ". . . et c'estoit une chose qui moult metoit le cuer le roi a aise et qui moult li fesoit mescroire les paroles que il ot oïes. . . ." (62: 11–13)

> ("This was a thing which went a long way to set the king's mind at rest and which led him to discount what he had heard. . . ." [p. 82])

His escape from reality is short-lived.

If one were to apply Jean Rychner's linguistic analysis of the *Mort Artu* to this situation in order to substantiate these arguments even further, the willingness of the King to close his eyes to the truth would become adequately clear. Rychner suggests:

Entre le pn sj sans conjonction [sujet pronominal: i.e., le pronom personnel, il, ele, et le pronom démonstratif cil, cele] et le pn sj avec
conjonction on peut être sensible à la même différence qu'entre sj nm
[sujet nominal] et 'et' + sj nm: plus de calme et de ponderation d'un
coté, et de l'autre plus de familiarité et de vivacité.

(Between the pronominal subject without a conjunction [i.e., the personal pronoun, *il, ele,* and the demonstrative pronoun *cil, cele*] and
the pronominal subject with a conjunction, one can be aware of the
same difference that exists between a nominal subject and "and" +
nominal subject: more calm and equilibrium on the one hand, and
on the other more intimacy and vivacity.)[9]

Elsewhere he refers to the ". . . entrée plus vive et plus dramatique . . ."
("more lively and dramatic opening")[10] of such phrases, and "Le syntagme
en 'et il' de même sujet est habituellement prospectif et pourvu d'une suite"
("The syntagma in "et il" of the same subject is usually prospective and provided with a continuation").[11] The thrust of the story is, therefore, clearly
in the direction of this clause rather than the preceding one and thus toward
Arthur's attempts to discredit what he has heard and seen. He continues to
close his eyes to the truth in the hope that the threatened confrontation with
Lancelot will somehow disappear. The presence of the "et" which introduces
this section looks ahead to the continuing attempts of the King to avoid
making an unwanted decision.

The episode of the poisoned fruit follows and Lancelot is called upon
to prove the innocence of the Queen in the death of Gaheris. Once he has
done so, however, he falls more hopelessly in love with her: "Et se Lancelos
avoit devant ce amee la reïne, il l'ama orendroit plus qu'il n'avoit onques
mes fet a nul jor, et ele ausint lui. . . ." (85:33–35; "And if Lancelot had loved
the queen before, from now on he loved her more than he had ever done in
the past, and so did she him" [p. 108]). Unfortunately, their lack of discretion makes this illicit relationship obvious to almost everyone and ultimately
leads to yet another crisis.

To some extent this crisis provides an interesting contrast with the
initial Arthur-Agravain episode, for this time, Agravain finds himself on
somewhat firmer ground. By now, the gravity of the situation is clear and
he deliberately allows Arthur to overhear the conversation between himself
and his brothers. Once he has captured the King's attention, he then allows
both Gaheriet and Gauvain to parry Arthur's questions in order to cover up
the truth about Lancelot and Guinevere. In spite of the King's anger, nei-

ther will yield to Arthur's pressure and tell him what they have been discussing. Significantly, he reacts to their refusal in a totally irrational way, demanding to know their secret, first, on the oaths they have sworn to him, and then, threatening them on pain of death if they should fail to inform him. In spite of these angry words, neither Gaheriet nor Gauvain gives in and both leave the King's presence; Arthur does nothing about it. Left in the room with the others, Arthur asks them, begs them and finally, beside himself with rage, stands ready to strike Agravain dead with a blow from his sword. No longer in control of himself, Arthur shows signs of cracking under the strain of his dilemma. However, as soon as Agravain has finally told him what he wants to know, Arthur recoils from the truth he fears; subconsciously, he does not really want to hear the truth: "Comment, fet li rois, me fet donc Lancelos honte? De quoi est ce donc? Dites le moi . . ." (86: 23–25) ("What," said the king, "is Lancelot dishonoring me? What are you talking about? Tell me . . ." [p. 110]). One would almost think that he was hearing this news for the first time! When Agravain assures him of the facts, Arthur turns pale, and as earlier in the initial Agravain scene, as well as in the scene with Morgan, falls silent, lost in deep thought. He can no longer take refuge in appearances; the truth is out and the reality of the situation known: ". . . car il set bien de voir que, se Lancelos est pris a cest afere et il en reçoit mort, onques si grant tormente n'avint en ce païs por la mort d'un seul chevalier" (87: 23–26; "He knew perfectly well that if Lancelot were caught in adultery and put to death, there would be such torment in the country as had never before been caused by the death of a single knight" [p. 111]). Once again in a position to make a choice (although admittedly the options open to him are not very attractive) Arthur is so emotionally involved because of the faithlessness of his wife, the deception of a friend, and the certain downfall of all his kingdom that he can hardly act with a clear and rational mind. Accepting the treacherous advice of Agravain, he rejects his loyal nephew, Gauvain, and from this point onward, acting out of "desmesure" ("lack of moderation"), he swears revenge upon Lancelot and the Queen. Unlike Morgan, who finds herself forced to remind Arthur constantly of the steps he must take, Agravain no longer needs to goad him into action. He merely capitalizes on a situation from which Arthur cannot escape. Once the oath has been sworn to him, there can be no turning back—the crisis which must inevitably lead to bloodshed has been reached.

The death of Gaheriet, a direct result of Agravain's hatred for Lancelot, is significant, falling as it does almost exactly in the middle of *La Mort le Roi Artu*. Once again, appearances play an essential role in the progress of the plot and lead to an irreversible turning point in it. Gaheriet's death is a simple case of mistaken identity, for he is not who he seems to be or Lancelot would never have slain him willingly. This single event, originating in appearances, irrevocably alienates Gauvain and sets him off on his senseless quest for revenge upon Lancelot. This, in turn, marks the beginning of the end and that which Arthur fears more than anything else: a confrontation between himself on the one hand, and Lancelot and Ban's kin on the other. The King is quite aware of the inevitable consequences of such a conflict for the Kingdom of Logres.

Lancelot's love for the Queen, while obviously important in itself, finds its real significance, not in adultery, but in the fact that it threatens to bring about the confrontation which Arthur has sought to delay as long as possible. The King is prepared to close his eyes to the truth, to accept the appearances of the situation, as long as he can postpone the inevitable. The pity he betrays when he sentences Guinevere to death is indicative of the genuine love he still has for the Queen, while the anger he shows at Lancelot's good fortune in the tournament at Karahés is a reflection of his frustration that the very knight he loves most should be the catalyst in his dilemma. Indeed, there are times, in particular when Lancelot's actions seem to contradict the reality of the situation, when Arthur's vacillations would seem to suggest that he could almost live with the shame of the Queen's adultery if only he could somehow avoid the impending conflict with Lancelot. Let there be no mistake; it is not because Arthur fears Lancelot, but because he loves him and because he is quite aware of the consequences of his choice that he finds himself on the horns of a dilemma. From a structural point of view, it is important to note that the adulterous love affair plays a less significant role in the second half of the story than the first, although that aspect of it which would lead to confrontation is retained and developed, not in the love affair itself, but in Gauvain's passionate hatred of Lancelot. The thread of unity in the work is thus maintained.

As we have seen, the love affair aggravates the dilemma in which Arthur finds himself by slowly but surely forcing a confrontation between Arthur and Lancelot del Lac. The "desmesure" of Gauvain takes up where this adulterous relationship leaves off and continues inexorably to force Arthur into a conflict which he knows will ultimately destroy himself and, more significantly, the Round Table. Gauvain's obsession for revenge plays an important role in the second half of the *Mort Artu* not only as an end in itself, for that is certainly important, but also insofar as it contributes to the death of Arthur and with him, the downfall of the entire Kingdom of Logres.

The death of Gaheriet is significant for our discussion of appearances and reality, for out of it arise the hatred and irrational behaviour of Gauvain, who, in a state of shock at the news of his brother's death, is unable to see the situation as it really is. Blaming Lancelot for slaying Gaheriet willingly, he does not realize that it was a case of mistaken identity and that Lancelot would never have killed the man he loved so much. Gauvain should have known this, but his inability to recognize the truth of the matter leads him to an "idée fixe"—a fatal aspect of "desmesure." He derives his very "raison d'être" from the thought of revenge upon Lancelot, and this grows so out of proportion that he cannot see clearly nor make rational decisions. He neither can nor will recognize the truth. Motivated by blind passion which originates in mistaken observations, Gauvain's subconscious quest for his own death which so dominates the second half of the romance begins, bringing with it the realization of Arthur's fears of an end to the glorious days of the Round Table. Overwhelmed by grief, he mistakenly lays the blame for his brother's death and his own sorrow on Fortune, for therein would seem to lie the source of the problem. But he fails to see that Agravain's hatred—a hatred which he, himself, has already warned against—has contributed directly to Gaheriet's death and that he is mistaken in his accusation of Lancelot. Gauvain, in emotional shock, is therefore deceived by the appearance of things.

When Gauvain lays the blame for his tragic loss upon the whims of Fortune, he is making a serious error, for Fortune is only the apparent cause of his troubles. Indeed, she almost becomes the scapegoat for his own weaknesses, since the real source of his dilemma lies within himself, in his "fol apel," his irrational behaviour, his inability to see things as they really are. But it is easier and perhaps more human for Gauvain to blame Fortune rather than himself. In this, the mediaeval author of the *Mort Artu* measurably broadens the scope of his characterization of Gauvain.

Arthur's reaction to Gaheriet's death is also significant, for even though the King has retreated somewhat into the background in a scene devoted primarily to insight into Gauvain's behaviour, the author has found it essential to re-emphasize those elements that retain the thread of unity throughout the work. As one might expect, Arthur views the events of the past few hours less in terms of the death of Gaheriet, himself, than in terms of his own personal loss. Still preoccupied with himself and his own dilemma, he considers Gaheriet's death an extension of his own problems. Since these problems, at least as far as he is concerned, find their origin in Lancelot, the King accuses him and holds him directly responsible. The inevitable confrontation has drawn closer; there can be no turning back once the oath of vengeance has been sworn from his followers. Thus, at this most critical of moments, both Gauvain and the King are confronted by a choice and both are incapable of acting rationally. The former, blinded by his emotional shock and his desire for revenge, and the latter, obsessed by his fears that the end of the Round Table is in sight, both fail to distinguish reality from appearances.

If King Yon's pleas for moderation are readily discounted, in particular at the urging of Mordred whose own motives are suspect, it is hardly likely that Lancelot's offer of explanation and submission to the will of the court can be accepted either. Once again, men are deluded and deceived by the appearance of things and are therefore vulnerable to the baseness of such men as Mordred. Consequently, they reject truth and reason. Repeated warnings have no effect: ". . . vos en seroiz destruiz er menez a mort, ou li sage home par maintes fois sont deceü" (110: 39–41; "You . . . will be destroyed and brought to death as a result of this war; you know that death often deceived wise men" [p. 137]); and Gauvain is admonished for his foolishness. Although the main thrust of the story is now, at least temporarily, carried by Gauvain, whose actions at times overshadow those of Arthur, the author of the *Mort Artu* never really loses sight of the King as the central figure in the story. Arthur continues to display the weakness that characterized him in the first half of the romance, wavering back and forth between love and hatred, admiration and contempt for Lancelot. Whenever the latter makes a chivalric gesture (quite in contrast to Gauvain's behaviour) by sparing Arthur's life or by willingly returning his Queen, Arthur's resolve begins to vacillate, much to the anger of his nephew. The King still hopes against hope that conflict can be avoided. Had he indeed the courage of his convictions, recognizing the senselessness of a war between his forces and Ban's kin, he would then reject those unreasonable demands that Gauvain is making upon him, but instead, he allows himself to be swayed by the apparent truth of Gauvain's arguments. "Puis que Gauvains le velt . . . il me plest bien" (119: 49–50; "Because that is what Gawain desires . . . it is what I want too" [p. 150]).

Thus the human weakness inherent in his own character inevitably leads to the tragedy Arthur would avoid. Finding himself in a situation for which there is now no satisfactory solution, he is obviously aware of the consequences of continued confrontation with Lancelot, and yet, by refusing to draw the line, he brings about his own destruction and that of the Round Table with him. In this he parallels Gauvain who is also accused of pursuing his own death. By this time, Arthur's passive acceptance of the inevitability of the conflict becomes clearer and he becomes an almost pitiful figure. He has had several opportunities to make a clear decision, but he has failed to avail himself of them. Now he almost seems to believe that only death can relieve him of his burden and so he is no longer willing to struggle against a situation he thinks he cannot control. Perhaps he is right. The events which have been set in motion could have been stopped only by a firm stand by the King himself and this is something beyond the capabilities of the older Arthur of *La Mort le Roi Artu.*

In the scene involving Arthur and Gauvain and the old woman, the King and his nephew are both criticized for their foolishness. To the King she says: "Saches veraiement que c'est grant folie et que tu crois fol conseil . . ." (131: 2–3; "I can tell you truly that it is a great madness and that you are ill-advised" [p. 158]). Gauvain, too, does not escape her remarks: ". . . vous porchaciez si durement vostre damage que vous jamais ne reverrés le roialme de Logres sains ne haitiés" (131: 9–11; "You are so resolutely pursuing your own destruction that you will never again in good health see the kingdom of Logres" [p. 158]). Her warnings represent the reality, the truth, of the situation in which they find themselves, but Arthur's weakness, indeed by now the loss of his desire to live, coupled with Gauvain's stubbornness, close their ears to her words. Arthur is still unsure of himself and Gauvain continues to cling stubbornly to the apparent truth that Lancelot deliberately killed his brother. In his anger and grief, Gauvain is unable to distinguish between appearances and reality and pursues his foe to the end, dragging with him Arthur and the remnants of the Round Table to their destruction. Not even Lancelot's magnanimous offer of penance can dissuade him. Thus "desmesure," "outrage," and "desreson" ("irrationality"), the most serious sins a knight could commit, bring about his death.

These are the root causes of the tragedy; man himself by his excesses, and not Fortune as an active force intervening in the affairs of men, is responsible. Although Gauvain blames his problems on Fortune, he does so mistakenly. It will be some time yet before he realizes that he does have a measure of control over his own destiny. But that moment will come and when it does, the moral lesson of the author will be clear: in spite of the seriousness of his sins, there is still hope for the true penitent which Gauvain ultimately becomes. Seeing the error of his ways, Gauvain recognizes his own guilt—not Fortune's—in this tragic situation. Rising above self-indulgence and ego, he soon attains the Kingdom of Heaven. When his quarrel with Lancelot is over, resulting as it does in the subsequent death of Gauvain, a man the King held most dear, there remains virtually nothing more for Arthur in this life. His loved ones and his Kingdom are gone. The fight with Mordred which must now follow serves only to wipe away the final remnants of a once glorious society.

It is significant at this point in the story that Arthur has not yet reached the level of awareness and understanding which Gauvain finally attains and still cannot recognize that the source of his problems lies within himself and his inability to see the reality of things. As Gauvain did before him, therefore, he, too, mistakenly shifts the blame for his own shortcomings upon the vicissitudes of Fortune:

> Hé! Fortune, chose contrere et diverse, la plus desloial chose qui soit el monde, por quoi me fus tu onques si debonere ne si amiable por vendre le moi si chierement au derrien? Tu me fus jadis mere, or m'ies tu devenue marrastre, et por fere moi de duel morir as apelee avec toi la Mort, si que tu en deus manieres m'as honni, de mes amis et de ma terre. Hé! Mort vileinne, tu ne deüsses mie avoir assailli tel home comme mes niés estoit qui de bonté passoit tout le monde. (172:45–55)

> ("Ah! Fortune, contrary and changeable, the most faithless thing in the world, why were you ever so courteous or so kind to me if you were to make me pay so dearly for it in the end? You used to be my mother; now you have become my stepmother, and to make me die of grief you have brought Death with you, in order to dishonour me in two ways at once, through my friends and through my land. Ah! base Death, you should not have attacked a man such as my nephew, who surpassed the whole world in goodness." [p. 200])

Arthur, to whom the weight of the plot now shifts, still must learn that Fortune, whom he blames for his predicament, is only the manifestation, the apparent cause of his troubles. In a sense, Fortune functions as a kind of symbol here. This becomes adequately clear in the scene in which she takes Arthur up on her wheel and tells him the real reason for his impending downfall. Arthur has just been admonished in another dream by the crowd following Gauvain. They tell the King that his nephew, as a true penitent, has indeed attained the Kingdom of Heaven: ". . . et fei aussi comme il a fet . . ." (176: 14–1; "follow his example" [p. 204]). In other words, overcome foolish earthly pride, and salvation will be guaranteed. But Arthur does not. Instead, he commits himself even more completely to the inevitable battle on Salisbury Plain. Lifting him up on her wheel, Fortune warns him of the consequences of his actions, the direct result of his own unwillingness to see the truth: "Mes tel sont li orgueil terrien qu'il n'i a nul si haut assiz qu'il ne le coviegne cheoir de la poesté del monde" (176: 73–75; "But such is earthly pride that no one is seated so high that he can avoid having to fall from power in the world" [p. 205]). The baseness of human actions, then, which overwhelms knightly virtue, and not the whimsical intervention of blind fate, leads to the rude awakening that Arthur experiences in his dream. There is no suggestion that the King could not have retained his lofty position even longer if he had acted in accordance with the chivalric code of behaviour. Arthur's worst fears, the final destruction of his Round Table, are about to be realized; the climax has been reached. He knows this but he also believes that he has come too far to turn back. Like Gauvain immediately before his fateful battle with Lancelot, he continues to deceive himself by trying to convince himself that victory is possible and that there is an apparent hope for him. The Battle of Salisbury Plain puts an end to these illusions.

From the initial scenes of the *Mort Artu*, the main thread of this story has dealt with the downfall of Arthur and with him the destruction of the Round Table. The events which began with Merlin, his prophecies and his relationship to Arthur at the beginning of the Vulgate Cycle (Sommer: Vol. II) have now come full circle. But it is important to stress that the prophecies that Merlin makes there are inevitable only insofar as Arthur's own behaviour makes them so. These events are destined to occur because they must, for after all, they are a part of the traditional story which the mediaeval author has inherited from his predecessors; but with a remarkable degree of sophistication, that same author has introduced a tangible motivation beyond that of Fate or Fortune to justify their occurrence. Arthur's own weakness and unwillingness to see the truth provide the story with another dimension—another of the "branches" to which Vinaver refers. When he finally does realize that the tragic end is near, he cannot go back. It is too late.[12]

NOTES

1. Jean Frappier, *Etude sur La Mort le Roi Artu* (Paris, 1961; 2nd ed.), p. 287. Translations of quotations from works of French and German scholarship have been added by E.D.K.

2. Jean Frappier, ed., *La Mort le Roi Artu* (Paris, 1964; 3rd ed.), p. xix.

3. Rudolf Voss has made this point in *Der Prosa Lancelot: eine strukturanalytische und strukturvergleichende Studie auf der Grundlage des deutschen Textes* (Meisenheim am Glan, 1970), p. 60: "Artus erfährt sich selbst wiederholt als ein unter der blinden Macht des Schicksals und ihres Helfers, des Todes, Leidender . . ." ("Arthur comes to know himself as one suffering under the blind power of Fate and her helper, Death"). Similarly Karl Josef Höltgen argues in "König Arthur und Fortuna" in *Anglia: Zeitschrift für englische Philologie* 75 (1957), 42: ". . . das Rad der Fortuna, das Zentralthema des Werkes, strahlt eine schicksalhafte Aura aus, die den Leser ständig auf den Tod des alten Königs und den Zusammenbruch seines Reiches hinlenkt" ("The wheel of Fortuna, the central theme of the work, radiates an aura of fate, which directs the reader constantly to the death of the old king and the

collapse of his kingdom"). Erich Köhler alludes to a ". . . willkürlich schaltenden Fortuna . . ." ("an arbitrary governing Fortuna") in *Ideal und Wirklichkeit in der höfischen Epik: Studien zur Form der frühen Artus- und Graldichtung* (Tübingen, 1956), p. 202 and n. 1 beginning p. 199. He continues: "Zurück bleibt die tragische, die ganze *Mort d'Artu* durchziehende Ahnung, nach dem Scheitern der ritterlichen Ideale in einer sinnentleerten Welt zu stehen. Fortuna ist wieder blind und kennt nur noch Opfer" ("After the chivalric idea fails to survive in a senseless world, the tragic presentment, extending throughout all of the *Mort d'Artu,* remains"). Finally, James Cable in his translation, *The Death of King Arthur,* Penguin Classics (Harmondsworth, Middlesex, 1971), pp. 12–13, blames much of the tragedy on the adultery of Lancelot and Guinevere but he still alludes to ". . . some supernatural hand, that of God or destiny" as being instrumental in the final analysis.

4. Eugène Vinaver, *The Rise of Romance* (Oxford, 1971), p. 89.

5. Vinaver, pp. 91–92.

6. Vinaver, p. 92.

7. Vinaver, p. 89.

8. *Mort le Roi Artu,* ed. Frappier, 6:26–29; *Death of King Arthur,* trans. Cable, p. 22. Future quotations from these books appear within parentheses in the text.

9. Jean Rychner, *Formes et structures de la prose française médiévale* (Genève, 1970), p. 58.

10. Rychner, p. 53.

11. Rychner, p. 59.

12. A publication by Atie Dingemans Zuurdeeg, *Narrative Techniques and Their Effects in "La Mort le Roi Artu"* (York, South Carolina: French Literature Publications, 1981) did not appear in time for consideration in this paper.

King Arthur and Fortuna

Karl Josef Höltgen

The way in which King Arthur is affected by Fortuna changes in the various works of Arthurian literature written in England in the Middle Ages. In the early period neither Geoffrey of Monmouth, Wace, nor Laʒamon mentions Fortuna as having any particular association with King Arthur. With the thirteenth-century French prose romance *Mort Artu,* however, Fortuna and her wheel emerge decisively in Arthurian legend and from thereon maintain their place. She appears to King Arthur in a dream; he climbs onto her wheel, is drawn up, and hurled down. The presentation of this dream vision and the significance given to it in individual works affect not only their content and form but also shed light on the position of Fortuna in the history of ideas. Fortuna functions almost as a touchstone that shows basic trends in Arthurian literature. Particularly with the alliterative *Morte Arthure,* she places the national, heroic, chivalric, and religious trends in a new relation to one another, while she herself appears as the chief agent in a new conception of Arthur that makes the alliterative *Morte Arthure,* more than previous works, an exemplum with historical and theological significance.

The significance of Fortuna will become clearer if the discussion of her treatment in literature is preceded by a brief account of the history of the creation and development of this lively and changeable symbolic personification.[1] While the early Greeks knew only the relentless ruler Tyche as the goddess of fate, in late antiquity she was joined by the friendly but incalculable sister goddess Fortuna, the good luck of the moment, embodying Opportunity or Kairos, and also honored as the goddess who protected individuals and the state. Later Seneca, Ovid, and Livy recommended courage, virtue, and wisdom as weapons against the unreasonable, ill-tempered decrees of Fortuna.

Originally published as "König Arthur und Fortuna," *Anglia*, 75 (1957), 35–54; translated by Edward Donald Kennedy.

The Church Fathers, especially Augustine, anathematized the heathen goddess since the deeds of irrational Fortuna could not be reconciled with God's providence, his plan for salvation. Fortuna, however, had the vitality she needed to endure. She could never have survived the beginning of the Christian era as a mere literary topos; but like the topos of personified Natura, she represented so much of universal human experience that she continued to live, even if in a frequently reinterpreted and modified form, throughout the Christian Middle Ages. Boethius, outwardly Christian, inwardly Stoic, in particular, helped give Fortuna, as modified by Christianity, powerful life. She appears to him and speaks:

> I turn my wheel in its ever changing circle, and it is my joy to bring the one on top to the bottom and the one on the bottom to the top. If you wish, get on the wheel, but with the understanding that when you fall down again according to the rules of my game, you will not consider it an injustice inflicted upon you. (*Consolatio Philosophiae* II, II, 28–31)

Here freedom of will is maintained since people can choose whether to trust the wheel or stay away from it, and thus the existence of a Christian Fortuna becomes possible for the first time. Moreover, in Boethius's *Consolatio* Fortune has for the first time a functional relationship with the wheel that prior to this was only one of her many attributes; she turns her wheel and watches its course. A Monte Cassino Boethius codex of 1100 shows the picture of the wheel of Fortuna, occupied by four kings, with the inscriptions: "regnabo" (for the rising king), "regno" (for the one on the throne), "regnavi" (for the one falling), and "sum sine regno" (for the one lying under the wheel). This became a standard model for the countless Latin and vernacular depictions of Fortuna in later literature and the visual arts. Richard Rolle, who some decades before the alliterative *Morte Arthure* meditated on the Wheel of Fortuna, offers an English example of this traditional four-part formula: "I regne shalle—I regne nobly—I falle — withouten regne am I."[2]

Certainly there had to be a far-reaching new interpretation and assimilation of the goddess Fortuna, in order that theologians might allow her a right to live under God's dominion in the medieval Christian region of demons and celestial intelligences that existed beneath Heaven. Thomas Aquinas rejected the goddess Fortuna, although he found her useful as a symbol for the apparently chaotic and, for man, incomprehensible distribution of good and bad fortune in the material world. He explains her rule through the Aristotelian "causa per accidens" ("cause by chance or accident"): what seems to be brought about by Fortuna has its true cause in itself and ultimately in God.[3]

Fortuna lives untouched by theological subtleties in folklore, art and literature, and there is often no clear distinction between allegorical abstraction and credible reality. Alan of Lille sketches a colorful picture of the princess Fortuna and her kingdom in the *Anticlaudian*[4] that seems almost heathen. Dante, on the other hand, creates the definitive Christian conception of Fortuna as a true "ancilla dei" ("maid-servant of God") who turns her wheel according to God's directions (*Inferno* VII, 61–97). At the same time he expands her function to the cosmic and universal dimensions of salvation and establishes the concept of the rise and fall of great men as part of the Christian interpretation of history. His definition of tragedy is generally valid for the Middle Ages and beyond: "tragoedia in principio est admirabilis et quieta, in fine sive exitu est foetida et horribilis" ("tragedy at the beginning is admirable and placid, but at the end or issue is foul and horrible").[5]

The tragic theme of an individual's rise and fall that is more or less clearly associated with the thought that earthly glory is in no way compatible with sinful pride and the hubris of Satan and that thus portrays the fall into misery as the punishment for these sins is behind the countless historical exempla in works concerned with Fortuna. Originally there are simple lists of the names of famous rulers; then, in Boccaccio's *De Casibus,* detailed descriptions of the lives and deaths—and of the sins—of these great men. These accounts are further developed by Boccaccio's successors, among them Lydgate. We frequently find exempla of Fortuna organized around the Nine Worthies, who are subdivided into three pagan (Hector, Alexander, Caesar), three Jewish (David, Joshua, Judas Maccabeus) and three Christian (Arthur, Charlemagne, Godfrey of Bouillon). We can again cite an English example, the dream vision *The Parlement of the Thre Ages* (ca. 1352–1370),[6] a work contemporary with *Piers Plowman* and possibly known to the author of the alliterative *Morte Arthure.* It tells of the fate of the Nine Worthies, who in spite of their earthly splendor fell without exception to death.

The Nine Worthies, augmented by other names including Merlin and Isolde, are found in the thirteenth-century Italian folk tale *Libro de Santo Justo paladino de Franza.*[7] This tale of Fortuna—one could just as easily call it a saint's legend—shows quite clearly the new roll of Christian Fortuna in leading men to salvation. The paladin Justo, accusing her for his great misfortune, seeks the improvement of his fate. She teaches him that every great man fell into death and destruction and that the worldly goods, riches, power, and beauty that he asks of her were the ruin of each. "Fleeting and frail is the life of man and of each worldly good" *(Ibid.)*. Deeply moved and converted, Justo arms himself with the spiritual virtues of obedience, humility, and chastity, and not with earthly goods. Resisting as a pious hermit the temptations of the devil, he is carried off to Heaven as a saint.

The golden wheel of Fortuna, which in an English monastery under the constant ringing of a little bell was turned by the monks "ad maioris excitationem devotionis" ("for the purpose of the exercise of greater devotion")[8] had the similar duty of awakening pious thoughts of rejection of this world and of hope for the next.

To be sure, the Janus-faced Fortuna does not completely lose her characteristic iridescent being; she appears as a radiant princess, comparable to the Queen of Heaven, and as a horrible Megaera and a deceitful devil, as mere allegory and as living, real figure, as both a lovely and a malicious creature; the heathen goddess of fate still often looks through the Christian robe. The Christian "ancilla dei" is, however, dominant throughout the Middle Ages: as servant of divine justice she leads men to salvation by turning their minds away from the vanity of earthly fortune toward eternity and by humbling the pride of the powerful through misfortune and death.

For comparison, the work of Machiavelli offers an example of the Renaissance conception of Fortuna that has been freed from the bonds of religion: his poem about Fortuna describes several wheels next to one another, and the clever individual is capable of deceiving Fortuna, as he leaps from one wheel to the other in order to remain at the top of the wheel and retain his good fortune (cf. *Principe,* chapter 25).

The most important literary forms for the presentation of Fortuna can be mentioned briefly. In addition to the moral tracts on Fortuna there is the dream vision or dream allegory, a genre that influenced by models from antiquity (Cicero's *Somnium Scipionis*) attained rich development in the Middle Ages *(Roman de la Rose)*. In these works the dreamer is led into the most splendidly described kingdom of Fortuna (Alanus, *Anticlaudian); frequently* there are complaints of misfortunes *(Lamenti)* or debates *(Altercationes),* often with the participation of a superior allegorical figure as arbiter ("Philosophy" in Boethius). These altercations are similar to the debates between Man and Death *(Ackermann aus Böhmen),* since both Fortuna and Death have the power to decide an individual's fate; indeed, Fortuna fulfills the work of Time and works hand in hand with Death.[9]

Fortuna enjoyed such popularity in the Middle Ages that there is scarcely a work of literature of any length in which her name is not at least mentioned. Thus Geoffrey's *Historia Regum Britanniae* (ca. 1136)[10] gives the old, unfortunate King Leir a lament about horrible Fortuna: "O irrevocabilia fatorum decreta, quae solito cursu fixum iter tenditis! . . . O irata fortuna! . . ." ("O irrevocable decrees of you fates who follow your preordained journey on an accustomed course! . . . O angry Fortuna!") (II, 12). Nevertheless, as noted above, Geoffrey, Wace, and Laȝamon do not mention Fortuna in the story of King Arthur. With all three authors the British kingdom begins with Brutus, the great-grandson of the Trojan Aeneas, and reaches its apex at the mid point of their books during the reign of Arthur; and yet, each has a different purpose and plan of organization.

Geoffrey intended his *Historia* as a historical work with a contemporary political message: the urgent need for unity and for strengthening the dynasty against the threat of civil war after the death of Henry I (1135).[11] Thus the ideal kingdom of the past, the kingdom of Arthur, and its collapse through the betrayal of the nephew Modred serve as an historical exemplum for the present. Geoffrey is not concerned with salvation history, but with political history, just as later English kings tried to justify political and dynastic claims by invoking the name of Arthur. Wace, as a Frenchman bound not to the English national interests but to the international ideal of the courtly knight, turns the learned historical work into an entertaining romance (ca. 1155). He refers to Fortuna several times, now together with her wheel: the lament of old Leir (ll. 1917 ff.) emphasizes her cruelty; the allusion to the Roman state, which has no counterpart in Geoffrey, demonstrates her inconstancy:

> De ceste ille Bretainne furent
> Belins e Brennes ki tant crurent . . .
> Fortune ad sa roe tornee
> E Rome rest esviguree. (ll. 3877–78, 3883–84)

("Belinus and Brennius who increased their power so much were from this British isle . . . [Fortuna had turned her wheel, and Britain rose and Rome fell from power. Now] Fortuna has turned her wheel and Rome is in turn strengthened.")[12]

Both references are presented as incidental remarks, within the bounds of rhetorical tradition, and they are insignificant so far as the outcome of the story is concerned. Nevertheless, Fortuna now has some relation to the misfortune of a king and the downfall of his kingdom (in Geoffrey and Wace), and the effect of what she does is clarified by the symbol of her wheel (in Wace). It is likely that both these details suggested the development of the theme of Fortuna and its application to King Arthur in the French *Mort*

Artu, just as the chivalric motif of the Round Table introduced by Wace is later given wider significance through its association with the Grail motif. Laȝamon's *Brut* (late twelfth to early- or mid-thirteenth century)[13] depicts a different, lost world. Laȝamon writes without any contemporary political purpose, but as an English patriot, who looks back to the glorious past in order to present to the English people an Arthur who is endowed with marvelous gifts and almost superhuman powers and who thus offers the historical exemplum of a national hero. The Germanic belief in fate is represented not by Christian Fortuna but by Merlin, who here acts as a mysterious and magical instrument of fate rather than as the almost omniscient advisor and helper that one finds in Geoffrey. The three authors intend Arthur to be an ideal ruler, the incarnation of the *regnum,* the prototype of noble knighthood, a national hero. This idealization of Arthur's character precludes any possibility of placing the figure of Arthur in the medieval Christian conception of tragedy, that "Fall from high to low," which Fortune causes as punishment for the sins of those who have climbed too high on her wheel. At this early stage Arthur is still glorified too much as hero of romance or national hero to be perceived as a tragic "casus" or exemplum with a religious and didactic significance. The consideration of his death as the result of guilt and punishment is still unthinkable.

The French *Mort Artu* (ca. 1230), the last part of the Prose *Lancelot* trilogy *(Lancelot, Queste del Saint Graal, Mort Artu),* takes the first step in this direction. This work centers on King Arthur, who in earlier works had been only the greatest of a long series of kings. It is not accidental that here for the first time the "Death of Arthur" appears as the title and from now on will be a part of the Arthurian story. The wheel of Fortuna, the central theme of the work, radiates an aura of fate, which directs the reader constantly to the death of the old king and the collapse of his kingdom. Here the "Fortuna of Death" plays her special role: "The tradition of Fortune's causing death is widespread and continuous, and takes an important place in all medieval elegiac poetry" (Patch, *op. cit.,* pp. 119–20). Fortuna and Death work together to take life and kingdom from Arthur.[14] In the dream he is enthroned on the highest seat of her wheel, and she speaks to him:

> "Voire, fet ele, tu le voiz, n'il n'i a granment chose dont tu n'aies
> esté sires jusques ci, et de toute la circuitude que tu voiz as tu esté
> li plus puissanz rois qui i fust. Mes tel sont li orgueil terrien qu'il
> n'i a nul si haut assiz qu'il ne le coviegne cheoir de la poesté del
> monde." Et lors le prenoit et le trebuschoit a terre si felenessement
> que au cheoir estoit avis au roi Artu qu'il estoit touz debrisiez et qu'il

perdoit tout le pooir del cors et des menbres.

("You see, there is nothing great over which until now you have not been ruler, and in the whole world, which you see, you have been the most powerful king that ever was. But thus is earthly pride, that no one is set so high, that he could not fall and lose his earthly power." And then she took him and threw him on the earth so roughly that it seemed to King Arthur that he was so injured from the fall that he had lost all power over his body and his limbs.)[15]

Arthur's dream of Fortuna is framed by two additional signs of disaster, which establish the gloomy atmosphere of death before the decisive battle against Modred on Salisbury Plain: the appearance of Gawain in a dream and the discovery of Merlin's prophetic inscription on a rock. In spite of the warnings of the Archbishop, who interprets the dreams and explains the inscription, Arthur fights the battle in which he receives his mortal wound. The dream of Fortuna symbolizes above all the fall of Arthur. However, it is still not the true medieval Christian tragic "casus," which clearly mirrors the causality of rise, guilt, and death. Although Fortuna alludes to the ominous nature of "earthly pride" and "earthly might," the destruction of the Round Table and the fall of the kingdom is caused not by Arthur's hubris, but by Lancelot's sinful love for Guinevere, the king's wife. The general significance of the *Mort Artu* lies in the fact that through the introduction and Christian interpretation of the Grail motif the redemption of secular Arthurian chivalry occurs through the new spiritual ideal of the Grail knights. The heroes of chivalric adventures fail on the Grail quest; they are humiliated and can not prevent the collapse of the Arthurian kingdom, because God no longer supports them. Other previously less prominent knights such as Galahad, Bors, and Perceval are privileged to recognize the deep mysteries of God. The *Mort Artu* presents not so much the individual tragedy of Arthur but, corresponding to religious concerns of the time, demonstrates the general tragedy of secular chivalry. This immutable general fate of a whole estate and way of life is here symbolized through Fortuna. In spite of the religious intention of the whole work, she proudly remains the player, a virtually independent executrix of Fate: "Sire, ce sont li geu de Fortune! . . ." (p. 218; "Sire, these are the games of Fortune").

The author of the alliterative *Morte Arthure* (ca. 1400),[16] probably a cleric and once thought to be the Scot Huchown, takes the decisive step toward an individual tragedy of Arthur that includes an exemplary "fall" and makes full use of the function of Christian Fortuna as one who urges men to repentance and conversion. The enthusiasm for heroic and national ideals that he shares with his predecessor Laȝamon is joined with the religious conceptions associated with Christian Fortuna. He takes the dream (ll. 3230–3455) from the *Mort Artu*[17] and expands it considerably (it runs to seven pages in the Brock edition) by describing the wonderful garden of Fortuna, her splendid clothing, and her wheel, by inserting that paradigm of destiny, the Nine Worthies,[18] who reveal their fates in impressive speeches, then by adding the dramatic dialogue between Fortuna and Arthur, and finally by giving the full explication of the philosopher, who uses the dream to guide Arthur toward salvation.

Within the story the dream appears in a different place than in *Mort Artu*. Arthur is not yet about to go into his final battle against Modred; in fact, he at this point knows nothing about Modred's betrayal and is still enjoying his good fortune with no premonition of the trouble to come. Because the Emperor Lucius demands tribute, he has gone to France and has defeated Lucius, and he now expects the Pope to offer him the emperor's crown before the gates of Rome. At this point in Laȝamon's account Arthur also had a dream that clearly foreshadowed Modred's rebellion and the infidelity of Queen Guinevere. If the poet had been concerned only with presenting a bad omen, he would simply have adapted the dream from Laȝamon. That he instead chose the dream of Fortuna reveals his intention to teach men something about the divine scheme of salvation. Structurally he makes the ominous dream of Fortuna, which points to death, a counterpart to a dream of a dragon, which pointed to victory before the battle against Lucius (ll. 757 ff.). Until the dream of Fortuna interrupts Arthur's streak of good luck, there is no intimation of the death of the king, since Merlin's prophecies of the earlier works are missing. The dream, however, marks the abrupt break in Arthur's good fortune, so that the structure of the alliterative *Morte Arthure* clearly reflects the tragic theme of rise and fall brought about by Fortuna. With its skilful arrangement of events, imaginative descriptions and dramatic heightening, this is indeed a work of considerable artistic merit. An analysis of the function of the dream of Fortuna in this poem is therefore necessary.

Arthur dreams that he is lost in the woods and, helpless, is attacked by fierce animals—an archetypal symbol for a dangerous situation in which one's fate is decided. Fleeing, he reaches the paradisaical garden of Fortuna, which in its colorful oriental splendor is clearly influenced by Alanus (ll. 3230–3249). Now Fortuna appears to him, as a splendid princess descending from the clouds: "Than discendis in the dale, downe fra the clowdezz, A duches dereworthily dyghte in dyaperde wediss . . ." (ll. 3250 ff.) This picture is reminiscent of portrayals of the Virgin Mary; the religious connotations of Christian Fortuna suggest the possibility of the amalgamation of both images[19] and the influence that poems about Mary and Fortuna had upon one another.

Fortuna turns a richly adorned wheel with her hands "as cho scholde" (l. 3260), that is, not according to her own arbitrary whim but according to a higher command, a first reference to her role as "ancilla dei." On the wheel are eight kings who later identify themselves, along with Arthur, as the Nine Worthies: Alexander, Hector, Caesar; Judas Maccabeus, Joshua, David; Charlemagne, Godfrey of Bouillon, and Arthur. Six of them suddenly fall off, their crowns broken, and each speaks the same words:

> That euer I regnede one thir rog, me rewes it euer!
> Was neuer roye so riche that regnede in erthe!
> Whene I rode in my rowte, roughte I noghte elles,
> But reuaye, and reuelle, and rawnsone the pople!
> And thus I drife forthe my dayes, whiles I dreghe myghte,
> And there-fore derflyche I am dampnede for euer! (ll. 3272–77)

Each considered himself to be the most powerful king on earth; however, Fortuna, the merciless leveler, overturns all, and they fall to death and damnation and must feel remorse for the continual dissipation and sin that they committed when they were at the height of their powers. In six individual speeches, which would impress listeners or readers through the striking contrast between past glory and present ruin, the kings express the morally instructive, exemplary significance of their "casus" (ll. 3284–3323). Two other kings now strive in vain to climb to the top of the wheel (ll. 3324–37); they are Charlemagne and Godfrey of Bouillon, who along with Arthur form the third group, the three Christian Worthies.

Here the poet encounters a difficulty. His nationalist pride and the fact that Arthur is the hero of both the poem and the dream demand that he be the last and greatest of the Nine Worthies to ascend the wheel. In order to draw attention away from this anachronism, he has Charlemagne and Godfrey, both of whom lived after Arthur, climb on the wheel before Arthur, but without reaching the throne at the top. In the philosopher's interpretation that follows the dream, the poet has the philosopher refer to the two other Christian Worthies by using the future tense: the one "salle Karolus be callide" (l. 3423) and "the tother salle be Godfraye" (l. 3430). These comments were suggested by the tradition of the wheel with the formula of four statements, which for the ascending king appeared in Richard Rolle as "I regne shalle." The anachronism is thus recognized but not eliminated, since when Arthur finally as the last fulfills the number of nine—"fore thy ffortune the fetches to fulfille the nowmbyre" (l. 3438)—it thus seems that Charlemagne and Godfrey have reached the throne on the wheel before him. The poet prefers to retain the anachronism than to abandon Arthur's preeminent position.[20] This is more than an anachronism, however, since the literary form of the dream vision in which it appears offers a revelation of the past, present, and future and with that an indication of the timeless, transcendental vision of the world and history. Thus the poet's concerns with both national and religious matters are shown in his treatment of the Nine Worthies. I shall now turn back to the actual presentation of the dream.

After the entrance of his eight predecessors, Arthur, dressed with royal insignia as a sign that he truly is ruler of the world (ll. 3338–60), is placed by Fortuna onto the throne of the wheel with all friendliness and favor. She promises him the possession of Rome, offers him exquisite fruits and delicious wine, indeed, even grants him her love (ll. 3361–81). After this high point of good fortune the Janus figure shows him her threatening, hostile face:

> Kyng, thow karpes for noghte, be Criste that me made!
> ffor thow salle lose this layke, and thi lyfe aftyre,
> Thow has lyffede in delytte and lordchippes inewe.

She immediately whirls the wheel around, and Arthur falls to the ground, breaks all of his limbs, and awakes full of fright (ll. 3382–92). Under the appointment of her creator Christ, Fortuna has revealed her second Christian face, the face of a warning and punishing power in the service of divine Providence, behind which the friendly smile of good fortune disappears as a deceptive mask. If riches and power were her first gifts, so death and damnation are her last.

The philosopher's interpretation that now follows plays a role similar to that of the allegorical figure who interprets events in other poems about Fortuna. Through direct speech the spiritual message achieves a strong impact. At the beginning and end stands the urgent admonition to repentance and conversion, between which the paradigms of the Nine Worthies are explained. The philosopher clearly states Arthur's sin: in his wanton greed for conquest he has shed much innocent blood:

> "Frekke," sais the philosophre, "thy fortune es passede! . . .
> Thow has schedde myche blode, and schalkes distroyede,

Sakeless, in cirquytrie, in sere kyngis landis;
Schryfe the of thy schame, and schape for thyne ende!"(ll. 3394–
99)

He must found abbeys in France and thus through active repentance
prepare for his certain death. However, now the poet shows himself to be a
Janus figure: his Christian piety must condemn Arthur's bloody acts of war;
his nationalist enthusiasm for heroic and chivalric achievements must glorify the same deeds. Two hearts beat in his breast: the one predicts eternal
damnation (l. 3386), the other eternal fame (l. 3445):

This salle in romance be redde with ryalle knyghttes,
Rekkenede and renownde with ryotous kynges,
And demyd on domesdaye, for dedis of armes
ffor the dougheste that euer was duelland in erthe,
So many clerkis and kyngis salle karpe of youre dedis,
And kepe your conquestez in cronycle for euer! (ll. 3440–45)

Now the philosopher briefly touches upon the present danger from which
the disaster will proceed, Modred's betrayal in England, and he concludes
his interpretation with repeated admonitions to repent and pray for God's
mercy: "Mane, amende thy mode, or thow myshappene, And mekely aske
mercy for mede of thy saule!" (ll. 3454–55). A re-examination of the dream
shows that its structure precisely mirrors the structure of the whole work
and with it that of the exemplary tragic "Fall from high to low." The transformation from the friendly to the angry Fortuna forms the climax and turning point of Arthur's fate (ll. 3382 ff.). Within the history of the Fortuna
figure the poet achieves the unique combination of the formula of the four
kings and the "Nine Worthies." Indeed the wheel with the four kings (cf.
Richard Rolle) and the account of the Nine Worthies (cf. *Parlement of the
Thre Ages*) were current themes. In accordance with his purpose of leading
men to salvation, the poet places the nine directly on the wheel, and in doing so explains in the clearest, strongest, and most concise way the lesson
of both themes. The story of the nine is narrated and at the same time en-
acted on the wheel—a striking "theatrum mundi"!

After the dream Arthur is disturbed by the predictions about his fate
(ll. 3464–67); he seems to take the warnings of Fortuna to heart and, like
the Paladin Justo of the previously mentioned Italian tale, wishes to devote
the rest of his life to pious preparation for death. There is, however, no sign
of conversion in the heroic and horrible deeds of the final battle against

Modred. Only afterwards, in the loneliness of the battle field, in the midst of his fallen knights, after he is mortally wounded, he prepares himself for grace. Trusting to God's mercy, he receives the sacrament and dies a truly Christian death with the words of Christ, "in manus," on his lips (ll. 4312–27). The apparent paradox of heroic and Christian elements next to one another can be explained. The heroic elements, inherent in the Arthurian story, particularly since Laʒamon, and strengthened by the nationalism of the Alliterative Revival, could not be completely sacrificed to the new Christian view of the poet, but they could be subordinated. Moreover, even the Christian point of view at times places a positive value on Arthur's heroic deeds, for instance in fighting the traitor and adulterer Modred, who now as a sacrilegious plunderer of monasteries and ally of pagan princes becomes the incarnation of evil. Without doubt the poet's chief concern was with the Christian view of salvation; that is the new interpretation that he adds to the old subject, and it has the final word. Through this interpretation Arthur receives a portrayal that is more deeply individualized than that of earlier works. The superhuman hero of the past becomes a Christian king with human failings and merits, the individual hero of a medieval Christian tragedy. The contradiction between the heroic and Christian view of the world is not completely eliminated, but this is not due to the incompetence of the poet but to the almost insoluble, even, in the modern sense, tragic problem of existence of the Christian knight, who is pulled between the world and God. He should serve God through his feats of arms; but in doing so he almost inevitably does wrong to the life and property of his fellow man.

Leaving the alliterative *Morte Arthure,* I shall briefly touch upon the use of the theme of Fortuna in other Arthurian works. The stanzaic *Morte Arthur* (ca. 1400)[21] and Malory's *Morte Darthur* (1469)[22] contain short versions of the dream of Fortuna (Bruce II, 3168–91; Vinaver, III, 1223.11–22) derived from the French *Mort Artu* rather than from the alliterative *Morte Arthure.* For both authors the dream represents only an incidental bad omen that has been transmitted from their source. The author of the stanzaic romance forgoes religious symbolism, since he wishes to narrate, in the manner of a minstrel, an interesting adventure; Malory omits it since he sees the fall of Arthur's kingdom resulting from the chivalric conflict of masculine loyalties and courtly love. A nostalgic look at the courtly ideal of the Round Table, prompted by a feeling of national pride, forms the chief impetus for his work.

However, the religious view is evident in some poems of the Alliterative Revival. The *Awntyrs off Arthure* (ca. 1400–1430),[23] written in imitation of the alliterative *Morte Arthure,* begins with a section in which moral and religious themes are emphasized. Gawain and Queen Guinevere are haunted by a frightening ghost while Arthur is out hunting. The apparition, which identifies itself later as the spirit of Guinevere's mother, has here taken on the function of the dream of Fortuna. She laments her sins—lechery and pride—which she committed while in the prime of her life; because of these she is now wretched and condemned to wandering about as a ghost and warns that, as the prophets teach, only humility and compassion can assure eternal salvation.

When Gawain considers an exemplary Christian way of life, he faces the crucial problem of the knight pulled between the world and God.[24] How can he fulfill the Christian ideal of life, if it is his profession to win fame through conquests and feats to arms?

> "How salle we fare," said the freke, "that fowndis to tyghte,
> That ofte foundis the folkes, in fele kyngis landis . . . ?" (st. XXI)

The ghost's answer ties in directly with the exemplum of the fall of King Arthur:

> Youre kynge es to couetous, I telle the, sir knyghte.
> Maye no mane stere hym of strenge, whilles the whele standis.
> When he es in his magestc hegheste, and maste es of myghte,
> He salle lighte fulle lawe, appone the see sandis . . .

As long as the wheel does not move,[25] his splendor seems secure; however, Fortuna, "that wondirfulle whele-wryghte," will overthrow him because of his greed for lands and his desire for conquest. After Arthur's greed for lands is condemned in the first, legendary part of the work, in the second, political part the question of the rightful possession of Scotland, which Arthur had conquered and given to Gawain, is settled by Gawain's duel with the Scottish knight Galleron. Through a peaceful arrangement, Arthur finally returns Scotland to Galleron as a fief, and Galleron becomes a knight of the Round Table, a kind of compromise for the conflicting religious and political views of the poet.

Death and Life (ca. 1450),[26] a dream allegory outside of the Arthurian tradition but with close affinities to the alliterative *Morte Arthure,* may again illustrate the previously mentioned relationship between Fortuna and Death. In a debate Death introduces himself as a servant of God, because through his intervention he keeps people from the most extreme wickedness. There the task of overthrowing the Nine Worthies, which is customarily given to

Fortuna (as in the *Parlement of the Thre Ages*), falls to Death, an indication that to a certain extent their functions are interchangeable.

In *Golagros and Gawain* (ca. 1470)[27] Arthur appears as a crusader, and the knight Golagros, whom Gawain has defeated, delivers a treatise on Fortuna that was probably influenced by the alliterative *Morte Arthure*. Fortuna has decided the duel between two equally noble and brave knights. Since here there can be no question of guilt and punishment, there is no possibility of presenting a tragic fall; there is only the insight that Fortuna, as a servant of Christ, sets limits for each individual:

> Quhat menis fortoune be skill,
> Ane gude chance or ane ill,
> Ilkane be werk and be will
> Is worth his rewarde. (ll. 1242–45)

Thanks to Arthur's generosity and Gawain's magnanimity Golagros's good fortune is restored. The romance ends not with death but with a nine-day feast.

Arthur's role as crusader in *Golagros* shows a further step in the direction of his becoming a kind of legendary Christian king. Arthur's battle against the oriental allies of Lucius in Geoffrey[28] provided a suggestion for the development of this legend. For its further development, misconceptions of geography (Geoffrey's "Aravius mons," VII, 85; X, 97) could have been responsible, as well as the fact that Arthur, in the group of the three Christian kings, was placed next to Charlemagne and Godfrey of Bouillon, both of whom, rightly or wrongly, were thought to be crusaders and were also described as such in the alliterative *Morte Arthure* (ll. 3422–35).

In the romance *Lancelot of the Laik* (ca. 1490)[29] we find not Fortuna herself, but the familiar motif of the interpretation of a dream with Arthur receiving religious and moral admonition and political instruction. First clerks and then Master Amytans, a special authority in this area, explain Arthur's disturbing dreams. He will fall into misfortune if the "water-lion," "leech," and "flower," representing God the Father, Christ, and Mary, do not help him. Eternal death is certain for him if he does not end the misery of his people and the oppression of the poor. Deeply dismayed by the incessant, powerful rebukes (that take up almost all of the second book), Arthur repents, confesses, and becomes a God-fearing king. This part of the work, whose artistic unity suffers from this extensive didacticism, points equally in the direction of the saint's legend and *speculum regis* literature.

These traits are even more pronounced in Lydgate's *Fall of Princes*,[30] which, although written earlier (ca. 1431), because of its general and far reaching significance for the medieval conception of history, can form the conclusion to this study. Using the *leitmotiv* of the transience of all earthly glory, Lydgate wants to record for the benefit of the princes of the present the tragedies of past princes caused by Fortuna. His definition of tragedy goes back beyond Boccaccio to Dante.[31]

However, these medieval Christian tragedies almost always implied the guilt of the hero. Lydgate acknowledges that Fortuna can bring about tragedy only because of "vicious lyvyng," that she has no power over good princes (II, 46). The goddess, who alternates between being an independent agent and a servant of divine justice, becomes very troubling for him (cf. III, 204–707; VI, 1–518). In any case, it is quite clear that the story of Arthur (VIII, 2661–3206), in contrast to that of the pagan princes, can not be a real tragedy: in a display of national and patriotic enthusiasm Lydgate can find no guilt in him. Guilt, in moral and religious terms, is attached only to the unnatural and horrible traitor Modred (VIII, 3165–178), against whom the full force of the accusation is directed. And while the fall of Arthur appears, in accordance with the plan of the whole work, in the long series of tragedies, he is actually portrayed in the tradition of the exemplary Christian king of the saint's legend. This is clearly shown in his final apotheosis: after his innocent death Arthur is taken up into Heaven, where he, as the greatest of the Nine Worthies, is enthroned in eternal glory (VIII, 3102–08). There is also a contemporary political allusion to the danger that the quarrels of highly placed relatives may bring to the kingdom and a nostalgic look back at the Round Table, which is seen as a moral and religious ideal (VIII, 3130–3206; cf. 2773–74). Thus the earlier religious, national, and chivalric trends in portraying Arthur, which often conflicted with one another, are brought together in Lydgate's idealized legendary figure. Arthur has been removed from the tragic causality of rise, guilt, and punishment, and Fortuna's envy (VIII, 2868 ff.) that leads to the fall of the British realm can only work through the misdeeds of others.

Looking back, we can see the absorbing historical spectacle of an almost cyclic change in the conception of Arthur under the influence of Fortuna. In Geoffrey, Wace, and Laȝamon national, chivalric, or heroic idealization excludes Fortuna. After an unobtrusive beginning in the French *Mort Artu* Fortuna, with her duty to warn and punish in order to lead to salvation, dominates the figure of Arthur, who thus becomes the hero of a tragic fall. At the same time a positive religious assessment of Arthur that points in the direction of the saints' legends begins to appear. Later writers develop with certain crucial changes the earlier characteristic features, and

Lydgate achieves their reconciliation through a renewed and more extensive idealization of Arthur.

NOTES

1. Cf. the instructive study by A. Doren that includes representation of Fortuna in pictorial art: *Fortuna im Mittelalter und in der Renaissance,* Vorträge der Bibliothek Warburg 1922–23, Pt. 1 (Leipzig and Berlin, 1924), p. 71; also see the study with extensive supporting material by H.R. Patch, *The Goddess Fortuna in Mediaeval Literature* (Cambridge, Mass., 1927).

2. Rolle, *Yorkshire Writers,* ed. C. Horstmann, (London, 1896), II, 70.

3. *Opera Omnia, jussu impensaque Leonis XIII, edita,* II, 77, 9.

4. Migne, *PL,* CCX, cols. 557–60.

5. *Epistola* X in *Dantis Alagherii Epistolae/ The Letters of Dante,* ed. and trans. Paget Toynbee (1920), 2nd ed. (Oxford, 1966), pp. 175, 200.

6. Ed. Sir I. Gollancz, SEEP, 1915. Cf. J.P. Oakden, *Alliterative Poetry in Middle English* (Manchester, 1935), p. 97. For the date, also see *Parlement of the Thre Ages,* ed. M.Y. Offord, EETS 246 (1959), pp. xxxvi–xxxvii; *Wynnere and Wastoure,* ed. Stephanie Trigg, EETS 297 (1990), pp. xxii–xxvii. For the "Nine Worthies," see also K.J. Höltgen, *"Die Nine Worthies,"* Anglia, 77 (1959), 279–309, and the definitive study by Horst Schroeder, *Der Topos der Nine Worthies in Literatur und bildender Kunst* (Göttingen, 1971).

7. "Beiträge zur älteren italienischen Volksdichtung IV, 2," *Zeitschrift für romanische Philologie,* LXIV (1944), 88. This includes further references to the Fortuna theme in literature.

8. Dugdale, *Monasticon Anglicanum,* I, 104; Gaidoz, *Rev. archéol.,* IV, 142 ff.

9. Dante, *Canzoni X,* 90. The less popular belief that Fortuna fears death alone is found in Watriquet de Couvin, *Dits,* ed. A. Scheler (Brussels, 1868), 77, 80.

10. Ed. J. Hammer (Cambridge, Mass., 1951).

11. W.F. Schirmer, "Geoffrey of Monmouth as a Political Writer," Address delivered to the International Association of University Professors of English (Cambridge, 1956); now in Schirmer, *Die frühen Darstellungen des Arthurstoffes* (Köln-Opladen, 1958).

12. Ed. I. Arnold (Paris, 1938–40). [Although "esviguree" can mean "weakened" (see Frédéric Godefroy, *Dictionnaire de l'ancienne langue française,* 3 [Paris, 1884; rpr. New York, 1961], 668b), its more common meaning is "strengthened"; and in the context in which it appears at this point in Wace's account, it appears to mean the latter: Caesar is here referring to the conquests of Belinus and Brennius as having occurred long ago and to people once again paying tribute to Rome. The passage indicates that although Fortuna has now turned her wheel in Rome's favor, she had once cast Rome down in favor of the British.—E.D.K.]

13. Ed. Sir F. Madden (London, 1847). For the date of Laȝamon's *Brut,* see E.G. Stanley, "The Date of Laȝamon's Brut," *Notes and Queries,* 213 (1968), 85–88; Françoise Le Saux, *Layamon's Brut: The Poem and its Sources* (Cambridge, 1989), pp. 1–13.

14. This conception would be supported by C.L. Brown's view that the Arthurian works still preserve traces of an old Celtic version, according to which Arthur's real opponent was "the principle of evil or death." ("Arthur's Loss of Queen and Kingdom," *Speculum* 15 [1940], 3). Brown's thesis, however, based chiefly on a few names and etymological speculations, seems weak.

15. Ed. J. Frappier (Paris, 1936), 3rd ed. (Geneva and Paris, 1964), p. 227. [The English translation is E.D.K.'s translation of Professor Höltgen's German translation of the French text that appeared in the original article.]; also see Frappier's study,

Étude sur la Mort le Roi Artu (Paris, 1936).

16. Ed. E. Brock, EETS OS 8 (1865). For the date, see Larry D. Benson, "The Date of the *Alliterative Morte Arthure,*" *Medieval Studies in Honor of Lillian Herlands Hornstein,* ed. J.B. Bessinger, Jr. and R.K. Raymo (New York, 1976), pp. 19–40; and Mary Hamel, ed., *Morte Arthure* (New York, 1984), pp. 53–58.

17. P. Branscheid overlooked the *Mort Artu* in his investigations of the sources of the alliterative *Morte Arthure* (*Anglia* 8 [1885], *Anzeiger,* 179) and could determine no definite source for the dream of Fortuna.

18. The author of the alliterative *Morte Arthure* seems to have derived the Nine Worthies from Longuyon's Alexander romance *Voeux du Paon* (ca. 1300) rather than from the previously mentioned *Parlement of the Thre Ages.*

19. In Hary's *Wallace* (VII, 90–132) the clerk who is to interpret the appearance of a lovely lady in a dream says:

> I can nocht witt quhat qweyn at it suld be,
> Quhethir fortoun, or our lady so fre.

See *Hary's Wallace,* ed. Matthew P. McDiarmid, 2 vols., Scottish Text Society, 4th series 4, 5 (Edinburgh, 1968), Vol. 1, p. 142. Cf. Patch, *op. cit.,* p. 61.

20. Caxton shows the same feeling of pride in the national hero in the Preface to Malory's *Morte Darthur,* whose publication he justified by pointing out that Arthur, the English king, had been the noblest and greatest of the Nine Worthies (*The Works of Sir Thomas Malory,* ed. E. Vinaver, 3 vols., 3rd rev. ed., P.J.C. Field [Oxford, 1990], p. cxliii).

21. Ed. J.D. Bruce, EETS ES LXXXVIII.

22. See n. 20 above.

23. Ed. F.J. Amours, *Scottish Alliterative Poems,* STS 27, 28. The *Awntyrs* was once tentatively dated ca. 1380 on the basis of allusions to hunting, armor, and costume that suggested the end of the reign of Edward III or the beginning of the reign of Richard II; Ralph Hanna, however, suggests in his edition that it was written ca. 1400–30 (*The Awntyrs off Arthure at the Terne Wathelyn* [Manchester, 1974], pp. 50–52).

24. How to combine service to God and service to the world is also a major concern in Middle High German chivalric poetry of the *Blütezeit* (Wolfram von Eschenbach, Hartmann von Aue, Walther von der Vogelweide).

25. The presentation of the motionless wheel goes back to Hildebert of Lavardin: "Stante rota Fortuna favet" (While the wheel stands still, Fortuna is favorable"; Migne, *PL* CLXXI, col. 1424 A).

26. Ed. Sir I. Gollancz, SEEP, 1930.

27. Ed. M. Trautmann, *Anglia* 2 (1879), 395.

28. Cf. J.S.P. Tatlock, "Certain Contemporaneous Matters in Geoffrey of Monmouth," *Speculum* 6 (1931), 206.

29. Ed. W. Skeat, EETS 6.

30. Ed. H. Bergen, EETS ES CXXI-CXXIV. Cf. W.F. Schirmer, *John Lydgate* (Tübingen, 1952).

31. W.F. Schirmer, "Lydgates Fall of Princes," *Anglia,* 69 (1950), 301.

MALORY'S KING MARK
AND KING ARTHUR

Edward Donald Kennedy

Readers with preconceptions of King Arthur as a great king are sometimes disappointed by Malory's Arthur and find him an inconsistent blend of strengths and weaknesses. Although most critics believe that Malory admired Arthur,[1] some have argued that Malory intentionally presented him as a weak king largely responsible for the downfall of his realm. In the words of one critic, "When one looks at the King's real actions, one may wonder indeed how he ever got his splendid reputation."[2] Such statements fail to give sufficient weight to Malory's praise for Arthur throughout his book as the "floure of kyngis" who does his "trew parte" in battle as a "noble kynge" should, as a king praised above all others as the "moste man of worshyp crystynde," whose "grete goodnes" caused the Pope to attempt to end the war between him and Lancelot.[3] Since no one has been able to argue that Malory created a narrator whose words are to be interpreted ironically, the logical conclusion is that although Arthur, like the other major characters—Lancelot, Guenevere, and Gawain—makes mistakes that contribute to the tragic destruction of his kingdom, Malory nevertheless had much greater admiration for him than some readers do.

I have elsewhere suggested that Malory was initially influenced by the positive portrait of Arthur found in English chronicles and because of this coped as best he could with the often negative portrait found in his sources.[4] Here I shall suggest ways in which the tyrant Mark (Marc) that Malory found in the French prose *Tristan* influenced the way Malory changed the portrait of Arthur that he found in one of his major sources, the French Vulgate *Mort Artu*. In fact, the often weak, vacillating King Arthur of the *Mort Artu* was, as Jean Frappier has shown, influenced by the portrait of

Revised by the author from "Malory's King Mark and King Arthur"; originally published in *Mediaeval Studies*, 37 (1975), 190–234; © 1975 by the Pontifical Institute of Mediaeval Studies, Toronto.

Mark found in some versions of the Tristan story.[5] Thus Malory would have found in this French source an Arthur who was at times quite similar to Mark, and while Malory retains the portrait of Mark as "le plus mescheant de tous les rois" ("the most wicked of all kings"),[6] his changes suggest that he wished to present in Arthur a sharply contrasting king.

MALORY'S KING MARK

Mark in the French prose *Tristan*[7] epitomizes the most salient characteristics of a tyrant. Although Mark's kingdom of Cornwall is dependent upon Tristan's ability to defend it, Mark repeatedly disregards Tristan's value to his realm and tries to have his nephew killed because of his jealousy over Tristan's love for his wife Isode. Mark appears as a ruler who lives for his *bonum privatum* instead of the *bonum commune,* who is dominated by feelings of hatred, envy, jealousy, and fear, who punishes according to his own whims, who acts treacherously, who starts a foreign war to keep his people from turning against him, and who, as a result of his actions, loses the best knight in his kingdom and faces a civil war.

In the early part of Malory's fifth tale and in the corresponding section of the French *Tristan* Mark does not display his treacherous nature. Instead, like a good king he appreciates Tristram's value to his realm.[8] Tristram is the hero of Cornwall, who saves the kingdom by mortally wounding Marhalte, the champion of Ireland. After Tristram is injured fighting Marhalte, "kynge Marke and all hys barownes" were "passynge hevy"; and when he recovers, King Mark was "passynge glad, and so were all the barownes."[9]

In both Malory and the source, however, personal animosity soon takes precedence over Mark's concern for the *bonum commune:* there arises "a jolesy and an unkyndenesse betwyxte kyng Marke and sir Trystrames," for they both fall in love with the same lady, the wife of Sir Segwarydes (p. 393; MS Bibliothèque Nationale Fr. 103, fols. 44r-v). Ignoring Tristram's defeat of Marhalte and overwhelmed by jealousy, Mark considers Tristram an enemy and unsuccessfully tries to kill him by treacherously attacking him at night.[10] He fails in his attempt, but "as longe as kynge Marke lyved he loved never aftir sir Trystramys" (p. 396; MS 103, fol. 46v). Mark's actions display the selfish motives of a tyrant and foreshadow his later reactions to Tristram's love for Isode.

Disregarding Tristram's value to his realm, Mark persists in his attempt to dispose of him. He sends Tristram to Ireland to bring Isode back as his queen because he knows that the relatives of Marhalte will attempt to avenge their kinsman and kill Tristram: "all this was done to the entente to sle sir Trystramys" (p. 403). This plan is taken with little change from Malory's French source; although Vinaver and Rumble maintain that the plan in the French *Tristan* was developed by the barons, the extant manuscript closest to Malory's text makes it clear that in the source as in Malory, Mark is the one who wants to kill Tristram.[11] In both Malory's version and the source, Tristram safely returns to Cornwall with Isode and gives her to Mark as a bride even though Tristram and Isode have by this time fallen in love.

Soon after the marriage Mark's role as a suspicious and jealous tyrant becomes more pronounced. Seeing Tristram and Isode sitting together in a window and taking "a swerde in his honde," he attempts to kill him. When Tristram takes the sword away from Mark, the King, ignoring in his rage Tristram's importance to the kingdom, orders his men to "sle this traytowre." But "there was nat one that wolde meve for his wordys." The men's inaction clearly illustrates the medieval political belief that a subject can forcibly resist the unjust demands of a tyrant; and it foreshadows a more serious rebellion against Mark later. Tristram threatens to strike the king; Mark flees, but Tristram pursues him, gives him "fyve or six strokys flatlynge in the necke," and rides into the forest with his men (p. 426). In the source Tristram at this point also threatens to kill Mark (MS l03, fol. 70r), but Malory omits this and thus makes Tristram less reprehensible. Mark asks his barons what he should do; they advise him to ask Tristram to return, and Dynas the Seneschal warns Mark of the probable consequence if he does not: ". . . many men woll holde with sir Trystrames and he were harde bestadde. . . . we know none so good a knyght but yf hit be sir Launcelot du Lake. And yff he . . . go to kyng Arthurs courte . . . he woll so frende hym there that he woll nat sette by your malyce" (p. 427). Mark, seeing the advisability of this warning, asks that Tristram be sent for so "that we may be frendys."[12] A comparison with the source shows that what is most original about Malory's version is the comparison of Tristram with Lancelot and the statement that a knight of Tristram's prowess would be welcome at Arthur's court.[13] The scene emphasizes both the support Tristram has among Mark's knights and Tristram's value to the realm, and it implies that if Mark alienates Tristram, "many men woll holde with sir Trystrames" and civil war will ensue. Mark in both Malory and the source wisely decides to forgive Tristram. This is one of the few occasions when Mark acts wisely as a ruler and places the good of his realm first. His kingly behavior here, however, is soon negated.

A later scene that occurs in both Malory's fifth tale and the source further illustrates Tristram's value to the *bonum commune* and consequently focuses attention upon the distinction between Mark as a wronged husband who might justifiably hate Tristram and Mark as a king who should value Tristram's past service to Cornwall and judge him unemotionally for the good of the realm. Tristram and Isode are found together in bed, and Tristram is condemned to death "by the assent of kynge Marke and of sir Andret and of som of the barownes." In both Malory's account and the French source, Tristram speaks of the past deeds he has done for Cornwall: "Remembir what I have done for the contrey of Cornwayle, and what jouparté I have been in for the wele of you all . . . . I was promysed to be bettir rewarded."[14] Tristram's speech stresses his value to the kingdom; subsequent events show that Mark, as a king, should have remembered these deeds and ignored the adultery with Isode.

Although Tristram at this time escapes from Mark, he is later captured and taken back to court. Mark has a trial for Tristram, but his manner of judging is a travesty of justice. Mark wants his barons to decide the case in a way that will gratify his desire for vengeance, and he does not give them much choice; he "lete calle hys barownes to geve jugemente unto sir Trystramys to the dethe." The barons, however, "wolde nat assente thereto" and instead advise that Tristram be banished for ten years (pp. 502–03). Malory appears to have given Mark a more villainous role here; in the source instead of wanting to have Tristram killed, Mark ignores Andret's advice to kill Tristram and instead wants to have him exiled forever.[15] When Tristram is preparing to leave Cornwall, he again emphasizes his past services to the realm: his battle against Marhalte; the trip to Ireland to bring Isode to Mark; the battles against Bleoberys, Blamoure de Ganys, Lamarok, the King with the Hundred Knights, the King of North Gaul, the giant Tauleas, and the battle against Palomydes to save Isode. He adds, "And many othir dedys have I done for hym, and now have I my waryson! . . . And telle kynge Marke that many noble knyghtes of the Rounde Table have spared the barownes of thys contrey for my sake" (pp. 503–04). Malory appears to have lengthened the list of heroic deeds that Tristram mentions in order to stress Tristram's value to Cornwall and to emphasize the folly of Mark's desire to execute him.[16]

Subsequent events illustrate the tyrant's fear and jealousy of others and the danger of placing desire for personal vengeance above the welfare of the kingdom. After Tristram leaves Cornwall, he goes to Arthur's court and wins fame as a knight. When Arthur's nephew Gaherys comes to Mark's court and tells of Tristram's success, Mark "in hys harte . . . feryd sore that sir Trystram sholde gete hym such worship in the realme of Logrys wherethorow hymselff shuld nat be able to withstonde hym" (p. 545; MS

334, fol. 265v). When Sir Uwayne challenges all the knights of Cornwall, the king at first has no knight to answer the challenge; Mark's nephew Andret and Dynas the Seneschal finally accept but are defeated (pp. 545–46). As Gaherys points out, Mark's vengeance has deprived Cornwall of the one man capable of saving it from dishonor: "Sir kynge, ye ded a fowle shame whan ye flemyd sir Trystram oute of thys contrey, for ye nedid nat to have doughted no knyght and he had bene here" (p. 547; MS 334, fol. 269ra). Uwayne's success, however, does not teach Mark anything, and he persists in his hatred of Tristram.

Malory begins the "King Mark" subdivision by reminding his readers of Mark's "grete dispyte" and "grete suspeccion unto sir Trystram bycause of his quene . . . for hym semed that there was much love betwene them twayne" (p. 577; MS 334, fol. 302va). A little later Lamarok condemns Mark for driving Tristram, "the worshypfullyst knyght that now is lyvynge" from Cornwall "for the jeleousnes of his quene" (p. 580). Malory seems to have added Lamarok's statement about Mark's "jeleousnes,"[17] a statement that emphasizes Mark's concern for his wife, his interest in his *bonum privatum,* and not in the *bonum commune* of the realm.

Another scene in both Malory's fifth tale and his source further illustrates Mark's treachery and selfish concerns. When Mark's spies tell him of Tristram's heroic accomplishments in England, Mark, with no regard for the law or justice, sets out to "destroy sir Trystram by some wylys other by treson." After he tells two knights of his plan, one of them, Bersules, rebukes him: "Sir Trystram is the knyght of worshyp moste that we knowe lyvynge. . . . I woll not consente to the deth of hym, and therefore I woll yelde hym my servyse and forsake you." Although Mark has been personally wronged by Tristram, he acts "shamfully" as a king in seeking vengeance on such a "knyght of worshyp." After Bersules rebukes Mark, the king displays the impulsiveness for which tyrants were noted by drawing his sword and killing Bersules. When the other knight Amant and his squires see that "vylaunce dede," they say: "Hit was foule done and myschevously, wherefore we woll do you no more servyse." Mark then becomes "wondirly wrothe" and tries to kill Amant, but he and the squires "sette nought by his malyce" (p. 578; MS 334, fol. 303rb-va). Like the previously cited passage in which Mark's men refuse to attack Tristram, this scene presents the individual's right to disobey a tyrant's evil command: "I woll . . . forsake you"; "we woll do you no more servyse." It also anticipates the later rebellion that Mark has to face.

After Mark arrives at Arthur's court, Arthur rebukes him: "Ever ye have bene ayenste me and a dystroyer of my knyghtes." Mark, however, "a fayre speker and false thereundir," falls "flatte to the erthe at kynge Arthurs feete," promises to "make a large amendys," and wins Arthur's trust.[18] Arthur tries to make peace between Mark and Tristram and asks Mark to be a "good lorde unto sir Trystram," and to "cherysh hym." Mark swears to do this, and he and Tristram, supposedly reconciled, return to Cornwall. At this point, however, Malory emphasizes Mark's tyrannous duplicity: "But for all this kynge Marke thought falsely, as hit preved aftir; for he put sir Trystram in preson, and cowardly wolde have slayne hym" (pp. 608–09; MS 334, fol. 330vb).

Soon after Mark and Tristram reach home, an event occurs which again shows Tristram's value to the realm and Mark's inability to set aside personal enmity. An army from "Syssoyne" invades Cornwall, and Tristram is needed to defend the realm; at first, however, Mark "wolde nat sende for sir Trystram, for he hated hym dedly." Because his council warns, "Ye muste sende for sir Trystram . . . other ellys they woll never be overcom," Mark finally asks Tristram to fight for Cornwall, but he is still "full lothe thereto." After Tristram fights for the kingdom in battle (pp. 618–19; MS 99, fol. 365vb), Elyas, the leader of the enemy, challenges Mark to send him a champion for single combat. Mark's other knights find this preferable to another full-scale battle: "To fyght in a fylde we have no luste, for had nat bene the proues of sir Trystram, hit hadde been lykly that we never sholde have scaped"; but none of the knights will volunteer to fight the champion of Syssoyne. Mark is forced to admit "than am I shamed and uttirly distroyed, onles that my nevew sir Trystram wolde take the batayle uppon hym" (p. 623; cf. MS 99, fol. 373r). Tristram agrees to fight Elyas and once again saves Cornwall. Malory adds the comment, "Yett for all this kynge Marke wolde have slayne sir Trystram" (p. 626; not in source), thus implying that in spite of the affair with Isode, Mark should have considered Tristram's heroism and set aside his enmity.

Mark persists in his villainy, and his efforts to kill Tristram have serious consequences for both himself and the realm. Malory begins the "Joyous Garde" subdivision of the fifth tale by having Mark attempt to have Tristram killed in a tournament; this attempt on Tristram's life was apparently not in Malory's sources and is one of the instances in which Malory seems to have actually blackened Mark's character.[19] In both Malory's account and the source, Mark then drugs Tristram and puts him "in a stronge preson," an act which produces immediate political repercussions in the realm. Hearing what the king has done, one of Mark's knights first attempts to assassinate him (p. 676; MS 99, fol. 398r), and, failing to do that, stirs up rebellion against him. Sir Dynas also defies "suche a kynge" and renounces loyalty to him; and "all maner knyghtes seyde as Sir Dynas sayde." The angry knights soon fortify towns and castles and raise an army to overthrow their king (p. 677; MS 99, fol. 398va). Thus the result of Mark's desire for personal vengeance against the best knight of his realm is civil war.

To solve the problem, Mark establishes a crisis; he tries to unite his people by calling them to war in the Holy Land. Mark has "countirfete lettirs from the Pope" written which order the army of Cornwall "to go to Jerusalem for to make warre uppon the Saresyns." He offers to release Tristram from prison if he will "go warre uppon the myscreauntes"; but Tristram is not deceived and says to Mark's clerk: "I woll nat go at his commaundemente! . . . for I se I am well rewarded for my trewe servyse." When the clerk returns with a second group of counterfeit letters, he gets a similar rebuff (pp. 677–78). The major change that Malory appears to have made here is that in his version both sets of letters are counterfeit; in the French *Tristan*, the first ones are genuine, but Tristan does not believe that the Pope would send letters to the "felon traitre roy marc" ("wicked traitor King Mark").[20] Tristram's statement about his "trewe servyse" also seems to be original with Malory and further emphasizes Tristram's importance to the realm.

Mark's ruse fails and the rebellion continues; some of his men ask, "Kynge, why fleyste thou nat? For all this contrey ys clyerly arysen ayenste the" (p. 678; MS 99, fol. 399rb). At this point Perceval arrives in Cornwall and after freeing Tristram tells Mark that "he had done hymselff grete shame for to preson sir Trystram so, 'for he is now the knyght of moste reverence in the worlde. . . . And yf he woll make warre uppon you, ye may nat abyde hit.'" Mark replies, "That is trouthe, . . . but I may nat love sir Trystram, bycause he lovyth my quene, La Beall Isode" (p. 679). In the source Perceval reminds Mark of the services Tristram has done for him and of the danger of offending him, but Mark's reply appears to be original with Malory.[21] This addition is important, for it shows that Mark is more concerned about Tristram's love for Isode than about a potentially disastrous civil war, and he is more willing to risk the destruction of his kingdom than forget a personal wrong.

Although Mark promises Perceval "never by no maner of meanys to hurte sir Trystram," as soon as Perceval leaves, the king thinks "of more treson"; and, finding Tristram with Isode, "by treson Kynge Marke . . . put hym in preson, contrary to his promyse that he made unto sir Percivale" (pp. 679–80; MS 99, fol. 399vb). Isode, however, hearing of this, has Dynas capture Mark and imprison him; then she and Tristram escape to Arthur's kingdom.[22] Thus the story of Mark in the fifth tale ends with the king in prison as a just reward for his tyrannous acts.

The narrative in both Malory and the source shows that Mark and Cornwall need Tristram and that although Mark as a husband has ample reason for hating Tristram, as a king he is wrong in trying to destroy him. Tristram's valor saves Cornwall from enemies like Marhalte and Elyas; his forced absence results in disgrace for Cornwall because Mark has no champion to defend it; and his imprisonment causes a civil war.

Mark's inadequacy as a king is revealed not only by his attacks upon Tristram but also by his relationship with others. He is reviled as a "grete enemy to all good knyghtes" (p. 580; similarly MS 334, fol. 305v) and a "dystroyer of good knyghtes" (p. 582; similarly MS 334, fols. 308vb-309r). At one point Mark secretly rides after Uwayne, smites him "allmoste thorow the body," and leaves him to die (p. 547; MS 334, fol. 270r-v). Shortly after this, he and Sir Andret attack Kay and Gaherys; and Gaherys turns on them and says, "Ye ar false traytours, and false treson have ye wrought undir youre semble chere that ye made us. For hit were pité that ye sholde lyve ony lenger" (pp. 548–49; MS 334, fol. 277ra). The political sentiments expressed here in both Malory and his source are the same: a king who is treacherous deserves to die. Mark's lack of chivalry and cowardice is emphasized by the knight Berluse: "ye slew my [fader] traytourly and cowardly . . . ye ar the moste vylaunce knyght of a kynge that is now lyvynge, . . . and all that ye do is but by treson" (p. 582; MS 334, fols. 308vb-9ra). Later after Berluse has been overcome in combat by Dynadan, Mark tries to kill him; for "this kynge Marke was but a murtherer."[23] Dynadan later angrily tells him, "Ye ar full of cowardyse, and ye ar also a murtherer, and that is the grettyst shame that ony knyght may have."[24]

Mark's jealousy is not restricted to sexual jealousy, and he epitomizes the tyrant's fear of others who might be more powerful or who might detract from his own glory. Some of his animosity toward Tristram, for example, is motivated by his fear of Tristram's prowess. Such fear is further shown in the story of Alexander the Orphan in the fifth tale. In this story Mark has a brother, Bodwine, "that all the peple of the contrey loved." When Cornwall is invaded by Saracens, Bodwine raises an army and defeats the invaders. Hearing of his brother's heroism, Mark "was wondirly wrothe that his brother sholde wynne suche worship and honour. And bycause this prynce was bettir beloved than he in all that contrey, and also this prynce Bodwyne lovid well sir Trystram, . . . he thought to sle him." Mark then plots to kill Bodwine, his wife, and their young son "for he was the falsist traytour that ever was borne." When Bodwine comes to dinner, Mark accuses him of raising an army "to wynne worship from me and put me to dishonoure."

He then "stroke hym to the herte wyth a dagger" (pp. 633–34).

The only known version of the prose *Tristan* that comes close to this is the account given in MS Bibliothèque Nationale Fr. 362.[25] Malory seems to have added the statement about the brother being a friend of Tristram, and he also seems to have given Mark a more specific and political reason for murdering his brother. Although in both cases the murder is caused by jealousy of the brother's popularity, in Malory's account the brother is a hero who, like Tristram, saves the country from foreign invasion. Malory indicates, moreover, that the Saracen invasion occurs "sone aftir these Sessoynes were departed" (p. 633). The Sessoynes were the invaders that Tristram had defeated after which Mark had tried to dispose of him. The Bodwine episode thus underlines Mark's disregard for those who work for the good of the country and further shows that Mark, controlled by his passions, tries to destroy the men that Cornwall needs most. In the case of Tristram, Mark is motivated primarily by jealousy over Isode, but his anger when he hears of Tristram's success at Arthur's court also indicates his jealousy of Tristram's prowess and his fear of retribution. In the case of Bodwine, Mark is again angry that someone other than himself "sholde wynne suche worship and honour." What he overlooks is the "trew servyse" of these two men to Cornwall; his concern is only with his *bonum privatum* and not with the *bonum commune* of the realm.

Mark's treatment of Bodwine and Tristram shows disregard not only for two champions of his realm but also for two kinsmen, his brother and his nephew; Mark should have been loyal to both men, not only because of their service to his kingdom but because of the blood bond between them. Malory, in fact, at least twice emphasizes Mark's neglect of his blood bond with Tristram. Malory says that Mark "chaced hym [Tristram] oute of Cornwayle (yette was he nevew unto kynge Mark)" (p. 577; not in source), and Perceval rebukes Mark for mistreating his nephew: "for shame . . . for ar nat ye uncle unto sir Trystram?"[26] Later in the story of the King of the Red City in the fifth tale Malory added references that were not in his source to the importance of ties of kinship: a ruler is destroyed because he neglects the lords "of his owne bloode"; one of his subjects says, "And all kyngis and astatys may beware by oure lorde; for he was destroyed in his owne defaute; for had he cheryshed his owne bloode, he had bene a lyvis kynge."[27] Malory may have added the emphasis upon the blood bond to the story of the King of the Red City in order to draw a parallel between that king's fate and Mark's. As will be shown later, Malory placed great importance on blood ties, and Mark was wrong to violate them.

Malory found most of Mark's villainy in his source; the additions that

Malory may have made—Mark's attempts to have Tristram executed, his hope that Tristram would be killed in the tournament, his counterfeiting both sets of letters from the Pope, the comments of Lamarok and Mark that emphasize Mark's love for Isode, the political reason for his hatred of his brother Bodwine, and his failure to regard his blood ties with Tristram and Bodwine—are not nearly as significant as the tyrannical aspects of Mark's character that appear in the source. The picture of Mark that the source provided must have suited Malory's purposes, and he saw little reason to make drastic changes in Mark's character. Of the changes that he did make, the most interesting are those that emphasize Mark's love for Isode and his disrespect for blood ties, for these changes suggest that while writing the fifth tale Malory had some interest in the political nature of Mark's role as king.

Malory found in the concluding section of the prose *Tristan* the culminating instance of Mark's villainy: the king discovers Tristram and Isode together and treacherously stabs Tristram in the back. Although Malory ends his fifth tale with Tristram and Isode together and omits most of the final part of his French source, he nevertheless works the murder of Tristram into his narrative at three different points. He first mentions it rather early in the fifth tale, concluding the story of Alexander the Orphan with a statement apparently not in his source: "this false kynge Marke slew bothe sir Trystram and sir Alysaundir falsely and felonsly."[28] But the most detailed accounts of the murder occur not in the fifth tale, but in the final tales, 7 and 8.

In the seventh tale Malory gives an account of the murder in his story of Sir Urry, for which there is no known source. Malory writes: "that traytoure kynge slew . . . sir Trystram as he sate harpynge afore hys lady, La Beall Isode, with a trenchaunte glayve." Malory at this point also tells of the fate of Mark: "Sir Bellynger revenged the deth of . . . sir Trystram, for he slewe kynge Marke" (pp. 1149–50). Although Malory would have found Tristram's murder in the prose *Tristan,* the account of the retributive slaying of Mark is not in any of the known versions of the *Tristan,* but it could have been suggested by his source for the first tale, the *Suite du Merlin.*[29] Malory thus lets his readers know that Mark's reward for his villainy is death, and he expresses no disapproval over the tyrannicide.

Malory adds the third account of the murder to his final tale; this account offers an explicit contrast between Mark and Arthur, a contrast that does not appear in Malory's sources. Lancelot's kinsman Bors, fearing that Guenevere will be burnt at the stake, suggests that Lancelot rescue her and take her back to Arthur when the king is no longer angry. Lancelot is reluctant to do this: "for by sir Trystram I may have a warnynge: for whan . . . sir Trystram brought agayne La Beall Isode unto kynge Marke . . . that false traytour kyng Marke slew hym as he sate harpynge afore hys lady." Bors replies: "All thys ys trouthe . . . but there ys one thyng shall corrayge you and us all: ye know well kynge Arthur and kynge Marke were never lyke of conducions, for there was never yet man that ever coude preve kynge Arthure untrew of hys promyse" (p. 1173; not in source). Bors's faith in Arthur is justified, for after Guenevere's rescue by Lancelot Arthur is willing to take the queen back and make peace with Lancelot (p. 1190). Mark reacts to the love affair by taking vengeance and killing his best knight; Arthur's attitude toward the affair between Lancelot and Guenevere shows willingness to forgive. Mark and Arthur, as Bors' comparison clearly shows, are quite different types of kings.

MALORY'S KING ARTHUR

Malory's Arthur has many of the best traits of the medieval ruler: interest in the common good, love of his men, courage, concern for law, a sense of justice. Although Malory found some of these traits in the Arthur of his sources, he added some to make Arthur appear in many ways a better king than he was in the sources. Arthur is a main character in only four of Malory's eight tales: 1, 2, 7, and 8; in the central tales he is in the background. Malory relies far less upon his sources in presenting the Arthur of Tales 7 and 8 than he did in presenting the Arthur of Tales 1 and 2. In discussing Malory's freer use of his sources in the final tales, Vinaver finds "a consistent, though somewhat slow, evolution towards a higher degree of independence in the interpretation of the narrative material, and even in the refashioning of that material for purposes of reinterpretation" (p. 1624). Development and reinterpretation of Arthur's role as king are especially important in Tales 7 and 8 and when he briefly appears in Tale 6. Although Malory derived some of his ideas from his sources, the Arthur of these final tales is more Malory's own creation than is the Arthur of the early tales.

The picture of Arthur that emerges in Tales 7 and 8 does not necessarily suggest that Malory originally intended to have Arthur develop into a better king as his book progressed. Malory apparently thought of Arthur as a good king in the early as well as the later parts of *Morte Darthur*. Although in the early tales Arthur has a number of weaknesses derived from the sources (the attempt to destroy Mordred by drowning all of the children born in the kingdom on May Day, some instances of acting rashly and vengefully),[30] he nevertheless has traits that, according to political theorists, a good king should have: a sense of justice and chivalry, courage and wisdom; Malory at times added to the early tales to emphasize these traits. In Tale 1, for example, the young Arthur shows that he is aware of the responsibility incumbent upon a king for he promises to rule with "true justyce" (p. 16; no source) and he charges his knights "never to do outerage nothir murthir and allwayes to fle treson, and to gyff mercy unto hym that askith mercy";[31] in this tale Malory also writes, "hit was myrry to be under such a chyfftayne that wolde putte hys person in adventure as other poure knyghtis ded" (p. 54; no source); in Tale 2, King Angwysshaunce exalts him above all kings for his "knyghthode" and "noble counceyle."[32] Instances of Arthur's regard for his men also appear in Tales 1 and 2 in, for example, Arthur's generous giving of "rychesse and londys" to his knights[33] and his care of them during the Roman campaign.[34]

In the final tales Malory's Arthur still has the good traits of a medieval king that he had shown earlier. In Tale 7 he is still the "floure of chyvalry of [alle] the worlde" (p. 1161; no source); and in Tale 8, in his final battle against Mordred, Arthur conducts himself as bravely as he had in the early tales: "ever kynge Arthure rode thorowoute the bat[a]yle . . . and ded full nobely, as a noble kynge shoulde do, and at all tymes he faynted never" (p. 1236; no source). Traits such as his love of his men and his sense of justice, however, receive more emphasis in the final tales and are less dependent on the source accounts than they were in the earlier tales.

One of Arthur's traits that becomes most prominent in the final tales is love for his men, especially for Lancelot and Gawain. Elizabeth Pochoda feels that Arthur, in demonstrating such love, is subject to "personal emotional ties" and is therefore unkingly; but as political theorists such as Aegidius Romanus and Gower noted, a ruler interested in the *bonum commune* valued the knights who protected his realm.[35] Such love enhances, rather than detracts from, Arthur's role as king; and it is nowhere so prominent as it is in Tales 6, 7, and 8 that tell of the deterioration and destruction of the realm.

Although Malory found in his sources instances of this love, in the final tales he adds to these to give the reader an overwhelming impression of the bond between Arthur and his knights, a bond that is a stark contrast to the relationship between Mark and his knights in the fifth tale. The importance of Arthur's relationship with his men appears emphatically at the beginning of Tale 6 when the knights depart for the Grail Quest. Malory follows his source in having Arthur mourn the departure of the "trewyst of knyghthode that ever was sene togydir" and in having his king say, "I have loved them as well as my lyff";[36] when the knights leave, however, Malory adds to his account, "the kynge turned away and myght nat speke for wepyng."[37] In Tale 7 Malory, without source authority, has Arthur tell Gareth how to be a good knight: "ever hit ys . . . a worshypfull knyghtes dede to help and succoure another worshypfull knyght . . . and he that ys of no worshyp and medelyth with cowardise never shall he shew jantilnes nor no maner of goodnes where he seeth a man in daungere, for than woll a cowarde never shew mercy" (p. 1114). In Malory's final tale Arthur's comments show his concern for his men: "I am sure the noble felyship of the Rounde Table ys brokyn for ever" (p. 1174; no source); "Alas, that ever I bare crowne uppon my hede! For now have I loste the fayryst felyshyp of noble knyghtes that ever hylde Crysten kynge togydirs."[38]

Arthur's concern for his men and for the *bonum commune* is especially shown in Tales 7 and 8 by his love for Lancelot and his appreciation of Lancelot's service to the realm. Malory, to be sure, found some references to Arthur's love for Lancelot in the sources of the final tales and he usually incorporates these into his account.[39] Malory, however, makes Arthur's love for Lancelot more pronounced than it is in the sources and also deletes references to Arthur's jealousy over the queen's relationship with Lancelot. The author of *Mort Artu* gives the affair much more emphasis than Malory does. In the beginning of this French romance, Agravaine warns Arthur of the adultery, but Arthur is unwilling to believe it (*Mort Artu*, p. 5); his fears are dispelled when Lancelot shows up at the tournament at Winchester instead of staying with the queen at Camelot as Arthur had suspected: "ge sei or bien que se Lancelos amast la reïne par amors, il ne se fust pas remuez de Kamaalot" ("I know now that if Lancelot were in love with the queen, he would not have left Camelot");[40] later, however, Morgan le Fay warns Arthur of the affair, and he swears that if her warning is true, he will avenge himself "si cruelment qu'il en seroit a touz jorz mes parlé" (p. 65; "with such vigor that it would always be remembered" [p. 73]). Malory omits these early allusions to the adultery, and when he does tell of Arthur's reaction to it, his account is far different from that of the French source: in the French account, for example, when Arthur hears his knights discussing the affair, he threatens to kill Agravaine if he does not tell him the truth and then threatens vengeance if Lancelot and Guenevere are taken together for it would be better for Lancelot to die than for his shame to go unavenged (pp. 110–11); from this point, in spite of a few references to Arthur's affection for Lancelot, the king is motivated largely by the desire to get vengeance on Lancelot and Guenevere or by his desire to win the queen again.

In Malory, on the other hand, when Arthur hears his knights discussing the affair, he simply asks "what noyse they made," and Agravaine willingly tells him. As in the source, Arthur wants proof of the affair, but Malory adds without source authority a statement about Arthur's love for Lancelot: "the kynge was full lothe that such a noyse shulde be uppon sir Lancelot and his quene; for the kynge had a demyng of hit, but he wold nat here thereoff, for sir Launcelot had done so much for hym and for the quene so many tymes that . . . the kynge loved hym passyngly well" (p. 1163). In the events that follow, Malory plays down instances of Arthur's animosity. Although Lancelot feels that Arthur is his foe and says that Arthur has shown "hete" [anger] toward the queen (pp. 1171–77, 1188), Arthur's actions show, on the whole, love for Lancelot. When Arthur is told that Lancelot and Guenevere have been found together, he expresses regret that "sir Launcelot sholde be ayenste me" (p. 1174; no source); later he wants to take the queen back "to have bene accorded with sir Launcelot"; in the sources, on the other hand, Arthur is willing to make peace because of his love for Guenevere.[41]

Malory also places more emphasis upon Arthur's concern for his men and the *bonum commune* by deleting allusions in the sources that show Arthur's love for the queen. Although Malory's Tale 1 shows Arthur as a loving husband, Tales 2–8, particularly 7 and 8, present Arthur as a king who has more love for his knights than for his wife and who is more concerned with his role as monarch than his role as husband.[42] In Tale 7 when Guenevere is falsely accused of killing one of Arthur's knights in the poisoned apple episode, both of Malory's sources place considerable emphasis upon Arthur's love for the queen and upon his emotional involvement in the case.[43] Malory, however, omits these allusions and instead presents in Tale 7 a king who, though convinced that his wife has been unfairly accused, must be a "ryghtfull juge" (p. 1050). Malory also omits references to Arthur's emotion when Guenevere is to be burnt at the stake, an affectionate parting scene between husband and wife when Arthur leaves to fight Lancelot, and references to the queen's fear of Arthur's jealousy (*Mort Artu*, pp. 122, 167, 217). Malory in fact presents an Arthur who clearly prefers his knights to his queen: "And much more I am soryar for my good knyghtes losse than for the losse of my fayre queen; for quenys I myght have inow, but such a felyship of good knyghtes shall never be togydirs in no company" (p. 1184). The changes that Malory makes in this relationship indicate that he was cutting down Arthur's personal role as husband in order to build up his public role as king.

Although the Arthur of Malory's sources regrets the war that breaks out between him and Lancelot,[44] he is often quite vengeful toward the queen and her lover. Malory, however, deletes most references in his sources to Arthur's vengeance toward Lancelot and Guenevere. Malory's Arthur suggests that he and Gawain get revenge for the deaths of Gaheris and Gareth, but the suggestion is much milder in Malory than in the source. In Malory's account, Arthur tells Gawain, "Launcelot slew them in the thyk prees and knew tham nat. And therefore lat us shape a remedy for to revenge their dethys" (p. 1185). Here, Malory's Arthur is acting out of a desire to do what honor demands and to avoid its opposite, shame. As Derek Brewer has pointed out, honor is not the same as moral goodness and the "distinction between right and wrong must go when honor is at stake."[45] Gawain then tells Arthur: ". . . frome thys day forewarde I shall never fayle sir Launcelot untyll that one of us have slayne that othir. . . . I requyre you, my lorde . . . dresse you unto the warres, for . . . I woll be revenged uppon sir Launcelot; . . . I shall sle hym, other ellis he shall sle me" (p. 1186). There is no basis for this scene in the English stanzaic *Morte Arthur*. In the French prose romance, Gawain says nothing at this point and Arthur is the one who eagerly seeks revenge: "Ceste perte [of his men] . . . m'est . . . avenue . . . par l'orgueill Lancelot . . . vos estes tuit mi home . . . por quoi ge vos requier . . . que vos me conseilliez . . . en tel maniere que ma honte soit vengiee" (pp. 133–34; "This . . . has befallen me . . . through Lancelot's pride. . . . You are all my men . . . Therefore I require you . . . to help me . . . so that my dishonor may be avenged" [p. 130]).

Malory at times follows his source in having Arthur show personal animosity toward Lancelot: during a battle after war has broken out between the king and Lancelot, "ever was kynge Arthur aboute sir Launcelot to have slayne hym, and ever sir Launcelot suffird hym and wolde nat stryke agayne." Lancelot, however, rescues Arthur and says in a speech original with Malory: "I pray you remembir what I have done in many placis, and now am I evyll rewarded." Arthur then "loked on sir Launcelot" and "the teerys braste oute of hys yen, thynkyng of the grete curtesy that was in sir Launcelot more than in ony other man."[46] Malory follows his source here in presenting an Arthur whose momentary vengefulness is replaced by affection for Lancelot and sorrow over the dissension between them. Arthur shows kingly appreciation for a knight who has been of great value to his realm.

In a number of other instances Malory tones down Arthur's desire for vengeance as it appears in the sources, particularly the French prose romance and gives Gawain the major responsibility for the war against Lancelot. Malory found in his sources instances of Gawain's hatred for Lancelot and desire for vengeance because Lancelot had accidentally killed his brothers; but he further emphasizes both Gawain's hatred and his ability to influence Arthur. When, for example, Arthur hears of Gareth's death, he says, "I am sure that whan sir Gawayne knowyth hereoff that sir Gareth ys slayne, I shall never have reste of hym tyll I have destroyed sir Launcelottys kynne and hymselffe bothe, othir ellis he to destroy me" (p. 1183). The hint for this in Malory's source was "Lette no-man telle Syr Gawayne/Gaheriet hys brother is dede hym fro" (Stanzaic *Morte Arthur,* ll. 1978–79). At one point in *Mort Artu* both Arthur and Gawain reject Lancelot's offer for peace (p. 142); Malory, however, follows the stanzaic *Morte Arthur* (ll. 2668 ff.) and has Gawain reject the offer (p. 1190). On a later occasion before Lancelot is exiled, he reminds Arthur and Gawain of his service in "dyverce placis" (p. 1198; *Mort Artu,* p. 161); and in a speech largely original with Malory, he complains, "truly me repentis that ever I cam in thys realme, that I shulde be thus shamefully banysshyd, undeserved and causeles! . . . in thys realme I had worshyp, and be me and myne all the hole Rounde Table hath bene encreced more in worshyp . . . than ever hit was by ony of you all."[47] Malory modifies the source account of Arthur's role in sentencing Lancelot on this occasion. In *Mort Artu,* Arthur himself tells Lancelot that he is pleased to do what Gawain wishes, and he threatens Lancelot with a great war (pp. 158–59). Malory has Gawain, not Arthur, do the talking: "in this londe thou shalt nat abyde paste a fiftene dayes . . . for so the kynge and we were . . . accorded ar thou cam" (p. 1200). In both Malory and the sources, Gawain pushes Arthur to resume the war against Lancelot, but in the French account Arthur promises Gawain that he will strike the lands of Lancelot so severely that not one stone will be left standing on another (pp. 165–66); this promise does not appear in Malory. In the English romance Arthur eagerly prepares to attack Lancelot's lands "to brenne and sle and make all bare" (l. 2507); Malory modifies this, however, to place more responsibility upon Gawain: "the Kynge . . . landed upon sir Launcelottis londis, and there he brente and wasted, thorow the vengeance of sir Gawayne" (p. 1211).

Malory incorporates instances from the sources which show Gawain's influence upon Arthur, and he also adds some of his own. Malory notes, "in no wyse he [Gawain] wolde suffir the kynge to accorde with sir Launcelot,"[48] and Lancelot tells Gawain, "Ye wolde [cause] my noble lorde kynge Arthur for ever to be my mortall foo."[49] Several other comments that cannot be traced to the sources further show Gawain's responsibility for the war: Lancelot tells Gawain: "ye . . . ar so myschevously sett. And if ye were nat, I wolde nat doute to have the good grace of my lorde kynge Arthure" (p. 1189); Malory notes that Arthur would have made peace with Lancelot, but "sir Gawayne wolde nat suffir hym by no maner of meane" (p. 1190); Lancelot's knights warn him: "sir Gawayne woll nevir suffir you to accorde with kynge Arthur" (p. 1191); and sir Lucan says, "Alas . . . my lorde Arthure wolde accorde with sir Launcelot, but sir Gawayne woll nat suffir hym" (p. 1213). Additions such as these emphasize Gawain's role in the war and also change Arthur into a king considerably different from the one who appears in the French source; while in *Mort Artu* the love affair is Arthur's chief motivation, in Malory's version Arthur's reason for beginning the war and persisting in it is clearly his loyalty to his nephew Gawain; the love affair itself is relatively unimportant.

Malory emphasizes not only Gawain's influence upon Arthur in pursuing the war with Lancelot, but also Arthur's love for his nephew Gawain, a love that has greater importance in Malory's account than it does in the sources. Robert H. Wilson has pointed out that Malory's changes in the sources indicate that he wished to show an especially close relationship between Gawain and Arthur.[50] Although the sources also suggest Arthur's affection for Gawain,[51] Malory adds to these references in Tales 7 and 8. At the tournament at Winchester in Tale 7, for example, "the kynge wold nat suffir sir Gawayne to go frome hym, for never had sir Gawayne the bettir and sir Launcelot were in the fylde" (p. 1069); in the source Arthur's concern is not only for Gawain but for Gawain's brother Gaheriez too (*Mort Artu*, p. 13). Later when Gawain realizes that Lancelot had been fighting in the tournament, Arthur says, "All that knew I aforehande . . . and that caused me I wolde nat suffir you to have ado at the grete justis" (p. 1080; no source). In Tale 8 Arthur's love for Gawain becomes all the more striking when he yields to his nephew's desire for a war of vengeance against Lancelot. A notable instance of the king's partiality for Gawain after the war has begun occurs when Gawain challenges Lancelot to single combat. Malory found in his sources an account of Gawain's miraculous strength which increased until noon (*Mort Artu*, pp. 197–98; stanzaic *Morte*, ll. 2802 ff.); but he uses the information to emphasize Arthur's love for Gawain:

> Kynge Arthur made an ordynaunce that all maner off batayles for ony quarels that shulde be done afore kynge Arthur shulde begynne at undern; and all was done for sir Gawaynes love, that . . . sir Gawayne . . . shulde have the bettir in batayle whyle hys strengthe endured three owrys. But there were that tyme but feaw knyghtes lyvynge that knewe thys advauntayge that sir Gawayne had, but kynge Arthure all only (p. 1217).

The reference to the ordinance made for Gawain's sake does not appear in the sources. Malory wished to show that Arthur's love for Gawain could lead him to give his nephew an advantage over other knights. While this partiality can be interpreted as a flaw in Arthur's character, it also helps make more plausible Arthur's willingness to follow Gawain's advice concerning the war against Lancelot.

Arthur's favoritism to Gawain and his consequent inability to resist

Gawain's desire for vengeance is one of the apparent weaknesses in Malory's Arthur that could detract from his being an effective king. Pochoda believes that such favoritism indicates that Malory was presenting Arthur as king dominated by private will instead of concern for the common good.[52] Malory's text and sources, however, suggest that Malory probably had a different objective. This weakness differs from those of the early tales, for it does not result from Malory's repeating information he found in his source; instead, it results from Malory's deliberate attempt to change the portrait of Arthur that he found in his sources for the final tales and particularly to make Arthur less tyrannical than the Arthur of *Mort Artu*.

In discussing Arthur's relationship with Gawain, Pochoda notes that Malory's Arthur cannot "stand apart from his personal ties" and he shows "unreasoned acquiescence to Gawain's influence."[53] There are, however, factors in the Arthur-Gawain relationship that should be considered. In waging the war against Lancelot Arthur is admittedly dominated by Gawain, and although he is unhappy about the war, he reluctantly fights Lancelot to satisfy his nephew. Malory's choosing to have Arthur influenced so strongly by Gawain is explained partly by Malory's sources. Malory found in both his French and English sources the account of the destruction of the realm, a destruction that results partially from the wrath of Gawain and partially from the king's desire for vengeance. He wanted to retell the story of the fall of the Round Table, and the changes he could make in this account were limited.[54] Malory apparently did not wish to present Arthur as the vengeful king he found in his chief source, the French *Mort Artu;* he consequently changed the character of Arthur and shifted most of the vengeance to Gawain. This change makes Gawain more directly responsible than Arthur for the destruction of the realm and removes from the king most of the desire for vengeance. Yet in departing from his sources in this way Malory presents an Arthur who seems at times to be a weakling controlled by his wrathful nephew. Although Malory makes Arthur's deference to Gawain understandable by emphasizing the king's love for him, Arthur's lack of independence surely seems to modern readers a flaw in his character. Malory, however, would probably not have considered Arthur's deference to his nephew as serious a flaw as the vengeance he found in his French source, for to Malory and his audience familial relationships were very important.

Malory emphasizes the importance of blood ties a number of times throughout *Morte Darthur*. In Tale 1, for example, Malory adds a reference to the blood relationship between Arthur and Gawain: Arthur says he will make Gawain a knight because he is his "sistirs son," while in the source only the narrator mentions that Gawain is Arthur's nephew and the king himself says nothing (*Works*, p. 99; Huth, Vol. 2, pp. 68–69). As noted earlier, the stories of Mark and of the King of the Red City in Tale 5 clearly show that a good ruler "cheryshed his owne bloode." In Tale 8 when Lancelot becomes ruler of France and distributes lands to his men, "firste he avaunced them off hys blood" (p. 1205; not in source); and Arthur appoints Mordred regent "bycause sir Mordred was kynge Arthurs son."[55] Similar respect for kinship would account for Arthur's loyalty to Gawain and alliance with him against Lancelot.

A.L. Morton has drawn parallels between the feuds of the "kindred and faction of Gawain and the kindred and faction of Lancelot" and the feuds of the Wars of the Roses. Gawain, Morton observes, represents "the ancient loyalty of the blood bond"; Lancelot, the "new loyalty of vassal for a lord," a loyalty that must give way when it conflicts with the blood bond.[56] Morton's point is well-taken; and the parallel between the "ancient loyalty of the blood bond" stressed by Malory and the ties of kinship adhered to during the Yorkist-Lancastrian disputes should be emphasized. Arthur's partiality toward Gawain would have been more sympathetically regarded in an age that understood the force of such ties. Although the Wars of the Roses would have shown Malory that allegiance to one's kin could have regrettable consequences, such allegiance was nonetheless a powerful fact of life. Loyalty to bonds of kinship was a part of the king's obligation, and ignoring them, as the King of the Red City did, could cause a great deal of trouble. Edward IV, who was ruling when Malory wrote *Morte Darthur*, ignored blood bonds and alienated some of his most powerful supporters.[57]

Malory's Arthur finds himself in a dilemma in which he must choose between his two favorite knights, the one a nephew and the other the champion of the realm. This dilemma is implicit in Malory's sources, but its significance was diminished there by Arthur's great concern for the queen. In Malory, however, the enmity between Lancelot and Gawain, not the liaison between Lancelot and Guenevere, presents the difficulty for Arthur. Although the king decides to honor the blood bond, his choice is not an easy one since he loves both men. His affection for them is most dramatically illustrated by his lament as Gawain is dying:

> Here now thou lyghest, the man in the worlde that I loved moste. And now ys my joy gone! . . . my nevew, sir Gawayne, . . . in youre person and in sir Launcelot I moste had my joy and myne affyaunce. And now have I loste my joy of you bothe, wherefore all myne erthely joy ys gone fro me! (p. 1230)

These lines are based upon a passage in the French *Mort Artu,* but there Lancelot is given less emphasis.[58] Malory's version emphasizes Arthur's dilemma, a dilemma that Malory's audience would have been able to understand.

Although Arthur's decision to honor his blood bond with Gawain and with Mordred leads ultimately to Mordred's rebellion and the downfall of the kingdom, the decision is not presented as an irresponsible one, and the readers are expected to sympathize with Arthur's predicament. This is indicated by the narrator's denunciation of the rebellion against Arthur and the fickleness of the English people:

> Lo ye all Englysshemen, se ye nat what a myschyff here was? For he that was the moste kynge and nobelyst knyght of the worlde, and moste loved the felyshyp of noble knyghtes, and by hym they all were upholdyn, and yet myght nat thes Englyshemen holde them content with hym . . . And the moste party of all Inglonde hylde wyth sir Mordred, for the people were so new-fangill. (p. 1229)

By Arthur, "the moste kyng and nobelyst knyght of the worlde," they "all were upholdyn," and they had no right to rebel against him.

Another apparent weakness occurs in Tale 8 when Arthur refuses to permit Guenevere to have trial by combat. When Lancelot and Guenevere are found together, Lancelot escapes after killing thirteen of Arthur's knights and wounding Mordred. Guenevere, however, is captured and is to be sentenced by Arthur. The scene is largely Malory's invention, and it occurs before Gawain's brothers have been killed and before Gawain turns against Lancelot. Gawain, in fact, defends the lovers in this case and says that Lancelot would fight for the queen in trial by combat:

> "peradventure she sente for hym for goodnes or for none evyll . . . For I dare sey . . . my Lady . . . ys to you both good and trew. And as for sir Launcelot, I dare say he woll make hit good uppon ony knyght lyvyng that woll put uppon hym vylany or shame."

Arthur replies:

> "That I beleve well . . . but I woll nat that way worke with sir Launcelot, for he trustyth so much uppon hys hondis and hys myght that he doutyth no man. And therefore for my quene he shall nevermore fyght, for she shall have the law. And if I may gete sir Lancelot . . . he shall have as shamefull a dethe." (p. 1175)

According to Pochoda, Arthur is here acting "not as king and judge but as a personal lord seeking revenge."[59] Arthur admittedly seems to be denying Guenevere her right to trial by combat, and the passage thus seems inconsistent with two earlier occasions when Arthur as a "ryghtfull juge" (p. 1050) permitted such trials.[60] Medieval readers tolerated some inconsistencies within works of literature;[61] and in this scene in the source trial by combat is not even mentioned although it had been used before. But this omission probably troubled Malory since he was careful to mention it at this time and give Arthur justification for not using it.

The scene that Malory found in his sources presents a picture of Arthur that would have been unpalatable to him and which he would have felt a need to change. Pochoda, following Vinaver's note, claims that in the source the barons decide to sentence Guenevere to death and that Malory "assigns the responsibility for the whole episode to Arthur."[62] In fact, however, in the stanzaic *Morte Arthur* both the king and knights take "there counselle" and decide to burn the queen (ll. 1920 ff.); in *Mort Artu* Arthur vindictively orders his barons to condemn the queen to death.[63] But in trying to ameliorate the picture of Arthur that he found in the sources, Malory still had to retain the essential features of the downfall of Arthur's kingdom. One might argue that if Malory wished to present a just king, he would have had Arthur give Guenevere a chance to escape, as he had on earlier occasions, by means of trial by combat. Here, however, Malory was bound by his source, for Lancelot's attempt to rescue the queen from the flames, the ensuing combat, Lancelot's accidental slaying of Gawain's brothers Gaherys and Gareth, and the subsequent downfall of the realm are all dependent upon the consequences of the condemnation of Guenevere. If Malory's Arthur had permitted trial by combat, Malory would have had two alternatives: either his hero Lancelot would have suffered defeat or Guenevere would have been proclaimed innocent and the whole course of the romance would have been changed. Since neither of these alternatives would have been acceptable to Malory, he could not include trial by combat at this point.

To make Arthur seem just, however, Malory gives him ample reason for not offering trial by combat. First, Arthur refuses to let Lancelot fight for the Queen because "he trustyth so much uppon hys hondis and hys myght." Though inconsistent with Arthur's procedure in the earlier trials, this would probably have seemed reasonable enough to Malory's readers since there was great distrust of trial by combat in England in the later Middle Ages,[64] and this distrust is reflected elsewhere in *Morte Darthur*.[65] Second, Malory without source authority gives Arthur legal justification for the sentencing of Guenevere without trial by combat:

> So than there was made grete ordynaunce in thys ire, and the quene
> must nedis be jouged to the deth. And the law was such in tho dayes
> that whatsomever they were, of what astate or degré, if they were
> founden gylty of treson there shuld be none other remedy but deth,
> and othir the menour other the takynge wyth the dede shulde be
> causer of their hasty jougement. And ryght so was hit ordayned for
> quene Gwenyver: bycause sir Mordred was ascaped sore wounded,
> and the dethe of thirtene knyghtes of the Rounde Table, thes previs
> and experyenses caused kynge Arthure to commaunde the quene to
> the fyre and there to be brente. (p. 1174)

Arthur thus tells Gawain that the queen "shall have the law."[66] This senti-
ment is similar to that which Malory expressed during Guenevere's earlier
trial scene during the poisoned apple episode of Tale 7: "for such custom
was used in tho dayes: for favoure, love, nother affinité there sholde be none
other but ryghtuous jugemente . . . as well uppon a quene as uppon another
poure lady" (p. 1055; not in source). Gawain assumes that Arthur could give
the queen a chance to escape with trial by combat; but Arthur says nothing
about a choice, and it is doubtful that a medieval audience would have
thought that he should have done anything other than what he did since "the
law was such in tho dayes." In both the sources and in Malory's account
the condemnation of Guenevere initiates the fall of the kingdom; Malory's
Arthur, however, condemns her in accordance with the law while the Arthur
of the sources is not bound by law and acts in accordance with his own
whim. When Gawain defends Lancelot in this scene, he tells Arthur,
"oftyntymys we do many thynges that we wene for the beste be, and yet
peradventure hit turnyth to the warste" (p. 1175). His statement is applicable to Arthur as well. In giving Guenevere the judgment prescribed by the
law, Arthur takes the initial step that leads to the destruction of his kingdom.

Malory further mitigates Arthur's actions in this scene by minimiz-
ing his personal concern for the adultery and by giving him the concern a
king should have, concern for the knights Lancelot has killed, the impending war with Lancelot, and the trouble it will cause his realm. When Arthur
hears that Lancelot and Guenevere have been found together, he shows the
same disregard for the adultery that he shows elsewhere in Morte Darthur.
He says nothing about the love affair, but instead says, "me sore repentith
that ever sir Launcelot sholde be ayenste me, for now I am sure the noble

felyshyp of the Rounde Table ys brokyn for ever" (p. 1174). Although Gawain assumes that Arthur is condemning the queen to death because of the adultery, Arthur says nothing about the queen. The "previs and experyenses" that, according to the passage on law, cause Arthur to condemn the queen are the wounding of Mordred and the "dethe of thirtene knyghtes of the Rounde Table." Guenevere is condemned to death because she is guilty of "treson," but "treson" seems to refer to the slaying of the thirteen knights instead of to the love affair.[67]

Thus, since the story that Malory found in his sources would not permit consistent use of trial by combat, Malory endeavors to put Arthur in a better light by noting that the law allowed "none other remedy but deth" in such a case, by showing Arthur's concern for such public problems as the war with Lancelot and the death of his knights, and by having Arthur show no concern for the adultery itself. These changes, like many others in Tales 7 and 8, make Arthur into a better king than he was in the corresponding scene in the sources.

Arthur's kingdom falls, but this was inherent in the story and was not due to Malory's re-creation of Arthur as an inadequate king. As Vinaver has pointed out, the tragedy results from the conflict of loyalties of many people;[68] although Arthur's decisions to follow the law and to side with Gawain contribute to the fall, the decisions are not irresponsible. There is, however, no reason to believe that the war could have been prevented even if Arthur had not sided with Gawain. The hostility of Agravain and Mordred, Lancelot's fateful killing of the unarmed Gareth and Gaheris, and Gawain's subsequent hatred of Lancelot are matters over which a king, no matter how good or bad, could have little control. The fact that Malory makes Arthur into a better king than he was in the sources makes the destruction of his realm all the more regrettable.

CONCLUSION

Malory's handling of the portrait of Mark that he found in the source of Tale 5 is, then, strikingly different from his handling of the portrait of Arthur that he found in the sources of Tales 7 and 8. Malory's Mark is essentially the same as he was in the source, a vengeful and jealous tyrant. The "blackening" of Mark that critics have emphasized amounts to only a few additions; Mark's villainy, including his hatred for Tristram and his jealous concern for Isode, is well developed in the source. Arthur, on the other hand, is in Tales 7 and 8 far different from the king of the French *Mort Artu* and somewhat different from the king of the stanzaic *Morte Arthur*. Although *Mort Artu* was the primary source for his final tales, Malory presented the milder king of the English stanzaic romance, or more often, made changes of his own. Most signs of Arthur's jealousy and sentimental love for the queen are gone; most instances of the king's vindictiveness toward Lancelot have been transferred to Gawain. Malory's Arthur has less affection for the queen and greater affection for his knights, particularly for Gawain and Lancelot.

Arthur, like Mark, loses his wife and the best knight of his kingdom and must face a civil war, but while Mark is a tyrant, Arthur usually lives up to the medieval conception of a good king. Mark heads the court at Cornwall where the "false knyghtes" are "naught worth" and are "no men of worshyp as other knyghtes ar."[69] Arthur, on the other hand, heads the court of the "moste nobelest knyghtes of the worlde" (p. 1252). Mark is reviled as a "murtherer," a "traytour," and "the falsyst knyght and kynge of the worlde."[70] Arthur is "the moste man of worshyp crystynde" (p. 1147) and the "nobelyst knyght of the worlde" (p. 1229). In ruling, Mark is a slave to wrath, pride, and jealousy; Arthur rules in accordance with the law. While Mark is a liar, Arthur is known for keeping his word. Mark's chief concern is his wife and her lover; Arthur's is the welfare of the knights who are necessary to his realm. Mark is an enemy to all good knights and lives in fear and suspicion that someone will win more honor than he; Arthur loves his men and respects them for their service to his kingdom.

Since Mark's traits are derived from the source and Arthur's are to a much greater extent the result of Malory's changes in the sources, it seems likely that the differences between Arthur and Mark are partially the result of Malory's deliberate attempt to set one king off against the other. Some of Malory's additions to Tale 5 indicate that when he was writing this tale he realized that the story of Mark provided material for an excellent contrast with Arthur. Mark's statement that he cannot love Tristram "because he lovyth my quene," Lamarok's condemnation of Mark for chasing Tristram out of the realm for "jeleousnes," and Mark's failure to respect his blood ties with Tristram and Bodwine all suggest that Malory wished to emphasize Mark's contrast with Arthur. Malory, moreover, adds to Tale 5 a statement that explicitly differentiates the two courts: Lamarok says that he had "lever stryff and debate felle in kyng Markys courte rether than in kynge Arthurs courte, for the honour of bothe courtes be nat lyke" (p. 443). Thus, these additions suggest that Malory, while writing his fifth tale, was looking ahead to the final ones. The references in both Tale 7 and Tale 8 to the murder of Tristram offer further evidence that Malory intentionally planned to have Mark contrast with Arthur. Although critics have suggested reasons for Malory's waiting until the final tale to give his most detailed accounts of Tristram's murder, they have concentrated upon the death of Tristram[71] and have ignored Mark's role. The reference to the murder in Tale 7 is important because, besides telling of Tristram's death, it also tells of the murder of Mark, and this provides an implicit contrast with the death of Arthur.[72] Just as there has been a great difference in the ways the two kings have lived, there is also a great difference in the ways the two kings meet death. Mark dies in a manner appropriate for a tyrant: he is murdered by a knight who wants to avenge the death of Tristram, and no one expresses regret. Arthur, on the other hand, dies in a manner appropriate for a king: he tries to save his kingdom and is mourned as "the floure of kyngis and knyghtes" (p. 1252). Although this contrast between the two kings is implicit, the one in Tale 8 is explicit. In the description of Tristram's death in Tale 8, Bors contrasts Mark and Arthur as being "never lyke of conducions" (p. 1173). The account of the murder of Tristram in both tales shows, in fact, the great difference in the two kings that is suggested by Bors's remark: while Mark kills his best knight because he is jealous of his love for his queen, Arthur wants to take Lancelot back and tries to ignore the adultery.

These allusions to Mark show that while writing the final tales Malory had Mark in mind. When this fact is considered along with the ways in which Malory changed his source accounts of Arthur's character, the contrasts between Arthur and Mark seem to be at least in part deliberate and Mark seems to have influenced Malory's conception of Arthur in these final tales.

First, the story of Mark may have influenced Malory's handling of the Arthur-Guenevere relationship in Tales 7 and 8.[73] The contrast between the two kings is best summed up in the statements, original with Malory, that they make about their queens: in Tale 5 Mark says, "I may nat love sir Trystram, bycause he lovyth my quene, La Beall Isode" (p. 679); in Tale 8 Arthur says, "more I am soryar for my good knyghtes losse than for the losse of my fayre quene; for quenys I myght have inow, but such a felyship of good knyghtes shall never be togydirs in no company" (p. 1184). These statements show the difference between the tyrant and the king; the one lives only for his *bonum privatum,* the other for the *bonum commune.* Thus the story of Mark's jealous concern for Isode probably helped shape Malory's contrasting presentation of Arthur's attitude toward Guenevere.[74] When reading *Mort Artu* and the stanzaic *Morte Arthur,* he would have found in Arthur's love for the queen and jealousy traits that would have made him similar to the tyrannous Mark. A desire to present a king that contrasted with Mark could have prompted Malory's changes in Arthur's love for Guenevere as he found it presented in *Mort Artu* and the stanzaic *Morte Arthur.*

Second, the story of Mark may have influenced Malory's presentation of Arthur's affection for Gawain and Lancelot in Tales 7 and 8. Throughout Malory's book, to be sure, Arthur shows affection for his knights, and such affection might have been inspired both by contemporary political conditions and by Malory's own concept of the proper relationship between a king and his knights. Malory's emphasis in the final tales, however, upon Arthur's love for both Gawain, his nephew, and Lancelot, the lover of his wife and champion of his realm, could have been influenced, not only by the sources for the final tales, but by Mark's different attitude toward Tristram who, like Gawain, is nephew to the king and, like Lancelot, is lover of the king's wife and champion of the realm. In fact, Malory's decision to remove the more aggressive, vengeful traits from the Arthur of the *Mort Artu* and to emphasize instead Arthur's love for and loyalty to Gawain may have been suggested by Mark's contrasting treatment of Tristram. Malory must have felt that such love for his nephew offered motivation for the king's actions that was preferable to the vengeance displayed by the Arthur of *Mort Artu,* who is too much like Mark. The ways in which Arthur and Mark treat Lancelot and Tristram further emphasize the contrast between them. Both knights twice remind their kings of their "trew servyse" to their respective kingdoms, and both knights are banished; but the reactions of the kings are quite different. As indicated earlier, on two occasions Tristram tells of his service to Cornwall and his importance to the realm, but to Mark the affair with Isode is more important and he banishes Tristram for a personal reason, "for jeleousnes of his queen."[75] Lancelot also twice emphasizes the service that he has done for the realm, and Arthur's reaction indicates that he can look beyond the personal injury done to him. On the first occasion, after Lancelot complains that he is "evyll rewarded," Arthur weeps and thinks of the "grete curtesy that was in sir Launcelot"; on the second, Arthur says nothing and Gawain has the vengeful speech that was Arthur's in the source.[76]

Thus, Malory presents in *Morte Darthur* two contrasting rulers, one a tyrant, the other a king, the vices of the one set against the virtues of the other. A desire to balance the events of the final tales with those of Tale 5 may have prompted some of Malory's additions to the final tales in Arthur's relationship with his nephew, his queen and her lover, his presentation of Lancelot's banishment as a parallel to Tristram's, and the condemnation of the rebellion against Arthur as opposed to the approval of the rebellion against Mark.

Mark's function in *Morte Darthur* is, of course, related to the question of the "cohesion" of Malory's work.[77] The story of Mark is not so organically related to the story of Arthur that it is essential to the whole; unlike a chapter of a novel or an act of a play, it could be omitted. Yet it does contribute to *Morte Darthur* in much the same way that the subplot of an Elizabethan play such as *Volpone* or *The Changeling* contributes to the whole: it is of value for the sake of contrast, and the work is a richer one if it is retained. The scenes concerning Mark contribute to the whole of *Morte Darthur* by presenting a king who acts in counterpoint to Arthur and thus sets off more sharply Arthur's virtues as king.

The power of Malory's narrative in Tales 7 and 8 has often been justly praised, and critics generally acknowledge that Malory's last tale in which he shows the most independence in the treatment of his sources, is his finest.[78] What should be noted, however, is that the "Tristan" was important to the development of Tales 7 and 8: it contributed markedly to Malory's greater independence in the use of his sources by influencing his conception of Arthur in these final tales.

NOTES

1. See, for example, Terence McCarthy, *Reading the Morte Darthur* (Cambridge, 1988); Mark Lambert, *Malory: Style and Vision in "Le Morte Darthur"* (New Haven, 1975); Derek Brewer, ed., *The Morte Darthur: Parts Seven and Eight* (Evanston, Ill., 1968), pp. 9–12; Larry D. Benson, *Malory's "Morte Darthur"* (Cambridge, Mass., 1976).

2. Peter Korrel, *An Arthurian Triangle: A Study of the Origin, Development and Characterization of Arthur, Guinevere, and Modred* (Leiden, 1984), p. 255; also see Elizabeth T. Pochoda, *Arthurian Propaganda:* Le Morte Darthur *as an Historical Ideal of Life* (Chapel Hill, 1971); Christopher Dean, *Arthur of England: English Attitudes to King Arthur and the Knights of the Round Table in the Middle Ages and the Renaissance* (Toronto, 1987), pp. 91–106; Ginger Thornton, "The Weakening of the King: Arthur's Disintegration in *The Book of Sir Tristram de Lyones*," *Sir Thomas Malory: Views and Re-views*, ed. D.T. Hanks, Jr. (New York, 1992), pp. 3–16, also in *The Arthurian Yearbook*, ed. K. Busby, 1 (1991), 135–48.

3. *The Works of Sir Thomas Malory*, ed. Eugène Vinaver, 3rd ed., rev. ed. P.J.C. Field (Oxford, 1990), pp. 188, 221, 1147, 1194, 1236, 1252. Other references to Malory's text are from this edition.

4. I discussed this in a plenary address "King Arthur in Malory and the Chronicles," at the ACTA Conference on Northern Europe in Buffalo, N.Y. on April 24, 1993. It is to be published in ACTA. Sources with negative portraits include the English alliterative *Morte Arthure* as well as some parts of the French prose romances.

5. See Frappier, *Étude sur La Mort le Roi Artu*, 3rd ed. (Geneva, 1972), p. 328, where Arthur is described as being in part a too faithful replica of Marc. The influence, of course, would not be from the prose *Tristan,* which was written after the Vulgate *Mort Artu.*

6. Critics have made misleading statements about Malory's "recharacterization" of Mark and have maintained that he "blackened" Mark's character. (See Thomas C. Rumble, "'The Tale of Tristram': Development by Analogy," *Malory's Originality: A Critical Study of* Le Morte Darthur, ed. R.M. Lumiansky [Baltimore, 1964], p. 153; Charles Moorman, *The Book of Kyng Arthur* [Lexington, Ky., 1965], p. 23; Donald G. Schueler, "The Tristram Section of Malory's *Morte Darthur*," *Studies in Philology* 65 [1968], 51–66; Pochoda, p. 98.) Although Malory made minor changes, to label them "re-characterization" is to give a misleading impression of Malory's contribution to Mark's character.

7. No extant manuscript of the French prose *Tristan* can be identified as the text Malory used for his fifth tale. Vinaver reconstructs the source from several manuscripts of the prose *Tristan:* Bibliothèque Nationale Fr. 103 for *Works,* pp. 371–512; B.N. Fr. 334 for *Works,* pp. 512–615; B.N. Fr. 99, Chantilly 646 (formerly 316), Fr. 41 of the Pierpont Morgan Library and F.V. XV.2 of the Leningrad Public Library for *Works,* pp. 615–846; and MS B.N. Fr. 362 for the "Alexander the Orphan" section of Tale 5. My comparison of Malory's text with the prose *Tristan* is based upon the first five of these manuscripts and the edition of the relevant portion of MS 362 in *Alixandre l'Orphelin: A Prose Tale of the Fifteenth Century,* ed. C.E. Pickford (Manchester, 1951); the Leningrad manuscript, which Vinaver first used in his 1967 edition of Malory, was not available to me. I also consulted the following Spanish and Italian versions: *Libro del esforzado caballero Don Tristan de Leonis* in *Libros de caballerias* primera parte, ed. Adolfo Bonilla y San Martin, Nueva biblioteca de autores españoles 6 (Madrid, 1907); *El Cuento de Tristan de Leonis,* ed. C.T. Northup (Chicago, 1928); *La leggenda di Tristano,* ed. Luigi di Benedetto, Scrittori d'Italia No. 189 (Bari, 1942). On reasons for consulting the Spanish and Italian versions, see Rumble, *Malory's Originality,* pp. 122–44 and my "Arthur's Rescue in Malory and the Spanish 'Tristan,'" *Notes and Queries,* 215 (1970), 6–10. I also used E. Löseth, *Le Roman en prose de Tristan, le roman de Palamède, et la compilation de Rusticien de Pise* (Paris, 1891), Vinaver, *Le Roman de Tristan et Iseut dans l'oeuvre de Thomas Malory* (Paris, 1925), and the notes to Vinaver's edition of Malory, cited in note 3 above. I based my comparison primarily upon the first five manuscripts that Vinaver used. When Malory's text agreed with the suggested manuscript, I checked only that manuscript; when Malory's text differed, I checked insofar as possible the corresponding sections of the other manuscripts. The manuscripts, however, are not equal in length and events found in one may be absent in another. MS 334, for example, does not carry the *Tristan* story nearly as far as MSS. 103 and 99; the Chantilly and Pierpont Morgan manuscripts do not include the early adventures of Tristan. Although details in Malory that appear in none of the above texts may represent Malory's contribution to the story, they could also represent changes that scribes made in manuscripts no longer extant; thus any attribution of these changes to Malory must be considered tentative. As will be seen, what is most significant about Malory's portrait of Mark is ways in which it agrees with the source.

Although there is no complete scholarly edition of the prose *Tristan,* several volumes have been edited: Renée Curtis, *Le Roman de Tristan en Prose,* 1 (Munich, 1963; rpt. Cambridge, 1985); 2 (Leiden, 1976; rpt. Cambridge, 1985); 3 (Cambridge, 1985); Le *Roman de Tristan en prose,* gen. ed. P. Ménard, 1–5 (Geneva, 1987–92). Since, however, no single manuscript closely represents Malory's source, the manuscripts Vinaver recommended still seem to be a better guide to Malory's adaptation. Brief references will appear in the text and longer ones in footnotes.

8. The prose *Tristan* begins with instances of Mark's villainy that do not appear in Malory; there Mark at the outset kills a younger brother, has assassins kill Tristan's father Meliodes, and attempts to dispose of Tristan (MS 103, fols. 28v, 30r; similarly MS 334, fols. 29v, 31rb–va; MS 99, fols. 36v, 39r; also see Löseth, pp. 17–18). The Italian version and one of the Spanish versions tell of Mark's murder of the brother, but Mark is not involved in the death of Tristan's father (see Benedetto, pp. 2, 12; Bonilla y San Martin, pp. 340, 344; *Cuento de Tristan* lacks the first five folios). MSS. Pierpont Morgan and Chantilly begin their narratives at later points. In all of the above accounts, however, Mark appreciates Tristan when he first comes to court.

9. *Works,* pp. 384, 393; similarly MS 103, fols. 35v–36r, 44ra. Although Vinaver says that in the source the barons at this point are hostile to Tristan, according to MS 103, both the king and the barons are happy to see him (fol. 44ra).

10. *Works,* pp. 394–96; MS 103, fol 46rb. Rumble cites this as an instance of Malory's blackening of Mark; he notes that in the source Tristan was accompanied

by two other knights and Mark attacks them, but that in Malory's account Mark is the one who has two helpers, not Tristram; thus the odds are reversed (*Malory's Originality*, p. 158). This is not, however, a major change, and Mark's basic treachery is derived from the source.

11. *Works*, p. 1461; *Malory's Originality*, p. 159. In MS 103 (fols. 49v–50r), Mark believes that sending Tristan to Ireland is a way to rid himself of Tristan, for Mark would prefer having him dead than alive. Although the barons advise the king to take a wife, it is Mark who asks for Iseult. When Tristan hears this, he realizes that Mark is sending him to Ireland so that he will be killed, not because the king wants Iseult as a bride. Similarly, MS 334, fol. 52r; MS 99, fol. 64v.

12. *Works*, p. 427. The Spanish *Tristan* is here closer to Malory's account than the French. See Bonilla y San Martin, p. 385; Northup, pp. 149–50. In the French, Andret advises Mark to lure Tristan back in order to kill him (Cf. MS 103, fol. 70v).

13. The idea for this may have come from a later section of the French source that tells of Tristan's madness and exile. There Andret advises Mark not to release Tristan from prison since he will go to Loegres where he, with the aid of good knights of the lineage of King Ban and King Arthur, will return to shame Mark and destroy Cornwall (MS 103, fol. 165v; similarly, MS 334, fol. 192v; MS 99, fol. 224r).

14. *Works*, p. 431; again the closest parallel is in the Spanish, not the French account. See Bonilla y San Martin, p. 286. In the French version the people of Cornwall praise Tristan, but he does not speak himself. See MS 103, fol. 75vb.

15. MS 103, fol. 165r; similarly, MS 334, fol. 192r–v; MS 99, fol. 224r.

16. In the source one finds only the battles against "morhoult . . . roy de norgules . . . roy des cent cheualiers . . . taulat de la montaigne"—MS 103, fol. 166r; similarly, MS 334, fol. 199ra; MS 99, fol. 225rb–va.

17. Not in MS 334, fol. 305va; MS 99, fol. 331r; MS 103, fols. 254v–255r; Chantilly, fol. 138vb.

18. *Works*, pp. 594–95; MS 334, fol 320rb–va; for comment on Mark, see fol. 330v.

19. *Works*, p. 675; the source does not have Mark attempt to have Tristan killed in this manner. See MSS. 99, fol. 397vb; Pierpont Morgan, fol. 95vb; Chantilly, fol. 231rb–va.

20. MS 99, fols. 398vb–399ra; Chantilly, fol. 233r; Pierpont Morgan, fol. 96vb.

21. Cf. MS 99, fol 399va, MS 103, fol. 300r; Pierpont Morgan, fol. 95r; Chantilly, fol. 234r.

22. *Works*, p. 680; MSS. 99 (fol. 399vb), Chantilly (fol. 234va), Pierpont Morgan (fol. 95rb) do not tell just how Isode saved Tristan. In some versions, including MS 103, Tristan is rescued by the people of Leonis. (See Vinaver's note, *Works*, p. 1509; Löseth, p. 203, n. 5.) In some MSS. Mark is imprisoned before Tristan escapes in order to make the escape plausible.

23. *Works*, p. 583; remarks about Mark being a murderer are not in MS 334, fol. 309v; Chantilly, fol. 144v; MS 103, fols. 258v–259r; MS 99, fol. 335r.

24. *Works*, p. 585; in the source Dynadan does not seriously rebuke Mark (cf. MS 334, fol. 310rb–va).

25. *Alixandre l'Orphelin*, p. 88.

26. *Works*, p. 679; in the source Perceval does not place as much emphasis upon the relationship; he simply asks how Mark can be so disloyal as to put his nephew Tristan in prison (MS 99, fol. 399v).

27. *Works*, pp. 711–12; not in source; cf. account in MS 99, fols. 431r ff.

28. *Works*, p. 648; not in MSS. 99, 362, Chantilly, Pierpont Morgan. MS 334 ends before this; MS 103 does not contain the Alexander story.

29. Mark's death is predicted in the *Merlin* of the Post-Vulgate *Roman du Graal*, which Malory had used for the source of his first tale, and this may have suggested Malory's addition of Mark's death to his account. See my "Malory's 'Noble

Tale of Sir Launcelot du Lake,' the Vulgate *Lancelot,* and the Post-Vulgate *Roman du Graal,*" *Arthurian and Other Studies presented to Shunichi Noguchi,* ed. Takashi Suzuki and Tsuyoshi Mukai (Cambridge, 1993), pp. 114–15 and n. 28. Accounts of Mark's death appear in a few other works: in a French MS of the Post-Vulgate *Mort Artu,* MS Bibliothèque Nationale, Fr. 340, he is killed by Paulart; in an Italian poem of the fourteenth century Lancelot kills him in combat; and in the Italian *Tavola Ritonda* he dies of overeating after having been kept in a cage and fed intensively. See Vinaver, *Works,* pp. 1503–04; C.E. Pickford, *L'évolution du roman arthurien en prose vers la fin du moyen âge* (Paris, 1960), pp. 197–98; Fanni Bogdanow, *The Romance of the Grail: A Study of the Structure and Genesis of a Thirteenth-Century Arthurian Prose Romance* (Manchester, 1966), p. 140, n. 3; E.G. Gardner, *The Arthurian Legend in Italian Literature* (1930; rpt. New York, 1971), pp. 186, 205, 263–64, 300–02.

30. On the drowning of the children, see *Works,* pp. 41, 44, 55–56; cf. Huth MS of the *Suite du Merlin,* published as *Merlin: Roman en prose du XIIIe siècle,* ed. Gaston Paris and Jacob Ulrich, 2 vols. (Paris, 1886), Vol. 1, pp. 154, 203, 207–09; in the *Suite* the children are rescued. For instances of rashness and desire for vengeance drawn from the source, see *Works,* p. 53 (*Merlin,* Vol. 1, p. 200), p. 146 (*Merlin,* Vol. 2, pp. 209–10); p. 157, (*Merlin,* Vol. 2, p. 250), p. 158 (*Merlin,* Vol. 2, p. 230).

31. *Works,* p. 120. This charge does not appear in the primary source for Tale 1, the *Suite du Merlin;* it could have been suggested, however, by the fifteenth-century *Chronicle* of John Hardyng or by Lydgate's *Fall of Princes.* See my "Malory's Use of Hardyng's *Chronicle,*" *Notes and Queries* 214 (1969), 167–70; John Withrington, "The Arthurian Epitaph in Malory's 'Morte Darthur,'" *Arthurian Literature,* 7 (1987), 124–44; Withrington, "King Arthur as Emperor," *Notes and Queries,* 233 (1988), 13–15.

32. *Works,* p. 188; similarly in the source; see *Morte Arthure,* ed. Mary Hamel (New York, 1984), 1. 291.

33. *Works,* p. 120; also pp. 113, 245–46. These are additions to the sources.

34. *Works,* pp. 211, 217, 222, 224. Examples one and three have some basis in the source; cf. alliterative *Morte Arthure,* ll. 1573–74, 2197 ff.

35. Pochoda, *Arthurian Propaganda,* p. 107; Aegidius Romanus, *De Regimine principum* (Rome, 1482), 3.iii.i, fol. 121rb–va and more extensively in the thirteenth-century French translation of Aegidius, *Li livres du gouvernement des rois* 3.iii.i, ed. S.P. Molenaer (New York, 1899), pp. 372–73; *Vox Clamantis* 5.1 in *The Complete Works of John Gower,* ed. G.C. Macaulay, 4 (Oxford, 1902), 201.

36. *Works,* pp. 866–68; similarly, *La Queste del Saint Graal,* ed. A. Pauphilet (Paris, 1923), pp. 16–25.

37. *Works,* p. 872. Modern readers are apt to consider tears a sign of weakness, but they were not necessarily considered that way in the Middle Ages. Dorothy Sayers, commenting on the excessive weeping in the *Song of Roland,* writes: "There are fashions in sensibility as in everything else. The idea that a strong man should react to great personal and national calamities by a slight compression of the lips and by silently throwing his cigarette into the fireplace is of very recent origin" (*Song of Roland,* trans. D. Sayers, Penguin Classics [Harmondsworth, Middlesex, 1957], p. 15).

38. *Works,* p. 1183; similarly, *La Mort le Roi Artu,* ed. Jean Frappier, 3rd ed. (Paris, 1964), p. 133; *Le Morte Arthur,* ed. S. Noguchi (Tokyo, 1990), ll. 1968–77. The French prose *Mort Artu* and the English stanzaic *Morte Arthur* are the major sources for Malory's Tales 7 and 8.

39. Cf. *Works,* p. 1051 and stanzaic *Morte,* ll. 818–20; *Works,* p. 1092 and stanzaic *Morte,* l. 711; *Works,* pp. 1200, 1216 and stanzaic *Morte,* l. 2437, *Mort Artu,* p. 191.

40. *Mort Artu,* p. 29; *The Death of King Arthur,* trans. James Cable, Penguin Classics (Harmondsworth, Middlesex, 1971), pp. 45–46. Translations from *Mort Artu* are from this edition. Malory's allusions to the adultery in the tournament episodes

are less specific so far as Arthur is concerned; see *Works*, pp. 1065–66.

41. *Works*, p. 1190; similarly p. 1194; cf. *Mort Artu*, p. 153; stanzaic *Morte Arthur*, ll. 2272–73.

42. For a discussion of this problem see my "The Arthur-Guenevere Relationship in Malory's *Morte Darthur*," *Studies in the Literary Imagination* 4 (1971), 29–40. This paragraph is based upon that article.

43. See *Mort Artu*, p. 101; stanzaic *Morte*, ll. 957, 1521, 1544–45.

44. See, for example, *Mort Artu*, p. 195; stanzaic *Morte*, ll. 2205, 2394–95.

45. Brewer, *Morte Darthur*, pp. 23–35. Also see C. David Benson, "Gawain's Defence of Guenevere in Malory's 'Death of Arthur,'" *Modern Language Review*, 78 (1983), 267–72.

46. *Works*, p. 1192; similarly, *Mort Artu*, p. 152; stanzaic *Morte*, ll. 2170–205.

47. *Works*, p. 1201; similarly *Mort Artu*, p. 163.

48. *Works*, p. 1194; cf. stanzaic *Morte*, ll. 2274–77.

49. *Works*, p. 1199; cf. *Mort Artu*, p. 165.

50. *Characterization in Malory: A Comparison with His Sources* (Chicago, 1934), pp. 106–09.

51. See *Mort Artu*, pp. 13, 212, 221; stanzaic *Morte*, ll. 3132–35.

52. Pochoda, pp. 134–36.

53. Pochoda, p. 136.

54. As Brewer notes, a medieval writer who based his narrative upon a source might "change the quality of personality of a given character . . . or the interpretation of an event," but he could "hardly change a principal event completely" (*The Morte Darthur: Parts Seven and Eight* [London, 1968], p 3).

55. *Works*, p. 1211; in the stanzaic *Morte*, the barons, not Arthur, choose Mordred because they think he is the best man to rule the realm (ll. 2516 ff.); in *Mort Artu* Mordred volunteers to guard the queen, and Arthur lets him, but the fact that he is Arthur's son is not mentioned (p. 166).

56. Morton, "The Matter of Britain: The Arthurian Cycle and the Development of Feudal Society," *Zeitschrift für Anglistik und Amerikanistik*, 8 (1960), 191.

57. See my "Malory and the Marriage of Edward IV," *Texas Studies in Literature and Language*, 12 (1970), 155–62.

58. In *Mort Artu* Arthur tells Gawain: "Biax niés, grant domage m'a fet vostre felonnie, car ele m'a tolu vos, que ge amoie seur touz homes, et Lancelot après" (p. 212; "Nephew . . . your wickedness has done me great harm because it has robbed me of you, whom I loved above all men, and also Lancelot" [p. 192]).

59. Pochoda, p. 134.

60. The earlier occasions in which Guenevere is permitted trial by combat are in the "Poisoned Apple" and "Knight of the Cart" episodes of Tale 7; Malory found these trials in his sources.

61. See Brewer, *Morte*, pp. 4, 22–23; Elizabeth Salter, "'Troilus and Criseyde': A Reconsideration," *Patterns of Love and Courtesy: Essays in Memory of C.S. Lewis*, ed. John Lawlor (London, 1966), pp. 90–91.

62. Pochoda, p. 134. Vinaver's note on this passage in the 1967 edition of *Works*, p. 1632 was misleading. Field corrected it in the 1990 revision.

63. In the French source Arthur swears to get vengeance. Although the barons formally pass the sentence, Arthur does not give them much choice: "ge vos commant . . . que vos esgardoiz entre vos de quel mort ele doit morir; que sanz mort n'en puet ele eschaper" (p. 120; "I command you . . . to determine among you how she should be put to death, because she will not escape with her life" [p. 119]).

64. See George Neilson, *Trial by Combat* (New York, 1891), pp. 147 ff.

65. At one point, for example, King Mark, though guilty of murder, wins the contest: "kynge Marke smote sir Amante thorow the body; and yet was sir Amaunte in the ryghtuous quarell"; no one believes that Mark is innocent and two maidens say,

"A, swete Jesu . . . Why sufferyst Thou so false a traytoure to venqueyshe . . . a trewe knyght that faught in a ryghteuous quarell" (pp. 592–93; similarly in the source: cf. MS 334, fol. 319 and Löseth, p. 163). Skepticism about this type of combat is also suggested by Malory's statement "worshyp in armys may never be foyled. But firste reserve the honoure to God, and secundely thy quarell muste com of thy lady" (p. 1119) and by statements such as Lancelot's "never was I discomfite in no quarell, were hit ryght were hit wronge" (p. 896; similarly, pp. 897, 1052, 1058, 1166). Ernest C. York discusses some of the instances of trial by combat in "The Duel of Chivalry in Malory's Book XIX," *Philological Quarterly*, 48 (1969), 186–91.

66. Brewer mentions that Arthur is later ready to take Guenevere back and forget about the law (*Morte*, p. 30); this, however, is after Lancelot explains: 1) that he has slain Arthur's knights only because "I was forced to do batayle with hem in savyng of my lyff"; and 2) that Guenevere "ys as trew a lady . . . as ys ony lady lyvynge unto her lorde" (p. 1188). The second part of Lancelot's explanation is a conventional courtly defense of a lady's honor; the first, however, deserves emphasis since this is the first time that Arthur hears that Lancelot was acting in self defense.

67. Malory defines treason in different ways. At times it is adultery: when Mellyagaunt believes Guenevere has been sleeping with a knight, he says: "I [wille] calle you of treson afore my lorde kynge Arthure" (p. 1132). At other times it is murder: "All maner of murthers in tho dayes were called treson" (p. 405); "at that tyme . . . all maner of shamefull deth was called treson" (p. 1050). Whether the death penalty was or was not used in cases of treason in the fifteenth century is irrelevant, since Malory here is referring to the law in Arthur's time.

68. Vinaver, *Works*, pp. xcv ff. and *The Rise of Romance* (Oxford, 1971), pp. 172 ff.

69. *Works*, pp. 547, 581; similarly, pp. 398, 404, 504. References to the worth-lessness of the Cornish knights also appear in the prose *Tristan*.

70. *Works*, pp. 583, 592; 633, cf. MS B.N. Fr. 334, fol. 318ra, where Mark is described in similar terms.

71. Rumble and Moorman maintain that the death of Tristram was added to Tales 7 and 8 to remind the readers of the adulterous relationship of Tristram and Isode and thus to show that such affairs were common in the declining days of Arthurian society (Rumble, pp. 146–47; Moorman, pp. 22–24). Malory's text, however, offers little evidence to support this interpretation. A better explanation is implicit in Brewer's remarks on why Malory did not include the murder in the fifth tale: it is "devoted to the glory and success of the knights of the Round Table," and a tragic ending would have been inappropriate at this point ("the hoole book," *Essays on Malory*, ed. J.A.W. Bennett [Oxford, 1963], p. 46). On the other hand, the addition of the story of Tristram's death to the final tales adds to their gloom.

72. On the death of Mark, see note 29 above. Malory's sources, of course, dictate Arthur's death in Tale 8.

73. Whether Mark might have influenced the Arthur-Guenevere relationship in the earlier tales is a moot point. Allusions to Tristram and Mark in Tale 1 are de-rived from Malory's source for this tale, the *Suite du Merlin* and not the prose *Tristan* (cf. *Works*, pp. 71–73; Huth, Vol. 1, pp. 230–32). Although Malory may have known the *Tristan* when he was writing this tale (see R.H. Wilson, "Malory's Early Knowl-edge of Arthurian Romance," *University of Texas Studies in English* 29 [1950], 36–37, and P.J.C. Field's suggestion that Malory's book was written during Malory's fi-nal imprisonment "with the help of a splendid library of Arthurian sources" ["The Last Years of Sir Thomas Malory," *Bulletin of the John Rylands Library*, 64 (1981–82), 438–39]), there is no evidence in it that Mark influenced Malory's conception of Arthur's attitude toward the queen, for there Malory deliberately makes Arthur a more loving husband. There also appears to be no influence in Tale 3 or Tale 4. When he was writing Tale 2, however, Malory may have been influenced by Mark's story; in any event Malory removes signs of Arthur's affection in this tale (see my "Arthur-

Guenevere Relationship," cited n. 42), and he also adds to his account references to Tristram that are not in the source of Tale 2, the alliterative *Morte Arthure* (see *Works,* pp. 185, 195).

74. As I have suggested elsewhere ("Malory and the Marriage of Edward IV," cited n. 57 above), Malory's attitude toward his wife and his emphasis upon the king's love for his knights could have been influenced by contemporary indignation over the marriage of Edward IV to Elizabeth Wydville and Edward's subsequent neglect of the nobility: a Lancastrian such as Malory may have wished to avoid presenting a King Arthur who was as uxorious as the Yorkist Edward IV; the rebellion of the nobility that followed Edward's marriage could have impressed upon Malory an important political lesson.

75. *Works,* pp. 431, 503–04, 580.

76. *Works,* pp. 1192, 1200–01.

77. "Cohesion" is a term better suited to Malory's book than "unity" since the latter too often connotes a tightly knit structure that *Morte Darthur* lacks. For objections to the term and alternatives, see Brewer, "hoole book," pp. 41–63 and *Morte Darthur,* p. 22; Arthur K. Moore, "Medieval English Literature and the Question of Unity," *Modern Philology,* 65 (1967–68), 296–99. For general criticism of the concept of organic unity, see Catherine Lord, "Organic Unity Reconsidered," *Journal of Aesthetics and Art Criticism,* 22 (1963–64), 263–68.

78. See Vinaver's comments, *Works,* pp. xciii–xcix, 1623 ff.

King Arthur in the Scottish Chronicles

Karl Heinz Göller

While the political intentions of Geoffrey of Monmouth's *Historia Regum Britanniae* have been thoroughly investigated, those of the Scottish chronicles have, for the most part, been neglected. An examination of the Scottish chroniclers' portrayals of King Arthur, who in Scotland was often perceived as the embodiment of the threat from the South, can give considerable insight into their political views. Instead of losing the British king in the mythical twilight of legend, they brought him into the political present. To Scottish nationalists Arthur was the embodiment of every English ruler who had hoped to conquer Scotland; to the minority with British sympathies, however, he was a symbol of the reconciliation and union of all races of the island.

For centuries the small, culturally backward country had nothing comparable to the legends about the British ruler and the claims to prestige associated with them. The *Historia Regum Britanniae* had treated the Scots as a second-rate people who were not to be taken seriously and who had been saved from complete destruction only by Arthur's mercy. The Scots, especially sensitive because of their long, painful experiences with England's interference in their affairs and its curtailment of their national independence, saw in this an insult and defamation; and the historians and others with vigorous national consciousness interpreted Geoffrey's account as an intentional attack on the dignity and cultural independence of their nation.

A history of Scotland, originating in the chronicle of J. Fordun (1384–1387) and completed in that of H. Boece (1527), was intended to correspond to the *Historia Regum Britanniae*. According to this work, Scotland had as distinguished an ancestry as Britain; in fact, the Scottish royal family was

Originally published as "König Arthur in den Schottischen Chroniken," *Anglia*, 80 (1962), 390–404; translated by Edward Donald Kennedy.

the oldest in Europe. This triumph over their neighbors was enjoyed fully by several generations of Scots and enhanced by Boece's translators Stewart and Bellenden who added new material. The latter were commissioned by the palace to write their great chronicles of the Scottish people, and while they differ from one another in style, temperament, and conception of history, they are in agreement in their depiction of Arthur, whose denigration becomes even more strongly evident when these works are compared with those of their predecessors.

The defenders and patrons of patriotic historical writing are usually found in the royal palace and its household. They were more interested in the prestige of the Scottish throne than in historical truth and thus did not share the views of those historians who disapproved of unsupported facts and legends. These apologists at court understood the meaning of historiographical work; for although authors such as Boece insisted upon the historicity of the reported events and closely associated the worth of the book with its claim to truth, anyone who at that time had studied Livy would have realized that in such chronicles the more august beginnings, the "primordia urbis augustoria," were the main incentive and that the purpose of such works was the exaltation of their own nation and the repudiation of the presumptuous Britons. The Scots, however, were not able to create a figure equivalent to Arthur; Boece's chronicle, although artistically fascinating, lacks a center comparable to the Arthurian section of the *Historia Regum Britanniae*.

The Scottish chronicles show that the conception of Arthur in England and Scotland is dependent on emotions and passions and that the king could become a vehicle for the expression of political opinions. From Fordun to Buchanan Arthur's reputation becomes increasingly diminished. Wyntoun and Major, who both present Arthur sympathetically, stand outside of this tradition; Wyntoun especially shows no sign of having been influenced by the biased Arthurian literature of the North and presents only a short summary of Arthur's life, which could have been derived from either a *Brut* chronicle or Geoffrey's *Historia*. Major, on the other hand, makes Arthur the protagonist of his program for the political integration of the island and thus reveals the true significance of the Arthurian story for Scotland.

I

Andrew of Wyntoun's chronicle is the first Scottish historical work written in English (ca. 1420).[1] The short summary of the deeds of the British kings could have been derived from any *Brut*: Arthur holds meetings of his Round Table, receives a challenge from Lucius, fights in France, and is betrayed by

Modred. More interesting is the closing remark about Arthur's death:

> Bot of his dede and his last end
> I fand na writt couþ mak it kend (ll. 4375–4376).

Thus Wyntoun wishes to say only what he knows:

> Bot quhen at he had fochtin fast
> Efter þat in ane Ile he past
> Saire woundit to be lechit þare
> And efter he wes sene na mare (ll. 4379–4382).

This information could be derived from the mysterious Huchown of the Awle Ryale,[2] whose *Gest Historiale* is repeatedly mentioned and praised. It is, however, possible that Wyntoun drew directly upon Geoffrey. Perhaps his source explicitly stated that more about Arthur's death could not be ascertained; such a remark appears in some versions of the *Historia*.[3]

II

The *Scotichronicon* (1384–1387) of John of Fordun[4] was written earlier than Wyntoun's chronicle, but was not a source for it. The facts in the chapters about Arthur are derived to a considerable extent from Geoffrey of Monmouth and also from the world histories that were admired and known in England. But while in the *Historia Regum Britanniae* the presentation of Arthur's reign takes up about a third of the whole book, it is compressed into a few pages in Fordun. The author is interested in only a very limited aspect of the character of the well-known British king, namely his significance for Scotland and the history of Scottish kings.

Thus he makes the past in Britain parallel to the history of Scotland. Just as King Gouramis in the thirty-fifth year of his reign was lured into an ambush and killed by his nephew Eugenius (or Eochodius Hebre), the British king Uter also died through the poison of the Saxons. Fordun shows with some understanding and sympathy the situations that arise from these events: interregnum, stronger Saxon invasions, danger of a destructive attack on the island. Fordun, however, has no sympathy at all for the measure that the British then considered necessary: the choice of Arthur as king. He is concerned above all with the unlawfulness of the succession. Arthur's sister Anna was the only legitimate child of Uter and Igerne and therefore only she had the right to inherit the throne. Fordun alludes here to the much discussed question of Uter's seduction of Ygerne and its chronology. It is not clear from

Geoffrey's "interea" whether Arthur was conceived while Gorlois was still alive or after his death. In any case, however, Fordun correctly concludes that Arthur was conceived outside of marriage and was therefore illegitimate.

The British king's character, however, is not denigrated. On the contrary, the picture of Arthur sketched by Fordun agrees in many points with Geoffrey's. Fordun also emphasizes the *virtus, largitas,* and *innata bonitas* which make Arthur's personality so attractive that all people love him. Arthur's court is portrayed as the center of chivalry that attracts nobles from all parts of the country.

Nevertheless this conception of Arthur is not uniformly the same in all manuscripts. Fordun apparently later reconsidered his presentation of Arthur and on the basis of different sources reached different conclusions. Not less than three divergent Arthurian chapters appear in the manuscripts of the *Scotichronicon.* MSS C and F conclude the text under discussion with a prophecy of Bede, which is associated with Arthur and Modred. Then follows the report of Arthur's being mortally wounded and his sailing to the island of Avallon to have his wounds healed ("ad sananda vulnera in insulam Avallonis evectus").[5] Geoffrey's *Historia* is the basis for this, and Fordun sometimes follows Geoffrey quite closely. MS F informs us that Arthur has been buried in the cloister at Glastonbury (Glasinbery). His epitaph reads: "Hic jacet Arthurus rex quondam rexque futurus" ("Here lies Arthur, the once and future king"). Fordun interprets this epitaph, known from romances, skeptically: "Credunt enim quidam de genere Britonum eum futurum vivere et de servitute ad libertatem eosque reducere" ("Some of the Britons believe that he will live again in the future and that he will deliver them from servitude to freedom").[6]

Manuscripts B and E, representing the author's last redaction, introduce a new chapter about Arthur. The information drawn from different sources for this section suggests that Fordun struggled with his presentation of Arthur. Although he does not follow his sources word for word, different parts of the chapter are drawn from Nennius, Bede, William of Malmesbury, and Giraldus Cambrensis. The last part borrows from Higden (whose name, however, is not mentioned) a concluding observation about Arthur's significance, which contradicts the preceding information both in details and in its general skeptical attitude and thus reflects Fordun's own ambivalence about Arthur.

Especially significant is Fordun's development of the Scottish claim to the English throne, which is claimed for the children of Loth and Anna. Fordun is not alone in advancing such arguments. In fact, Edward I had, on similar grounds, claimed the throne of Scotland. The Scottish claim was to remain politically insignificant; and this new interpretation of the Arthurian story stood no chance of gaining acceptance outside of Scotland.

III

One of the most significant and influential Scottish chronicles of the sixteenth century is that of Hector Boece (1527).[7] It is the Scottish counterpart to Geoffrey's *Historia* written almost exactly 400 years later.

The Arthurian section begins with an account that emphasizes the illegitimacy and disgrace of the conception of Arthur out of wedlock: "Suscepit Uter eo ex concubitu statutos post menses, filium Arthurum: is *que* post patrem regnauit in Britannia" ("Uther received from this cohabitation his son Arthur, who reigned in Britain after his father").[8] Afterward, in Boece's first notable departure from Geoffrey's account, Uter's first concern is that the lawful husband be murdered: "ut vxore eius liberius potiretur occidi mandauit" ("he ordered him to be killed in order to enjoy his wife more freely").[9] The fact that Arthur was illegitimately conceived will be repeated several times for the reader: "Constat omnium sententia . . . Vterum regem ex aliena conjuge suscepisse Arthurum" ("It is generally accepted that King Uter received Arthur from another's wife").[10] Departing from English tradition, Uter summons the nobles of the kingdom and persuades them to recognize Arthur as successor to the throne. Boece suppresses the spontaneous acclaim of the people, which, according to his own doctrine, would have legitimized the king in spite of his questionable conception.

A further significant change from Geoffrey's account is that Loth, who in Boece is king of the Picts (no longer a military leader of the British), appears at the outset as Arthur's opponent because of the unjust denial of his sons' claim to the throne. All battles consequently are attributed to Arthur's conception and illegitimacy, factors that were treated as insignificant or positive in the works produced outside of Scotland. Boece even interprets the Saxon wars—originally the starting point and impetus for the Arthurian story—from this point of view in order to give them a new meaning.

Arthur is portrayed as being treacherous and easily influenced by others. He retains some of his good qualities: his generosity is praised to almost the same extent as it is in Geoffrey's *Historia*. In Kent, Boece says, Arthur distributed such a great amount of silver among the people freed from the Saxons that he scarcely had enough left for his own needs.[11] Boece also praises Arthur's strategic capabilities, which he demonstrated particularly in the long battles against the Saxons. The outnumbered barons are themselves strengthened by the brilliant commander. That the British fail again and again is not the king's fault but must be ascribed to the weakness of his soldiers, who do not prove themselves worthy of Arthur. Occasionally Arthur must check their desire to kill, as for example, at the taking of York, where the king saves the lives of many people by preventing the massacre of the besieged.[12] The responsibility for the profanation of the Christmas feast, however, is attributed to Arthur himself. "Ab Arthuro sub idem tempus" ("From the time of King Arthur")[13] Christmas feasts began to be transformed into the shameful Bacchanalia, Floralia, and Priapalia that were still current in Boece's time.

Naturally Boece knew that his portrait of Arthur did not correspond to current conceptions of the king. He hastened therefore to assert that he did not wish to slander any of the past authors and certainly did not want to deprive a British king of his glory: "Non enim hic detrahende alicuius gloriae partes agimus" ("We do not report this in order to disparage the fame of some one").[14] Arthur had no less renown than the British kings before him: "Fuit rex Arthurus rerum egregie gestarum gloria & amplitudine, non minus quam Britanniae reges qui ante eum vixere insignis" ("King Arthur was in his deeds a man of fame and greatness, certainly not inferior in rank to the renowned British kings who lived before him").[15]

IV

The tendency toward Scottish nationalism is shown still more clearly in the Arthurian section of the translation of Boece that William Stewart prepared for Margaret Tudor, the widow of King James IV.[16] The scholar first of all distances himself from the conception of Arthur prevailing in England: one can find no more about Arthur in authentic sources ("storie autentik") than in his account. Although much fulsome praise comes from the pens of imaginative fools, their stories are so improbable that any rational individual can perceive their mendacity. For Stewart such distorted pictures of Arthur should be placed alongside those of Robin Hood and the Ossian hero Fyn-Mak-Coull, about whom just as many lies were circulating.

Stewart emphasizes more than Boece the negative aspects of Arthur's character. He does not say a word about Arthur's conquests, which Boece had mentioned with a skeptical "sunt qui scribant" ("some people write"). Loth remains King of the Picts, and Arthur apparently never left the island of Britain. His role is diminished to that of a tribal prince, who indeed advanced himself through personal bravery, strategic skill, and generosity, but who nevertheless was only one of many rulers of the British island.

Stewart's final assessment of Arthur is that he was Britain's most unfortunate ruler (l. 27979), and his misfortunes were caused by his disloyalty. He had broken his oath with Modred, and for that reason the hand of

God had severely punished him. The formerly proud Britons lost through him both crown and kingdom.

John Bellenden presented views similar to those of Stewart in the translation of the *Scotorum Historiae* that he prepared for King James V of Scotland (ca. 1591).[17] To be sure, he followed Boece more closely in the Arthurian section than in many other parts of the rest of the work. Basically he made the story tighter and more concise and added better motivations. In some cases there remains only the mere skeleton of what he found in his source. Many of the abbreviations concern Arthur whose virtues and achievements are repeatedly suppressed. Thus Bellenden cuts Arthur's devotion to the Virgin Mary, omits Boece's praise of his skill in war, and shortens the list of the lands he had conquered. Moreover, the inclusion of Gawain among Arthur's friends seemed to Bellenden useless and not essential for his purposes.

V

The unbiased reader might have expected an objective, scholarly presentation of the Arthurian story from the learned humanist George Buchanan. However, his *Rerum Scoticarum Historia* (1582)[18] also basically follows Boece; his professed critical relation to his source is often illusory. Thus Buchanan describes the story of Arthur's conception not as a fiction created by Geoffrey, but by Uther and Merlin: in order to diminish the shame of Igerne, they invent a fable "non dissimilem ei quæ de Jove & Alcmena in theatris sæpe actitata fuerat. Uterium scilicet arte Merlini in faciem Gorloidis versum primam cum Igerne habuisse consuetudinem" ("not dissimilar to the one that was often performed in the theatres concerning Jupiter and Alcmena. That is to say, Uter was through the art of Merlin changed into the likeness of Gorlois when he first cohabited with Igerne").[19] Thus Arthur is presented as a British Hercules.

The deviations from Boece's account consist partly of a blackening of Arthur's character or partly of hidden passing shots at the British. Thus Buchanan puts Arthur's wife in the enemy camp by indicating that she knew the plans of his opponents, but did not reveal them to her husband because she was having a secret affair with Modred. It is not to Buchanan's credit that he presented such a coarse vulgarization of Guinevere's involvement in a situation that is portrayed in many Arthurian stories as one in which she has little choice.

Nothing more remained of Laʒamon's brilliant hero, of the courtly leader of the Round Table, nothing, in short, of the *matière de Bretagne*. Arthur perhaps makes a journey "ad res in minore Britannia componendas" ("in order to settle things in Brittany").[20] Buchanan, however, does not know why the King went there. Geoffrey's depiction of the alleged events in France "nullam habent umbram ne dicam verisimilitudinem veritatis" ("have not even the shadow let alone the semblance of truth").[21] Arthur is a bastard, who through unlawful machinations came to the throne; during his reign he achieved little fame, and he fell in battle against the northern clans.

Like Boece, Buchanan also knew that such a picture of Arthur could be received by his countrymen with astonishment or indignation. He concludes therefore with a kind of apology: "De vita et morte Arcturi a multis fabulose tradantur" ("Events of the life and death of Arthur are conveyed by many as fables").[22] Such tales obscure historical truth, for they are told again and again with claims that they are worthy of being believed. Buchanan's concluding remarks about Arthur are not quite in agreement with his own portrayal of the king: Arthur was a great man, a gifted military commander, and a good Christian. He has given him more space than his subject permitted because "plaerique eas (= res Arcturi) partim per invidiam nimis parce, partim per vanitatem nimis verbose persequantur" ("some report on him too sparingly out of envy, others too verbosely out of vanity").[23] But Buchanan also could not free himself from the Scottish mindset.

VI

John Major, whose British chronicle first appeared in 1521,[24] is quite different. This surprisingly independent thinker, following no historiographical tradition, reveals his political philosophy in the title of his book, *Historia Majoris Britanniae tam Angliae quam Scotiae*. One hundred years earlier *Britannia major* would have meant something quite different (namely Britain proper as opposed to Brittany, *Britannia minor*), and the author must surely have thought that some of his contemporaries would also have misunderstood, because he explains: "tam Angliæ quam Scotiæ." Britons are for him not only the descendants of the original Celtic inhabitants (because they would be called Welsh), but all inhabitants of the British island, including the Scots. Major is the first advocate of the English-Scottish union and the champion of a politically united Great Britain.

This interest in unification is shown in his portrait of Arthur, about whom minds in Scotland were divided. For the adherents of Boece he was a symbol of the threat from their southern neighbor and a reminder of the British claims on Scotland. On the other hand, Major, who considered himself a Briton in the sense defined above, perceived Arthur as a congenial, positive figure, a model for the future kings of the country, who, following in his footsteps, could establish the unity of the nation in spite of popular opposition to it.

He therefore extols the king as the most powerful, bravest, noblest, and most chivalrous ruler of the world. He remarks with satisfaction that Arthur drove the Saxons from the island and conquered all native tribes, including the Picts and the Scots. Major would forgive much from a ruler of such importance, perhaps even the plan for the complete annihilation of the Scots. In any event, he reports without a word of anger Arthur's decision to kill all Scots. Although, according to Geoffrey, only a small part of the people were spared because the bishops and priests begged Arthur to show mercy, Major says that the people were spared because they finally submitted to Arthur.

Major adds as an incidental remark that Arthur's seat of government was at Edinburgh. There is no known source for that. People had, in fact, often incorrectly identified the *Urbs Legionum* and had placed it in different parts of the country; except for Dunbar[25] only Major and authors who drew upon him associate Arthur with Edinburgh. The direct influence of Dunbar is improbable; therefore we must assume that even such an apparently unimportant fact reflects Major's political inclination: the unification of the hostile races of the country, with one ruler for both groups of people, but with a government located in Edinburgh.

Substantial parts of the Arthurian section are a paraphrase of the corresponding sections of Geoffrey's *Historia* with the addition of occasional incidental remarks and insertions from other sources. The description of Arthur and his armor is apparently derived from Jacques-Phillipe Foresti.[26] Major mentions this chronicler elsewhere, but does not cite him as a source for this part of his account.[27]

Major agrees with the Britons' inclusion of Arthur among the Nine Just Men. The account of the nine presents the opportunity for historical excursuses and critical remarks about the worthiness of the individual kings and their claims to such a high honor. Arthur's position among the nine, however, is not disputed.

Major's interest in a settlement with the British is also apparent in his account of Anguischel, the king of the Scots, of whom it is said that he participated in Arthur's foreign wars, fought by Arthur's side against the Roman emperor, and finally returned with him to Britain.

Since Scotland and Britain have a legitimate ruler, Modred must be presented in a less favorable light. He again becomes—as in so many romances after Geoffrey—the treacherous, untrustworthy regent who betrays Arthur during the Roman campaign and who seduces Arthur's wife Guinevere. Major finds it difficult to understand how Modred could raise such an enormous army to fight against Arthur. He explicitly says that the king of the Scots loved Arthur because of his uprightness and honor. Thus for Major there is only one explanation: Modred bribed the Scots, who were ready to do any shameful thing for money, even to fight against the feudal lord to whom they had sworn everlasting fidelity.

The account of Arthur's decisive battle against Modred is derived from Geoffrey and shows little change. Modred was killed; Arthur received a severe wound and went to a certain island where he hoped to be healed. Before he left he predicted that he would return. Therefore the Britons hoped for hundreds of years for the return of their renowned king and for freedom from the Saxon yoke. Major, however, distances himself from such a hope and describes it as absurd and born out of excessive dependence on the king. And he adds an interesting proverb that was still current in his time: "Unde in fabulam ductum est, quando aliquis, qui numquam veniet, expectatur, hunc expectas, sicut Arthurum Britanni" ("From there it became a kind of saying that if you expect someone who will never come, you expect him as the British do Arthur").[28]

Tales of this type are on the same level as "Arthuri vota illa quae de lecto periculoso recitantur" ("as the solemn vows to King Arthur made from the sickbed").[29] Here we have evidence that Arthur would be called upon to help the sick;[30] however, Major thinks no more highly of that than of "multa alia quae illa tempestate in Britannia contigisse dicunt" ("many other things which are said to have happened in Britain at that time"). Unless they have been brought about by demons, they can be only *figmenta*. Finally there are many, among them the chronicler of Bergamo, Jacques-Philippe Foresti, who consider Arthur himself to be a magician.[31] "Sed huic de tam claro rege haud assentior" ("But I cannot agree to this, said about so famous a king").[32]

Major considers it wrong to devaluate the brilliance of the historical king and to diminish or even deny his heroic deeds simply because of the many fables and stories about him. Arthur was for him a great, perhaps the greatest king of the British island. But he was a mortal; his grave is located at Glastonbury. It bears the epitaph that was sung by the people attending his funeral and which corresponds fully to popular belief: "Hic jacet Arthurus Rex magnus Rex futurus" ("Here lies Arthur, the once and future king").

In summary, the accounts of Arthur in the Scottish chronicles indicate that they were derived, in both their contradictions and agreements, from Geoffrey's *Historia Regum Britanniae*, the political intention of which appears not to have gone unnoticed in the nations immediately affected. Boece and his successors saw in that epoch-making work a type of national epic that had been written for the glorification of a society in the British island that excluded the Scots. In this context the answer to the question for which nation the *Historia* was intended as an epic is superfluous.[33] According to Geoffrey, the Scots had a place only as a subjugated people.

That Scotland has in the *Historia* a relationship to Arthur's kingdom different from that of, for example, Wales, might be based on hostility that Geoffrey felt toward the Scots, but it can also be mere accident. In any case, the brief parts of the *Historia* that concern Scotland had a powerful historical effect. When Edward I in 1301 defended his claim to Scotland against Pope Boniface VIII, he drew his arguments chiefly from the *Historia:* The Scottish king Auguselus was placed on the throne by Arthur and at Pentecost in Caerlion had carried out the *servitium debitum* for Scotland. Scottish historians, however, rejected the claims of the *Historia* and as a countermove demanded in addition to political autonomy even the British throne, at least for Loth and his successors. This claim to hegemony, however, remained historically insignificant because of its utopian and theoretical nature. Today we still can not say what actual influence the Scottish chroniclers had on historical development. They at least contributed to the development of Scottish national feeling. While the English, as descendants of the Saxons, soon forgot that the old Britons had been the enemies of their ancestors and made Arthur one of their own, the Scots persisted in their defensive position against the "patron of England."[34] Major and his adherents would for a long time remain in the minority.

NOTES

1. *The Original Chronicle of Andrew of Wyntoun*, ed. F.J. Amours, STS (London and Edinburgh, 1902–1914). The story of Arthur is in No. 54 (1906), pp. 18 ff. Cf. Robert Huntington Fletcher, *The Arthurian Material in the Chronicles, especially those of Great Britain and France*, (Harvard) *Studies and Notes in Philology and Literature*, 10 (Boston, 1906), pp. 241 ff.

2. See H.N. MacCracken, "Concerning Huchown," *PMLA* 25 (1910), 507 ff.; W. Geddie, *A Bibliography of Middle Scots Poets*, STS 61 (Edinburgh and London, 1912), pp. 40 ff.

3. See, for example, the Welsh MS LXI in Jesus College, Oxford; *The Historia Regum Britanniae of Geoffrey of Monmouth*, ed. A. Griscom (London and New York, 1929), p. 501.

4. W.F. Skene's critical scholarly edition compared the known manuscripts: *Chronica Gentis Scotorum* (Edinburgh, 1871). The chronicle is known as *Scotichronicon.* Cf. L. Keeler, *Geoffrey of Monmouth and the Late Latin Chroniclers 1300–1500* (Berkeley and Los Angeles, 1946), pp. 76 ff.; Fletcher, *The Arthurian Material in the Chronicles*, pp. 242–43; J. Bain, *The Edwards in Scotland* (Edinburgh, 1901); H.M. Paton, *The Scottish Records* (Edinburgh, 1933). For Fordun's sources, also see Macpherson's introduction to his edition of Wyntoun.

5. Skene, I.111.

6. *Ibid.* Karl Heinz Göller translated most of the Latin quotations in this article.

7. The following edition was used: Hector Boethius, *Scotorum Historiae a prima Gentis Origine* (Parisiis, 1575), B.M. 1473. dd.12. Also see W. Douglas Simpson, "Hector Boece," in *University of Aberdeen: Quatercentenary of the Death of Hector*

Boece, *First Principal of the University* (Aberdeen, 1937), pp. 28 ff.

8. Boece, f. 155 v.
9. Boece, f. 155 v.
10. Boece, f. 155 r.
11. Boece, f. 159 v.
12. Boece, f. 160 r.
13. Boece, f. 160 r.
14. Boece, f. 163 v.
15. Boece, f. 163 v.

16. William Stewart, *The Buik of the Chronicles of Scotland, or a Metrical Version of the History of Hector Boece,* ed. W.B. Turnbull, R.S. 6, 1–3 (London, 1858).

17. *The Chronicles of Scotland,* compiled by Hector Boece, trans. into Scots by John Bellenden (1531), ed. R.W. Chambers and E.C. Batho, 2 vols, STS III. 10, 15 (Edinburgh and London, 1938–1941).

18. *Rerum Scoticarum Historia auctore Georgio Buchanano Scoto* (Abredoniæ, 1762).

19. *Ibid.,* p. 117.
20. *Ibid.,* p. 119.
21. *Ibid.,* p. 119.
22. *Ibid.,* p. 120.
23. *Ibid.,* p. 120.

24. *Historia Majoris Britanniae tam Angliae quam Scotiae, per Joannem Majorem, nomine quidem Scotum, professione autem Theologum e Veterum Monumentis concinnata . . . etc.,* Editio Nova (Edinburgh, 1740). Major is punning on his own name in the title; in the foreground, however, is the effort to find an equitable and acceptable term for the Scots and the English.

25. Cf. *The Poems of William Dunbar,* ed. W. Mackenzie (London, 1932), "The Flyting" (ca. 1500), l. 336. Cf. R.S. Loomis, "Scotland and the Arthurian Legend," *Proceedings of the Society of Antiquaries of Scotland,* LXXXIX (1955–1956), 1 ff. Loomis does not mention Edinburgh as the residence of Arthur; the *Castellum Puellarum,* however, has a close association with Morgain.

26. J. Ph. Foresti, *Historia Novissima congesta . . . Supplementum Cronicarum* (Brixie, 1485), Lib. Nonus, fol. 205–206.

27. Foresti again refers to Geoffrey's *Historia Regum Britanniae,* IX.4ʳ.

28. Major, p. 67.
29. Major, p. 67.

30. On the veneration of Arthur as a saint, see Karl Heinz Göller, "Saint Arthur," *La Bretagne,* 802 (1962), 2.

31. I found no remark of this type in the edition of Foresti.

32. Major, p. 67.

33. See E.K. Chambers, *Arthur of Britain* (London, 1927), p. 128; also W.F. Schirmer, *Die frühen Darstellungen des Arthurstoffes* (Köln and Opladen, 1958), p. 32; for references to the political significance of the *Historia,* see p. 20.

34. Chambers, *Arthur of Britain,* p. 128.

Polydore Vergil and John Leland on King Arthur

The Battle of the Books[1]

James P. Carley

The question of how the Tudor dynasty deployed the Arthurian myth is one that continues to be debated.[2] From a literary historian's perspective, however, there is one key fact: without doubt, Spenser's great poem, *The Faerie Queene,* linked the Arthurian legend with an imperial vision of the English monarchy.[3] Nor was Spenser alone in his interest in Arthur: Michael Drayton's *Poly-Olbion,* for example, examined the topographical aspects of the story, and other minor poets and playwrights throughout the period wrote about *la matière de Bretagne*.[4] Even if the situation is not entirely clear in all its political ramifications, then, Arthur certainly played an important role as symbol of the monarch and imperial splendour in the literature of the reigns of Henry VIII and Elizabeth I.[5] And this widespread association of Arthur with the Tudor throne, nationalism, and cultural concerns forms the backdrop to a particularly vehement scholarly battle between the Italian historian Polydore Vergil and the English antiquary John Leland.

Polydore Vergil (1470?–1555) first came to England from his native Italy in 1502 and, apart from brief absences, spent most of his life there until his final return to Italy in 1553.[6] Although he seems to have been interested in English antiquities from the time of his arrival, he did not begin composition of his *Anglica Historia* until about 1506–07, and the earliest manuscript copy of the text can be dated to 1512–13. The first printed version, which involved considerable rewriting, appeared in 1534; a second revised edition came out in 1546; a third, containing an additional book dealing with Henry VIII's reign to 1537, was printed in 1555.

Vergil's researches convinced him that Geoffrey of Monmouth, whose accounts of early Britain had constituted the *fons et origo* of much English

Revised by the author from "Polydore Vergil and John Leland on King Arthur: The Battle of the Books," *Interpretations*, 15 (1984), 86–100.

historical writing for almost four centuries, was not an accurate historian, and that the *Historia Regum Britanniae* was, in much of its narrative, a work of fiction. In the *Anglica Historia* Geoffrey's two chief heroes, Brutus and Arthur, came in for special scrutiny: Brutus was dismissed altogether and Arthur emerged with considerably diminished stature. In fact, the account of Arthur's reign occupied only one short paragraph in Vergil's text. All Vergil was willing to grant as ascertainable about Arthur was that he ruled after Uther and that he might well have reunited Britain for a time if he had lived longer. These are the only facts that can be established according to Vergil's reckoning; the rest is, at best, speculation. To state that the Arthur was buried at Glastonbury Abbey, in particular, was an indefensible piece of anachronism, Vergil argued, since the monastery was not even founded until after Arthur's death.

The response of John Leland (1503?-1552) to Vergil's account was swift and vehement; from his perspective, Vergil's diminution of Arthur struck at the very identity of the English nation.[7] As a loyal subject and dedicated "antiquarius"—the very term reflects his humanist training and continental models of scholarship—Leland challenged Vergil's interpretation of British history in two different Arthurian tracts and other writings as well: "Haec ego de Polydoro modeste satis, ut arbitror, & candide retuli, quem interim aperte de me male loqui & sentire certe scio, id quod susque deque fero" ("I have responded to those statements from Virgil modestly enough, as I think, and clearly. I know for certain that he meanwhile thinks badly of me and speaks openly against me, which I report up and down").[8] Polemical though his writings might have been—and in the *Cygnea Cantio* he would proudly assert: "Ego interea loci strenue caussam meae patriae defendam, & famam ejusdem modis quibus possim omnibus promovebo, augebo, ornabo" ("Meanwhile I shall vigorously defend the cause of my country on the proper occasion and shall honor, advance, and increase its fame in every way I can")[9]—Leland nevertheless saw himself as an objective historian; truth was his goal, facts were his weapons: "An other way, do equity, honesty, the rule of fame, and heerehence a iust loue to my country, yea truth it selfe (then which one thing, nothing more deare I loue) fully moue me."[10]

The *Codrus sive Laus et Defensio Gallofridi Arturii contra Polydorum Vergilium,* written perhaps in 1536, was never issued as a separate work, but came ultimately to form the section on Geoffrey of Monmouth in Leland's *De viris illustribus,* the comprehensive biographical and bibliographical study of British writers that was nearing completion when insanity overtook him in 1547.[11] The *Codrus* began and ended with biographical material about Geoffrey, but the bulk of the text was concerned with Arthur. Leland saw that an attack on Geoffrey's interpretation of British history, in which Arthur played such a pivotal role, was an attack on the foundations of English nationalism. He accepted without doubt, moreover, Geoffrey's statement concerning the ancient British book given him by Walter, archdeacon of Oxford.[12] In a certain sense we see here the voice of the ancients—those who would appeal to the world of textual scholarship, retrieval of lost documents from the distant past—asserting itself against the puny moderns, of whom Vergil, addressed under the pseudonym of Codrus (the name applied by the Roman poets to those poetasters who annoyed other people by reading their productions to them), constituted a prime example.

In the *Codrus* Leland touched on much of the evidence that he would analyse more fully in the *Assertio Arturii*. He first listed the many Arthurian remains that he had discovered throughout the kingdom. He noted, for example, that in Wales Caerleon is associated with Arthur, discussed the origin of the place name *Cather* or *Cair Arthur* and mentioned various other surviving Welsh written records. In the south of England, Dover provided Arthurian evidence through certain relics in its castle and through its chronicles. At Westminster there was an old wax seal with the provocative inscription PATRICIVS ARTVRVS BRITANNIAE GALLIAE GERMANIAE DACIAE IMPERATOR.[13] Not surprisingly, Glastonbury Abbey provided the largest collection of significant material. Taking the accounts of William of Malmesbury and Gerald of Wales found in the Glastonbury library, supplemented by chronicle references, Leland reconstructed a coherent account of Arthur's reign, which could be substantiated by the relics *in situ:* the famous leaden cross, an ancient seal, and the tomb itself.[14] The cumulative effect of all the evidence, in Leland's opinion, was to expose the folly of Vergil's doubts: "At ego tam certis, claris, veris argumentis, non dicam tam multis, probare possum, Arturium fuisse, quam Codrus Caesarem" ("But I can prove that Arthur existed with as certain, as clear, as true, not to mention as many, arguments as Codrus can prove Caesar to have existed").[15]

The *Assertio Arturii* (first published in 1544) took up the same themes in more detail and was Leland's most comprehensive statement on Arthur. It provides for the modern reader a detailed statement of intelligent sixteenth-century English opinion about the Arthurian legends and shows just what historical and archaeological resources (many subsequently lost) existed at the time.

In this text Leland made clear that he was willing openly to concede that not everything written about Arthur was necessarily true. As freely as the sceptics, he lamented the fables which had crept into the historical accounts:

It is no noueltie, that men mixe triflinge toyes with true thinges, and surely this is euen done with a certaine employment that writers might captiuate ye simple common people with a certaine admiration at them when they heare of marueylouse matters. So was *Hercules,* so was *Alexander,* so *Arthure,* and so also Charles commended.[16]

But, just because the romances are corrupt—containing exaggerations and sometimes falsehoods too—this does not mean that the whole story must be abandoned. Such an attitude, Leland observed, represents a kind of *reductio ad absurdum* and suggests a credulity of its own kind, one from which William of Newburgh, Hector Boece, and Polydore Vergil all suffered. Not unexpectedly, Leland rested his case upon authority:

> How much better is it . . . to reade, scanne vpon, and preserue in memorie those thinges which are consonant by Authorytie. For, that which nowe a long time is embraced of Learned men with greate consent: ought not in what soeuer moment of time barcking against it, together with faith or credite thereof, to be quite taken away.[17]

Authority for Leland, however, involved active scholarship and careful analysis of sources—all the techniques of humanist editing of the classics which he had learned in Paris—not just mindless spouting from the first materials to hand. Most importantly, Leland examined more than one kind of evidence and tried to weigh relative importance: he used materials contained in ancient—and some modern—books, etymologies, physical remains, and oral traditions.[18] In each category his research was thorough, his learning immense.[19]

Modern writers have pointed to a number of early texts that discuss Arthur or Arthurian events. For the early period scholars cite pseudo-Nennius and discuss why Bede is silent about Arthur and why Gildas refers to the Battle of Mount Badon without naming Arthur. Leland, too, seized on these problems and tried to grapple with them. For Leland, as for us, Geoffrey of Monmouth is a key figure in terms of the development of the late medieval version of the story. William of Malmesbury seems the most trustworthy twelfth-century witness. For the Glastonbury episode the two accounts by Gerald of Wales form the chief authorities, although Ralph of Coggeshall provides a more or less contemporary version which conflicts in some details.[20] In these essential aspects, then, the *Assertio Arturii* tallies with modern textual scholarship.

Where Leland differs from the modern tradition is in his acceptance of the evidence of more obscure writers: in his archival researches he discovered an almost overwhelming number of supporting documents for his Arthurian thesis. He was not interested in what he recognized to be fables per se, but he did devote a chapter to early poets and historians, most of whom would be considered apocryphal characters nowadays: individuals such as Taliesin, Melkin the Bard, Merlin Ambrosius, and Merlin Caledonius.[21] St. Patrick is treated in the context of establishing the antiquity of Glastonbury Abbey. Samuel Britannus, a contemporary of "Nennius," is credited with linking Arthur to the constellation Arcturus; he is also the authority for Arthur's putative trip to Jerusalem.

Apart from the predictable references to Geoffrey of Monmouth, William of Malmesbury, and Gerald of Wales many less reliable later medieval writers are cited: Alfred of Beverley, Henry of Huntingdon, Jacobus de Voragine, Thomas Gray, Joseph of Exeter, and John de Hauvilla. In his discussion of Arthur's burial, Leland listed, among other documents, the lives of Gildas, of St. Illtyd, and of St. David, as well as the writings of John Bever, Matthew Paris, Matthew of Westminster, Ranulf Higden, Glastonbury chroniclers, and the history of Dover Castle. Malory and Caxton are also quoted. Many distinguished historians abroad praised the name of Arthur, as Leland observed with pleasure: the anonymous chronicler of Dijon, for example, and, most famous of all, Boccaccio. In the *Assertio Arturii* there is, as well, a sprinkling of citations from modern writers. The effect of all these authorities is, as Leland planned, daunting:

> If these witnesses of sure credit make not sufficient for most apparant knowledge of the truth, surely there can nothing at any time auaylably serue. For not to be satisfied with these being receyued and knowen at full, is neyther the parte of a wise head, no nor yet of a good iudgment.[22]

As in the *Codrus*, Leland used etymologies as a means of establishing the legitimacy of the Arthurian legends. These are cited in the text, and there is also a long "Elenchus antiquorum nominum" ("List of ancient names"). Leland's interest in Welsh—a language with which his friend John Bale stated him to be familiar—is apparent.[23] Several place name attributions, moreover, led Leland to ingenious speculations.[24] Leland thought, for example, that the name of one of Arthur's major battle sites came into existence as a result of manuscript corruption: Camlann, he posited, was actually a misreading for the name Allen, the river that rises near Padstow in Cornwall.[25] There were ancient legends among local inhabitants about a great battle at this location, and these tended to confirm the etymological research. The rumours were strengthened, moreover, by the evidence of old coins turned up by ploughmen and fishermen and by horse trappings and bits of armour.

In the case of Camelot, Leland was prepared to debunk the popular association with Winchester by means of what modern scholars would call archaeological fact. The hill at South Cadbury—whose neglected state forcefully reminded him of Troy—was, in his opinion, indubitably the site of Camelot. The names of nearby places, such as Queen's Camel, provided added linguistic clues for the identification. The location, he noted, was obviously suited for fortification; the inhabitants retained trace memories of the legend and old coins confirmed it.[26] Leland was the first known modern writer to identify South Cadbury with Camelot, an identification accepted—in the most general sense—by some twentieth-century historians and archaeologists.[27]

In his discussion of Glastonbury Abbey, Leland demonstrated his sharp powers of observation, his attention to detail, and his breadth of knowledge. He had examined the library carefully[28] and could quote the many authorities whose works were found there, ultimately passing judgement on conflicting accounts of the same events.[29] He walked on the grounds, studied the sequence of Arthurian burials, discussed local legends with the monks, and handled the relics. The leaden cross, he affirmed, had the following wording: HIC IACET SEPVLTVS INCLYTVS REX ARTHVRIVS IN INSVLA AVALONIA ("HERE LIES BURIED THE RENOWNED KING ARTHUR IN THE ISLAND OF AVALON").[30] He was also interested in the inscription on the later and most elaborate tomb:

> Hic iacet Arturi coniunx tumulata secunda
> Quae meruit coelos, uirtutum prole saecundo.[31]

("Here lies buried the second wife of Arthur who merited heaven through the happy consequence of her virtues.")

Leland was, in fact, dubious about the tradition of a second wife, and decided that the whole story of Guinevere's burial at Glastonbury should be given considerably less credit than the account of Arthur's own disinterment and reburial.[32]

The structure of the *Assertio Arturii* is relatively straightforward; Leland narrated his story *ab ovo*, supporting the statements made in each segment by the weight of many authorities. He regularly quoted classical authors and used, on one occasion at least, direct discourse at length.[33] The *Assertio Arturii*, in its attention to detail and in its wide erudition, shows one use to which Leland's years of antiquarian research could be put. Although it is repetitive on occasion and often lacks the polish of his poetic works, it stands in other respects as a model of how Leland might have used his massive compilations of notes in other projects had his sanity held.[34]

An assertion, it must be remembered, is usually written against a negation; it fits, in other words, into the dialogue form.[35] Leland was acutely aware of Vergil's anti-Galfridian position and the text is full of attacks on his opponent:

> . . . and with the same dilligence to leane vnto the Brittish history interpreted by *Geoffrey* of *Munmouth* a man not altogether vnlearned, (what soeuer otherwise persons ignorant of antiquitie, which thinke themselues to haue knowledge, shall say) as vnto a firme defence, rather then vnto the fond fables or base stuffe of forraine writers.[36]

More specifically, Leland realized that there were at least two areas in which Vergil had seriously challenged the Arthur story, and that these needed to be directly confronted. The first concerned the date of the founding of the church at Glastonbury, and whether Arthur could, indeed, have been buried there. To answer Vergil's negative allegations, Leland had recourse to two types of evidence. The first consisted of an account given in the forged Charter of St. Patrick of the second-century evangelization of Avalon by Phaganus and Deruvianus.[37] This ancient, and to Leland's mind authentic, document was supported by references in a charter by Henry II to early benefactions to Glastonbury. The two charters are used together to build up an objective case: Vergil is silenced not by abuse but by the weight of greater learning.[38]

That Gildas, the most nearly contemporary witness to events in the Arthurian period, did not mention Arthur by name poses a serious problem to those wishing to maintain Arthur's historicity. Vergil had observed this and brought out an edition of the *De excidio Britanniae* in 1525, partly in order "to prepare the public for the anti-Arthurian position he was to take up in the *Anglica Historia.*"[39] Leland, however, was far from daunted by Gildas's silence. First, as he established, the manuscript tradition surrounding the *De Excidio Britanniae* is a corrupt one:

> *Gildas* his historie is published abroade of *Polidorus,* vndoubtedlie a fragment of ye old *Gildas,* but it is lame, out of order, and maimed,

so farre forth, as if he were now againe restored to life, the father would scarce knowe his chylde.[40]

Furthermore, Leland argued, other works by Gildas are now lost, so we really do not know the extent of his writings: he may well have discussed Arthur in works which have subsequently disappeared. In any case, even if Gildas never did mention Arthur, why should this be so surprising? After all, Gildas was not born until the year after the battle of Badon, he lived a secluded life, and he was bitter about the Britons.[41] To negate Arthur's existence because Gildas ignored him would, therefore, be a wild misuse of logic: "*Gildas* makes no mention at all of *Arthure: Ergo* he was neuer liuing."[42] Using this sort of reasoning, one would have to eliminate a large percentage of the individuals making up the British (or any) past. Perhaps, Leland concluded with irony, this is the Italian method of logic. If so, it was enough to make him wish to repudiate his own epithet of "ultramontanus."

In the final analysis, modern scholarship has not moved far beyond Leland in its approach to the question of Arthur's historical existence. Not every document cited by Leland would be accepted by modern scholars, of course, and not every etymology is accurate.[43] On the other hand, his approach resembles ours.[44] What he wrote prefigured E.K. Chambers's classic text, *Arthur of Britain,* or perhaps more specifically the archaeological/historical formulation put forward by Leslie Alcock in *Arthur's Britain.*[45] The conclusions reached by most historians in the twentieth century may be closer to Vergil's—or even more radically, as some scholars suggest, it may be impossible to ascertain anything much at all about what was going on in the period[46]—but the methodology resembles Leland's, and in this sense he is indeed the victor in the battle of the books.[47]

Although Leland clearly felt that he had successfully silenced Vergil, he did not think that his opponent was altogether unworthy; he conceded that Vergil was a man of intelligence, a practitioner of *bonae litterae* whose Latin style, at least, deserved admiration.[48] This estimation was not, however, shared by Leland's followers who reacted to Vergil's supposed insult to the British past with varying degrees of fury.[49] Although it refers to another episode in the *Anglica Historia,* the notorious passage in John Bale's *King Johan* shows the direction of the attacks and, equally significantly, holds Leland up as the sure defender of the British heritage and reformed church:

> I assure ye, fryndes, let men wryte what they wyll,
> Kynge Iohan was a man both valeaunt and godlye.
> What though Polydorus reporteth hym very yll

At the suggestyons of the malicyouse clergye?
Thynke yow a Romane with the Romanes can not lye?
Yes: Therfor, Leylond, out of thy slumbre awake,
And wytnesse a trewthe for thyne owne contrayes sake.[50]

In his *Acts and Monuments* John Foxe initiated the rumor that Vergil had either burned medieval manuscripts detrimental to his arguments or shipped them to Italy, and this supposition soon gained wide currency.[51] Ultimately, Vergil came to be viewed as a thorough rogue:

> *Polydore Vergilius*—that most rascall dogge knave in the worlde, an Englyshman by byrth, but he had Italian parents: he had the randsackings of all the Englishe lybraryes, and when he had extracted what he pleased he burnt those famouse velome manuscripts, and made himself father to other mens workes—felony in the highest degree; he deserved not heaven, for that was too good for him, neither will I be so uncharitable to judge him to hell, yet I think that he deserved to be hanged between both.[52]

Vergil's challenge to national pride (and ultimately to a concept of ecclesiastical purity stretching back well before the "contamination" of the Roman church) as exemplified in the heroic Arthurian past, then, continued to disturb English writers throughout the Elizabethan age and into the next century. Understandably, the sense of the tenuousness of any secure hold on the past had deepened. Leland, at least, had seen the great libraries and their manuscripts before the Dissolution and had attempted to save what he could from the general carnage.[53] The next generation had no way of knowing what might have been lost, and it was tempting to transfer blame from Henry's own domestic policies to foreign enemies.[54]

The generations immediately after Leland's death are the ones that produced Spenser and Drayton. The continued availability—and presumed readership—of the *Assertio Arturii* is, therefore, a point well worth establishing and it is to this which I wish finally to turn. As already noted, the *Assertio Arturii* was translated by Richard Robinson and reissued by John Wolfe, the son and heir to Leland's own publisher Reginald Wolfe, in 1582; this was, of course, the period when Spenser was seriously addressing himself to his great epic poem. Robinson himself is a deservedly obscure figure, a poor hack known almost exclusively for his translations and compilations.[55] Even taking into account the constraints imposed by pecuniary exigencies and the need to please patrons, Robinson's writings suggest a strong

Protestant bias, combined with a pronounced nationalism. Apart from the translation of the *Assertio Arturii,* there is one other book which deserves attention here: *The Auncient Order, Societie and Vnitie Laudable of Prince Arthure, and His Knightly Armory of the Round Table. With a Threefold Assertion Frendly in Fauour and Furtherance of English Archery at this Day,* also published by John Wolfe, in 1583. The London "fellowship of Prince Arthurs knightes" described by Robinson enjoyed a continuous existence from the time of Henry VIII through the reign of Elizabeth (except for a brief period under Mary) and seems to have made some sort of occult link between Arthur, archery, the Protestant religion, and the rainbow as Ark of the Covenant.[56] A number of influential figures—including Richard Mulcaster—were active members.[57] The allusion to Prince Arthur provides both a tribute to the Tudor dynasty, with its recollection of Prince Arthur, brother of Henry VIII, and a perpetuation of the noble fellowship of the Round Table. As in the nineteenth-century return to Camelot, there is a link between military prowess and religious devotion.[58] The Arthurian theme suggests, of course, that there might be some sort of general connection between Robinson's translation of the *Assertio Arturii* and his book on the Society of Archers. There are, however, even more specific links, since the earlier work is dedicated to three individuals, one of whom is Thomas Smith, the Society's Prince Arthur. The other two dedicatees are also significant: Arthur Lord Gray de Wilton, Spenser's patron, and Sir Henry Sidney, the father of Sir Philip. Finally, in the preface to the translation of the *Assertio Arturii* Robinson referred specifically to the Society and gave an interpretation of its origin and function:

> Hereupon by patent of his [Henry VIII's] princely prerogatiue ordayned, graunted, and confirmed hee vnto this honorable Citie of London, free election of a Chieftaine and of Citizens representing the memory of that magnificent King Arthure, and the Knightes of the same order, which should for the mayntenance of shooting onely, meete together once a yeare, with solemne and friendly celebration therof. So much in his noble minde preuayled all prouident care of princely prowesse, valiancie, cheualrie, and actiuitie, that he not onely herein imitated the examplers of godly K. Dauid for his Israelites as before, and of that noble Emperour Leo in ouerthrowing idolatrie, and exalting archerie maugre the mallice of that Romane Antichrist, and all his members: but also inuincibly maintayned the praiseworthie practize of this shooting in peace & wars by the examples of his princly progenitors.[59]

Aside from a strong anti-Catholic streak, which seems a natural development of the apocalyptic vision of John Bale and other of Leland's immediate successors,[60] there are associations between King David, the monarch as heir to "that magnificent King Arthure," and the church in England as well as hints of an esoteric brotherhood.[61]

Several other individuals are named by Robinson in his prefatory notes. First comes Stephen Batman, translator, author, and domestic chaplain to Archbishop Matthew Parker (for whom he was commissioned to collect ancient books).[62] As Robinson reported it, Batman found at Avalon/Glastonbury records which showed that Joseph of Arimathea had come to Glastonbury in apostolic times, and that Arthur was descended from his stock. Batman's source was presumably John of Glastonbury's *Cronica sive Antiquitates Glastoniensis Ecclesie*.[63] The information contained in John's "ancient" chronicle could easily be manipulated to show a link between English independence from Rome and the Arthurian tradition, a link which Leland's *Assertio Arturii* also seemed implicitly to suggest. John Stow and William Camden, not unexpectedly, receive acknowledgment for their help in dealing with place name identifications. Both appear as well in marginal notes, and their comments are sometimes incorporated into the text.[64]

Little, I think, needs to be said about the translation itself. John Leland was an accomplished humanist, educated first at St. Paul's School, then at Cambridge and Oxford, and finally in Paris, where he consulted with the great scholars of the day—Guillaume Budé, Jacques Lefèvre d'Etaples, Paolo Emilio, Jean Ruel, Jan Lascaris, Nicolas Bérault, and François Du Bois.[65] His prose is, for the most part, sophisticated and humanist (i.e., classical rather than medieval in style)—he was, after all, a student of William Lily. Robinson, whose background was humbler, and whose learning was considerably more rudimentary, produced a much rougher text. He was somewhat careless[66] and had various problems with details of translation—usually with the identification of names but sometimes with more fundamental grammatical issues. Certain of his changes—paraphrase, abbreviations and expansions—led to a misrepresentation of the sense of the original passage. When Leland ended his address to his readers with the admonition:

> Hinc procul at fugiant Codrino felle tumentes,
> Ne proprio crepitent ilia rupta malo.[67]

> ("Let those swelling up with Codrus-like bitterness flee far away from here/Lest their burst intestines rattle with their own evil.")

Robinson rendered it as:

> Farre hence flee those their spyte which spew,
> Least their Intestines burst with their owne ill.[68]

Leland's allusion here was to Polydore Vergil in the Codrus persona which he had given him, and Leland thus set up his dialogue format, which is important to a reading of the assertion itself. By omitting Codrus as a character, Robinson's translation robbed the text of a small but significant component.

This hortatory couplet also indicates that Leland could be both polemical and emotional in his writing. The tone in the greater part of the actual *Assertio Arturii* is, nevertheless, relatively restrained. Robinson is considerably more volatile; his prose at times downright scurrilous. The following example, taken from his own preface to the work, is representative:

> . . . euen one English Leyland for his learned laboure laudable, hath perfectly polished him [Arthur] in all poyntes. Chusing a cheefe & most perspicuouse, a valiant & most victoriouse, a couragiouse and most conquerouse, a religiouse and redoubted Royall soueraigne king Henry the eight, as sole supreme Patron and protector thereof against the cankered currish kinde of caueling carpers.[69]

Euphues appears to have met his match! Some of the bumbling quality which has been associated with Leland's *Assertio Arturii*, then, should probably be redirected at the translation, and it might well be interesting to ascertain how many of the modern commentators on this tract have inadvertently addressed themselves to Robinson rather than to Leland.

At several points in this paper I have suggested connections between Leland and the poets of the succeeding generations. Specific borrowings can be found both in *The Faerie Queene* and in Drayton's *Poly-Olbion*.[70] These links are, indeed, significant in themselves, but there is another component that is even more important. In the period after his death, Leland was greatly venerated as an authority on the British past, and his papers were treated with the highest regard and had a wide circulation and influence.[71] In his career as antiquary and topographer, he developed a passion for the past—closely linked with a pride in the present—quite unlike that of his predecessors. His treatment of the Arthurian legend was the first indication of a new way of looking at Arthur, one in which the romances of the Middle Ages have been replaced by a "topo-chrono-graphicall" mode.[72] Leland saw a new kind of romance in historical fact, a myth buried in loving description of actual landscape.[73] His adulation of Arthur as a man and his attraction to contemporary geography as a witness to the hero's reality prefigure many elements of later Arthurian trends in literature, in history, and in archaeology.

NOTES

1. For the version of this essay printed in this volume I have updated references and made stylistic changes, but the arguments remain basically the same. The conceit of a battle of the books to characterize the sixteenth-century controversy is taken from a paper written by Edwin Greenlaw and published posthumously in his *Studies in Spenser's Historical Allegory* (Baltimore, 1932), pp. 1–58. My paper is directed toward an examination of the writings of the two principal combatants (and Leland especially) and is not a general survey of Arthurian materials of the period, for which see Christopher Dean, *Arthur of England: English Attitudes to King Arthur and the Knights of the Round Table in the Middle Ages and the Renaissance* (Toronto, 1987), pp. 107–27; also T.D. Kendrick, *British Antiquity* (London, 1950), pp. 78–98.

2. For a long period the normally accepted view was that there was a strong and officially sanctioned cult of King Arthur in the Tudor period: see C.B. Millican, *Spenser and the Table Round: a Study in the Contemporaneous Background for Spenser's Use of the Arthurian Legend* (Cambridge, Mass., 1932). In "The *British History* in Early Tudor Propaganda," *Bulletin of the John Rylands Library*, 44 (1961), 17–48, Sydney Anglo challenged this thesis. He believed that the early Tudor use of Geoffrey of Monmouth's Arthurian history "should be regarded not as a continuous and expanding cult but, less dramatically, as an early efflorescence and subsequent decline" (p. 40). See also David Carlson, "King Arthur and Court Poems for the Birth of Arthur Tudor in 1486," *Humanistica Lovaniensia*, 36 (1987), 147–83. Carlson has observed (p. 165) that:

> the Arthur myth was viable propaganda for the urban middle class, but not for an aristocracy jealous of its prerogatives and perhaps vaguely resentful of bourgeois usurpations in general, nor for an educated élite, increasingly humanist in its orientation and increasingly skeptical about King Arthur.

3. See Greenlaw's "Elizabethan Fact and Modern Fancy," *Studies in Spenser's Historical Allegory*, pp. 59–103; also David Galbraith's forthcoming Ph.D. Dissertation (University of Toronto), "The Imitation Zone: Poetry and History in Spenser, Daniel and Drayton." Laurie A. Finke, "Spenser for Hire: Arthurian History as Cultural Capital in *The Faerie Queene*," in *Culture and the King: the Social Implications of the Arthurian Legend*, ed. Martin B. Shichtman and James P. Carley (Albany: State University of New York Press, 1994) has observed that "Arthur, while rarely in the forefront of the action in the poem and often absent from long stretches of text, provides the universal equivalent that orders and gives value to all the allegorical signifiers in the poem" (p. 214).

4. For a detailed discussion of sixteenth-century Arthurian writings see W.E. Mead's introduction to his edition of Christopher Middleton's *The Famous Historie of Chinon of England*, Early English Text Society, OS 165 (London, 1925), pp. xxv–xlvi; also Josephine Waters Bennett, *The Evolution of "The Faerie Queene"* (Chicago, 1942), pp. 61–79; Dean, *Arthur of England*, pp. 107–27. For an analysis of the Jacobean revival of interest in King Arthur as an imperial symbol see Frances A. Yates, *Shakespeare's Last Plays: A New Approach* (London, 1975), pp. 17–37.

5. On the *translatio imperii* theme see A. Kent Hieatt, "The Passing of Arthur in Malory, Spenser, and Shakespeare: The Avoidance of Closure," in *The Passing of Arthur: New Essays in Arthurian Tradition*, ed. Christopher Baswell and William Sharpe (New York, 1988), pp. 173–92. The continuation of *The Faerie Queene*, so Hieatt sug-

gests (p. 183), would have dealt with Arthur's conquest of Rome:

> Given the relation to the realities of politics and patronage, such a work would
> have pointed to the Protestant destruction of contemporary Spanish-dominated,
> Roman Catholic power and the founding of a Universal Reformed
> Church. . . . At the literal level the sequel would have built on a central Brit-
> ish tradition of great antiquity, concerned with the most important British hero,
> leading a host in the cause of national honor and the right, to world-triumph
> over the greatest power ever known.

6. My chief source for the details of Polydore Vergil's life is Denys Hay,
Polydore Vergil: Renaissance Historian and Man of Letters (Oxford, 1952); but see
also Richard Koebner, "The Imperial Crown of His Realm: Henry VIII, Constantine
the Great, and Polydore Vergil," *Bulletin of the Institute of Historical Research*, 26
(1953), 29–52.

7. Leland's biography remains to be written: see, however, James P. Carley,
"John Leland in Paris: The Evidence of his Poetry," *Studies in Philology*, 83 (1986),
1–50. Leland spent the 1530s and early 1540s traveling throughout England and Wales,
examining monastic and collegial libraries, describing buildings and monuments and
noting topographical features county by county. Among modern scholars his merit as
a historian is still debated. Kendrick (*British Antiquity*, p. 63) formulated dramatically
what has been a generally accepted stance when he characterized Leland as

> two faced, in one direction looking hopefully forward into a new era of em-
> pirical research and practical survey, and at the same time looking with affec-
> tion backward to the writing-desk of the medieval scholastic chronicler-anti-
> quary where a traditional fable might be repeated without unrestful inquiry
> or impertinent sixteenth century doubt.

In *Tudor Historical Thought* (San Marino, 1967) F.J. Levy took an opposing
view (pp. 130–31) and argued that Leland fell very much within the new humanist
tradition and that he was certainly a better historian by modern definitions than was
Polydore Vergil.

8. *Cygnea Cantio* (London, 1545; rpt. *The Itinerary of John Leland the Antiquary*, ed. Thomas Hearne, 9 vols. [Oxford, 1710–12], Vol. 9, pp. 1–108), p. 76; translation of this and other Latin quotations by James P. Carley.

9. *Cygnea Cantio*, rpt. Hearne, p. 49.

10. This statement is taken from Leland's *Assertio inclytissimi Arturii regis
Britanniae* (London, 1544), which I quote in Richard Robinson's translation—*A
Learned and True Assertion of . . . Prince Arthure, King of Great Brittaine*—reprinted
in Mead's edition of *The Famous Historie of Chinon of England*, p. 17. For Leland's
original see *ibid.*, 97: "Alio me aequum, honestum, famae ratio, hinc & amor patriae
iustus, ac ipsa veritas, qua nil mihi charius vna, perducunt."

11. Parts but not all of the chapter were published by A. Hall in his edition of
the *De viris illustribus,* which he entitled *Commentarii de Scriptoribus Britannicis* (2
vols. [Oxford, 1709], Vol. 1, pp. 189–91). The complete text, taken from Leland's
autograph manuscript, was printed as a separate *libellus* by Thomas Hearne in his
edition of *Joannis Lelandi Antiquarii de rebus Britannicis Collectanea*, 6 vols. (Oxford, 1715; London, 1770, 1774), Vol. 5, pp. 2–10. It will be included in the new edition of *De Scriptoribus* being prepared by Caroline Brett.

12. Leland's faith in Walter's book is not surprising, since Leland himself devoted the better part of his life to the examination of monastic libraries and their medieval manuscripts. Although most modern scholars would deny the reality of Walter's
book, Geoffrey Ashe has made a spirited attempt to prove its existence: see his "'A
Certain Very Ancient Book': Traces of an Arthurian Source in Geoffrey of Monmouth's

History," *Speculum*, 56 (1981), 301–23.

13. *Codrus*, ed. Hearne, p. 6. In *The Pastyme of People*, which first appeared in 1529, John Rastell expressed his disbelief in the authenticity of this seal (London, 1811, pp. 106–08). In 1531, when the Duke of Norfolk showed a copy of the seal to Eustace Chapuys, Charles V's imperial ambassador, Chapuys replied:

> "my answer was that I was sorry to see that he [Arthur] was not also entitled Emperor of Asia, as he might have left the present King Henry for his successor in such vast dominions; but that as all things in this world were so subject to change, it was reasonable that an English monarch of our days should conquer a portion of the provinces above named, since in those very countries men had been found who had conquered and held for a long time this very kingdom of England, where the succession of William of Normandy still lasted. If by showing me the inscription the duke meant that the present King Henry might be such a conqueror as King Arthur, I could not help observing that the Assyrians, Persians, Macedonians, and Romans had also made great conquests, and everyone knew what had become of their empires."

(See Charles T. Wood, "At the Tomb of King Arthur," *Essays in Medieval History. Proceedings of the Illinois Medieval Association*, 8 [1991], 11–12, 14.) See also John Selden's remarks on Leland's discussion of the seal in his commentary to Drayton's *Poly-Olbion* (*The Works of Michael Drayton*, ed. J. W. Hebel, 5 vols. [Oxford, 1931–41]), Vol. 4, p. 87.

14. On Glastonbury's Arthurian associations see James P. Carley, *Glastonbury Abbey: The Holy House at the Head of the Moors Adventurous* (Woodbridge, 1988), pp. 36–37, 124, 147–150, 154–166, 178.

15. *Codrus*, ed. Hearne, p. 5.

16. *A Learned and True Assertion*, p. 84. For the original see *Assertio Arturii*, p. 143: "Non est nouum fabulosa veris miscere, studio certe hoc quodam factum, vt scriptores plebem simplicem admiratione quadam detinerent, auditis rerum miraculis. Sic Hercules, sic Alexander, sic Arturius, sic Carolus laudati."

17. *A Learned and True Assertion*, p. 27. For the original see *Assertio Arturii*, p. 104: "Quanto rectius . . . quae ex autoritate consonantia sunt legere, discutere, conseruare. Nam quod longo iam tempore a doctis receptum magno consensu est non debet momento temporis quocunque oblatrante, vna cum fide e medio tolli."

18. In *Humanism and History: Origins of Modern English Historiography* (Ithaca and London, 1987) Joseph M. Levine discusses William Caxton's preface to Malory's *Morte Darthur* (1485). Like Leland Caxton tried to silence doubters and in so doing he used much of the same evidence. Nevertheless, Caxton's attempt failed "because the evidence was counted, not weighed. But what else could Caxton do? There was nothing in his training, nothing in all his culture, that could help him to evaluate the motley assortment of objects and testimonies, words and things, that had accumulated over the centuries" (p. 45). As Levine observes, it was not until humanist techniques were imported into England that the evaluative process, the "distinction between history and fiction," began to be applied. The contrast between Caxton and Leland's defence shows the profound changes in historiographical method that occurred in the space of half a century.

19. A particularly revealing example of his response to Vergil—one that indicates his own methodology—occurs in the *Cygnea Cantio*, rpt. Hearne, pp. 75–76, where he discussed the place of origin of the "Isis," one of the two rivers which come together to form the Thames. Disagreeing with Vergil on the topic, he emphasized the need for careful fieldwork coupled with bibliographical research, dismissing Vergil as one "qui domi sedens, & numeroso veterum auctorum de rebus in Britannia gestis scribentium praesidio destitutus. . . ." In *De Scriptoribus* I: 9, 51, Leland contradicted Vergil over the identification of *Mons Badonicus*—which, like Geoffrey of Monmouth,

Leland located at Bath; in *De Scriptoribus* I: 204, he reprimanded Vergil for follow-ing William of Newburgh. He corrected Vergil in *De Scriptoribus* II: 332 and his at-tack in *De Scriptoribus* II: 339 was especially harsh. See also James P. Carley, "John Leland's *Cygnea Cantio*: A Neglected Tudor River Poem," *Humanistica Lovaniensia,* 32 (1983), 235–36.

20. Leland quoted from Gerald's work in the *Collectanea* III: 10–16, 85–114, but did not seem to have seen Ralph's description of King Arthur's exhumation. For a good discussion of the differing accounts see Richard Barber, "Was Mordred Bur-ied at Glastonbury? Arthurian Tradition at Glastonbury in the Middle Ages," *Arthurian Literature,* 4 (1985), 37–63.

21. On Melkin's prophecy, probably put together in the late-thirteenth or early-fourteenth century, see James P. Carley, "Melkin the Bard and Esoteric Tradition at Glastonbury Abbey," *The Downside Review,* 99 (1981), 1–17.

22. *A Learned and True Assertion,* p. 39. For the original see *Assertio Arturii,* p. 112: "Hi tam certae fidei testes si non satis ad excussisimam veritatis cognitionem faciunt, nihil profecto vnquam faciet. Nam his auditis, & percognitis non adquiescere, nec sani capitis, sed neque iudicii erit."

23. *Inter alia* he provided etymologies for the names *Gallouinus* (*walle* = strang-ers; *guin* = white) and *Guenhere* which is the equivalent for "belle dame" (*guen* = white = beautiful).

24. Like many of his contemporaries Leland was an indefatigable philologist and the origin of place names especially fascinated him, as the commentary to the *Cygnea Cantio* in particular makes obvious.

25. Geoffrey of Monmouth was the first to locate the Battle of Camlann at the River Camel. There is a tributary of the Camel called the Allen, but in Leland's time, so it appears, the two names were used to designate the main river. Leland's spe-cific reference is to Slaughterbridge, an identification rejected by modern archaeolo-gists—on which see Leslie Alcock, *Arthur's Britain: History and Archaeology, AD 367–634* (London, 1971), pp. 67, 164–65.

26. Leland referred to Cadbury/Camelot elsewhere in his writings. See *The Itinerary of John Leland in or about the Years 1535–1543,* ed. Lucy Toulmin Smith, 5 vols. (London, 1906–10), I: 151:

> At the very south ende of the chirch of South-Cadbyri standith Camallate, sumtyme a famose toun or castelle, apon a very torre or hille, wunderfully enstrengtheid of nature. . . . Much gold, sylver and coper of the Romaine coynes hath be found ther yn plouing: and lykewise in the feldes in the rootes of this hille, with many other antique thinges, and especial by este. Ther was found *in hominum memoria* a horse shoe of sylver at Camallate. The people can telle nothing ther but that they have hard say that Arture much restorid to Camalat."

27. On this topic see Alcock, *Arthur's Britain,* esp. pp. 218–27, 347–49. What Alcock concluded was that: "Within our present framework of knowledge, it seems plain enough that Cadbury-Camelot played some special part in the warfare of south-ern Britain in the late fifth and sixth centuries." More recently, however, Alcock has distanced himself from any Arthurian associations generated by *Arthur's Britain* and has declared himself an agnostic, even though he would still see Cadbury as a special site: see his "Cadbury-Camelot: A Fifteen-Year Perspective," *Proceedings of the Brit-ish Academy,* 68 (1982), 355–88.

28. For Leland's list of books in the Glastonbury library see James P. Carley, "John Leland and the Contents of English Pre-Dissolution Libraries: Glastonbury Abbey," *Scriptorium,* 40 (1986), 107–20.

29. He argued, for example, that Arthur must have been buried in an alder trunk rather than in oak—as Gerald alone affirmed—since alder grew more profusely

in the moist ground at Glastonbury and would be less susceptible to rot. Not having seen Ralph of Coggeshall's account Leland rejected Matthew Paris's description of the monk who had wished to be buried at the spot where Arthur's tomb was subsequently discovered.

30. *Assertio Arturii*, p. 127. This reading is very close to that found in the copy made by William Camden, published in the sixth edition of the *Britannia* (1607). On these and other readings see Alcock, *Arthur's Britain*, pp. 74–80.

31. *Assertio Arturii*, p. 130. See Carley, *Glastonbury Abbey*, pp. 36–37, for the sequence of excavations and reburials. Leland described the tomb as being in black marble, with two lions at each end and an effigy of the king at the foot. For a discussion of the epitaph and a medieval illustration of the monument see John Withrington, "The Arthurian Epitaph in Malory's *Morte Darthur*," *Arthurian Literature*, 7 (1987), 103–44.

32. See, in particular, *Collectanea* III: 106, where Leland flatly contradicted Gerald of Wales's reading: "cum tamen in cruce, quam nunc ostentant, nulla mentio ejus conjugis" ("since, however, on the cross which they now show there is no mention of his wife"). On the tradition of a second wife see also *The Chronicle of Glastonbury Abbey. An Edition, Translation, and Study of John of Glastonbury's "Cronica sive Antiquitates Glastoniensis Ecclesie,"* ed. James P. Carley, trans. David Townsend (Woodbridge, 1985), pp. 182–83, 297–98. In his otherwise favourable review of *The Chronicle of Glastonbury Abbey* (*Speculum*, 62 [1987], pp. 426–30) Charles T. Wood took exception to the translation of *secunda* as fortunate, observing that Gerald of Wales quite clearly read it as second. Since then he has modified his position (private communication) and suggests that "Gerald is the one who got it wrong. The cross said *coniux secunda*, all right, but the monks themselves could well have intended that adjective in its sense of fortunate. Gerald, not knowing that, then proceeded to misconstrue it in his own discussion."

33. Hay, *Polydore Vergil*, p. 105, pointed out that direct speech was much used by humanist historians in their accounts of past events.

34. For the works envisaged by Leland see James P. Carley, "The Manuscript Remains of John Leland, 'The King's Antiquary,'" *Text*, 2 (1985), 111–20.

35. On the dialogue form as it developed in England in the Renaissance see K.J. Wilson, *Incomplete Fictions. The Formation of English Renaissance Dialogue* (Washington, D.C., 1985).

36. *A Learned and True Assertion*, p. 17. For the original, which is somewhat less flowery, see *Assertio Arturii*, p. 97: ". . . & eadem opera Britannicae historie a Galfredo Monaemuthensis viro non omnion inerudito, quicquid alias calumnientur scioli antiquitatis ignari, interpretatae praesidio inniti firmo, potius quam externorum ficulneo."

37. Interestingly, Leland claimed to have a copy of this charter in his own possession; one must presume he acquired it from Glastonbury itself. For a discussion of the charter see *The Early History of Glastonbury. An Edition, Translation and Study of William of Malmesbury's "De Antiquitate Glastonie Ecclesie,"* ed. and trans. John Scott (Woodbridge, 1981), pp. 34–35. In general Leland tended to be somewhat gullible, at least by modern standards, about medieval forgeries.

38. Although no modern scholar would accept the evidence of St. Patrick's Charter, there is still considerable dispute about the date of the founding of Glastonbury Abbey, and Leland is not necessarily completely naive in his reading of the evidence. For a summary of the historical materials see Sarah Foot, "Glastonbury's Early Abbots," in *The Archaeology and History of Glastonbury Abbey*, ed. Lesley Abrams and James P. Carley (Woodbridge, 1991), pp. 163–89. See also C.A.R. Radford, "Glastonbury Abbey Before 1184: Interim Report on the Excavations, 1908–64," *Medieval Art and Architecture at Wells and Glastonbury*, The British Archaeological Association Conference Transactions, 4 (London, 1981), 110–34.

39. Hay, *Polydore Vergil*, p. 30.

40. *A Learned and True Assertion*, p. 79. For the original see *Assertio Arturii*,

p. 140: "Gildas a Polidoro editus, fragmentum indubie Gildae veteris, sed mancum, luxatum, & mutilum, vsque adeo, vt, si iam vitae restitueretur, vix foetum agnosceret parens."

41. Leland also touched upon the tradition, first suggested in Caradoc of Llancarvan's *Life of Gildas,* that Gildas did not mention Arthur out of anger, because Arthur killed Gildas's brother Hueil.

42. *A Learned and True Assertion,* p. 79. For the original see *Assertio Arturii,* p. 140: "Gildas nullam prorsus Arturii mentionem fecit: ergo non fuit."

43. Even in the next generation William Camden was less willing to accept medieval etymologies than was Leland, as in the case, say, of Marlborough: "the derivation of this place from *Merlin's* Tomb, which *Alexander Necham . . .* hammer'd out in this Distich, is ridiculous" (William Camden, *Britannia: or, a Chorographical Description,* trans. and ed. Edmund Gibson, 2 vols. [London, 1753], Vol. 1, p. 129).

44. As Levine observed (*Humanism and History,* pp. 80, 82):

> A classical education combined with patriotic and religious motivation was an excellent prescription for studying English antiquities. . . . Leland understood thoroughly the interrelationship of word and object, and he believed that the study of Celtic and Saxon antiquities could be modeled upon the Roman precedent; it was his particular genius to discover how the techniques of classical scholarship could be extended to the Middle Ages. In short, he understood clearly and before anyone else in England that the many new devices of Italian humanism could be employed not only to resuscitate classical antiquity but to recover the whole of the British past.

45. In "Wanton Discourse and the Engines of Time: William Camden—Historian among Poets-Historical" (*Renaissance Rereadings. Intertext & Context,* ed. M.C. Horowitz, A.J. Cruz, and W.A Furman [Urbana, 1988], p. 156, n. 19) Wyman H. Herendeen observed that "Camden was among the first in England to examine archaeological material for its historical significance." In this, as in so much, Camden was very much Leland's disciple. Herendeen's statements about the *Britannia* ("Wanton Discourse and the Engines of Time," p. 149) apply equally forcefully, moreover, to Leland's writings: "The *Britannia* is the first such work to include literature as part of our cultural history: it is presented rather like an 'histoire des mentalités' and not as narratives pretending to truth."

46. David N. Dumville's observation concerning the earliest Arthurian texts— "The Historical Value of the *Historia Brittonum,*" *Arthurian Literature,* 6 (1986), 14— has, I think, gained wide acceptance:

> In general, our ignorance of the political history of the British fifth century is almost total; in my view, it is not legitimate to seek to lighten this darkness by the use of unhistorical sources offered by a writer whose ignorance *was* complete and whose concept of history did not require him to distinguish between certain types of evidence, as we must do.

47. In this context, see Levine, *Humanism and History,* p. 49:

> To be sure, it was another humanist [than Vergil], John Leland, who tried to defend the Arthurian story early in the century, but he failed in the long run precisely because he agreed to play the same historiographical game: to collect all the original sources archaeological and literary, and to date and sift and compare them. "If these witnesses of some credit make not sufficient for most apparent knowledge of the truth," he insisted correctly, "surely there can nothing at any time availably serve." Put to the test, it became gradually clear that all the evidence for the historicity of the British story—not only Geoffrey of

Monmouth and the medieval romances but Arthur's seal, floating traditions, gravestones at Glastonbury, even the Round Table itself—were equally untenable.

48. See, for example, *Cygnea Cantio,* rpt. Hearne, p. 76, where he referred to Vergil's writing as "tersus, nitidus, elegans." In the *De Scriptoribus,* however, he was somewhat less objective and could be fairly rancorous in his appraisal of his opponent.

49. A very thorough discussion of the reaction to Vergil is contained in Millican, *Spenser and the Table Round;* see also the notes to Greenlaw, "The Battle of the Books," pp. 180–84.

50. *John Bale's "King Johan,"* ed. Barry B. Adams (San Marino, 1969), ll. 2193–99.

51. The accusation is perhaps prefigured in Leland's earlier fear "ne homo *Italus* in nostris rebus titulo eloquentiae nimium sibi tribuat" ("lest an Italian assign too much of the title of eloquence to himself in our affairs"; *De Scriptoribus,* Vol. 2, p. 339).

52. This passage, quoted in Hay, *Polydore Vergil,* p. 159, is found in the margin of a copy of Bale's *Scriptorum Illustrium Maioris Brytanniae Catalogus.*

53. On Leland's attempt to set up a national archive for the preservation of monastic manuscripts see James P. Carley, "John Leland and the Foundations of the Royal Library: The Westminster Inventory of 1542," *Bulletin of the Society for Renaissance Studies,* 7 (1989), 13–22.

54. There was also an increased nostalgia for the past, which released itself in renewed literary activity and historical research: see Margaret Aston, "English Ruins and English History: The Dissolution and the Sense of the Past," *The Journal of the Warburg and Courtauld Institutes,* 36 (1973), 231–55.

55. Apart from the *Dictionary of National Biography* entry on Robinson see G.M. Vogt, "Richard Robinson's *Eupolemia* (1603)," *Studies in Philology,* 21 (1924), 629–48. Robinson translated several works which have been doubtfully attributed to Leland in their original Latin form.

56. The most thorough discussion of this order to date is found in Millican, *Spenser and the Table Round,* pp. 54–64. Shortly before she died Frances Yates made a strong plea (personal communication) for more research on the symbolism of this order and its possible occult links.

57. In the preface to his translation of the *Assertio Arturii* Robinson referred to the discussion of archery in the *Toxophilus.* Mulcaster's association with Spenser makes the connection particularly germane.

58. For a thorough discussion of this latter topic see Mark Girouard, *The Return to Camelot: Chivalry and the English Gentleman* (New Haven, Conn., 1981).

59. *A Learned and True Assertion,* p. 8.

60. For a general summary, with references included, of Bale's view of history and its relationship to Leland's methodology see *Index Britanniae Scriptorum. John Bale's Index of British and Other Writers,* ed. R.L. Poole and Mary Bateson, with an introduction by Caroline Brett and James P. Carley (Cambridge, 1990), pp. xi–xv.

61. In his letter of Raleigh, of course, Spenser explained why the epithet "magnificent" was particularly suited to Arthur: moreover, as Finke, "Spenser for Hire," observes: "For Spenser, Arthur becomes a synecdoche for all princely virtue by reason of his 'magnificence.'" More generally, on the cult of magnificence in sixteenth-century England see Gordon Kipling, *The Triumph of Honour: Burgundian Origins of the Elizabethan Renaissance* (The Hague, 1977), pp. 28–30, 64–65, 160–68. On Henry VIII's identification with King David see Pamela Tudor-Craig, "Henry VIII and King David," in *Early Tudor England. Proceedings of the 1987 Harlaxton Symposium,* ed. Daniel Williams (Woodbridge, 1989), pp. 183–205.

62. Robinson described Batman as "a learned Preacher and friendlie fauourer

of vertue and learning" (*A Learned and True Assertion*, p. 12). On Batman see the entry in the *Dictionary of National Biography;* also Janet Backhouse, "Sir Robert Cotton's Record of a Royal Bookshelf," *The British Library Journal,* 18 (1992), 48, 50, n. 16; D. Galbraith, "Stephen Batman," in *Dictionary of Literary Biography: 16th-century Non-dramatic Authors,* ed. David A. Richardson, forthcoming.

63. On John's sources see *The Chronicle of Glastonbury Abbey,* ed. Carley, pp. xlviii–liii, 54–55, 280–81, n.83.

64. Camden and Stow had access to Leland's papers—and indeed Stow's transcripts are our only source for some papers subsequently lost or destroyed—and both followed in the antiquarian tradition he established. For an examination of differences of methodology between Leland and Camden and ways in which Camden stands as Leland's heir in matters historiographical see W.H. Herendeen, "William Camden: Historian, Herald and Antiquary," *Studies in Philology,* 85 (1988), 192–210; also "Spenserian Specifics: Spenser's Appropriation of a Renaissance *Topos,*" *Medievalia et Humanistica,* NS 10 (1981), 159–88; and *From Landscape to Literature: the River and the Myth of Geography* (Pittsburgh, 1986), pp. 186–204.

65. See Carley, "Leland in Paris," 12–18, 35–48.

66. When he named King Arthur's knights, for example, he listed 150 but miscounted as 149.

67. *Assertio Arturii,* p. 91.

68. *A Learned and True Assertion,* p. 10.

69. *A Learned and True Assertion,* p. 7.

70. Millican, *Spenser and the Table Round,* pp. 145–46, discusses the relationship between Leland's view of Henry VIII as "Arturius alter" and "Arturius rediuiuus" and Spenser's interpretation of Elizabeth as Arthurian majesty. See also James P. Carley, "John Leland," *The Spenser Encyclopedia,* ed. A.C. Hamilton, et al. (Toronto, 1990), p. 433. For Drayton see *Poly-Olbion,* Song 1, ll. 169–203; Song 4; Song 10. B.H. Newdigate, *Michael Drayton and His Circle* (Oxford, 1941), p. 170, comments on Drayton's acceptance of Leland's defence of British history. Herendeen ("Wanton Discourse and the Engines of Time," p. 151) has observed that:

> . . . while usually considered Spenserian in inspiration, Drayton's *Poly-Olbion* and Daniel's *Civile Wares,* as historical poems, are closer to the *de Connubio* [*Tamae et Isis*] than to *The Faerie Queene:* both poets are troubled by the proper assimilation of the historical material as Spenser was not, and ultimately they both weave the threads of history and poetic invention together in ways very different from Spenser, so that generically their debt to Camden the historian is greater than it is to Spenser the poet.

Here, I would suggest that the debt is also to Leland the historian and for *de Connubio* I would be tempted to substitute *Cygnea Cantio.*

71. Tradition has it that Edward VI was concerned about Leland's literary remains and consigned his papers to the care of Sir John Cheke. Whatever else, John Foxe certainly testified to the fact that Cheke possessed the *De Scriptoribus:* see Brett and Carley, *Index Britanniae Scriptorum,* p. xiv, n. 14. It is also worth noting in his notes to the *Poly-Olbion* John Selden characterized Leland as "our most judicious antiquary of the last age." See *The Works of Michael Drayton,* Vol. 4, p. 23.

72. Leland's river poems are even more influential in the development of this new mode, on which see Carley, "Leland in Paris," pp. 18, 48–49; *id.,* "John Leland's *Cygnea Cantio,*" 238–40; Herendeen, "Spenserian Specifics." For George Wither's use of the term "topo-chrono-graphicall" to describe Drayton's poetry see "Spenserian Specifics," p. 187, n. 6.

73. In another sense too he is a precursor of Camden, whom Spenser viewed as a reconciler of the opposition between historians and poets, an individual able to mediate the opposition between fact and fiction in the epic form.

The Arthurs
of the *Faerie Queene*

Merritt Y. Hughes

Modern criticism of *The Faerie Queene* begins its creed with Hurd's remark in the *Letters on Chivalry and Romance* that Arthur was "but an after-thought."[1] Professor Josephine Bennett's analysis of the poem opens its discussion of Spenser's "failure in unity and action" by quoting Hurd's dictum.[2] Professor W.L.Renwick acknowledges that Arthur's "place in the epic-romance was never clearly worked out; his appearances are fitful and unrelated."[3] B.E.C. Davis regards him as a crude device for gathering up the "scattered threads of allegory"—"an abstraction of a personality" and "a false cornerstone" in an "ethical scheme that starts at the wrong end."[4] With a single important exception, critics agree that Spenser was throwing dust in his readers' eyes when he wrote to Raleigh in 1590 that "in the person of Prince Arthure" he "sette forth magnificence . . . according to Aristotle and the rest," as a virtue containing all other virtues and therefore peculiarly fitting a hero whose rôle it is to succor the champions of other virtues.

In the chorus of condemnation of Arthur the outstanding exception is Janet Spens's defense of him as the cornerstone of the moral allegory and of the original structure of the poem. Unfairly perhaps, her sensitive appreciation of Arthur as the Neo-Platonic lover of Gloriana has been slighted because it is involved in her unconvincing suggestion that originally the work was planned in eight books of eight cantos each, with "Prince Arthur's quest of the Faerie Queene as its main theme."[5] Her treatment of Arthur fails to convince even her friendliest critic, C.S. Lewis, who has pronounced his conduct "inexplicable," and objected that, "if Arthur is Aristotelian 'Magnanimity' in search of earthly glory, his deliverance of St. George is arrant nonsense. 'Magnanimity' in this sense," he adds, "cannot rescue Holiness, for

Reprinted from *Études anglaises*, 6 (1953), 193–213. The final division of this article was read before the "Newberry Library Renaissance Conference," in Chicago, on Saturday, April 25, 1953.

whatever in the pagan character of the μεγαλόψυχοσ [great-souled man] is not sin, belongs already to the saint."[6] Lewis's jealous love for Spenser's allegory and his devotion to the Arthurian tradition contrast strangely with his contempt for the Spenserian Arthur. The key to his dislike of Spenser's figure may be found in the widening gulf that scholarship has opened between him and the mediaeval Arthur.

There can, of course, be no doubt that modern research has reversed Thomas Warton's view that "the adventures of his [Spenser's] knights are a more exact and immediate copy of those which we meet in the old romances, or books of chivalry [among which he put Malory's *Morte d'Arthur* first], than of those which form the *Orlando Furioso.*"[7] As late as the publication of Marie Walther's thesis on Malory's influence on Spenser, Warton's opinion prevailed, but as early as 1897 the attack on it was begun by Neil Dodge, and in 1921 it was continued by Professor Blanchard in his Harvard thesis *Italian Influence on "The Faerie Queene."* In 1942 Bennett gave the older doctrine its *coup de grâce* by her proof that Spenser's Arthur owed little to the King Arthur of Gildas, Nennius, or even Geoffrey of Monmouth, and nothing important to Malory.[8]

From mediaeval sources Bennett turned to Chaucer's Sir Thopas as the first seminal influence on Spenser's Arthur. She acknowledges that his prototype must be in love with glory, as indeed he must be, up to the degree to which Aristotle's magnanimous man was held to be its lover. But Bennett also acknowledged that her Sir Thopas-Arthur lacked the spirit of the King Arthur of the romance—"der nach Ehre strebenden König" ("the king striving for honor") whose Gestalt a German scholar has described as the embodiment of *Ehregefühl* ("sense of honor"):

> Mult ama pris, mult ama glore,
> Mult vult son fait metre en memore.[9]

> (He loved fame very much, he loved glory very much,
> He very much wanted his deeds to be remembered.)

Nor is Bennett interested in the Aristotelian μεγαλόψυχοσ or the channels of his impact on the Renaissance epic hero. She looks for the key to his love of glory in Ariosto and compares Arthur's haphazard pursuit of Florimel in Book III, cantos i and v, with Rinaldo's pursuit of Angelica. Angelica, she recalls, seemed to Sir John Harington to represent "the honor that brave men seek."[10] But in fact, though Ariosto's editors loaded his poem with allegory, they could have given Spenser no conception very like his hero. Between his

Arthur and Rinaldo there is a gap bridgeable only by a revelation nowhere to be found in the *Orlando Furioso* of that "Idea of pure Glory" that Bennett regards as the "final exaltation of Sir Chastity's (Thopas') dream" of Gloriana.[11] If the illumination behind Arthur's devotion to the Fairy Queen can be traced to any allegorical source, it must be to such dreams as those of the suitors of the Queen of the Fortunate Isles in Cardinal Bembo's *Asolani*.[12] Those of them who dreamed of earthly honors were granted careers deserving them, but those who dreamed of the Queen herself lived forever in her court and in a vision of her as beatific as Arthur told Una that he had once beheld of his Fairy Queen.

Whether or not Bembo's dreamers in the Fortunate Isles were precursors of Spenser's Arthur, the *nach Ehre strebenden König* of the romances must be recognized in the genealogy of the imperial Arthur whose popularity Bennett agrees with Greenlaw in dating from the revival of *Arthur of Little Britain* in the 1580s. To the vogue of the popular Arthur she partly attributes Spenser's treatment of his magnificent Prince, who is as frankly a political symbol as he is an image of the Neo-Platonic "Idea of pure Glory." So the question arises whether the purity of Arthur's passion for glory will bear scrutiny in contrast with his political role in *The Faerie Queene*. The problem must be stated before we can accept Arthur's claim to have seen the Christian vision of Glory or even to incarnate Aristotle's ideal of magnanimity or true magnificence.

The Imperial Arthur

The imperial Arthur of Spenser's political allegory has been a phoenix too frequent among commentators who wish to make his poem into a *roman à clé*. Though no one now follows Upton in identifying him simply with the Earl of Leicester, some scholars still would like to explain him as "shadowing forth" the impossible Sidney or the more plausible Essex. It was Greenlaw who first denied that "a shadow of proof exists"[13] for Arthur's identification with Leicester in more than one or two episodes in *The Faerie Queene*. To this position Millican yielded when he ended his survey of the contending theories about the legendary Arthur among Tudor historians from Polydore Vergil to Camden by acknowledging that "if Spenser's Arthur did not serve as a humble prototype for Robert Dudley, Earl of Leicester," he was at least "a complete picture of an Elizabethan captain moving about Fairyland in quest of Gloriana, England's Tudor Fairy Queene."[14] Similarly Isabel Rathbone has qualified her identification of the Arthur of the later books of the poem with the Earl of Essex by recognizing in him a composite topical Arthur[15] from whom it is not a long step to a symbolic Arthur surcharged with ethical as well as political significance.

A symbol pretending to unite political with ethical ideals should be irreproachable, but Spenser's Arthur is an obvious target for democratic idealists. Sociological critics such as Dr. Levin Schücking treat him roughly as an idol of the Elizabethan courtiers who can be sweepingly stigmatized as

> ... a group that strives to distinguish itself from the common herd in language, style, clothing, bearing, and behavior; a group, moreover, whose taste, in accordance with its whole training, seeks association with the antiquity of which the common people have no comprehension, strives after difficult and artificial forms, is esoteric, abominates realism, despises simplicity, and goes in search of humanism and culture.[16]

There is irony in the fact that Millican, who shared Greenlaw's admiration for Spenser's imperial Arthur, should have contributed to Schücking's view of him by investigating the Tudor genealogies that flattered Elizabeth by making him her ancestor. There is irony too in J.W. Saunders's recent substitution of a new sociological-democratic interpretation of *The Faerie Queene* for Schücking's. Saunders treats the Arthur of the last three books of the poem as a crass surrender of the aristocratic Prince of the first three to bourgeois prejudice and sentimentality.[17] This attempt to interpret Arthur sociologically may be over-ingenious. Over-ingenious or not, it should serve to remind us that in Aristotle's portrayal of the magnanimous man there was an unmistakable mixture of the bourgeois with the aristocratic. In the Aristotelian portrait the famous passion for honor was clearly tinged with the primitive pride of the Homeric heroes, but its essence was a nicely balanced psychological conception of the social virtues—that "theory of friendship which in the *Nicomachaean Ethics* is expanded into a general sociology of the manifold forms of human relationship."[18] The truth is that neither the Aristotelian nor the Spenserian embodiment of magnanimity can be cut to fit the Procrustean modern definition of the bourgeois. Of the two, Aristotle's μεγαλόψυχοσ is closer to the civic ideal—the ideal of the *sittlich* ("ethical") which a German analyst of his conception of honor has made central in the *Ethics*.[19]

Behind the sociological strictures on Spenser's Arthur is the dislike for the Elizabethan conception of magnanimity which is voiced by J. Bronowski, who pities the Elizabethan proneness to hanker "after acts like Sidney's death, of gallant glory and magnificence; they would not face the evil extravagance, the lust for glory of heroic villains, which these acts bred."[20] Bronowski sees Spenser's public darkly as naïvely snobbish, imperialistic, and militaristic. And he is uneasy about an Arthur who loves a Gloriana whose realm is glory, and "Whose Kingdomes seat Cleopolis is red" (*F.Q.*, I, vii, 46). Though in the moral allegory Cleopolis may signify the City of God manifesting itself "in the history of several famous cities, of which London is the last,"[21] Elizabeth's London, the Troynovant of the poem, is a Utopia very different from Blake's

> Jerusalem
> In England's green and pleasant land.

Or Herbert Read's

> Crystal city in the age of peace a
> limpid source of love.

If the sociological critics would delve a bit more deeply than is their wont into literary sources, they might strengthen their case against the "magnificence" of Spenser's Arthur. They might appeal to Aristotle's description of that virtue as a monopoly of rich men, and as consisting in the tasteful outlay of money on public building or display. Italian popularizations of Aristotle—such as those of Patrizi, Pontano, and Allessandro Piccolomini—accept the Aristotelian account and adapt it to the Italian scene. Aristotle's warning of the vulgar degradation of the virtue is remembered. But, as students of Machiavelli remind us, Italian *magnificenza* ("magnificence") could be fulsomely identified with *suntuosità* ("sumptuousness"), and in *The Prince* it was frankly treated as the shrewd price that Cosimo de' Medici paid for his tyrannic power in Florence.[22] The worldly conception of the "virtue" as an instrument in practical politics emerged in Francesco Patrizi's *De Regno et Regni Institutione*[23] when he praised Caesar's public tables and games as supreme examples of the magnificence becoming a ruler. On the level of the Italian courtier Castiglione honored large means display; while on that of the English nobleman who, "to sustain his reputation, must live more magnificently than others," Sir Thomas Smith candidly said that wealth was as essential as virtue or learning.[24] Although in quoting Sir Thomas Smith in her *Doctrine of the English Gentleman* Ruth Kelso had a better perspective than do most Marxist explorers of the Renaissance, she saw the Elizabethan conception of magnificence and magnanimity as stemming too simply from the "boundless ambition and thirst after greatness" which seemed so characteristic of the period to Burckhardt.

Too few students of the Italian Renaissance share Burckhardt's comprehension of the passionate fusion of opposites—of ambition and idealism in the conception of honor that drew theoretical sanction from the Aristotelian virtues of magnificence and magnanimity. In our stereotype of the Elizabethan magnate the idealism is often under- or over-valued; its cohabitation with pride is hard for us to understand in a figure like the Earl of Essex—"deeply influenced by two contradictory ideals, 'Magnificence' and renunciatory Puritanism."[25] We think of even the noblest Elizabethans in terms of *trascuratezza* ("negligence") and *virtu* ("virtue") and see them as specimens of "the Renaissance Magnificent Man" whom William Empson recognizes in Shakespeare's Sonnet XCIV:

> They that have powre to hurt, and will doe none,
> That doe not do the thing, they most do showe,
> Who mouing others, are themselves as stone,
> Vnmoued, could, and to temptation slow . . .

In the brimming cup of irony that the sonnet offers to Empsonian interpretation there is a portrayal of "the Machiavellian, the wicked plotter who is exciting and civilized and in some way right about life."[26] It is easy to confuse the Machiavellian with the proud side of the Aristotelian μεγαλόψυχοσ and so to invest Essex, Sidney, and all the Elizabethan worthies whose composite portrait we have in Spenser's Arthur with a kind of magnanimity that is alien to Christian humility. Then, as Professor Ernest Sirluck points out, since the pride in Aristotle's ideal amounts to an "affront to Christian humility," it seems to follow that Spenser's "Arthur does not really correspond to Aristotle's proud man."[27] Yet he is the true descendant of that proud man, the mainspring of whose conduct was passion for civic honor; but his blood has been so altered by Roman, Chivalric, and Christian admixtures that in *The Faerie Queene* he transforms the cold preference of Aristotle's magnanimous man for doing rather than receiving favors into a passion for offering miraculous help to the distressed in all ranks of life. He is more paradoxical than the gilded youth of Shakespeare's sonnet who "has powre to hurt and will doe none." Class-conscious or imperially ambitious though he is, in most situations he is also a minister of grace.

The Minister of Grace

That Arthur "functions as a symbol or personification of the grace of God"[28] is a fact hardly needing proof by scholars such as Professors Jones, Woodhouse, Whittaker, and Melan, who have traced its significance to its roots in Christian theology, Catholic and Protestant. Professor Woodhouse holds that Arthur signifies grace only in Book I and stands elsewhere in *The Faerie Queene* for Aristotelian magnanimity; but he is nearest the truth in concluding that there is an ultimate synthesis of nature and grace in Prince Arthur. He is rarely the simple minister of grace that he seems to have been when, finding Amoret half dead, he drew forth the

> pretious liquor
> Which he in store about him kept alway,
> And with few drops thereof did softly dew
> Her wounds, that vnto strength restor'd her soone anew.
> (*F.Q.*, IV, viii, 20, 6–9)

In his first adventure, his rescue of Redcross from Orgoglio, Arthur is the "magnificence, or literally the great-doing of the Kingdom of England"[29] against Rome, but he is also Christian magnanimity defeating pride. In defending Guyon against Pyrochles and Cymochles he is again a minister of grace, and here no worldly shadow seems to fall across his spiritual symbolism. His ministry was, of course, consecrated by that beatific vision of the Fairy Queen of which we hear in his first account of himself to Una:

> Was neuer hart so rauisht with delight,
> Ne liuing man like words did euer heare,
> As she to me deliuered that night.
> (*F.Q.*, I, ix, 14, 6–8)

Toward the end of Book III Arthur suffers an inversion of his vision of the Fairy Queen. His benighting there may be compared with his beatific vision in Book I. It is more than mere embroidery on the theme of night as we have it in Shakespeare's *Rape of Lucrece* for Arthur's imprecation upon "Night, thou foule Mother of Annoyance sad, Sister of heauie death, and nourse of woe," (*F.Q.*, III, iv, 55, 1–2) is more universal than Lucrece's diatribe against "Comfort-killing Night, image of hell," (l. 764).

Though the benighting is but an incident, it implies a threatened loss and recovery of the Truth that Arthur calls the daughter of Day. His imprecation recalls More's reflections on the ninetieth Psalm, "The Terror by Night and of Pusillanimity" in *A Dialogue of Comfort against Tribulation* (II, xi–xvi), while it also recalls Hesiod's mysterious roster[30] of the daunting children of Night against whom men need metaphysical aid. Hesiod mingles daemonic powers such as Nemesis and the Fates with abstractions such as those that Arthur tries to exorcize:

Light-shonning theft, and traiterous intent,
Abhorred bloudshed, and vile felony,
Shamefull deceipt, and daunger imminent;
Foule horror, and eke hellish dreriment.
(*F.Q.*, III, iv, 58, 2–5)

Arthur's omission of Hesiod's supernatural beings may be due to rationalization on Spenser's part. He was familiar with the debate over the existence of the gods in Cicero's *De Natura Deorum* (III, 17–18) and with the plea of the Academician, Cotta, that those who accept the divinity of the heroes of myth such as Hercules, Aeasculapius, and Bacchus. For Spenser Night was a symbol to be felt as deeply as Sacheverell Sitwell's "night of day . . .

> that deeper and tremendous gloom,
> The spirit's cold prison, with the heart for tolling bell,
> Never, never ceasing, for every hour is wasted."

In Arthur's benighting Spenser may have had no thought of the "Dark Night of the Soul" that Evelyn Underhill recognized as separating the Illuminative from the Unitive states for all true mystics, but his portrayal of Arthur in the following canto as fired with renewed love for "the highest and the worthiest" (III, v, 2, 5) recalls Underhill's theory of the Dark Night as finally leading to "mystical energy and supernatural effects."[31] If Spenser owed nothing to the experience of mystics such as Richard Rolle and Heinrich Suso, he learned something of their wisdom from Cotta's faith in the divinity of the conquerors of the children of Night, and from mythographers such as Natale Conti, who made her a symbol of the night of the mind that spawns all human calamities.[32] Or Spenser may have remembered Boccaccio's explanation of Night as the dam of the blind heart, or his allegorical fancy that Homer called Night the conqueror of the gods because magnanimous men who meditate great deeds find their surging spirits oppressed by a night of unendurable darkness.[33]

Arthur's benighting occurs in his pursuit of a lady who, as we have seen, was perhaps accepted as a symbol of the honor of brave men. In most of his encounters with strange ladies, however, he is less a knight errant in quest of glory than he is a minister of grace. So it is when he meets Una and visits Alma. Some of his adventures with ladies involve him in battles that make him less a spiritual than a political symbol. Two such cases are his encounters with Samient and Serena—particularly if Greenlaw and Pauline

Henley were right in taking both damsels for precursors of Cathleen-Ni-Houlihan. Samient's enemy is obviously Philip II or his kingdom, Spain, the foe of her queen, Mercilla, who is Elizabeth. If Samient represents Ireland, Arthur is involved in the most urgent of Spenser's political interests. His task is to "free Samient from fear" (V, viii, Argument), and his performance of it implies chivalry in his creator. Indeed, Henley has suggested that in associating Arthur with her country Spenser achieved in him a true symbol of national magnanimity. And in the story of Serena in the Legend of Courtesy she saw "the Poet, in one of his softer moods, dreaming of a peace" that has been violated by the slanderous "propaganda of both sides, tending to fan the flames of racial hatred" that have wounded Serena.[34] Her suffering has innocently arisen from her efforts "to establish friendly relations between the Salvage Man, or the ordinary people of Ireland, and Arthur, the representative of English government in Ireland." Proof is impossible, but if Henley is right, her thought falls into line with W.B. Yeats's conviction that Spenser "drew from the book of the people," and so she may illuminate Yeats's sympathy for "the practical and ferocious author of *A View of the Present State of Ireland.*"[35]

On the political level Henley implies a degree of humility in Arthur's treatment of Samient and Serena that contrasts sharply with Kelso's account of the virtue of magnanimity as "self-expansion, self-assertion."[36] Kelso found the evidence for her view in the Italian Aristotelians and especially in their justification of display and aggressiveness in high places on the strength of Aristotle's account of the great-souled man in the *Nicomachaean Ethics* (IV, iii) as self-sufficient, aloof, and moved solely by the passion for honor. Evidence for a different view can be found both in humanistic tradition and in scholastic thought. Though Spenser may not have read the mediaeval theologians, he can hardly have been ignorant of their view of Aristotelian magnanimity as equivalent to the "human will when it supports the Christian virtues"—a doctrine which has been traced[37] through many writers from Alanus de Insulis to the Lutheran Melancthon. In the *Summa Theologica* and elsewhere St. Thomas Aquinas laid heavy emphasis on the humility of magnanimity—"Magnanimitas et humilitas non sunt contraria" ("Magnanimity and humility are not contrary to one another")[38] though "Propria enim materia magnanimitatis est honor" ("The characteristic substance of magnanimity is indeed honor"). St. Thomas transformed Aristotle's proud, ironical μεγαλόψυχοσ, who is unwilling to accept favors though covetous of the honor of bestowing them, into a Christian ironist who modestly hides his greatness of spirit from inferiors though he never blenches before men of high estate. Among the many heirs of St. Thomas the most influential upon

Spenser may have been Alessandro Piccolomini, whose *Institution Morale* paraphrased the treatment of magnanimity in the *Nicomachaean Ethics;*[39] yet his last words on the subject echo St. Thomas's doctrine of the virtue as consisting in pure humility. Though at one point he followed Aristotle closely, he later represented the great-souled man as aloof from inferiors not through scorn for them but simply from single-minded devotion to the good.[40] But Piccolomini, famous though he was for several learned works that better became him as a titular bishop than *La Raffaella,* was not the best exponent of magnanimity in either the Scholastic or the humanistic tradition.

Among humanists the greatest *doctor magnanimitatis* was the Neapolitan poet and philosopher, Pontano, who proved his grasp of the Aristotelian ethic by his vision of happiness as a full life of the mind living in accordance with virtue—"felicitatem mentis esse effectionem secundum virtutem perfectam" ("Happiness of mind is to be achieved after virtue has been achieved").[41] In his *De Magnanimitate* he deferred to Aristotle by making the virtue the sum of all the others and by rooting it in moderation in pursuit of honor. He wrote eloquent pages on liberty, justice, and the courageous devotion to truth that he regarded as typically Roman virtues.[42] As examples of them he names men such as Fabricius and Publicola with a respect like Milton's for

> Quintus, Fabricius, Curius, Regulus,
> > men so poor
> Who could do mighty things, and could contemn
> Riches though offer'd from the hand of Kings. (*Paradise Regained,*
> > II, 446–449)

Pontano's Roman instances do not mean that his magnanimous ideal was unchristian; it was as pious as Milton's when in the *De Doctrina Christiana,* II, ix, he defined the virtue as "a right attitude towards worldly honors, particularly as shown by Christ on Mount Hermon."

Pontano's doctrine of magnanimity was an article in the humanist creed. From a statesman's point of view Francesco Patrizi promulgated it in his *De Regno Principum,* making the pride and preference for conferring to receiving favors of Aristotle's μεγαλόψυχοσ into a king-becoming excellence of spirit seeking honor for itself in the public good.[43] From Patrizi it is but a short step to popular moralists like Giraldi Cinthio, in whose *Dialogues of Civil Life* Magnificence and Magnanimity appear as emblematic figures adorning the path that leads the soul to God.[44] Giraldi treated magnanimity primarily as a safe-guard of public peace. Opposing it to the duelists' code of honor, he glorified it as an aspect of Aristotle's high-minded man's contempt for insult. This version of the great-souled man became commonplace in the form that it took in *The French Academie,* where he is made good, gentle, and courteous even toward his greatest enemies, and—like Plato—a despiser of the "ambitious desire of vain-glory, honour, and power."[45] Similarly, in *The Governour* Sir Thomas Elyot defined magnanimity in Platonized Aristotelian terms as "the doynge all thynge that is vertuous for the achieuynge of honour."[46] He was, of course, also echoing St. Thomas's definition of it as "doing those things that are worthy of honour."[47] Though Elyot's main source was Cicero's chapter on the virtue in *De Officiis,* I, xx, his treatment of it had a Thomistic color that also tinged Spenser's conception of Arthur. Elyot was attracted by St. Thomas's figure of magnanimity as the "ornament" of the other virtues, which he elaborated into the "garment of Vertue, wherewith she is set out . . . lyke wise as a lady of excellent beautie, thoughe that she be all wayes fayre, yet a ryche and fresshe garment . . . causeth her naturall beautie to be the better perceyued."[48] Ultimately, the image of magnanimity as a crowning ornament (κόσμοσ [ornament]) of all other virtues goes back to the *Nicomachaean Ethics* (IV, iii, 15–16). Perhaps we have a shadow of it in Spenser's statement to Raleigh that Arthur's virtue was "the perfection of the rest, and conteineth in it them all."

With the spread of the view that magnanimity was an ornament as well as an arduous virtue men became sensitive both to its counterfeits and to its beauty in the elevation of spirit to what Aristotle called "a heroic and divine kind of nature, such as Homer attributed to Hector."[49] We remember Spenser's confession of a desire to invest Arthur with the perfection of the Homeric heroes. Behind Spenser's words we should hear Patrizzi's warning that, "It is wrong to say (pinguiore Minerva ["without learning"]) that magnanimity is the ornament of the virtues; without them it cannot exist."[50] We do not know how well Spenser was aware that, in France if not in England, the ideals of magnanimity and magnificence had been brought into some contempt among courtly audiences. A recent study of Philibert de Vienne[51] has shown that as early as 1547 the degradation of Castiglione's ideals in *Il Cortegiano* had gone so far in courtly circles on the continent that their perversion was attacked in the first of a series of satires. One of their main targets was the false magnificence of courtiers who were bent upon "inspiring sympathy, which is the key to success." Spenser was aware of the difficulty that he faced in undertaking to create true magnificence in Prince Arthur and a convincing semblance of it in the "glitterand armour" that he wears in *The Faerie Queene.*

To accept the accoutrements in Arthur's portrait in Book I, vii, 29–37, a modern reader needs to share the Elizabethan taste for emblematic armorial splendor; he must be able to drown all doubt of their fitness to be worn by any human being in response to their symbolic reflection of the beauty of holiness as well as of the virtue that is the ornament of all the rest. In such a portrait realism was impossible; if the reader suspended his disbelief, he must perform an act of something like religious faith. He accepted Arthur as a synthetic symbol and found pleasure in responding to components that he would expect to total up to super-human magnificence. In the diamond shield he would recognize a symbol of humility and repentance as well as a match for the aegis of Homer's Athene or Ariosto's Ruggiero.[52] In the lady's head on the baldric he might conflate the faces of the Fairy Queen and the Virgin Mary. In the armor he saw St. Paul's "armor of light" or "righteousness" or "whole armor of God."[53] Behind the sword and spear he might recollect Arthur's fabulous accoutrements in *Kilhwck and Olven*: Caledvwlch, his sword; Rhongomyant, his lance, etc.,[54] which stemmed from unfathomed depths of Celtic faith, playful or half-serious, in mighty men of old. In the "magnificent" synthesis pagan and Christian elements unite, and the resulting portrait can hardly be matched anywhere except in the parallel symbolic portrayal of Hercules in full chivalric panoply in the *Ercole* of G.-B. Giraldi. Though Spenser was probably uninfluenced by Giraldi's work and even unaware of it, he was moved by a reverence for the myth of Hercules as the vaguely historical personage whom Pontano had declared to be, of all traditional heroes, the worthiest of the honor of divinity. As subject and symbol in a myth of magnanimity Spenser resolved that his Prince Arthur should rival and perhaps overgo Hercules.

THE RIVAL OF HERCULES

A mystery about Spenser's Arthur is his closer resemblance to the mythological Hercules than to the Arthur of the romances. His first triumph, the victory over Duessa's "fruitfull-headed beast," recalls the Lernaean Hydra. Conventional though the allusion was, it was not perfunctory. Spenser used it because he shared the indignation that made Giordano Bruno describe Jove as awarding the Corono Borealis to any prince who would use club and fire to "bring back the rest so much desired by this miserable and unhappy Europe, smashing the heads of this worse than Lernaean monster which is scattering the fatal venom of its multiform heresy."[55] Bruno wrote as a disillusioned fellow-traveler of the Reformation who had once hailed Luther as "the new Alcides,"[56] but later come to regard his doctrine of justification by faith as the venom of the hydra. In reverse, the hydra's venom became a

Protestant metaphor for the doctrine of Rome, and in the character of a Protestant reformer Henry VIII was awarded the crown of Hercules, "the chief daunter of monsters," for his "moste famous subduyng of the Romayne monster Hydra."[57] In a doctrinal quarrel a symbol like the hydra is at the disposal of both parties, and Spenser knew that it had served two masters. Its prestige came from Plato's reference to it in the *Republic* (IV, 426) as symbolic of demagoguery. All Europe was familiar with Alciati's emblem of Hercules and the interpretation of the hydra as representing the eristic sophists of the *Euthydemus*. As a symbol of sophistry it appeared in most of the mythographies from Boccaccio's *Genealogy* (XIII, i) down, and Boccaccio set the example of interpreting Hercules as a symbol of intelligence penetrating and destroying fraud. So Arthur's laying of Duessa's "fruitfull headed beast" is an emblem of the intelligence militant and triumphant. However unsavory its political allegory may seem, its basic symbolism entitles it to enduring respect.

In scenes where Hercules's labors are recalled by Arthur's exploits the political allegory is often less obvious than might be expected. An exception to this rule is the Legend of Justice, in which the career of the titular knight, Artegal, is announced as rivaling those of Hercules and Bacchus; but it is Arthur rather than Artegal whose adventures prove Herculean.[58] Spenser wrote with Hercules constantly in mind, suggesting similes and twice influencing the form of episodes. Like Raleigh, he accepted as fact the core of the myth that Hercules "slew many theeves and tyrants," though he may not have gone all the way with Raleigh in believing that the legends were "truly written, without adition of Poeticall vanitie."[59] When

> the brave Prince for honour and for right
> Gainst tortious Powre and lawlesse regiment,
> In the behalfe of wronged weake did fight," (*F.Q.*, V, viii, 30, 6–8)

he is England defeating the Spanish Armada; but his conquest of the Souldan recalls that

> Thracian tyrant, who, they say,
> Unto his horses gave his guests for meat,
> Till he himselfe was made their greedie pray,
> And torn in peeces by Alcides great. (V, viii, 31, 3–4)

In that following canto Arthur's tussle with the robber, Malengin, seems patterned on Hercules's struggle with the thief, Cacus, as Virgil tells the tale in the *Aeneid*. At least the detail about Malengin's lair,

> hewen farre under ground
> A dreadfull depth, how deepe no man can tell;
> But some doe say, it goeth downe to hell (V, ix, 6, 3–5)

recalls the lines describing Cacus's cave:

> ac si qua penitus vi terra dehiscens
> Infernas reserat sedes et regna recludat
> Pallida, dis invisa, superque inmane barathrum
> Cernatur . . . (*Aeneid,* VIII, 243–46)

> (. . . as if the earth,
> ripped open by some violence, unlocked
> the house of hell and all its pallid kingdoms,
> so hated by the gods, and one could see
> deep down into that dread abyss. . . .)[60]

Again, in the next two cantos, Arthur's defense of Belgé against Geryoneo, though it patently celebrates England's intervention against Spain in Flanders, is made a sequel to Hercules' war with the three-bodied giant, Geryon, his cruel cowherd and two-headed dog, when "Hercules them all did overcome in fight" (V, x, 10, 9). The parallel with the myth is explicit. In Spenser's chronology Arthur belongs to the generation after Hercules, for Geryoneo

> was borne and bred
> Of gyants race, the sonne of Geryon,
> He that whylome in Spaine so sore was dred . . . (V, x, 9, 1–3)

Behind these evocations of the saga of Hercules in Spenser's treatment of Arthur lay ramifications all the way from Boccaccio's *Genealogy of the Gods* (ca. 1360) and Coluccio Salutati's *De Laboribus Herculis* (ca. 1450) to the *Vita Herculis* of Lilius Gregorius Gyraldus (1589). They all accepted him as the hero who, in the words of Chaucer's Boethius, "disservide eftsones the hevene to ben the pris of his laste travaile."[61] The mythographers' darling became the hero of the most extravagantly idealized of the Italian epics of the Counter-Reformation, G.-B. Giraldi's *Ercole* (1554). The keynote of that enormous poem is the "aria di magnanimità" ("aria of magnanimity") which Guerrieri-Crocetti has traced in every episode. Ercole is the flower of "nobiltà e magnanimità" ("nobility and magnanimity"), the *honnête homme* and *varón ilustre* ("the honorable man, and illustrious man") without peer, the prototype of Goffredo, Belisario, and the Cornelian Cid.[62] Though Arthur is not among his epigones, he is comparable with "un cabaliere d'Artù" ("one of Arthur's knights") because

> . . . qualche avventura brama
> Con la qual giovar possa a l'human stuolo,
> Et ch'i pericoli et le fatiche ama,
> Per levarsi, ad altrui giovando, a volo,
> Et che compagno alcun seco non chiama,
> Perché vuol che l'honor sia di lui solo.

> (He desires some adventures with which he can assist the human kind; he loves danger and labor, so that he can fly up high, while helping others; and he wants no companions next to him, so that the honor can only be his.)[63]

To make the chivalrous Arthurian likeness unmistakable, a sharp contrast emerges between Giraldi's hero and the "instinctive and individualistic" heroes of the *Orlando Furioso*. In Giraldi's epic Hercules, though he is as magnificently accoutered as Spenser's Arthur, is no less generous than Arthur to defeated enemies and indeed to "all humble creatures."[64] The unctuous tone of Giraldi's stress on the humility of his Hercules exceeds anything like it in Spenser, and it is revolting when his hero is fulsomely compared to the most modest of monarchs, the Emperor Charles V, to the latter's advantage.

Giraldi's flattery of Charles should surprise no one who is familiar with the ascription of the title of Hercules to rulers from the Emperors Commodus and Probus down to the time when the Swiss Reformer Zwingli assured Francis I that in heaven he would find himself beside Hercules, Socrates, and Aristotle.[65] From childhood Henry VIII of England was matched with Hercules, as he seems first to have been by Castiglione.[66] Sir Anthony Coke's comparison of him to Hercules for slaying "the Romayne monster Hydra" illustrates the process that made the mythological hero into an instrument of political propaganda and royal compliment and at the same time prepared for his rebirth in Neo-Platonic allegory as the Arthur of *The Faerie Queene*. If Henry could be likened to Hercules, the worthies of his daughter's court might enjoy the same comparison; if not directly, then through Spenser's Herculean Arthur. For—as Fuller observed in *The Worthies of England*[67]—Arthur might be "called the British Hercules" for his "painful life" and divine birth as well as his violent end.

In an illuminating study Rathborne has reminded us that "all heroic virtue whose reward is immortal fame" found its "prototype" in the Hercules who was the "ancestor of Spenser's Prince Arthur."[68] Her main interest is in the pseudo-historical Hercules looming behind Spenser's imperial Arthur—the Libyan Hercules of the spurious chronicle of "Berosus the Chaldaen," in whom the Elizabethans saw both an ancestor of their queen and a conqueror of western Europe whose empire outmatched that of the legendary Arthur and inspired Spenser to recreate Dante's dream of a new Holy Roman Empire with Elizabeth's London, Troynovant, as its capital. If there was truth in the fables that made Hercules the progenitor of a Trojan-British dynasty, what could be more natural than to reincarnate him in an allegory that was both historical and moral? But in such an allegory politics must come second to ethics. Arthur's foe Geryoneo may represent the Spain that Elizabeth held at bay, but he must be explicitly sib to Typhaon and the cosmic monsters which Hesiod describes Hercules as destroying.[69] In Spenser's allegory Arthur never meets Typhaon though in the mutability cantos he is twice mentioned as making war on Jove. As the strongest opponent of all the kindred of Typhaon, Arthur becomes a kind of cosmic symbol of magnanimity or the valiant beneficence of the superman whom L.-G. Gyraldus recognized as archetypal when he declared that in primitive times "men called all brave spirits that extirpated monsters Hercules."[70]

The Euhemeristic view of Hercules went back, as Coluccio Salutati recalled in *De Laboribus Herculis* (III, i), to Cicero and Varro. Varro's computation of forty-three different Hercules in the mythology of Egypt, Chaldaea, Greece, and Rome pleased Salutati because he liked to think of the figure as a magnet attracting the glory of human greatness to itself in all ages. The *De Laboribus* made Hercules a symbol of all virtue, intellectual as well as moral, of all human learning, science, and wisdom, and of all the spiritual energy that the story of his begetting by Jove upon Alcmena might imply. A mystic justification for his idea might, he thought, be found in his favorite etymology for the name *Hercules: heris cleos*—the glory of struggle or of the wars of the spirit. Similarly, Natale Conti declared that for him the name was a symbol of "honor, courage, and virtuous excellence of mind and body alike."[71] The etymology was ancient—perhaps as ancient as those lauds of Hercules to which Eryximachus refers in Plato's *Symposium*. Spenser may have been familiar with it in Boccaccio's *Genealogy*.[72] Certainly its prestige among the mythographers played a part in his invention of an Herculean Arthur in love with glory.

Though Spenser may never have heard of Salutati, it is worth remarking that in the *De Laboribus* the myth of Geryon is treated as a spiritual allegory and its villain as "a symbolic fomenter of vice."[73] So it is with all the other labors. Cerberus at hell's gate represents sensuality—not the fear of death. Among all the monsters slain by Hercules we should expect the giant Antaeus to be Salutati's most ingeniously treated symbol of sensuality or materialism. And with the help of Fulgentius and a score of other ancient writers, every detail of his struggle with Hercules is allegorized to make him a symbol of lust.[74] His renewal of strength at every fall means lust's nourishment by its gross, earthly mother, and his final strangling aloft in Hercules's arms means virtue's triumph over lust by starving it of food. The allegorical cycle is complete when Salutati etymologizes Antaeus as meaning "virtue's opposite" and cites the authority of Lucan and Statius for regarding the giant's bout with Hercules as a supreme instance of virtue militant.

As a symbol of embattled virtue Hercules's bout with Antaeus had long been a motif in Italian literature and art. Its symbolism was essentially like that in Prudentius's *Psychomachia* or allegory of the sin-besieged soul. Spenser did no violence to either motif in combining them in his Antaeus figure, Maleger, who leads the bestial armies that beset the castle of Alma.[75] In making their rout by Arthur the setting for his victory over their captain in a wrestling bout resembling that of Hercules with Antaeus, Spenser knew that he would remind his readers of sculptural groups like Pollaiuolo's bronze (now in the national museum in Florence). In such groups Antaeus is "large of limbe, and shoulders brode," as Spenser describes his counterpart, Maleger. Both wrestlers seem to express simply the sculptor's pleasure in magnificent anatomy and the drama of the ring. There is no suggestion of Spenser's paradoxical account of the large-limbed Antaeus as being

> of such subtile substance and vnsound,
> That like a ghost he seem'd, whose graue-clothes are vnbound.
> (*F.Q.*, II, xi, 20, 8–9)

Maleger's strength consisted in his bloodless flesh and

> bodie without might,
> That could doe harme, yet could not harmed bee,
> That could not die, yet seem'd a mortall wight,
> That was most strong in most infirmitee . . . (II, xi, 40, 5–8)

Maleger is hard to match among the sculptural groups of Hercules and

Antaeus, but he has a counterpart in the etching of the Master of 1515, with its nobly robust Hercules at grips with a mysteriously withered Antaeus. Like Spenser's Maleger, the Antaeus seems to symbolize weaknesses subtler than the mere carnality that Salutati and the mythographers were satisfied to see in Hercules's opponent.

The three main Herculean scenes in the career of Spenser's Arthur—the slaying of Duessa's hydra-like beast, the defeat of Geryoneo, and the strangling of Maleger—coupled with other traces of the Hercules saga in Arthur's story, leave no doubt that Spenser intended to add another Hercules to the forty-three that Varro distinguished in ancient tradition. Conflating them, Spenser derived an image of

> that great Champion of the antique world,
> Whom famous Poetes verse so much doth vaunt.
> And hath for twelue huge labours high extold. (*F.Q.*, I, xi, 27, 1–3)

Cicero, he knew, made the divinization of that hero by popular faith a part of the argument of the Stoic, Balbus, in the *De Natura Deorum* for a divine government of the universe.[76] He may have remembered that in the same dialogue the sceptical Cotta inverted the Euhemeristic view of Hercules as a synthetic hero representing all the benefactors of mankind and ridiculed the popular faith in his divinity.[77] Spenser may have been aware that continental thinkers, heirs of the second-century Platonist, Celsus,[78] were drawing the most skeptical conclusions from Euhemeristic premises to cast doubt upon the divinity of Christ and rank him with Moses and Hercules among man-made deities. Spenser may also have recalled a tradition associating the worship of Christ with Hercules that went back as far as the Emperor Alexander Severus, who was said to have images of Abraham, Orpheus, Hercules, and Jesus standing together in his oratory. Severus's eclectic pantheon is mentioned in Bodin's *Heptaplomeres* (1593) in a way that seems indicative of the author's religious position.[79] The context of Spenser's interest in Hercules was thinking akin to Bodin's rationalism, which his editor hesitates to call "natural religion." Bodin had much in common with the later Stoics for whom Hercules was a divine agent for human service. The great Neo-Stoic Justus Lipsius seems to have been near Bodin's position when he wrote in the *Physiologia Stoicorum* (1604) approving Seneca's theology in a passage in the *De Beneficiis* (IV, viii) which declares that God "may be called Providence, World, Destiny, Hercules, or Mercury."[80] The Neo-Stoics of the later sixteenth century in France did their best to reconcile Christian faith with the rational pantheism of Seneca.[81]

It is significant that, though Spenser could speak of Hercules in *The Ruines of Time* and *An Hymne in Honour of Love* as divine and sharing heaven's joys with "Venus' dearlings," he did not follow the Neo-Stoics in coupling Hercules with Jesus. Nor did he yield to the literary convention of the Italian Neo-Platonists for whom Professor Walzel observes that the blurring of the distinction between Hercules, Bacchus, Mercury, and the Christian God was an esthetic principle.[82] Yet divinity was the essence of the Hercules that Spenser acclimatized in Fairy Land in the person of Arthur. Like Cicero's Hercules,[83] Arthur is a symbol of the magnanimous human spirit attaining immortality. In terms of Aristotle's magnanimous man, as Professor Ernest Sirluck points out, Arthur may be regarded—particularly in his battle with Maleger's feral hosts—as incarnating the "heroic and divine kind of nature" that Aristotle opposed to brutishness.[84] How consistently Spenser reflected the Aristotelian doctrine that "a state evidently opposed to a brutish state" implied virtue enough to make a man divine.

For Spenser the divinity of Aristotle's high-minded man was most obvious in his love for doing favors—a trait that he identified with Hercules' motive in the famous labors. In the plan of his poem he found that Herculean magnanimity was convenient as well as appropriate for a character with a commission to unify the plots of his vaguely related books by graciously supervening at their crises. No matter if his appearances were as little interrelated as the labors of the mythical Hercules; they had an integrity of their own for his readers. Spenser understood Herbert Read's distinction between a myth and a poem; while a poem lives only in forgettable words, a myth "persists by virtue of its imagery."[85] No more potent images than some of the labors of Hercules existed in the minds of the Elizabethans.

Whether Spenser's Arthur really suffuses *The Faerie Queene* with the magnanimity that Dryden said "shines throughout the whole poem"[86] is a question that the present study does not try to answer; nor does it try to settle that other persistent question whether Spenser intended to complete his unfinished poem with a Legend of Magnanimity with Arthur as its central figure. Doctors disagree. W.F. De Moss thought that "under Spenser's plan, as set forth in the Letter to Raleigh, the virtue assigned to Arthur could have no book."[87] Lewis is certain that Spenser "intended a final book on Arthur and Gloriana which would have stood to the whole poem as such central or focal cantos [as the Garden of Adonis and the Temple of Venus] stand to their several books."[88] If Lewis is right, an interesting possibility occurs for in that book the rival of Hercules would certainly reenact some of the famous labors that have left no trace in the existing *Faerie Queene*. What they would have been we cannot tell, but it may be surmised that they would have included a counterpart of Hercules's invasion of hell to rescue Perithous—a situation that is paralleled with Christ's harrowing of hell by Ronsard in his *Hercule Chrestien*. If among other possibilities Spenser meditated an Arthurian analogue to Hercules's deliverance of Prometheus from his chain on Mount Caucasus, we may be sure that he had no thought of drawing the parallel that Ronsard did between Prometheus and

> Nature humaine
> (J'entends Adam) que Christ a détaché
> Par sa bonté des liens de péché,
> Lors que la Loy comme une aigle sans cesse
> Luy pincetoit son ame pécheresse.[89]

> (Human nature [I mean Adam] that Christ through his goodness freed from the bonds of sin, when the Law like an eagle unceasingly cut away from him his sinful soul.)

We may be sure (regardless whether Spenser knew Plotinus directly) that he would have preferred the Plotinian interpretation of the myth as an allegory of the deliverance of the soul from matter or its own creation.[90] He would not have forced an analogy with Christ, as Ronsard did throughout his poem. In Spenser's potential Legend of Magnanimity we should expect to find Arthur's quest of glory becoming a search for truth and the soul's goal in the intelligible world, where Plotinus says that Hercules ultimately arrives.[91]

The climax of Arthur's legend would perhaps have been a version of Hercules's death in flames of his own kindling on Mount Oeta. Although Spenser was attracted to the story of "that great Oeten knight,"[92] he never told it. He must have known Castiglione's allegory of the soul's quest for intellectual beauty in "the great fire in which (the Poets write) Hercules was buried on the toppe of the mountaine Oeta: and through that consuming with fire, after his death was holy and immortall."[93] The motif of the pyre was used in many a poem developing the theme of the quest for true beauty, like—for example—Du Bellay's sonnet on Hercules building his pyre to attain "Une beauté plus parfaitement belle" ("a beauty more perfectly beautiful"):

> Rien de mortel ma langue plus ne sonne:
> Ja peu à peu moismesme' j'abandonne,
> Par cete ardeur, qui me faict sembler tel
> Que se monstroit l'indomté fils d'Alcméne,

Qui dedaignant nostre figure huméne,
Brula son corps, pour se rendre immortel.[94]

[My tongue no longer speaks of mortal things; little by little I already abandon myself through this ardor, which makes me seem like the undaunted son of Alcmene, who, disdaining our human form, burnt his body in order to make himself immortal.]

Some such act of heaven-storming self-immolation we may imagine as the last scene in the Legend of Spenser's Herculean Arthur. From it we may picture him ascending to the skies as Tasso pictured the dying Ercole Gonzaga, Cardinal of Mentova, rising from his funeral pyre to the heavens.[95]

And we may imagine Spenser's contemporaries reading the Legend of his Herculean Arthur with the delight that Sidney makes Argalus and Parthenia feel in "reading . . . the stories of Hercules"[96] at the crisis of the *Arcadia* when they are both unexpectedly summoned to prove their magnanimity by death in the wars against Amphialus.

Notes

1. 2nd ed. (London, 1762), p. 75.

2. Josephine W. Bennett, *The Evolution of "The Faerie Queene"* (Chicago, 1942), p. 25.

3. W.L. Renwick, *Edmund Spenser, an Essay in Renaissance Poetry* (London, 1925), p. 175.

4. B.E.C. Davis, *Edmund Spenser, A Critical Study* (Cambridge, 1933), p. 68.

5. Janet Spens, *Spenser's "Faerie Queene." An Interpretation* (London, 1934), p. 32.

6. C.S. Lewis, *The Allegory of Love* (Oxford, 1936), p. 337.

7. Thomas Warton, *Observations on the Fairy Queen of Spenser* (London, 1762), Vol. 1, p. 17.

8. Bennett was partly anticipated by Professor Edwin Greenlaw in *Studies in Spenser's Historical Allegory* (Baltimore, 1932) and by Charles B. Millican's survey of Tudor concurrence in Ascham's view of the *Morte d'Arthur* as a tissue of "murder and bold bawdry," Tudor prejudice against it as a work of Papists, and Tudor criticism of it as "a poor criterion of literary form" (*Spenser and the Table Round,* Harvard Studies in Comparative Literature, VIII, 1932). Though modern scholarship may agree with Howard Maynadier's statement in *The Arthur of the English Poets* (Boston, 1907, p. 262) that Spenser "felt the influence of the Arthurian legends," it cannot agree that "he knew them best through Malory."

9. August Bruno Höppner, *Arthurs Gestalt in der Litteratur Englands im Mittelalter* (Jena, 1892), p. 28. [The quotation is from Wace, *Le Roman de Brut,* ed. Ivor Arnold, 2 vols. (Paris: Société des Anciens Textes Français, 1940), Vol. 2, p. 476, lines 9025–26. The spelling in Arnold's text is different from that of Höppner's quotation.—E.D.K.]

10. Bennett, *Evolution of "The Faerie Queene,"* pp. 140–41.

11. *Ibid.,* p. 52.

12. *Gli Asolani* di Monsignor P. Bembo (In Venetia, XDXL), pp. 98v–99r.

13. Greenlaw, *Studies in Spenser's Historical Allegory,* p. 66.

14. Millican, *Spenser and the Table Round*, p. 126.

15. Isabel E. Rathborne, *The Meaning of Spenser's Fairyland*, Columbia University Studies in English and Comparative Literature, n. 131 (New York, 1937), p. 235.

16. Levin L. Schücking, *The Sociology of Literary Taste* (London, 1944), pp. 11–12.

17. J.W. Saunders, "The Facade of Morality," in *ELH, a Journal of Literary History,* 19 (1952).

18. Werner Jaeger, *Aristotle: Fundamentals of the History of his Development,* trans. Richard Robinson (Oxford, 1948), p. 243.

19. In *Der Ehrbegriff der Nikomachischen Ethik* (Prague, 1889) Josef Lugert noted (p. 24) "ein Stück der alter Ritterlichkeit" ("a bit of the old chivalry") of Homeric times in Aristotle's *Ehrbegriff* ("concept of honor") which he saw (p. 7) as consisting in the "Glückseligkeit, Tugend, und Lust" ("bliss, virtue, and delight") on which the entire work rested.

20. J. Bronowski, *The Poet's Defence* (London, 1946), p. 100.

21. Rathborne, *Meaning of Spenser's Fairyland,* p. 106.

22. Allan H. Gilbert, *Machiavelli's "Prince" and its Forerunners* (Durham, N.C., 1938), p. 85.

23. Patrizi's work was written probably shortly before his death in 1494. The reference is to the Paris edition of the *De Regno* (1567), pp. 244v–245r.

24. Ruth Kelso, *The Doctrine of the English Gentleman in the Sixteenth Century,* University of Illinois Studies in Language and Literature, 14 (1929), 27.

25. Geoffrey Bullough, "Bacon and the Defense of Learning," in *Seventeenth Century Studies Presented in Honor of Sir Herbert Grierson* (London, 1938), p. 17.

26. William Empson, *Some Versions of Pastoral* (London, 1935), p. 90.

27. Ernest Sirluck, "Aristotle's *Nicomachaean Ethics* and *The Faerie Queene,*" *Modern Philology,* 49 (1951), 88–89.

28. Virgil K. Whittaker, *The Religious Basis of Spenser's Thought,* Stanford University Publications, University Series, Language and Literature, Vol. 7, no. 1 (1950), p. 42. Cf. A.S.P. Woodhouse's "Nature and Grace in *The Faerie Queene,*" *ELH* 16 (1949), 194–228; F.M. Padelford's *Political and Ecclesiastical Allegory of the First Book of "The Faerie Queene"* (Boston, 1911); and T.P. Nelan's New York thesis on Spenser's theology (1943).

29. Ruskin, *The Stones of Venice* (London, 1853), Vol. 3, pp. 204–05.

30. *Theogony,* II.211–235.

31. Evelyn Underhill, *Mysticism. A Study in the Nature and Development of Man's Spiritual Consciousness,* 2nd ed. (London, 1911), p. 466.

32. Natale Conti, *Mythologiae, sive Explicationis Fabularum Libri decem* (Frankfurt, 1596), III, xii, p. 233.

33. *Genealogiae Jonannis Baccatii: cum demonstrationibus in formis arborum designatis* (Venice, 1511), II, ix, p. IIr.

34. Pauline Henley, *Spenser in Ireland* (Cork, 1928), p. 145.

35. T.R. Henn, anent Yeats's interest in Spenser, in *The Lonely Tower* (London, 1950), p. 37.

36. Kelso, *Doctrine of the English Gentleman,* p. 95.

37. By H.S.V. Jones in "Magnanimity in Spenser's Legend of Holiness," *Studies in Philology,* 39 (1932), 203–04 and in *"The Faerie Queene* and the Mediaeval Aristotelian Tradition," *The Journal of English and Germanic Philology,* 25 (1926), 282–98.

38. *Summa Theologica,* II, ii, 129, 2 and 3.

39. Cf. J.J. Jusserand's "Twelve Private Morall Vertues as Aristotle Hath Devised," *Modern Philology,* 3 (1906), pp. 373–83.

40. Alessandro Piccolomini, *Della Institution Morale* (Venice, 1569), Book VI, Chapter ix, and VII, xv–xvi. In VII the abuse of magnificent dress and personal splen-

dor by the ambitious is condemned.

41. The maxim is attributed to Pontano by Giuseppe Zonta in *Storia della Letteratura Italiana* (Bologna, 1930), Vol. 2, p. 480.

42. Ionnis Ioviani Pontani, *Opera Omnia* (Venice, 1518), pp. 229r–256v, and *passim*.

43. Francisci Patricii Senensis, *de Regno et Regis Institutione Libri* IX (Paris, 1567), Book VII, Chapter viii.

44. *Hecatommithi*, ouero Novelle di M. Giovanbattista Giraldi Cinthio, nobile Ferrarese . . . Et vi sono tre *Dialoghi della Civile* . . . (Venice, 1580). Dialogo Primo (p. 19r) makes a point about magnanimity versus the duellists' code. It was suggested by Jusserand that Spenser was acquainted with this dialogue. Cf. note 39 *supra*.

45. Pierre de la Primaudaye, *The French Academie*, newly trans. T. B(owes) (London, 1586), pp. 297–98.

46. Sir Thomas Elyot, *The Boke Named the Governour*, Everyman's Library, p. 239.

47. S. Thomae Aquinatis, *In decem libros Ethicorum Aristotelis ad Nicomachum Expositio* (Turin, 1934), IV, viii, 749, p. 253.

48. *The Governour*, p. 240.

49. *Nicomachaean Ethics*, IV, iii, 16.

50. *De Regno et Regis Institutione*, p. 236r.

51. C.A. Mayer, "L'Honnête Homme," *The Modern Language Review*, 46 (1951), 202.

52. The symbolism of the diamond shield is studied by D.C. Allen in "Arthur's Diamond Shield in *The Faerie Queene*," *The Journal of English and Germanic Philology*, 36 (1937), 234–43.

53. Romans, 13, 12; 2 Corinthians, 6, 7; Ephesians, 6, II.

54. *The Mabinogion*, trans. Lady Charlotte Guest, Everyman's Library (London, 1910), p. 100.

55. Giordano Bruno, *Lo Spaccio de la Bestia Trionfante*, *Opere Italiane*, ed. Giovanni Gentile (Bari, 1927), Vol. 2, p. 64.

56. Cf. Gentile in *Giordano Bruno e il pensiero del rinascimento* (Florence, 1925), p. 169. As Luther became the Hercules Germanicus, Zwingli was honored as the Hercules Helveticus and later lampooned in the *Triumphus Herculis Helvetici of the two moste noble captaines of the worlde, Anniball and Scipio* (1544), p. 33r.

57. Sir Anthony Coke in the preface to *The Historie*.

58. Though Artegal's imprisonment by Radegund parallels Hercules's enslavement by Omphale, the resemblance ends when Britomart rescues him and ends the "monstrous regiment of women," as if she reincarnated Alcides, whom Bruno imagined in *Lo Spaccio* (p. 69) as subduing "a new Amazonian queen and her rebel forces."

59. Sir Walter Raleigh, *The History of the World* (London, 1652), p. 402.

60. *The Aeneid*, trans. Allen Mandelbaum (New York: Bantam, 1972), ll. 317–21, p. 199.

61. *The Complete Works of Geoffrey Chaucer*, ed. F.N. Robinson (Boston, 1933), p. 435.

62. Camillo Guerrieri-Crocetti, *G.-B. Giraldi ed il Pensiero Critico del Secolo XVI* (Milan, 1932), pp. 435, 554, 557, and 558.

63. *Ercole*, Canto II, quoted by Guerrieri-Crocetti, p. 566. Translation by Dino S. Cervigni, Dept. of Romance Languages, The University of North Carolina at Chapel Hill.

64. Guerrieri-Crocetti, p. 571.

65. Originally the practice was Greek; it was ridiculed by Plutarch, in *How a Man May Discern a Flatterer from a Friend* (*Moralia* 56f). For Commodus's assumption of the title "Invictus Romanus Hercules" see Giovanni Costa's "Giovi ed Ercole" in *Bilychnis* (II Serie, n. 17, 1919), p. 17. Zwingli's act is recorded by M.H. Pinard de la Bouillay in *Histoire des Religions* (Paris, 1922), pp. 136–37.

66. *The Book of the Courtier* by Count Baldassare Castiglione, done into English by Sir Thomas Hoby, Everyman edition, pp. 289–90.

67. Thomas Fuller, *The History of the Worthies of England,* ed. P. Austin Nuttall (London, 1840), Vol. 1, pp. 311–12.

68. Rathborne, *Meaning of Spenser's Fairyland,* p. 113.

69. *Theogony,* Vol. 2, pp. 287–311.

70. Lilius-Gregorius Gyraldus, *Herculis Vita* (Basle, 1589), p. 2.

71. *Mythologiae libri decem,* Book VII, Cap. I, p. 708.

72. In the *Genealogia,* XIII, I (p. 96r) Boccaccio impartially offers the meanings *terra, heros,* and *erix* as etymons for the first element in the name *Hercules.*

73. *De Laboribus Herculis,* ed. B.L. Ullman (Zurich, 1952), III, xxviii; Vol. 1, p. 328.

74. *Ibid.,* p. 322.

75. If Spenser's moral seems morbid, it should be compared with the emblem of Antaeus on the seal of the Academy of the Elevati in Ferrara and with its unctuous interpretation by their orator, Bartolomeo Ferrino, in *Delle Orationi Volgarmente Scritte da molti huomini de nostri tempi* (Venice, 1575), pp. 138 r and v.

76. *De Natura Deorum,* II, xxiv.75; *Ibid.,* III, xv, xvi, xix.

77. *Ibid.,* III, xv, xvi, xix.

78. Cf. Henri Busson, *Les Sources et le Développement du Rationalisme dans la Littérature française de la Renaissance* (Paris, 1922), pp. 196–98.

79. *Colloque de Jean Bodin des Secrets cachez des choses sublimes, entre sept scavans qui sont de differens sentimens,* traduction française du *Colloquium Heptaplomeres,* par R. Chauviré (Paris, 1914), p. 24.

80. Justi Lipsii V.C. *Opera Omnia* (Velasiae, 1675), pp. 852–53.

81. L. Zonta, *La Renaissance du Stoïcisme au XVIᵉ Siècle* (Paris, 1914), p. 229.

82. Oskar Walzel, "Plotins Begriff der Aesthetischen Form," *Vom Geistesleben alter und neuer Zeit* (Leipzig, 1922), pp. 49–50.

83. Cf. *De Natura Deorum,* II, xxiv, and *Disputationes Tusculanae,* I, 25–26 and 32.

84. Cf. Sirluck, "Aristotle's *Nicomachaean Ethics* and the Second Book of *The Faerie Queene,*" 93.

85. Herbert Read, *Collected Essays in Literary Criticism* (London, 1938), p. 103.

86. Thomas Warton quoted the remark from Dryden's Dedication to his translation of Juvenal in *Observations on the Fairy Queen of Spenser* (London, 1762), I, 7, only to deny it and declare that, instead of shining everywhere in the poem, magnanimity "bursts forth but seldom, in obscure and interrupted flashes."

87. W.F. De Moss, *Influence of Aristotle's "Ethics" and "Politics" on Spenser,* p. 44.

88. C.S. Lewis, *The Allegory of Love,* pp. 336–37.

89. Pierre de Ronsard, *Œuvres complètes,* textes établi et annoté par Gustave Cohen (Paris, 1938), Vol. 2, p. 210.

90. Plotinus, *Ennead IV,* iii, 14.

91. *Ennead IV,* iii, 32.

92. *F.Q.,* V.viii, 2, 4.

93. *Book of the Courtier,* p. 320.

94. The sonnet (tenth of the *XIII Sonnets*) is quoted by Robert V. Merrill in *The Platonism of Joachim Du Bellay* (Chicago, 1925), pp. 43–44. [For an edition see Joachim du Bellay, *Oeuvres Poétiques,* Vol. I, ed. Henri Chamard (Paris: Nizet, 1982), p. 146.—E.D.K.]

95. *Le Rime di T. Tasso,* a cura di Angelo Solerti (Bologna, 1899), Vol. 3, p. 24.

96. Sir Philip Sidney, *The Countess of Pembroke's Arcadia,* ed. Ernest A. Baker, p. 322. The importance of this passage in Sidney's treatment of magnanimity is noted by John F. Dandy in *Poets on Fortune's Hill* (London, 1952), p. 52.

THE FEMALE KING

TENNYSON'S ARTHURIAN APOCALYPSE

Elliot L. Gilbert

> Yet in the long years liker must they grow
> The man be more of woman, she of man.
>
> Tennyson, *The Princess*

> Dr. Schreber believed that he had a mission to redeem the world and
> to restore it to its lost state of bliss. This, however, he could only bring about
> if he were first transformed from a man into a woman.
>
> Freud, "A Case of Paranoia"

> The happiest women, like the happiest nations, have no history.
>
> George Eliot, *The Mill on the Floss*

> Queen Victoria, there's a woman . . . when one encounters a toothed
> vagina of such exceptional size. . . .
>
> Lacan, "Seminar, 11 February 1975"

> La femme est naturelle, c'est-à-dire abominable.
>
> Baudelaire, *Mon Cœur mis à nu*

I

Sooner or later, most readers of the *Idylls of the King* find themselves won-
dering by what remarkable transformative process the traditionally virile and
manly King Arthur of legend and romance evolved, during the nineteenth
century, into the restrained, almost maidenly Victorian monarch of Alfred
Lord Tennyson's most ambitious work. Many of the earliest of these readers of the *Idylls* deplored the change, noting in it disquieting evidence of the

Reprinted by permission of the Modern Language Association from *PMLA*, 98 (1983),
863–78.

growing domestication and even feminization of the age.[1] And more recent critics, though they may have moderated the emotionalism of that first response, continue to see in Arthur's striking metamorphosis a key element in any analysis of the poem. I will argue here, however, that such a metamorphosis was inevitable, given the nineteenth-century confluence of what Michel Foucault has called "the history of sexuality" with what we may call the history of history, and that Tennyson's Arthurian retelling, far from being weakened by its revisionary premise, is in fact all the stronger and more resonant for depicting its hero as a species of female king.

Tennyson was attracted to the legend of King Arthur as a prospective subject for literary treatment almost from the beginning of his career; "the vision of Arthur had come upon me," Hallam Tennyson quotes his father in the *Memoir*, "when, little more than a boy, I first lighted upon Malory" (2:128). *Poems, Chiefly Lyrical,* published in 1830, when Tennyson was just twenty-one, contains the picturesque fragment "Sir Lancelot and Queen Guinevere," and by 1833, when his next volume appeared, the poet had already written, or was in the process of writing, two of his best-known Arthurian works, "The Lady of Shalott" (1832) and the ambitious rendering of King Arthur's death that, at its first publication ten years later, he called "Morte d'Arthur."

By this time, however, Tennyson had come to question the propriety of a nineteenth-century artist devoting his energies to the reworking of medieval materials. That is, he came to feel that only some contemporary significance in the Arthurian retellings, only "some modern touches here and there" (as he puts it in "The Epic"), could redeem his poetry "from the charge of nothingness," from Thomas Carlyle's characterization of it as "a refuge from life . . . a medieval arras" behind which the poet was hiding "from the horrors of the Industrial Revolution" (quoted in Priestley, 35) or from John Sterling's judgment that "the miraculous legend of 'Excalibur' . . . reproduced by any modern writer must be a mere ingenious exercise of fancy" (119).[2]

The idea that nineteenth-century artists ought to concern themselves with nineteenth-century subjects was a pervasive one (see Gent). When, for example, Matthew Arnold omitted *Empedocles on Etna* from a collection of his poetic works, he found it necessary to explain that he had not done so "because the subject of it was a Sicilian Greek born between two and three thousand years ago, *although many persons would think this a sufficient reason*" (italics mine). In the Preface to *Poems* (1853), Arnold goes on to quote "an intelligent critic" as stating that "the poet who would really fix the public attention must leave the exhausted past, and draw his subjects

from matters of present import, and therefore both of interest and novelty"(1, 3). Four years later, in a long discourse on poetics in *Aurora Leigh*,
Elizabeth Barrett Browning takes a similar position. "If there's room for poets
in this world," Barrett Browning declares in Book 5 of her blank-verse novel:

> Their sole work is to represent the age,
> Their age, not Charlemagne's
>
> . . . .
>
> To flinch from modern varnish, coat or flounce,
> Cry out for togas and the picturesque,
> Is fatal—foolish too. King Arthur's self
> Was commonplace to Lady Guenevere:
> And Camelot to minstrels seemed as flat
> As Fleet Street to our poets. (200–13)

That Tennyson himself was influenced by such attitudes is plain from
the fact that when he published "Morte d'Arthur" in 1842, he set his medieval story in a modern framing poem, "The Epic," whose only partly ironic
theme is the irrelevance of such a historical subject to the contemporary
world. Edward Fitzgerald asserts that Tennyson invented this setting "to give
a reason for telling an old-world tale" (quoted in H. Tennyson, 1:194). Otherwise, as poet Everard Hall remarks in "The Epic," explaining why he has
burned his own long Arthurian poem:

> Why take the style of those heroic times:
> For nature brings not back the mastodon,
> Nor we those times; and why should any man
> Remodel models?

The lapse of fifty-five years between the writing of the "Morte d'Arthur"
in 1833 and the publication of the complete *Idylls of the King* in 1888 suggests how difficult a time Tennyson had finding the contemporary significance he was looking for in his medieval material. Nevertheless, nearly all
readers agree with the poet that "there is an allegorical or perhaps rather a
parabolic drift in the poem" that permits the work to be read as "a discussion of problems which are both contemporary and perennial" (H. Tennyson,
2:126–27).

The exact nature of that discussion remains an open question, though
a few facts about the allegory do seem clear. The book, proceeding season-
ally as it does from spring in "The Coming of Arthur" to winter in "The

Passing of Arthur," is certainly about the decline of a community from an original ideal state, about the corruption and nihilism that overtake a once whole and healthy social order. Just as surely, an important agency of this decline is identified by the story as human sexuality and, in particular, female passion. The four idylls published by Tennyson in 1859—"Vivien," "Guinevere," "Enid," and "Elaine"—under the general title *The True and the False* focus on the polar extremes of feminine purity and carnality, and however the author may have altered his plans for the book in the following years, his emphasis on the corrosiveness of female sexuality never changed. "Thou has spoilt the purpose of my life," Arthur declares grimly in "Guinevere," about to part forever from the queen and plainly placing the whole blame for the decay of the Round Table and the fall of Camelot on his wife's unfaithfulness.

The association of marital fidelity with the health of the state did not please all the first readers of the *Idylls*. Swinburne, for one, condemned what he felt was the reduction of Sir Thomas Malory's virile tales of chivalry to a sordid domestic quarrel. To him, Victorian King Arthur was a "wittol," or willing cuckold, Guinevere "a woman of intrigue," Lancelot "a co-respondent," and the whole story "rather a case for the divorce court than for poetry" (57). In the same essay, Swinburne refers to the *Idylls* as "the Morte d'Albert" (56), alluding to Tennyson's 1862 dedication of his poem to the recently deceased prince consort but, even more than that, to the royal family's celebrated bourgeois domesticity.

Swinburne was right to see that Tennyson's idylls turn on the issue of domestic relations and specifically on the willingness or unwillingness of men and women to play their traditional social and sexual roles in these relations. He was wrong, however, to think such a subject contemptible. Indeed, his sardonic reference to "the Morte d'Albert" inadvertently calls attention to a major theme in the poem as well as to one of the central problems of Victorian society: the growing assertion of female authority.

In his Dedication of the *Idylls of the King* to Prince Albert, Tennyson describes a relationship between husband and wife that on the surface is entirely conventional. Albert is presented as an active force in national life, as "laborious" for England's poor, as a "summoner of War and Waste to rivalries of peace," as "modest, kindly, all-accomplished, wise," and, most important, as the ultimate pater familias, "noble father" of the country's "kings to be." Victoria, by contrast, appears in the Dedication principally in the role of bereaved and passive wife, whose "woman's heart" is exhorted to "break not but endure" and who is to be "comforted," "encompassed," and "o'ershadowed" by love until God chooses to restore her to her husband's side.

What lies behind this traditional domestic relationship is, of course, a very different reality. In that reality, Victoria is the true holder and wielder of power, the repository of enormous inherited authority, while Albert possesses what influence and significance he does almost solely through his marriage. This reversal of the usual male-female roles, superimposed on the more conventional relationship depicted in Tennyson's Dedication, produces a curious dissonance, much like one that came to sound more and more insistently in the culture as a whole as the nineteenth century progressed and that received powerful expression in the *Idylls of the King*. Indeed, Tennyson's very contemporary poem can be read as an elaborate examination of the advantages and dangers of sexual role reversal, with King Arthur himself playing, in a number of significant ways, the part usually assigned by culture to the woman.

II

Such revision of the female role in the nineteenth century is closely associated with the period's ambivalent attitude toward history. It was during the nineteenth century that the modern discipline of history first came fully into its own as a truly rigorous inquiry into the past, demanding, as Frederic Harrison puts it, "belief in contemporary documents, exact testing of authorities, scrupulous verification of citations, minute attention to chronology, geography, paleography, and inscriptions" (121). Defined in this new way, history had a distinctly male bias. This was true for a number of reasons. To begin with, its "disavowal of impressionism" (Douglas, 174) in favor of a preoccupation with hard facts permitted it for the first time to rival the natural sciences as a "respectable" career for intellectual young men. Francis Parkman, American student of the Indian Wars, "defiantly chose history," one commentator tells us, "as a protest against what he considered the effeminacy of the liberal church" (Douglas, 173). In addition, as a record of great public events, history had always tended to dwell almost exclusively on the activities of men. "It should not be forgotten," writes Arthur Schlesinger, "that all of our great historians have been men and were likely therefore to be influenced by a sex interpretation of history all the more potent because unconscious" (126). In *Northanger Abbey*, Jane Austen alludes sardonically to this fact when her heroine dismisses history books for being full of "the quarrels of popes and kings, with wars and pestilences in every page; the men all so good for nothing, and hardly any women at all" (108).

But nineteenth-century history was male-oriented in an even deeper and more all-pervasive sense than this; for to the extent that historians were principally concerned with recording the passage of power and authority through the generations, their work necessarily preserved the patrilineal forms and structures of the societies they investigated. "The centuries too are all lineal children of one another," writes Thomas Carlyle in *Past and Present,* emphasizing the intimate connection that has always existed between history and genealogy (45). In *The Elementary Structures of Kinship,* Claude Lévi-Strauss argues that culture, and by extension history, can only come into existence after the concept of kinship has been established. But this means that in those societies where family structure is patrilineal, women must inevitably play a secondary role in history, since they do not have names of their own and therefore do not visibly participate in the passing on of authority from one generation to the next. The rise of "scientific" history in the nineteenth century, then, might have been expected to confirm, among other things, the validity of the traditional male-dominant and female-subordinate roles.

But in fact, those roles came more and more frequently to be questioned during the period, as did the new history itself. Ironically, it was the very success of scientific history at reconstituting the past that provoked this resistance. For what soon became clear was that, seen in too much detail and known too well, the past was growing burdensome and intimidating, was revealing—in Tennyson's metaphor—all the models that could not be remodeled. John Stuart Mill's celebrated dismay, reported in his *Autobiography,* that all the best combinations of musical notes "must already have been discovered" was one contemporary example of this anxiety. Another was George Eliot's declaration, in *Middlemarch,* that "a new Theresa will hardly have the opportunity of reforming a conventual life . . . the medium in which [her] ardent deeds took shape is for ever gone." For a nineteenth-century woman like Dorothea Brooke, George Eliot tells us, it is often better that life be obscure since "the growing good of the world is partly dependent on *un*historic acts" (612; italics mine).[3] Such a conclusion follows inevitably from the idea that history, simply by existing, exhausts possibilities, leaving its readers with a despairing sense of their own belatedness and impotence. And this despair in turn leads to anxious quests for novelty, to a hectic avant-gardism, and in the end to an inescapable *fin de siècle* ennui. "The world is weary of the past,/Oh, might it die or rest at last," Shelley declares in *Hellas,* expressing a desire for oblivion, a longing for the end of history. Only through such an apocalypse, the poet suggests, can life be made new and vital again.

The great apocalyptic event for the nineteenth century was the French Revolution, at its most authentic a massive and very deliberate assault on history. To be sure, regicide is the ultimate attack on the authority of the past, but if it is dealt with merely on a political level, its deeper significance is likely to be missed. To be fully understood, it must, rather, be placed in the context of the many other revolutionary acts whose collective intent was to overthrow not only the old historical regime but history itself. Among these acts were laws that abolished the right to make wills and that declared natural children absolutely equal with legitimate offspring. Both struck directly at the power of the past to control the present and, just as important, at the right of patrilineal authority to extend itself indefinitely into the future. Revolutionary calendar reforms were an even more literal attack on history. By decree, official chronology, for example, began at the autumn equinox of 1792; the first day of the new republic thus became the first day of the new world. Even the names of the months were changed in the revolutionary calendar, with the seasons replacing the Caesars—nature replacing history—as the source of the new nomenclature.

From these revolutionary activities two important principles emerged. The first is that wherever intolerable social abuses are the consequence of history, reform is only possible outside of history.[4] The French Revolution sought to incorporate this idea, at least symbolically, into an actual working community, a community for which not history but nature would provide the model. In that new dispensation, each person would be self- authorized, independent of genealogy, and each day would have the freshness of the first day or, rather, of the only day, of *illo tempore,* a moment in the eternal present unqualified and undiminished by an "exhausted past." Such an ambition has never been entirely fanciful. Mircea Eliade, for one, reminds us of "the very considerable period" during which:

> . . . humanity opposed history by all possible means. . . . The primitive desired to have no "memory," not to record time, to content himself with tolerating it simply as a dimension of his existence, but without interiorizing it, without transforming it into consciousness. . . . That desire felt by the man of traditional societies to refuse history, and to confine himself to an indefinite repetition of archetypes, testifies to his thirst for the real and his terror of losing himself by letting himself be overwhelmed by the meaninglessness of profane existence. (*Cosmos* 90–91)

The Revolution's famous exchange of "fraternity" for "paternity" makes the same point. The father-child relationship is generational and thus principally a product of history. Brothers, on the other hand, are by their nature contemporaries, and their relationships are therefore more "spatial" than temporal. In *Parsifal,* Wagner describes the realm of the Grail knight brotherhood in just these terms. "Zum Raum," Gurnemanz explains to the at-first uncomprehending Parsifal, "wird hier die Zeit" ("Time changes here to space"). Significantly, James R. Kincaid finds this same idea built into the very structure of Tennyson's *Idylls.* "The overlaid seasonal progress in the [poem]," he writes, "suggests not so much objective, physical time as the spatial representations of time in medieval tapestry or triptychs. This emphasis on space seems to imply the absence of time, the conquest of time" (151–52). It is a conquest that Ann Douglas believes was, for the nineteenth century, inescapably gender-identified; distinguishing between "scientific" historians and feminine and clerical historians, she remarks that the latter, "in their well-founded fear of historicity . . . substituted space for time as the fundamental dimension of human experience" (199).

As the Douglas comment shows, the second principle established by the Revolution is closely related to the first, asserting that the apocalyptic end of history signals the end of a system in which women are instruments of, and subordinate to, patrilineal continuity. In particular, the revolutionary law making natural children the absolute equals of so-called legitimate offspring had the effect of taking from men their familiar right to direct and subdue female sexuality. In the saturnalia of sexual "misrule" that followed, with its release of aboriginal energy and its invitation to self-discovery and self-assertion, traditional gender roles were radically reexamined. Eliade's study of ceremonial transvestism describes this symbolic sex role reversal as:

> . . . a coming out of one's self, a transcending of one's own historically controlled situation, a recovering of an original situation . . . which it is important to reconstitute periodically in order to restore, if only for a brief moment, the initial completeness, the intact source of holiness and power . . . that preceded the creation. (*Mephistopheles,* 113)

Interestingly, 1792, the first year of the new French Republic, was also the year in which Mary Wollstonecraft published her *Vindication of the Rights of Woman,* inaugurating the modern era of feminism. Wollstonecraft would later include in her own study of the French Revolution descriptions of the part women played in overturning the monarchy. "Early . . . on the fifth of October," she reports, "a multitude of women by some impulse were collected together; and hastening to the *hôtel de ville,* obliged every female they met to accompany them, even entering many houses to force others to follow in their train." The women are only temporarily delayed by national guardsmen with bayonets. "Uttering a loud and general cry, they hurled a volley of stones at the soldiers, who, unwilling, or ashamed, to fire on women, *though with the appearance of furies,* retreated into the hall and left the passage free" (*Historical and Moral View,* 133; italics mine).[5]

One can perhaps find in these latter-day Eumenides the originals of Dickens's Madame Defarge and her ferocious female companions of the guillotine. The same image seems to have occurred independently to Edmund Burke, who equated the insurrection on the Continent with the dismemberment of King Peleas of Thessaly by his daughters, an act contrived by the vengeful Medea (109).[6] Clearly, the nineteenth century perceived the French Revolution as juxtaposing two key contemporary themes, the attack on history and the assertion of female authority. The reading of Tennyson's *Idylls of the King* proposed here focuses precisely on this juxtaposition; on the rich potential for a new society that emerges from the original association of these two themes and on the disaster Tennyson says overtakes such a society once all the implications of the Arthurian apocalypse are revealed.

III

The coming of Arthur at the beginning of the *Idylls* is plainly an apocalyptic event, recognized as such by the whole society.[7] The advent of a king who proposes to reign without the authorization of patrilineal descent is an extraordinary and threatening phenomenon. "Who is he/That he should rule us?" the great lords and barons of the realm demand. "Who hath proven him King Uther's son?" The community first attempts to see if the situation can be regularized, to see, that is, if some evidence can be found that Arthur is, after, all, the legitimate heir of an established line of kings. Leodogran, the king of Cameliard, is particularly anxious for such confirmation since Arthur has asked to marry his daughter, Guinevere. "How should I that am king," Leodogran asks, "Give my one daughter saving to a king,/And king's son?" In seeking evidence of Arthur's legitimacy, Leodogran, parodying the methodical inquiries of a historian, tracks down one source of information after another: an ancient chamberlain, some of Arthur's own closest friends, a putative stepsister. None can supply the absolute assurance the king wants, and over against their only partly convincing stories stands the undoubted truth that, while Arthur's supposed parents, Uther and Ygerne, were dark-haired and dark-eyed, the new monarch is himself "fair/Beyond the race of Britons and of men."

What emerges from all this investigation is the fact that Arthur represents not a continuation and fulfillment of history but rather a decisive break with it. Indeed, the failure of Leodogran's conventional historical research to establish some connection with the past suggests that in Arthur's new dispensation even the traditional methods for acquiring knowledge have become ineffectual. "Sir and my Liege," cries a favorite warrior after one of Arthur's victories, "the fire of God/Descends upon thee in the battlefield./ I know thee for my King!" Here is a way of recognizing authority very different from one requiring the confirmation of genealogy. Arthur's fair coloring also confounds genealogy. Not only does it set him apart from the people most likely to have been his parents, it isolates him as well from all other Britons and even, we are told, from all other men. Radically discontinuous with the past in every one of its aspects, Arthur is like some dramatic mutation in nature, threatening the integrity of the genetic line as the only means of infusing new life into it.

In fact, nature does replace history as the sponsor of the new king. Tennyson affirms this idea both in what he chooses to drop from the traditional account of the coming of Arthur and in what he invents to replace the omission. Perhaps the best known of all legends associated with the identification of Arthur as England's rightful king is the story of the sword in the stone. In Malory, for example, young Arthur wins acceptance as lawful ruler because he is the only person in England capable of removing a magic sword from a marble block on which have been inscribed the words "Whoso pulleth out this sword of this stone and anvil is rightwise king born of all England."

In nearly every retelling of the Arthurian stories down to our own time, this dramatic incident plays a prominent part. Tennyson's omission of the anecdote from his own rendering of the Arthurian material, then, is at least noteworthy and may even be a significant clue to one of the poet's principal intentions in the *Idylls*. For what the phallic incident of the sword in the stone emphasizes is that Arthur, though not as incontrovertibly a descendant of the previous king as the people of England might like, is nevertheless the inheritor of some kind of lawful authority, the recipient of legitimate power legitimately transferred. And the participation in this ritual of the church, with its traditional stake in an orderly, apostolic succession, further ensures that such a transfer is, at least symbolically, patrilineal. Tennyson's rejection of this famous story, therefore, may well suggest that the poet was trying to direct attention away from conventional continuity in the passing of power to Arthur and toward some alternative source of authority for the new king.

What that alternative source of authority might be is hinted at in "Guinevere," the eleventh of the twelve idylls, an unusual work in that, as

Jerome Buckley points out in his edition of the poetry, it draws on little "apart from Tennyson's own imagination" (536). This "self-authorized" and so-to-speak "unhistorical" idyll contains a striking description of the early days of Arthur's reign—the account of a magical initiatory journey, invented by Tennyson, we may conjecture, as a substitute for the omitted episode of the sword in the stone. We hear this story from a young novice, who repeats the tale her father had told her of his first trip to Camelot to serve the newly installed king. "The land was full of signs/And wonders," the girl quotes her father's narrative of that trip. By the light of the many beacon fires on the headlands along the coast:

> . . . the white mermaiden swam,
> And strong man-breasted things stood from the sea,
> And sent a deep sea-voice thro' all the land,
> To which the little elves of chasm and cleft
> Made answer, sounding like a distant horn.
>
> So said my father—yea, and furthermore,
> Next morning, while he past the dim-lit woods
> Himself beheld three spirits mad with joy . . .
>
> And still at evenings on before his horse
> The flickering fairy-circle wheel'd and broke
> Flying, and link'd again, and wheel'd and broke
> Flying, for all the land was full of life.
>
> And when at last he came to Camelot,
> A wreath of airy dancers hand-in-hand
> Swung round the lighted lantern of the hall;
> And in the hall itself was such a feast
> As never man had dream'd; for every knight
> Had whatsoever meat he long'd for served
> By hands unseen; and even as he said
> Down in the cellars merry bloated things
> Shoulder'd the spigot, straddling on the butts
> While the wine ran.

This visionary scene both celebrates and ratifies the coming of Arthur, affirming that the young king's authority over the land proceeds directly from the land itself, from the deepest resources of nature, and that "all genealogies founder," as J.M. Gray puts it, "in that 'great deep.'" (11). Metaphors of depth and interiority are everywhere: seas, woods, chasms, clefts, cellars. All the spirits of nature rejoice in Arthur, seeing in him their rightful heir, the repository of their power. In Tennyson's remarkable vision, radically departing as it does from historical sources, Arthur's coming fulfills that revolutionary law of the French National Convention which declared "natural children absolutely equal with legitimate."

This Romantic idea that the true source of kingly power is natural and internal rather than historical and external is more fully developed in the first of the idylls. There, Arthur's legitimacy is shown to derive from two sources: an inner strength, of which his successful military adventures are symbols, and the depths of nature, themselves metaphors for the young king's potent inwardness. When we first meet Arthur in the *Idylls,* he is a newly fledged warrior, driving the patriarchal Roman Caesars from his land as determinedly as the French would later drive them from the calendar.[8] Later, we see the young monarch receiving the sword Excalibur from the Lady of the Lake, a mystic wielder of subtle magic who "dwells down in a deep" and from whose hand, rising "out of the bosom of the lake," the new king takes the emblem of his authority.

To the extent that such derivation of power from the deep symbolizes access to one's own interior energy, Arthur's kingly mission is ultimately self-authorized; and in particular it is authorized by that part of himself which, associated with creative, ahistorical nature, is most distinctly female. Tennyson emphasizes this idea not only by assigning the Lady of the Lake a prominent role in the establishment of Arthur's legitimacy but also by introducing the mysterious muselike figures of the "three fair queens" who attend the young king at his coronation: "the friends/Of Arthur, gazing on him, tall, with bright/ Sweet faces, who will help him in his need."[9] In his Preface to *The Great Mother* Erich Neumann declares that the "problem of the Feminine [is important] for the psychologist of culture, who realizes that the peril of present-day mankind springs in large part from the one-sidedly patriarchal development of the male intellectual consciousness, which is no longer kept in balance by the matriarchal world of the psyche" (xlii). Clearly, the new dispensation promised by the coming of Tennyson's nineteenth-century Arthur will involve, as an important part of its program, the freeing of that matriarchal psyche, of feminine energy, from its long subservience to male authority and consciousness. Everything we know about the new king makes this certain. The very manner of his accession directly challenges such authority and consciousness, and his establishment of the community of the Round Table can best be understood as an attempt to assert the wholeness of the human spirit in the face of that sexual fragmentation described by Neumann.

What the dominance of male consciousness over female psyche can lead to in society is made plain in the *Idylls* through Tennyson's description of the all-male community of King Pellam in "Balin and Balan," the last of the books to be written. Pellam, a rival of King Arthur's, determines to outdo the court of Camelot in piety, and as a first step he pushes "aside his faithful wife, nor lets/Or dame or damsel enter at his gates/Lest he should be polluted." As a manifestation of abstract male reason and will, such suppression of the feminine renders the society moribund. The aging Pellam, described by Tennyson as "this gray king," has "quite foregone/All matters of this world" and spends his listless days in a hall "bushed about . . . with gloom," where "cankered boughs . . . whine in the wood." Nature here, rejected as a source of energy and replenishment, takes suitable revenge on its sullen oppressor.

King Pellam is the guardian of a most appropriate relic. The old monarch, who "finds himself descended from the Saint/Arimathaean Joseph," is the proud possessor of "that same spear/Wherewith the Roman pierced the side of Christ" as he hung on the cross. Death-dealing, Roman, phallic, linear, the spear—its ghostly shadow haunting the countryside—symbolizes the desiccated male society of Pellam's court; indeed, it is very literally the male "line" through which Pellam—who, unlike Arthur, is deeply interested in genealogy—traces the source of his authority back to Joseph of Arimathaea. Significantly, as a symbol of the linear and the historical, the spear belies the cyclical promise of the resurrection represented by the Grail, the companion relic from which, in the sexually fragmented culture described both by Neumann and by Tennyson, it has long been separated.[10]

As the country of King Pellam is the land of the spear, so Arthur's Camelot is the court of the Grail. At least, it is from Camelot that the knights of the Round Table, tutored in Arthur's values,[11] set out on their quest for the sacred cup, familiar symbol both of nature and of the female, a womblike emblem of fecundity associated with what, in pagan legend, is the Cauldron of Plenty, an attribute of the Goddess of Fertility.[12] Such female energy is, in traditional mythography, ahistorical, a fact to which the Grail also testifies. The vessel's circular form, like that of the Round Table itself and like the "flickering fairy circles" and "wreaths of airy dancers" associated with the coming of Arthur, mimics the timeless cycles of nature, a timelessness in which the Round Table knights themselves participate. As we noted earlier, fraternal relationships are necessarily contemporaneous ones, expressing themselves in space rather than in time. The whole of Camelot partakes of this anachronistic quality. The young knight Gareth, catching his first glimpse of the sculptured gates of the city, marvels at how intermingled—how contiguous rather than continuous—all the events depicted there seem to be: "New things and old co-twisted, as if Time/Were nothing." His intuition of the ahistorical character of Camelot is confirmed by the "old seer" at the gate, who speaks of the city as a place "never built at all,/And therefore built forever." Significantly, the principal subject of "Gareth and Lynette" is young Gareth's commitment "to fight the brotherhood of Day and Night" in "the war of Time against the soul of man," a war in which, in this early idyll, the soul signally triumphs.[13]

IV

The optimism expressed in the early idylls about the joyous and lively new society that would result from an apocalyptic release of natural and, by extension, female energy into a world heretofore dominated by history and male authority was largely a product of one form of nineteenth-century Romantic ideology. Traditionally, nature has been seen as the enemy of rational and historical human culture. Indeed, it has been argued that culture functions to permit human beings to assert their independence of—and superiority to—nature. In examining the origins of kinship, for example, Lévi-Strauss suggests that the whole elaborate and extended structure of the family can best be understood as a means by which "culture must, under pain of not existing, firmly declare 'Me first,' and tell nature, 'You go no further'"(31).[14] In this view, nature is dangerous, anarchic, indifferent to human concerns. Its frightening power may have to be placated or invoked on special occasions, but it must always be treated warily, must be controlled and even suppressed.

The Romanticism of the early nineteenth century, as one of its most striking innovations, managed momentarily to suspend the traditional enmity between nature and culture. In the benign natural world of the Wordsworthian vision, for example, breezes are "blessings," vales are "harbors," clouds are "guides," groves are "homes." Where human culture is a burden, it wearies the poet precisely because it is "unnatural." Under such circumstances, Wordsworth attempts to reconcile these traditionally polar opposites, submitting his cultivated sensibility to a sustaining and unthreatening nature in order to receive a new infusion of energy. It is nature in this ameliorative sense that underlies the scene in the *Idylls* in which the coming of Arthur is celebrated by all the mermaidens, elves, fairies, spirits, and merry bloated things we would naturally expect to find inhabiting a land that is "full of life."

The same Romantic optimism that permitted nature to be so readily domesticated in many early nineteenth-century works of art, that allowed nature's powers to be courted so fearlessly, also made possible the hopeful invocation of female energy that is such a striking feature of the *Idylls*. Historically, this benignant view of female power is unusual. Both in history and in myth women have for the most part been associated with the irrational and destructive forces of nature that threaten orderly male culture. As maenads, bacchantes, witches, they express in their frenzied dances and murderous violence an unbridled sexuality analogous to the frightening and sometimes even ruinous fecundity of nature. Indeed, the control of female sexuality is among the commonest metaphors in art for the control of nature (just as the control of nature is a metaphor for the control of women; cf. Smith and Kolodny). And as Lévi-Strauss points out, the earliest evidences of culture are nearly always those rules of exchange devised by men to facilitate the ownership and sexual repression of women.

Tennyson's departure, in the early idylls, from this traditional fear of female sexuality coincides with a dramatic development in modern cultural history. "Between the seventeenth and the nineteenth centuries," Nancy F. Cott remarks about this change, "the dominant Anglo-American definition of women as especially sexual was reversed and transformed into the view that women were less carnal and lustful than men" (221). Or as Havelock Ellis put it more succinctly in his *Studies in the Psychology of Sex,* one of the most striking creations of the nineteenth century was "woman's sexual anesthesia" (3:193–94). Cott substitutes for Ellis's "anesthesia" her own term "passionlessness," linking it with Evangelical Protestantism, which "constantly reiterated the theme that Christianity had elevated women above the weakness of animal nature for the sake of purity for men, the tacit condition for that elevation being the suppression of female sexuality" (227). Plainly, Tennyson's nineteenth-century re-creation of Camelot depends to a considerable extent on this contemporary theory of female passionlessness— what another critic calls woman's "more than mortal purity" (Christ, 146)— and its ameliorative influence on male sensuality.[15] Unlike the society of King Pellam, which preserves the earlier view of women as sexually insatiable and which adopts a grim monasticism as the only defense against feminine corrosiveness, Arthur's court welcomes women for their ennobling and now safely denatured regenerative powers. In this respect, Camelot seems to resemble the many nineteenth-century utopian communities that attempted to experiment with a new and higher order of relationship between the sexes and that Tennyson himself had already commented on obliquely in *The Princess.*[16]

It is in his own "passionlessness" that Arthur most clearly embodies the nineteenth-century feminine ideal on which he seeks to build his new society.[17] "Arthur the blameless, pure as any maid," he is called, sardonically but accurately, in "Balin and Balan," and it is in these terms that he becomes a model for all his knights, urging them:

> To lead sweet lives in purest chastity,
> To love one maiden only, cleave to her,
> And worship her by years of noble deeds.

Such sexual restraint will, according to Arthur, win for the Round Table knights the moral authority to purify a land "Wherein the beast was ever more and more,/But man was less and less." These lines perfectly express the Evangelical Protestant belief, just noted, that "Christianity had elevated women above the weakness of animal nature for the sake of purity for men," and they confirm that it is on the female ideal of passionlessness that Arthur means to found his new community. Tennyson even goes so far as to alter his sources in order to make this point, rejecting Malory's designation of Modred as Arthur's illegitimate son and instead having the king refer to the usurper as "my sister's son—no kin of mine."

<h2 style="text-align:center">V</h2>

The scene would now appear to be set for the triumph of the Round Table experiment. With the apocalyptic overturning of history and male authority and the substitution for them of a benign nature and a safely contained female energy, Arthur's new society ought certainly to flourish. How, then, are we to account for the famous decline of this ideal community into corruption and nihilism, how explain the fall of Camelot? Tennyson's revision of the story of Modred's origins may offer one answer to these questions. As I have suggested, the point of the poet's departure from Malory is to maintain unblemished the record of Arthur's sexual purity. But the textual change has unexpected ramifications that reveal a serious flaw in the Arthurian vision. For if Modred is not Arthur's son, illegitimate or otherwise, then in the story as we receive it, Arthur has no children at all. He and Guinevere produce no offspring, and even the foundling he brings to his wife to rear as her own dies.

Such sterility, appropriate symbol of a denatured sexuality, means the end of Arthur's dream of a new society; the rejection of history and patriarchy that is the source of the young king's first strength here returns to haunt the older monarch, who now perceives that without the continuity provided by legitimate descent through the male line, his vision cannot survive him.[18]

This point has already been made obliquely in the passage from "Guinevere" describing the natural magic that filled the land when Arthur first began to rule. The story, we know, is recounted by a young novice who explains that she is repeating a tale her father had told her. Thus, even this early in Arthur's reign, the dependence of the king's authority on the preservation of a historical record is recognized, a preservation that in turn—the passage reminds us—requires men capable of begetting children through whom to transmit that record.[19]

It is precisely Arthur's incapacity to propagate his line that renders his new society so vulnerable. In "The Last Tournament," for example, the Red Knight calls tauntingly from the top of a brutally phallic tower:

> Lo! art thou not that eunuch-hearted king
> Who fain had clipt free manhood from the world—
> The woman-worshipper?

The Red Knight's equation of Arthur's sterility with a worship of woman suggests how enfeebling the king's sentimentalizing of nature has become. The female ideal worshipped by Arthur (and scorned by the Red Knight) is tame, disembodied, passionless, itself the product of an abstract male rationalism and no real alternative source of strength. Lancelot, describing to Guinevere, in "Balin and Balan," a dream he has had of "a maiden saint" who carries lilies in her hand, speaks of the flowers as "perfect-pure" and continues:

> As light a flush
> As hardly tints the blossom of the quince
> Would mar their charm of stainless womanhood.

To which Guinevere replies, resenting such an imposition of the ideal on the natural,

> Sweeter to me . . . this garden rose
> Deep-hued and many-folded! sweeter still
> The wild-wood hyacinth and the bloom of May!

In the end, Guinevere's reality triumphs over Arthur's and Lancelot's abstraction in the *Idylls of the King,* just as her irresistible sexual energy at last defeats her husband's passionlessness.

Given the subject and the theme of the *Idylls,* this outcome is inevitable. Indeed, Tennyson's profoundest insight in the poem may be that nature cannot be courted casually, that the id-like energy of the deep must not be invoked without a full knowledge of how devastating and ultimately uncontrollable that energy can be. Again, for the nineteenth century it was the French Revolution that most dramatically embodied this insight. We have already seen how that event, for all its celebration of myth over history, nature over culture, female over male, itself began by trying to contain the outburst of insurrectionary energy it had released within a number of easily manipulated abstractions: new laws governing the inheritance of property, new names for the months of the year. Even regicide was intended as a kind of abstract statement, the removal of a symbol as much as of a man.

But unaccountably, the blood would not stop flowing from the murdered king's decapitated body. It poured into the streets of Paris from the foot of the guillotine and ran there for years, as if newly released from some source deep in the earth. From the first, the bloodstained Terror was associated with female sexuality. The key symbol of the Revolution was the figure Liberty, later memorably depicted by Eugene Delacroix as a bare-breasted bacchante striding triumphantly over the bodies of half-naked dead men. The Dionysian guillotine haunted the imagination of Europe; a mechanical *vagina dentata,* it produced, with its endless emasculations, an unstoppable blood flow, the unhealing menstrual wound curiously like the one suffered by the maimed king in the story of the Grail. In primitive societies, such menstrual bleeding is the ultimate symbol of a polluting female nature, an unbridled sexual destructiveness that the power of patriarchal authority must at all costs contain. In nineteenth-century England, the bloody denouement of the French Revolution produced a similar reaction, a suppression of sex and a repression of women that to this day we disapprovingly call Victorian.

From the beginning of his career, Tennyson had been preoccupied with these issues—with what Gerhard Joseph has called the poet's "notion of woman as cosmic destructive principle" (127)—and in particular with the point at which the themes of nature, blood, and female sexuality converge. An early sonnet, for example, begins:

> She took the dappled partridge fleckt with blood,
> And in her hands the drooping pheasant bare,
> And by his feet she held the woolly hare,
> And like a master-painting where she stood,
> Lookt some new goddess of an English wood.

This powerful figure of female authority, bloody, dangerous, but curiously attractive, springs from the imagination of a young poet already moving toward a post-Wordsworthian view of nature as "red in tooth and claw." In "The Palace of Art," the protagonist, withdrawing too deeply into self, approaching too closely the dark, secret springs of nature, comes "unawares" on "corpses three-months-old . . . that stood against the wall" and on "white-eyed phantasms weeping tears of blood." In the *Idylls,* the doom of the Round Table is sealed at the moment during "The Last Tournament" when, to defeat the bestial Red Knight, Arthur's men give themselves up to the almost erotic appeal of blood lust, when:

> . . . swording right and left
> Men, women, on their sodden faces, [they] hurl'd
> Till all the rafters rang with woman-yells,
> And all the pavement streamed with massacre.

But the dismantling of the brotherhood had begun even earlier, as a direct result of the Grail quest. The blood-filled holy cup, itself a menstrual symbol, first appears in the *Idylls* to Percival's sister, a young nun in whose description the vessel seems almost explicitly a living female organ:

> Down the long beam stole the Holy Grail,
> Rose-red with beatings in it, as if alive,
> Till all the white walls of my cell were dyed
> With rosy colors leaping on the wall.
> ("The Holy Grail")

It is when the Round Table knights abandon themselves to the visionary pursuit of this symbol of the "eternal feminine" that Camelot, literally "un-manned," begins to fall into ruin.

"Creator and destroyor," Robert M. Adams comments on the Victorian image of the *femme fatale:*

> . . . but more fascinating in the second capacity than the first, woman
> for the late nineteenth century . . . is both sacred and obscene, sacred
> as redeeming man from culture, obscene as content with a merely
> appetitive existence that declines inevitably from the high fever of Eros
> to the low fever of dissolution and decay. (185)

In the end, Arthur's dream of a natural community is destroyed, Tennyson suggests, by the carnality to which such a dream must necessarily lead, is spoiled by an irrepressible female libidinousness that, once released by the withdrawal of patrilineal authority, can be neither contained nor directed. The second half of the *Idylls* is one long record of licentiousness: the faithless depravity of Gawain and Ettarre, the crass sensuality of Tristram and Isolt, the open adultery of Lancelot and Guinevere. "Thou hast spoilt the purpose of my life" we have already heard Arthur declare bitterly to the queen at their last meeting, a key passage in the long-standing controversy about the psychological and moral sophistication of the *Idylls*. For if Christopher Ricks, among others, is right that in this speech Guinevere is made "too much a scapegoat [since] the doom of the Round Table seems to antedate her adultery," he is surely wrong to find, in such an attack on her, evidence of "a root confusion in Tennyson" (272). Rather, what the poem preeminently shows is that the confusion here is Arthur's. It is Arthur's naiveté about the dynamics of the human psyche that dooms his ideal community from the start; it is his own well-intentioned but foolish binding of his knights "by vows . . . the which no man can keep" that threatens his dream long before the adultery of Guinevere and Lancelot can precipitate its destruction.[20]

In his isolation from reality, the king resembles other self-authorizing post-Renaissance heroes, from Faust to Frankenstein, who begin by creating the worlds in which they live out of their own private visions and end by succumbing to the dark natural forces they have raised but fail to understand or control. The solipsistic isolation of such figures becomes their fate as well as their failing, their retribution as well as their sin. For where the historical record provides individuals with a context independent of themselves, a past and a future in which they need not participate to believe, a variety of experiences unlike their own but just as real, myth asserts the sovereignty of the eternal moment, which is forever the present, and the ubiquitousness of the representative human, who is always the same, without antecedents or heirs. It is into this reductive timelessness and silence of myth that characters like Merlin and Arthur ultimately fall in the *Idylls* for having cut their connections with patriarchal history.

Merlin, Tennyson tells us in the sixth idyll, derives his power from an ancient volume that is the paradigmatic book of history, passed down through the generations from one male magician to another. The first owner we hear of is a little, shriveled, Pellam-like wizard whose strength comes from his rejection of sensuality in favor of the intensest possible concentration on the text. (The seer's principal use of this text is to help a local king exercise absolute control over his queen.) The book then "comes down" to Merlin, who describes it as

Writ in a language that has long gone by.
. . . .
And every margin scribbled, crost, and cramm'd
With comment, densest condensation, hard
. . . .
And none can read the text, not even I;
And none can read the comment but myself;
And in the comment did I find the charm.

Here is the perfect symbol of what we have been calling patrilineal continuity, continuity dependent on a bequeathed historical record that is both the ultimate source of male power and, with its antiquity and its accumulating burden of interpretation, a constant reminder of the belatedness of the present. Shut out of history by her gender, a vengeful Vivien determines to seduce Merlin from the satisfactions of male tradition with the blandishments of female sexuality. For a long while the old magician holds out against the woman, but in the end he yields, revealing to her the secret of the ultimate charm. The next moment, Vivien has turned the spell back on him, robbing him—significantly—of "name and fame," the two best gifts that patrilineal history can bestow on a man, and casting him into the eternal isolation of myth, "Closed in the four walls of a hollow tower/From which was no escape for evermore."[21]

In his final battle, Arthur suffers a fate much like Merlin's. Because he has received authorization from no father and conveyed it to no son, the king is trapped in the reflexiveness of the prophecy that has governed him all his life: "From the great deep to the great deep he goes." That same solipsistic reflexiveness characterizes Arthur's last hallucinatory battle against his sister's son, a war, he tells us:

. . . against my people and my knights
A king who fights his people fights himself.
. . . .
I perish by this people that I made. ("The Passing of Arthur")

The war is fought in "a death-white mist" in which the solid reality of the world proves an illusion, "For friend and foe were shadows in the mist,/And friend slew friend not knowing who he slew."

Ironically, the reign that began with the whole world doubting the legitimacy of the king ends with the king himself doubting it. "On my heart," says Arthur:

> . . . hath fallen,
> Confusion, till I know not what I am,
> Nor whence I am, nor whether I be king;
> Behold, I seem but king among the dead.

In the end—Tennyson summarizes the central theme of the *Idylls*—all certainty is impossible for a man who rejects the stability of patrilineal descent and seeks instead to derive his authority from himself, to build a community on the idealization of nature and female energy.

VI

The resemblance of this scene, in which "friend slays friend," to the equally confusing struggle of "ignorant armies" on "the darkling plain" in Matthew Arnold's "Dover Beach" reminds us that, in writing the *Idylls of the King,* Tennyson was participating in an elaborate symposium with his fellow Victorians on the troubling state of their world. But where Arnold's poem focuses on a particular moment in the history of that world, Tennyson's *Idylls* provide, in John D. Rosenberg's phrase, "the chronicle . . . of a whole civilization" (34) as it passes from the Romantic optimism of its first days— about which Wordsworth could exult, "Bliss was it in that dawn to be alive"—to the *fin de siècle* disillusionment of the last hours—which found, in Walter Pater's words, "each man keeping as a solitary prisoner, his own dream of a world." The springtime innocence and eagerness of the first idylls wonderfully convey the excitement of the Romantic rediscovery of nature, and the Arthurian credo of passionlessness embodies the early Victorian belief in the benevolence and controllability of that nature. But just as the Victorians' famous efforts to suppress female sexuality only succeeded in generating a grim and extensive sexual underground, so Arthur's naive manipulations of nature conclude in the society of the Round Table being swept away on a great wave of carnality.

Despite the failure of the Arthurian assault on history, Tennyson persists at the end of the *Idylls,* as he does elsewhere, in seeking a rapprochement with myth. Thus, against the linear and historical implication of the king's famous valedictory, "The old order changeth, yielding place to new," the poet reiterates the traditional cyclical promise of Arthur's eventual return as *rex quondam rexque futurus.* In the same way, at the end of *In Memoriam* Tennyson sets the historical and progressive "one far-off, divine event/To which the whole creation moves" within a cycle of seasons. To be sure, the hero of "Locksley Hall" seems to offer the definitive disavowal of myth when he declares, "Better fifty years of Europe than a cycle of Cathay."

But it is significant that the narrator of that poem lives long enough to discover how the inevitable alternation of "chaos and cosmos" in the universe
renders even the most intense vision of historical progress trivial.

Such ambivalence about history, our starting point for this consideration of the *Idylls*, marks the history of the poem itself, a history that records
the poet's entrapment in a familiar nineteenth-century dilemma, one with
its own broader ramifications. Like Merlin, Tennyson is committed—since
"first light[ing] upon Malory"—to the authority of a historical test of which
he is his generation's principal interpreter:

> And none can read the comment but myself;
> And in the comment did I find the charm.

But no belated expositor such as he, no descendant of patriarchal exegetes,
can hope to make the unimaginable backward leap through commentary to
the mystery of the text itself. Indeed, it is the very weight of traditional commentary—"densest condensation, hard"—that renders such a leap impossible, precisely that burden of the past that unmans where it means to em-
power. For in exhausted latter days, as Merlin informs us, "None can read
the text, not even I." Yet Tennyson's attempt, in the face of this exhaustion,
to reject traditional sources in favor of a contemporary, ahistorical representation of Arthurian materials—his refusal, that is to "remodel models"—
courts another kind of weakness, risking, in the absence of patrilineal reso-
nances, the domesticity and effeminacy of "Morte d'Albert."

A similar ambivalence toward history characterizes the century for
which Tennyson wrote. Already during the early decades Viconian cyclical
theory was becoming influential, Thomas Carlyle was denouncing scientific
reconstructions of the past as "tombstone history" and time as "a grand anti-
magician and wonder-hider," and the First Reform Act, Britain's bloodless
version of the French Revolution, had dramatically rejected genealogy as
society's sole authorizing principle. In the light of such reformist impulses,
Tennyson's investigation of a natural community in the *Idylls of the King,*
one in which the female energy of myth substitutes for the male energy of
history, seems inevitable. Equally inevitable, however, is the failure of that
community, given the growing Victorian disillusionment with the Romantic experiment.[22] For Carlyle, for instance, who in his own way shared the
fate of Tennyson's Arthur, the magic creativity of *Sartor Resartus* unavoid-
ably declined into the solipsistic self-imprisonment of the *Latter-Day Pam-
phlets.* Just as inescapably, the First Reform Act led to the Second and toward that "anarchy" which Matthew Arnold prophesied and deplored and

of which the developing women's movement was seen by the Victorians as a powerful symbol. And, despite eager celebrations of myth, over this perceived decline brooded a sense of the enervating, irreversible historicity of things. Particularly in the *Idylls,* Tennyson depicts a disintegration of society from which there can be no reasonable expectation of a return. From his long, dark Arthurian speculation, Tennyson seems to be saying, the century can only move inexorably forward through *fin de siècle* hedonism into the fragmentation and alienation of a modernist waste land.

NOTES

1. Cf. George Meredith's description of Arthur as a "crowned curate," quoted in Martin, 423–24. "Tennyson was criticized," Mark Girouard writes, "both at the time and later for turning Malory's king and knights into pattern Victorian gentlemen" (184).

2. See also John Ruskin's comment to Tennyson about the *Idylls* in a letter of Sept. 1859: "So great power ought not to be spent on visions of things past but on the living present. . . . The intense, masterful and unerring transcript of an actuality . . . seems to me to be the true task of the modern poet" (36: 320–21).

3. The complete passage from *Middlemarch* reads: "[Dorothea's] full nature, like that river of which Cyrus broke the strength, spent itself on channels which had no great name on the earth. But the effect of her being on those around her was incalculably diffusive: for the growing good of the world is partly dependent on unhistoric acts; and that things are not so ill with you and me as they might have been, is half-owing to the number who live faithfully a hidden life, and rest in unvisited tombs" (613). In speaking of Theresa at the end of the novel, George Eliot implies that it is the girl's childish innocence, analogous to the innocence of her time, that made possible her great work. By contrast, the present is so burdened with knowledge of the past that "its strength is broken into channels," and people like Dorothea Brooke are effective precisely because they are "unhistoric." Were they to be historic—that is, memorable—they would only add to the burden of the next generation, become one more influence for the future to be anxious about. Their importance, then, derives from the fact that their lives are "hidden" and their tombs "unvisited." Note that unhistoric people are likelier to be women than men (history remembers more Cyruses than Theresas), women's "hidden" influence being "incalculably diffusive," like nature, rather than immediate and focused, like history. In this connection, consider the puns on Dorothea's "nature" and on her last name, closer in meaning to channel than to river.

4. Cf. National Socialism's twentieth-century exploitation of this nineteenth-century idea in support of its own revolutionary theories. "I, as a politician," Hitler is quoted by Hermann Rauschning, "need a conception that enables the order that has hitherto existed on an historic basis to be abolished and an entirely new and antihistoric order enforced" (229).

5. "The Revolution," writes Virginia Woolf of Mary Wollstonecraft, "was not merely an event that had happened outside her; it was an active agent in her own blood" (143).

6. G.P. Gooch writes that "in combating the French Revolution, Burke emphasized the continuity of historic life and the debt of every age to its predecessors" (9), just those patriarchal values under attack by the apocalyptic female energy Burke associated with the Revolution.

7. See John D. Rosenberg's discussion of Tennyson's deep interest in apocalyptic subjects, an interest evident as early as the poet's fifteenth year in the fragment "Armageddon" (14–19).

8. Indeed, the early nineteenth century found victory over Rome a particularly compelling metaphor. When Napoleon seized the crown from Pius VII at Reims and placed it on his own head, he was attacking the most venerable patriarchy in Europe, substituting for an "apostolic" descent of royal power a self-authorizing kingship that may well have influenced Tennyson's depiction of Arthur in the *Idylls*.

9. Tennyson himself refused to be tied down to a specific identification of the three queens; he responded to readers who saw them as Faith, Hope, and Charity that "they mean that and they do not. . . . They are much more" (quoted in H. Tennyson, 2:127).

10. Some forty years earlier, Tennyson had dealt with this same fragmentation in "Tithonus." In that poem, he sets the Pellam-like figure of the aged male protagonist—unable to die, obliged to move always forward in time burdened more and more by his own past, his own history—against Aurora, the female representation of the dawn, a natural phenomenon who, existing out of time in Eliade's *illo tempore* and always circling back to her beginning, continually renews her youth. In the end, Tithonus's dearest wish is to awake from the nightmare of history, to which he had willfully consigned himself, and to reenter the restorative cycle of nature, even though that change can only be inaugurated by his own death.

11. That Arthur is himself dismayed at how the embodiment of those values in the Grail quest must necessarily destroy the Round Table brotherhood prefigures the king's later despair at the final collapse of his ideal.

12. See Jessie L. Weston's discussion of this symbol (72–76). See also Robert Stephen Hawker's contemporary "Quest of the Sangraal" (1863), where the poet writes about Joseph of Arimathaea, keeper of the Grail, that "His home was like a garner, full of corn/and wine and oil: a granary of God" (184).

13. "The timelessness of myth was one of its greatest attractions to the Victorians," writes James Kissane. "It was the realm of myths and legends that came closest to constituting an idealized past that could solace Tennyson's imagination as a kind of eternal presence" (129).

14. If Lévi-Strauss does not explicitly equate culture and history, he clearly links the two through his association of culture with genealogy.

15. See also Ward Hellstrom's comment that "if the *Idylls* fail to speak to the modern world, that failure is the result to a great degree of Tennyson's attempt to preserve a lost and perhaps ultimately indefensible ideal of womanhood" (134). As my own essay tries to establish, it is Arthur rather than Tennyson who futilely defends this ideal. I fully agree with Hellstrom, however, that "the woman question is more or less central to all the books of 'The Round Table'" and even with his more daring assertion that it is "perhaps the most significant and revolutionary question of the nineteenth century" (109).

16. "In the *Idylls,* Tennyson takes up with complete seriousness, although not without irony, the question of woman's role in private and public life—a topic that in *The Princess* he treated half seriously, half satirically" (Eggers, 144).

17. Tennyson had also dealt with the issue in *The Princess,* where he dramatizes "a pattern of feminine identification in his portrayal of the Prince" (Christ, 154). Such mildness would also be appropriate, of course, to the more conventional association of Arthur with Jesus. But the attack on mid-nineteenth-century Christianity for its effeminacy, already noted, suggests that the familiar image of Arthur as Christ and Tennyson's new depiction of him as female king were beginning to coincide.

18. Margaret Homans makes a similar point, speaking of Arthur as "a victim of continuity: his origins, from which he has endeavored all his life to escape, have successfully reasserted the claim that the past makes on the future" (693).

19. Interestingly, Robert B. Martin sees this issue reflected in what he calls the poet's "slackened language" in the *Idylls,* a neglect of grammatical cause and effect that "robs the characters of any appearance of *'real man'* because there is no feeling of behavior resulting from antecedents" (496; italics mine).

20. Jerome Buckley comments that Arthur is "ineffective" in dealing with Lancelot and the queen "despite his ideal manhood, or perhaps because of it" (177).

21. Henry Kozicki describes this passage as portraying "the lotos death of old historical form through its hero's withdrawal into self" (112). Kozicki's study comments usefully on Tennyson's vision of, and attitude toward, history during the course of his career.

22. "With its lesson that the world is irredeemable," writes Clyde de L. Ryals, "the *Idylls of the King* seems to reflect much of the pessimism of nineteenth-century philosophy" (94).

WORKS CITED

Adams, Robert M. "Religion of Man, Religion of Woman." In *Art, Politics, and Will: Essays in Honor of Lionel Trilling*. Ed. Quentin Anderson, et al. New York: Basic, 1977, 173–90.

Arnold, Matthew. Preface to *Poems* (1853). In *On the Classical Tradition*. Ed. R.H. Super. Ann Arbor: University of Michigan Press, 1961.

Austen, Jane. *Northanger Abbey*. In *The Novels of Jane Austen*. Ed. R.W. Chapman. Vol. 5. London: Oxford University Press, 1923.

Browning, Elizabeth Barrett. *The Poetical Works of Elizabeth Barrett Browning*. Ed. Ruth M. Adam. Boston: Houghton, 1974.

Buckley, Jerome. *Tennyson: The Growth of a Poet*. Cambridge: Harvard University Press, 1960.

Burke, Edmund. *Reflections on the Revolution in France*. Ed. Thomas H.D. Mahoney. New York: Bobbs-Merrill, 1955.

Carlyle, Thomas. *Past and Present*. Ed. Richard D. Altick. Boston: Houghton, 1965.

Christ, Carol. "Victorian Masculinity and the Angel in the House." In *A Widening Sphere*. Ed. Martha Vicinus. Bloomington: Indiana University Press, 1977, 146–62.

Cott, Nancy F. "Passionlessness: An Interpretation of Victorian Sexual Ideology, 1790–1850." *Signs* 4 (1978): 219–36.

Douglas, Ann. *The Feminization of American Culture*. New York: Knopf, 1977.

Eggers, J. Philip. *King Arthur's Laureate*. New York: New York University Press, 1971.

Eliade, Mircea. *Cosmos and History*. New York: Harper, 1954.

———. *Mephistopheles and the Androgyne*. Trans. J.M. Cohen. New York: Sheed & Ward, 1965, 78–124.

Eliot, George. *Middlemarch*. Ed. Gordon S. Haight. Boston: Houghton, 1956.

Ellis, Havelock. *Studies in the Psychology of Sex*. 2nd ed. Philadelphia: F.A. Davis, 1913.

Gent, Margaret. "'To Flinch from Modern Varnish': The Appeal of the Past to the Victorian Imagination." In *Victorian Poetry*. Ed. Malcolm Bradbury and David Palmer. Stratford-upon-Avon Studies 15. London: Edward Arnold, 1972, 11–35.

Girouard, Mark. *The Return to Camelot*. New Haven: Yale University Press, 1981.

Gooch, G.P. *History and Historians of the Nineteenth Century*. London: Longmans, 1913.

Gray, J.M. *Man and Myth in Victorian England: Tennyson's "The Coming of Arthur."* Lincoln, Nebr.: Tennyson Society, 1969.

Harrison, Frederic. "The History Schools." In his *The Meaning of History*. 1894; rpt. New York: Macmillan, 1908, 118–38.

Hawker, Robert Stephen. "Quest of the Sangraal." [2nd ed.] In *The Cornish Ballads and Other Poems*. Oxford, 1869, 180–203.

Hellstrom, Ward. *On the Poems of Tennyson.* Gainesville: University of Florida Press, 1972.

Homans, Margaret. "Tennyson and the Spaces of Life." *ELH* 46 (1979): 693–709.

Joseph, Gerhard. *Tennysonian Love: The Strange Diagonal.* Minneapolis: University of Minnesota Press, 1969.

Kincaid, James R. *Tennyson's Major Poems: The Comic and Ironic Patterns.* New Haven: Yale University Press, 1975.

Kissane, James. "Tennyson: The Passion of the Past and the Curse of Time." In *Tennyson.* Ed. Elizabeth A. Francis. Englewood Cliffs, N.J.: Prentice-Hall, 1980, 108–32.

Kolodny, Annette. *The Lay of the Land.* Chapel Hill: University of North Carolina Press, 1975.

Kozicki, Henry. *Tennyson and Clio: History in the Major Poems.* Baltimore: Johns Hopkins University Press, 1979.

Lévi-Strauss, Claude. *The Elementary Structures of Kinship.* Boston: Beacon, 1969.

Martin, Robert B. *Tennyson: The Unquiet Heart.* New York: Oxford University Press, 1980.

Neumann, Erich. *The Great Mother.* Princeton: Princeton University Press, 1955.

Priestley, F.E.L. "Tennyson's *Idylls.*" *University of Toronto Quarterly* 19 (1949): 35–49.

Rauschning, Hermann, ed. *Hitler Speaks.* London: Butterworth, 1939.

Ricks, Christopher. *Tennyson.* New York: Macmillan, 1972.

Rosenberg, John D. *The Fall of Camelot: A Study of Tennyson's* Idylls of the King. Cambridge: Belknap-Harvard University Press, 1973.

Ruskin, John. *The Works of John Ruskin.* Ed. E.T. Cook and Alexander Wedderburn. 39 vols. London: George Allen, 1909.

Ryals, Clyde de L. *From the Great Deep: Essays on* Idylls of the King. Athens: Ohio University Press, 1967.

Schlesinger, Arthur. "The Role of Women in American History." In his *New Viewpoints in American History.* New York: Macmillan, 1921, 126–59.

Smith, Henry Nash. *The Virgin Land.* Cambridge: Harvard University Press, 1950.

Sterling, John. Rev. of Tennyson's *Poems* (1842). *Quarterly Review,* Sept. 1842, 385–416. Rpt. in *Tennyson: The Critical Heritage.* Ed. John D. Jump. London: Routledge & Kegan Paul, 1967. 103–25.

Swinburne, Algernon Charles. *Under the Microscope.* In *Swinburne Replies.* Ed. Clyde K. Hyder. Syracuse, N.Y.: Syracuse University Press, 1966. 33–87.

Tennyson, Alfred Lord. *Poems of Tennyson.* Ed. Jerome H. Buckley. Boston: Riverside, 1958.

Tennyson, Hallam. *Alfred Lord Tennyson: A Memoir by His Son.* 2 vols. London, 1897.

Weston, Jessie L. *From Ritual to Romance.* New York: Anchor-Doubleday, 1957.

Wollstonecraft, Mary. *An Historical and Moral View of the Origin and Progress of the French Revolution and the Effect It Had Produced in Europe.* In *A Wollstonecraft Anthology.* Ed. Janet M. Todd. Bloomington: Indiana University Press, 1977, 125–41.

Woolf, Virginia. *The Second Common Reader.* New York: Harcourt, 1932.

To Take Excalibur

King Arthur and the Construction

of Victorian Manhood

Debra N. Mancoff

In "The Coming of Arthur," (1869) Alfred Tennyson tells of young Arthur's acquisition of the sword Excalibur. Given to him by the Lady of the Lake, Arthur, like others after him, stood in awe of its magnificence, "With jewels on the rim, elfin Urim, on the hilt, / Bewildering heart and eye—the blade so bright / That men are blinded by it" (ll. 298–300). But the sword was more than a simple gift; in taking it Arthur agreed to a pact of use and return. The sword itself bore the contract. "On one side, Graven in the oldest tongue of all this world, / 'Take me,' but turn the blade and ye shall see, / And written in the speech ye speak yourself, / 'Cast me away!'" (ll. 300–04). With this inscription, Arthur acquired not just a weapon, but a pattern for his life, acting as an agent of ancient ideals in the modern world, bridging the past to the present with noble actions.

The construction of British manhood was an all-pervasive theme in Victorian culture. No greater subject existed in the arts than that which exemplified the true, high virtue and actions of a man. Based in the era's intersecting needs to recognize national character and revere national heroes, the cultural discourse centered around a single question: What makes a man? The answers emerged in the arts, in letters, and in codes of behavior. Both a social critique and a self-celebration, the idealized portrait contained a pattern for the life of a man. From the directed energy of youth, to the tempering obligations of wife, home, and family, to the responsibilities of work, and the memories left to posterity, the fulfilled cycle of a man's years were seen as enduring and as universal as the seasons. The Arthurian legend was revived as part of this quest for the timeless model for manhood. But, as Eve Sedgwick has observed, "to identify *as* must always include multiple processes of identification *with*."[1] And, in this, the renewal of the King and his legend became an act of self-construction.

For Tennyson and his Victorian audience, Arthur's actions cast a matrix for British manhood. The inscription on Excalibur encoded the obligation the Victorian gentleman saw in his position: to bring ancient, honorable standards to life in the modern world. In Tennyson's poems, and the paintings they inspired, each phase of Arthur's life was offered to the Victorians as a lesson in manly action: the bold youth transformed to tempered manhood through the acquisition of Excalibur; the true lover faithful to his marriage vows; the public servant who placed duty over private gain and pleasure; and the fallen hero dying in fellowship and dignity, leaving his life's example as his legacy. The Victorians drew a sharper, stronger portrait of Arthur than earlier generations. Cast in their own image, the new Arthur encoded and confirmed their own definition of manhood. In this the pact of Excalibur was fulfilled, and the message of "oldest tongue of all this world" sounded in a new and vibrant voice.

There is a duality in the act of cultural self-definition. The process is both critical and congratulatory. But the two are never equal. At the dawn of the Victorian era, Britain held a position of power unsurpassed in its history. The victories in the Napoleonic wars were still vivid in the public consciousness; led by heroic commanders such as Admiral Nelson and the Duke of Wellington, British forces brought safety and stability to Europe. Britain was also a world leader in industry, transforming its financial base from agriculture to manufacture in a full embrace of Industrial Revolution technology. The growth of the vast colonial empire gave Britain a global sovereignty, adding wealth and worldwide influence to military and financial security. The success of the nation's strength was seen in its organization, a paternalistic, ordered society, based on the authority and natural rule situated in the traditional bases of power: class and gender.[2]

Although the dominant tone of Victorian self-construction was congratulatory, it also served to confront and correct the problems of the era. The rise of the middle class as a force in finance and politics assaulted the traditional security of upper-class hegemony. The shift of the national interest from agriculture to industry resulted in a movement of population from the estate to the city, replacing the old, familiar pattern with one both untried and uncertain. The expansion into world markets and world leadership changed the society from isolated to cosmopolitan, instilling diversity where uniformity was long the rule. And significantly, the new sovereign was a woman, no more than a girl at the time of her accession. At a time when traditional male prerogative had won its greatest victories, existing circumstances seemed to erode its foundations.

The cultural discourse on character responded to this circumstantial duality. No contemporary writer on this subject was more outspoken and eloquent—or, for the modern reader, more telling—than Thomas Carlyle. In his essay "The English" (1843) he seated national character, and the very future of the nation, in a male virtue: practical sense.

> What a depth of practical sense in thee, great England! A depth of sense, of justice, and courage; in which, under all emergencies and world-bewilderments, and under this most complex of emergencies we now live in, there is hope, there is still assurance![3]

While Carlyle admitted that his nation was "dumb," he praised this as a strength, resulting in the course of actions rather than the promise of words. The appearance of this silent force, "Nature's fact," was deceptive. A "burly figure, . . . thick-skinned, seemingly opaque . . . almost stupid," this "Man of Practice" did not reveal his worth until pitted against the "Man of Theory," "light adroit," "all equipt with clear logic, and able anywhere to give you Why Wherefore!" (p. 153). But the unprepossessing Man of Practice gets the job done; his efforts give tangible results, not hollow promise.[4] His contribution to society is his work in it, and work, to Carlyle, is essential to the character of a man. "A man that can succeed in working is to me always a man" (p. 153). Praising "toughness of heart" and "toughness of muscle" (p. 154), Carlyle sketched a powerful portrait of directed energy and stalwart resolve, a working man who propelled a working society.[5]

In this nation of practical men, extraordinary individuals combined pragmatic force with vision and virtue. These were the great men of the past and present who, endowed with the energy, tenacity, and focus of national character, rose above the rest to serve, to lead, and to inspire. These were society's heroes. And hero worship was a potent force of Victorian ideation. Carlyle saw hero worship as "a most valuable tendency . . . the main impetus by which society moves, the main force by which it hangs together."[6] He defined "hero-worship" as "instinctual, a source of strength in frail human nature." It rose as "the primary creed" of an honorable society, and would prove to be "the ultimate and final creed of mankind." For Victorian society, and especially for the upper-middle- and upper-class male, hero worship was a potent constructive force; it taught virtue through example. To admire a hero incorporated the desire to strive for heroic belief and action, wedding practical energy to romantic association. The man who could recognize a hero in society could recognize the heroic in himself. And, as recognition *of* the hero was inseparable from identification *with* the hero, it was central to the construction of contemporary manhood.

The Neo-medieval movement provided potent symbols in this quest for construction and identity. For almost a century, British culture had been fascinated with its own past. The Gothic Revival, beginning in sham castles and "Gothick" tales of horror in the mid-eighteenth century, led to serious exploration of the national literary and material heritage.[7] By the nineteenth century, an image of the Middle Ages emerged that gave form to modern desire and ambition. Seen as a more stable time, when the hierarchy was benevolent and society was a macrocosm of the family, an invented medieval past seemed to offer a corrective to the present. Evidence of this was wide ranging: as part of the High Church Movement John Keble and John Henry Newman revived an older and more extensive role for ritual in worship, and A.W.N. Pugin gothicized the church setting. The Neo-medieval movement in literature sought less to entertain than to instruct, as seen in the exemplary but plain-spoken heroes of Walter Scott's novels and in the vastly popular *Broadstone of Honour,* written by Kenelm Digby in 1823 as a guide to chivalry for the modern English gentleman. Neo-feudalism was promoted in the political arena, seen in policies of Lord John Manner's Young England Party, overtly seeking to return social responsibility to the upper classes through *noblesse oblige* and covertly striving to limit the influence of the middle class.[8] Just as the Gothic Revival church employed new technology to ensure soaring height and structural stability, the knight of the chivalric revival drew on motivations of a thoroughly modern invention. This, more than any romantic association or degree of authenticity, inspired the Victorian public to reverence the idea of the knight in society. Seeing their own image in the gleam of shining armor, the Victorian public chose the knight as their favored icon for the construct of hero.

These three cultural issues—national character, hero worship, and Neo-medieval invention—converged in Alfred Tennyson's earliest Arthurian poetry. In 1842 he published "Morte d'Arthur," the first poem that established the epic tone and pattern for his life's work the *Idylls of the King.* Using a framing poem, "The Epic," Tennyson offered the saga of Arthur's last battle as the eleventh book of a lost Arthuriad. In the prologue, the writer Everard Hall, an embittered poet who discarded his epic with his ideals, is coaxed to read a portion of his poem at a Christmas reunion of university friends. Despite his dismissal of the poem as "'Faint Homeric echoes, nothing worth, / Mere chaff and draff, much better burnt'" (ll. 38–39), Hall reads with "Deep chested music" (l. 51). In the epilogue, the narrator recounts a dream of Arthur's return, in a form "Like a modern gentleman / Of stateliest port" (ll. 345–46), received by a cheering crowd ready to reverence the king who "cannot die" (l. 347).

It is widely known that Tennyson used "The Epic" as an advance response to critics who might question the revival of an old subject, but Linda K. Hughes notes that it functioned as well to announce the poet's intentions. The poem within the frame is identified as the eleventh of a set of twelve, implying that the rest of the epic would be forthcoming. At the same time, the frame allowed Tennyson both to close and to reopen the cycle, reversing the passage to oblivion described in the "Morte d'Arthur."[9] But Tennyson did more than reverse the action; he replaced the king. The grand but dying warrior of the "Morte d'Arthur" is seen transformed in "The Epic" into the "Modern gentleman / Of stateliest port," vibrant, vital, and familiar. The recognition of the heroic in Tennyson's newly forged Arthur succeeded on his audience's identification with this incarnation of the king.

History, and specifically historicity, had little relevance in the construction of the Victorian king. Tennyson acknowledged his debt to Malory but stressed that the image of the king was his own creation. He told his son, "The vision of Arthur as I have drawn him . . . had come upon me when, little more than a boy, I first lighted on Malory."[10] As David Staines reminds us, Malory's Arthur is a noble figure, "a great warrior," a "leader of men, and exemplary monarch," but at the same time he is profoundly human, given to the sins and failures associated in the medieval era with the human condition.[11] But Tennyson was a man of his own era, and his idea of the human condition did not allow acts of incest, marital infidelity, or filial betrayal in the life of an exemplary man.[12] Tennyson characterized his king as "blameless," and urged his readers not to "press too hardly on details whether for history or allegory." To Tennyson, Arthur was not a symbol, but a man, "a man who spent himself in the case of honour, duty, and self-sacrifice, who felt and aspired with his nobler knights, though with a stronger and clearer conscience as his king" (as quoted in Hallan Tennyson, Vol. 1, p. 194). Tennyson's readers were to see in Arthur an image of themselves improved, and they were urged to improve their own condition according to this enhanced reflection.

The modern reader feels estranged from the Victorian Arthur. More likely to see the King as William Morris portrayed him, as distant and cold, with his "great name and his little love,"[13] rather than as Tennyson formed him, "the highest and the most human too" ("Guinevere," l. 644), he is currently perceived in opposition to Tennyson's intentions, more as a symbol and less as a man. But Hughes suggests that this may be due to the order in which we read the *Idylls* today (p. 48). The current shape of the narrative, progressing from Arthur's emergence as a king to his retreat into Avalon, was not established until Tennyson gave the poems their present order in 1892. The first *Idylls* ("Enid," "Elaine," "Vivien," and "Guinevere") were published in 1859, and they were united in character and setting rather than through a lineal construction. Hughes notes that to the Victorian audience, "*Idylls of the King* meant from the start a human-centered, accessible, vivid set of stories about attractive characters," and suggests that this so strongly colored the way Tennyson's Arthurian world was received that the poems published in 1869 ("The Holy Grail and Other Poems"), despite "metaphysical themes and heavily symbolic patterns," were seen "within a framework of identifiable and lively human interest" (p. 48). Critical opinion affirms this assertion. *The Examiner* (July 16, 1859, p. 452) described each of the first four *Idylls* as "inscribed with a woman's name," with "a woman's heart as the center of its action," but graced by the presence of Arthur, "an image of pure manhood." To the Victorian reader "pure manhood" was a significant term, both human and heroic, a point of recognition and a force of inspiration. There was a reciprocity between Tennyson and his audience. Through "The Epic" he prepared them to see themselves in his King, and their predisposition to do so enhanced the humanity of Arthur's character in the ongoing publication of the *Idylls*.[14]

Reception offers one form of evidence that Tennyson's Arthur was read through identification and admiration. Subject selection for visual imagery offers another. In the early 1860s, Arthurian painting and illustrations enjoyed an unprecedented popularity in the visual arts. Although several editions of Malory's *Le Morte Darthur* were available to the Victorian public, Tennyson's early Arthurian poetry and his first four *Idylls* proved the more popular source.[15] Subjects about Arthurian women—especially Enid, Elaine, and the Lady of Shalott—dominated, owing, no doubt to the popularity of the first four *Idylls*.[16] The boy knight Galahad, as portrayed in the 1842 poem, was favored among male subjects. Arthur's image, in this early phase of the Arthurian Revival, appeared more often than the other knights excepting Galahad. And the subjects selected confirmed the cycle of a contemporary man's life: passage to manhood, marriage, manly responsibility, honorable death. In art, as much as in poetry, Arthur was the paradigmatic Victorian gentleman.

To the Victorian public Arthur's youth was encoded in a single subject: the taking of Excalibur. Tennyson gives it scant attention in his "Morte d'Arthur" of 1842. A fuller description of the scene would not be published until 1869 ("The Coming of Arthur," ll. 294–306). But the early version cast the iconic form for the image: On a summer day, Arthur saw the sign that changed his life. Out of the lake rose an arm holding a sword, "Cloaked in white Samite, mystic, wonderful," and as the arm brandished the powerful blade, Arthur rowed to the center of the lake to take what was offered, gaining his weapon and sealing his fate (ll. 80–86).

Daniel Maclise was the first artist to take up this subject. The context for his interpretation was significant. He was commissioned, with eight other artists, to provide illustrations for Tennyson's early poems in a small but luxury edition, published by Edward Moxon in 1857.[17] Maclise had a reputation as a chivalric painter. He led the first wave of popularity for subjects featuring knights and their ladies in the 1830s and 1840s and had been commissioned by the government to paint an allegory, *The Spirit of Chivalry* (1848), in the Lords Chamber in the new Palace at Westminster.[18] Of

Figure 1. *Daniel Maclise. "Arthur Obtains Excalibur," Poems. London: E. Moxon, 1857. Courtesy of The Newberry Library, Chicago.*

all the artists in the project, he was the obvious choice to illustrate the most heroic poem, "Morte d'Arthur." The poem appeared with "The Epic," which now served not as a frame but as a prologue. Maclise provided two illustrations, *Arthur Obtains Excalibur* and *Arthur in the Death Barge*, which were positioned at the beginning and the end of the poem.

Although the artists for the "Moxon *Tennyson*" were assigned their poems, they were given full liberty of artistic interpretation. Maclise's decision to frame Arthur's life with his pictures (and, in a sense, replacing the function of "The Epic") was his own. In this, Maclise marks the beginning of Arthur's life with his passage from youth to manhood (Figure 1). Maclise positions the young King in his boat. Approaching the brandished sword, Arthur drops his oars and clasps his hands in reverence. His awe, expressed in his hesitancy, suggests that he is fully aware of the obligations that come with the magnificent and magical weapon. The Lady of the Lake is seen beneath the water's surface, turning in the waves and waiting for Arthur to grasp his destiny.

The composition succeeds in its masterful economy. Maclise limited his expression to those details necessary to tell the tale: the King, the boat, the sword, and the Lady. It is the figure of Arthur, in form and posture, that conveys the meaning. He is not a youth but a bearded man, with a strong, mature physique. His powerful body is eloquent in its tension. He leans toward the sword but, at the same time, recoils. This palpable, physical conflict speaks of the challenge before him. To take the sword is to take its obligations. But Maclise implies the transfer of power from one powerful figure to the other. The line of Arthur's gaze describes the sword and bonds him to the Lady of the Lake churning below the water. No text is needed to pronounce the act and its consequences. Maclise embedded his meaning in pictorial choices: the axes, the gestures, and the muscular force of his figures in action.

The image of Maclise's manly youth even influenced artists who chose sources other than Tennyson. In *How Arthur by the Meanes of Merlin Gate His Sword of Excalibur of the Lady of the Lake* (1862; Figure 2), James Archer used an arcane title to suggest an older source. Archer claimed to use a medieval text, identified only as the *Romance of Arthur* in the Royal Academy catalogue, but his imagery links him to Maclise's vision, and through that, to Tennyson. Archer casts Arthur as a stalwart man—tall, broad, athletic—rather than a youth just realizing his power. The firm stance and torque of his body are monumental; here is a classical hero disguised in medieval costume. The fierce profile, the muscular tension, even the mustache, suggest manhood. Archer, like Maclise, leaves no doubt that Arthur's passage

Figure 2. *James Archer.* How Arthur by the Meanes of Merlin Gate His Sword of Excalibur of the Lady of the Lake *(1862). Engraving after the painting. F. Kemplen,* Art Journal 33 *(April 1871). Courtesy of The Newberry Library, Chicago.*

from childhood is complete. But unlike Maclise's interpretation, Archer allows no moment of hesitancy. The single-minded tenacity of Archer's king is forged in the spirit of Tennyson's, whose altruistic vision had the passionate focus of a divine mission. In Victorian England passage to manhood was defined by the ability of a boy to recognize purpose and marshal all energies in the direction of attaining that purpose. Arthur, taking up Excalibur, shows the youth of England the way.

It may seem curious that the young Arthur is always depicted with the physical attributes of a man. Invariably, whether taking Excalibur or, as William Riviere portrayed him, gaining his first victories with his sword (1859; Oxford Union Hall), Arthur's form holds no vestige of youth. His physical maturity is always realized: he towers in height; he is massive in breadth; he is bearded and his face is already rugged and weathered. The youthful King is in marked contrast to the way the boy knight Galahad is portrayed—delicate, fine-boned, and feminized.[19] This is neither an accidental difference nor an aesthetic choice. Galahad, while marking the purity and promise of youth, also encodes an arrested development. He will never know a woman, he will never head a household, he will never be a leader of men. In short, to the Victorian mind, he was condemned to perpetual boyhood.

He would never be a man. Arthur's form and countenance acted to assure his audience that he, like them, would endure a natural cycle. Manhood cast the mode for the artists' image and was encoded in Arthur's iconography.

Modern readers have difficulty seeing Arthur as a model for husbands. And there is no denying that Arthur's marriage was problematic. In the early *Idylls* Arthur and Guinevere are rarely presented together. Instead, their marriage offers a metaphor for the discord and misunderstanding ("The Marriage of Geraint") or the suspicion and treachery ("Merlin and Vivien") that are nurtured in the court. When Guinevere speaks of the marriage, as she does in "Lancelot and Elaine," she offers a testament of her dissatisfaction. Arthur's cool reserve has both hurt her and hardened her. She reads his failure to confront her indiscretions as a lack of interest, based in a lack of love. "He never spake word of reproach to me, / He never had a glimpse of mine untruth, He cares not for me" (ll. 124–26). After reading the joyous description of Arthur and Guinevere's wedding in "The Coming of Arthur," when dressed in white in the dazzling May sunshine, the King and Queen vowed to guard their love to the death (ll. 455–469), Guinevere's laments and Arthur's detachment suggest failed hopes and broken promises. But "The Coming of Arthur" was not published until 1869, and the audience of the first *Idylls* saw Arthur and Guinevere in a very different light.

The centrality of marriage in Victorian life, and the roles defined for husband and wife, positioned Arthur and Guinevere for readers in 1859. Home and family anchored and fulfilled a man, tempered his passions, and renewed his spirit. Home, as Walter Houghton observed, was more than a place for a night's rest; "It was a place apart, a walled garden," the sanctuary for virtues and morality "too easily crushed by modern life" (p. 343). John Ruskin painted an image of the family home as a haven:

> It is the place of Peace, the shelter, not only from all injury, but from all terror, doubt, and division. In so far as it is not this, it is not home; so far as the anxieties of the outer life penetrate into it, and the inconsistently-minded, unknown, unloved, or hostile society of the outer world is allowed by either husband or wife to cross the threshold, it ceases to be home.[20]

Although Ruskin's evocation of the ideal home did not appear until 1865, the belief that home was the moral center of society and the wife was the moral center of the home had been current from the first years of the Victorian era, embodied in the marriage of the Queen to Prince Albert and held up to British subjects as a model for domesticity.[21]

A woman's responsibilities, and her individual success, were defined in the realm of the home. There she was to provide her husband a private domain, a personal retreat from public life, and a place of restoration for the body and soul. As wife and mother she guarded husband and children from the nagging or painful tribulations of daily life—discord, illness, even death—and tempered their existence with her uplifting spirit and her moral example.[22] If the home failed to offer a sanctuary of tranquility and morality, it was the wife's fault, even if the husband's behavior was a contributing factor. Although the home positioned and defined the woman, it did so in relationship to the man, and it was *his* comfort, *his* pleasure that offered the test of her accomplishment.

The first four *Idylls* appeared at a crucial time in the forging of male and female roles in marriage. Recognition of woman's inequality in the institution had its first effect on law, in the Divorce Act of 1857, allowing women the possibility (albeit slim) of initiating divorce on the grounds of the husband's adultery or desertion. The act also granted women some small measure of financial independence after separation through limited control of property, rights to be elaborated and expanded in future legislation (the Married Women's Property Acts of 1870, 1874, and 1882). Tennyson's early *Idylls* were read within these changing circumstances for women, seen by some as a threat to the natural social order. It was also a time that defined female sexuality. In *The Functions and Disorders of the Reproductive Organs* (1857), William Acton characterized normal women as above sexual desire. A modest wife was serviceable, but almost asexual, submitting "to her husband, but only to please him . . . and for the desire of maternity."[23] Susan P. Casteras interprets Acton's categorization of wives as sexless and mistresses as sexy is consistent with broad parameters of marital responsibility: "In a sense, the wife was also a moral savior for her spouse, for she 'saved' her libidinous husband from the 'sins' of his own sexuality" (p. 53). Guinevere's readiness to express her own taste in physical desire, "For who loves me must have a touch of earth; / The low sun makes the color" ("Lancelot and Elaine," ll. 133–34), positioned her as an unnatural woman to the audience of 1859. She was better suited to the ignoble role of mistress than to the honorable role of wife.

It was Guinevere's failure as a wife that revealed Arthur's exemplary role as husband to the *Idylls'* original audience. The scene of confrontation between wronged husband and guilty wife in Tennyson's "Guinevere" makes this perfectly—and painfully—clear. David Staines calls Arthur's explosive entry into Guinevere's sanctuary "the fullest and most direct presentation of the King in Tennyson's poetry" (p. 46). This is no accident, nor is it coincidental that Arthur's accusations, condemnations, and forgiveness of his wife mark the longest passage in the *Idylls* in which the King and Queen appear together (ll. 408–576). The harsh light Tennyson turns on Guinevere illuminates the King, whose fury at betrayal seemed justified in a time when marital stability and service were so central to the social order. Modern readers find this scene in the *Idylls* difficult, even distasteful, but to the Victorian audience it displayed the capacity and magnanimity of Arthur's heroic character.

Figure 3. *James Archer.* The Parting of Arthur and Guinevere *(1865). Oil sketch. Private Collection. Photograph Courtesy of the* Forbes *Magazine Collection, New York.*

This is evident in the interpretation of the confrontation at Almesbury as a subject in painting and the decorative arts. While the subject enjoyed enduring popularity through the beginning of the next century, James Archer's *The Parting of Arthur and Guinevere* (1865) seems to have set the visual type.[24] The original work, now lost, is known through a highly finished oil sketch (Figure 3). Archer consolidated the climactic events of the passage—Arthur's furious intrusion into Guinevere's refuge, his damning accusations, her pleading, and his final conciliation—into one telling image: the king at his moment of forgiveness. Although Guinevere, in her lush green gown, with her magnificent blonde hair spilling around her and hiding her anguished face, presents an image of pathetic beauty, it is Arthur who is the focus of the painting. His presence is monumental. He is both heroic and tragic. Archer conceived his king on a grand scale. His massive physique, broadened by the dark mantle over his surcoat and mail, and his lofty height, exaggerated by his gold-crowned helmet with dragon crest, embody the scope of his character. He is a tower of righteous indignation.

In Archer's painting, every facet of Arthur's character is portrayed: the strong king, the noble warrior, the enraged husband, the agent of earthly order. But as his body encodes the range of his powers, his face betrays his capacity for forgiveness. Arthur is the magnanimous husband. While he cannot deny that Guinevere failed him as a wife, he also cannot deny his unshakable devotion as a husband. The nature of this devotion transcends physical love: "I cannot touch thy lips, they are not mine, / But Lancelot's" (ll. 547–48). It is seated in commitment. "I am thine husband—not a smaller soul, / Nor Lancelot, nor another" (ll. 563–64). For Arthur, Guinevere was his first, his last, and his only love; and even though her betrayal destroyed his home, his order, and his kingdom ("For thou hast spoiled the purpose of my life," l. 450), he finds his own way to forgive her. Through Guinevere's late recognition of Arthur's worth, "Thou art the highest and the most human too" (l. 644), Tennyson instructs his audience that Arthur is a model of husbandly virtue. Arthur's commanding presence and marital steadfastness, thus presented in poetry and painting, contributed the ideal male role to the prevalent discourse on marriage, home, and the family.

Just as a tranquil home proved a woman's worth, work was the measure of the Victorian man. In considering the social emphasis on work—specifically man's work—in England in the mid-nineteenth century, Walter Houghton called it the "most popular word in the Victorian vocabulary," that is "except for 'God'" (p. 242). The significance of work transcended its prosaic function: the productive use of time and the contributive role in the social order. As it came to be regarded as a trait of national character—

recall Carlyle's Man of Practice for whom work was a test of manhood ("A man that can succeed in working is to me always a man," p. 153)—the idea of work moved from the realm of endeavor to the realm of virtue. As a virtue, work helped define its antithetical vice in idleness, offering another scale to measure and mark men. "The glorification of work as a supreme virtue, with the accompanying scorn of idleness, was the commonest theme of the prophets of earnestness, for the full meaning of life was identical in outward action with a life of moral earnestness" (Houghton, p. 243).

Any reader of the *Idylls,* from its first publication to the present day, knows that Arthur was always working. In the early *Idylls* Tennyson drew attention to his unceasing activity through Guinevere's complaints. When she first saw him, she was disappointed at his lack of response to her; he seemed "High, self-contained," his mind on other things ("Guinevere," l. 403). She justified her inclination toward Lancelot, insisting her husband had no time for her, "Rapt in this fancy of his Table Round, / And swearing men to vows impossible, / To make them like himself" ("Lancelot and Elaine," ll. 128–30). For Tennyson, Guinevere's complaints had a dual function: just as they damned Guinevere as an unnatural woman, they praised Arthur as a virtuous and hardworking man.

It is not until the later *Idylls* that Arthur's selfless attention to his work is used to mark the conflict with his knights' selfish indulgence in idleness. Tennyson painted the nature of idleness with a broad brush. It encompassed any activity that placed individual reward above community sacrifice. For example, in "The Last Tournament" (1871), Arthur departs from the court to lead his forces against the Red Knight Pelleas's rampage of destruction, leaving Lancelot to preside over a tournament, aptly named "The Tournament of Dead Innocence." News of Arthur's struggle reaches Camelot at regular intervals, marking a strong counterpoint to Lancelot's self-absorption in his own grief and guilt and Tristram's openly defiant pursuit of adulterous love.

Tennyson's deepest reflection on the nature of work and the nuances of endeavor is found in "The Holy Grail" (1869). For the poet, the Grail Quest offered a set of challenges that tested and sorted men. But while Galahad attained the Grail and Percivale and Bors were privileged by a vision, the three traditional Grail knights were grouped by Tennyson with Lancelot and Gawaine, those who failed in the Quest. It was Arthur who triumphed, for he shunned a mission that would force him to abandon his kingly duties and turn his energies from public service to private pursuits. Arthur knew his role and place, and Tennyson has him close the Quest with an articulation of his duties:

> The King must guard
> That which he rules, and is but as the hind
> To whom a space of land is given to plow,
> Who may not wander from his allotted field
> Before his work is done. (ll. 901–5)

Arthur had no time to chase a spiritual vision if it did not serve the community. In this, Tennyson equates the quest for spiritual reward with the indulgence in physical pleasure. Public service is a greater virtue than private pursuit, no matter the nature of the latter's reward. Again, Arthur sets a model. He is the Man of Practice, whose worth to the nation is greater than that of the Man of Theory, whether that realm be science or the spirit.

As a subject in art, Arthur's sense of obligation took one potent form: his dismay at his fellowship of knights choosing to seek the Grail. The image entered the artist's repertoire long before Tennyson put those sentiments into words. William Dyce's watercolor of 1849, *Piety: The Knights of the Round Table Departing on the Quest for the Holy Grail* (Figure 4), captures all the tension, excitement, and emotion associated with the Grail narrative. The setting is a courtyard at Camelot. The knights, some already mounted and eager to go, assemble for the rituals of departure. At the far right, Arthur bids farewell to his champions. Here, he is an aging man, grand and solid as a Renaissance patriarch, resplendent in his jeweled cloak. Arthur's massive form bears the weight of all his hard-won glories. His broad shoulders bend with the burden of leadership. He bows his head and clasps his left hand to his heart in the realization that the Quest would lead to the dispersal of his table. All his work would now begin to unravel, but his outstretched right hand indicates that he accepts his inevitable fate.

Later in the era, the subject emerged in a standard form. The scene of departure was replaced by the moment that the knights swore to seek the Grail. H.H. Armstead's oak bas-relief, *The Knights of the Round Table Vowing to Seek the Sancgreall* (1870; Figure 5), is a typical example. The work was carved as part of the decorative scheme for the Queen's Robing Room in the new Palace at Westminster, to complement the Arthurian cycle of frescoes painted by William Dyce on the walls. Armstead positions the King at the center of the panel. Arthur rises from the table and stands rigidly still, the only point of stability in the dynamic composition. All around the table the knights declare their intentions through their gestures. They raise their hands in oaths, they turn to each other for support, they kneel in prayer, they point in the direction that their inclinations lead them. The randomness of their actions marks a strong contrast to Arthur's stillness. He is the

Figure 4. *William Dyce.* Piety: The Knights of the Round Table Departing on the Quest for the Holy Grail *(1849). Watercolor. National Gallery of Scotland, Edinburgh.*

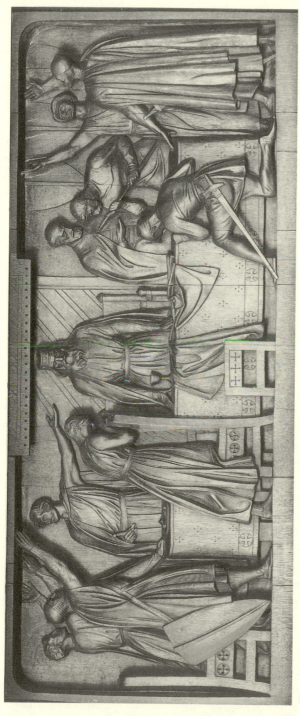

Figure 5. *H.H. Armstead. The Knights of the Round Table Vowing to Seek the Sancgreall (1870). Oak bas-relief. Queen's Robing Room, Palace at Westminster, London. British Crown Copyright. Reproduced with the permission of the Controller of Her Britannic Majesty's Stationery Office.*

only figure to be presented fully frontal, and he leans forward to the table, his arms like the powerful columns of a temple. Like Dyce, Armstead saw him as a patriarch, aged but strong, tempered rather than depleted by his years of struggle. Armstead leaves no question as to who is the support of the Order. Like an old but stable edifice, Arthur's stalwart presence stands as a reminder of the society he built and the obligations his knights so readily abandon.

As the era progressed the vision of the hard-working King chafed rather than inspired. Tennyson unwittingly opened himself for such criticism when he used Arthur's image to praise a real public servant, the late Prince Albert. Early in 1862, shortly after the untimely death of the Prince, who was only 42, Tennyson dedicated the first four *Idylls* to his memory. In his "Dedication," he praised the Queen's consort as "Scarce other than my own ideal knight" (l. 7).[25] Tennyson measured the Prince's endeavors against the oaths of Arthur's knights and found Albert as good as the best of them.

> Who reverenced his conscience as his king;
> Whose glory was redressing human wrong;
> Who spake no slander, no, nor listen'd to it;
> Who loved one only and who clave to her. (ll. 8–11)

Readers in 1862 found these lines familiar. Arthur reminded Guinevere of them, how he swore his knights to follow his example at the time of the founding of the Order ("Guinevere," ll. 464–80). But in the same passage, and observed elsewhere by Guinevere ("Swearing his men to vows impossible, / To make them like himself," ["Lancelot and Elaine," ll. 130–31]), it is clear only Arthur measured up to that standard. For some critics Tennyson's equation of Albert with Arthur diminished his portrait of the mythic King. Swinburne acidly dismissed Tennyson's poetry as "the Morte d'Albert" and the "Idylls of the Prince Consort," accusing Tennyson of pulling legend down to the level of reality.[26] As well as revealing the change in the climate of reception, Swinburne's comments show the extent to which the men of Victorian England identified with the *Idylls*. In recognizing Arthur as one of their own, Victorian male readers remade him in their own image, draining his romance and giving him, in its stead, reality.[27]

The style of death in Victorian England was as important as the style of life. In the nineteenth century, thoughts of death were ever present. Killing epidemics, inadequate medical and sanitation services, and high infant mortality made death a constant specter. To cope with that specter, death acquired a romantic rationale. It marked the point of accountability, the time when temporal worth would be counted and recognized. Nowhere was this better demonstrated than in the popularity of the deathbed scene in fiction. John Reed explains that "Deathbed scenes were common in Victorian literature because they were an important practical and moral feature of life."[28] Fictional representations gave proof to a comforting belief, that death epitomized the actions of life. The sinner suffered an agonizing end, while the good man enjoyed a well-earned release from mortal burdens. In "Life's End," Martin Tupper reflected, "When the bad man dieth, all his sins rise up against him / Clamouring at his memory with imprecated judgments; / But when the good departeth, all his noble deeds / Surround him like a cloud of light to sphere his soul to glory."[29]

The greatest legacy a man could leave his family and his friends was his memory. Those good deeds that accounted for his life and earned him a rewarding and respectable death offered more than comfort; they gave the good man the opportunity to exercise influence even from the grave. The man who died alone died in sadness. No one would see the full account of his life, and no one would perpetuate his memory. The man who died in the company of family and friends died in peace, knowing that his time on earth, all its value and all its instruction, would not be lost when he departed.

In the "Morte d'Arthur," Tennyson gave his King a model death. Only alluding to the confrontation with Mordred, Tennyson opens his poem with the deeply-wounded King reflecting on the loss of his chivalric fellowship. Arthur recognizes the gravity of his wound: "I am so deeply smitten thro' the helm / That without help I cannot last till morn" (ll. 76–77). He commands Bedivere, his last loyal companion, to return his brand Excalibur to the Lady of the Lake and then instructs him to carry him to the shore and wait with him for his final journey. When the death barge appears, "Dark as a funeral scarf from stem to stern" (l. 245), Arthur is taken aboard by three queens, who cradle him in their arms and try to ease his pain. The King draws his last strength to admonish Bedivere to bravery and remembrance:

> The old order changeth, yielding place to new,
> And God fulfills himself in many ways,
> Lest one good custom corrupt the world.
> Comfort thyself: what comfort is in me?
> I have lived my life, and that which I have done
> May He within himself make pure!
> If thou shouldst never see my face again,
> Pray for my soul. (ll. 291–98)

Arthur, assured that his life's work was completed, confident that he had always acted in good faith and served his purpose without self-interest or hesitation, experiences his epitome as apotheosis. His actions in this world earned him reward in the next, a reward of rest and remembrance.

In *Mort d'Arthur* of 1862 (Figure 6) John Mullaster Carrick was the first to paint the scene of Arthur and Bedivere waiting for the death barge. It is the moment between life and passing. Arthur, drained of all strength, lies exhausted on the marshy shore, resting in the arms of his companion. Bedivere's loyalty, tested for one last time through the return of Excalibur, gives the fallen hero comfort. The barge, a dragon-headed galley, is no more than a shadow in the distance. The transparent sail lends a ghostly quality, implying the otherworldliness of Arthur's impending departure. Turning his gaze out to sea, Bedivere sights the ship and gently rouses his king. But in that moment of rest, Arthur relives his life's endeavor, and Bedivere's presence is proof that his life will not be forgotten. In Carrick's large and graceful figures—with their noble bearing, their bond of friendship, their gestures of comfort and trust—Victorian men saw that the purpose of death was to prove the meaning of life. Even in his passing, Arthur proved that dignity and heroism was inherent in the pattern of manhood.

Throughout the *Idylls of the King,* Arthur and his knights are challenged, tested, and ranked. In this, the Victorian audience saw the lives of the legendary heroes as parallel to their own. Tennyson stressed this notion of testing and ranking, so central to the construction of Victorian manhood, in an exphrasis in "The Holy Grail." Merlin crafted a sculptural program for the gathering hall of the knights. Mute but eloquent, it reminded Arthur and his fellowship that there were types of men, and that they must choose what type to follow:

> And four great zones of sculpture, set betwixt
> With many a mystic symbol, gird the hall:
> And in the lowest are the beasts slaying men,
> And in the second are men slaying beasts,
> And on the third are warriors, perfect men,
> And on the fourth are men with growing wings. (ll. 232–37)

The tragedy of Tennyson's Grail story reveals that it is the third rank, not the fourth, that men should seek. His ghostly evocation of Galahad is proof that men should strive for the real goal, to become "warriors," the perfect men. And Arthur, in his oaths and his actions, gives his life as a pattern to follow.

Figure 6. *John Mullaster Carrick. Morte d'Arthur (1862). Oil on canvas. Private Collection. Photograph Courtesy of Sotheby's, Inc. 1988.*

The *Idylls of the King* and the whole Arthurian Revival in England embody the force of remaking as much as, if not more than, the spirit of revival. Even the charge that Tennyson inscribed on Excalibur indicated that to fulfill the legend was to change it. And his agent of change was the character of the King. In depicting Arthur—a Victorian gentleman in chivalric disguise—Tennyson and the painters he inspired were working in a surprising genre in the legend's tradition. The genre they used was the self-portrait, making the noble image they identified *as* Arthur, a telling document of the processes of identifying *with* Arthur. To take Excalibur was to be a man, and the question of manhood in Victorian England was answered and ennobled in a single incarnation.

NOTES

1. Eve Kosofsky Sedgwick, *Epistemology of the Closet* (Berkeley: University of California Press, 1990), p. 61.

2. For a discussion of the role and aspects of paternalism in this period, see David Roberts, *Paternalism in Early Victorian England* (London: Croom Helm, 1979).

3. Thomas Carlyle, "The English," *Past and Present* (London: Dent, 1919), p. 151.

4. Carlyle describes James Brindley, the channel builder, as his exemplary Man of Practice, who "has little to say for himself," but has "chained seas together" (p. 153). The "rugged Brindley" is offered as a national type, a John Bull, that pugnacious symbol to be promoted in the pages of *Punch* as the spirit of the nation.

5. For further discussion of Victorian character, see Walter Houghton, "The Worship of Force," in *The Victorian Frame of Mind 1830–1870* (New Haven: Yale University Press, 1985), pp. 196–217.

6. Carlyle, "Sir Walter Scott," in *Critical and Miscellaneous Essays,* 5 vols. (London: Chapman and Hill, 1842), Vol. 5, pp. 231–33.

7. For the standard history of the Gothic Revival, see Kenneth Clark, *The Gothic Revival, An Essay in the History of Taste* (New York: Scribner's, 1929).

8. See Alice Chandler, *A Dream of Order. The Medieval Ideal in Nineteenth-Century Literature* (Lincoln: University of Nebraska Press, 1970), pp. 12–82; 152–67; Mark Girouard, *The Return to Camelot, Chivalry and the English Gentleman* (New Haven: Yale University Press, 1981), pp. 15–110; and Debra N. Mancoff, *The Arthurian Revival in Victorian Art* (New York: Garland, 1990) pp. 3–64, for the causes and results of the Neo-medieval movement in early Victorian England.

9. Linda K. Hughes, "Tennyson's Urban Arthurians: Victorian Audiences and the City Built to Music," in *King Arthur Through the Ages,* ed. Valerie M. Lagorio and Mildred Leake Day, 2 vols. (New York: Garland, 1990) Vol. 2, pp. 41–42.

10. As quoted in Hallam Tennyson, *Alfred, Lord Tennyson, A Memoir by His Son,* 2 vols. (New York: Macmillan, 1897), Vol. 2, p. 128.

11. David Staines, *Tennyson's Camelot: The "Idylls of the King" and its Medieval Sources* (Waterloo, Ontario: Wilfrid Laurier Press, 1982), p. 3.

12. This was a common problem for Victorian revitalizers of the legend. William Dyce, the first Victorian painter to undertake an extended cycle of Arthurian imagery, wrote that the saga recorded in Malory's *Le Morte Darthur* turned on "incidents which, if they are not undesirable for representation under any circumstance, are at least scarcely appropriate in (the Queen's) apartment" (Dyce to C.L. Eastlake, August 15, 1848, in James Stirling Dyce, "Life, Correspondence, and Writings of William Dyce, R.A. 1806–1864, Painter, Musician, and Scholar, by His Son," 4 vols., in

the City Art Gallery of Aberdeen, Department of Manuscript, Vol. 3, p. 51). He was decorating the Royal Robing Room in the new Palace at Westminster. For a discussion of how Dyce edited the legend, see Debra N. Mancoff, "Reluctant Redactor: William Dyce Reads the Legend," in *Culture and the King: The Social Implication of the Arthurian Legend,* ed. James P. Carley and Martin B. Shichtman (Albany: State University of New York Press, 1994), pp. 254–73.

13. William Morris, "The Defence of Guenevere," in *Early Romances in Prose and Verse* (London: Dent, 1973), l. 110.

14. Walter Houghton sees this reciprocal relationship between the predisposition of the reader and what was read as a significant factor that differentiates the Victorian and the late-twentieth-century audience. Allowing that the reader today can enjoy heroic literature while rejecting the worship of heroes, he feels that separation was not possible in the Victorian era. "At that time, the enjoyment of heroic stories and the worship of heroes tended to merge, each encouraging the other, and both grew out of the same social and intellectual milieu" (p. 310, n. 20).

15. Until the 1850s, three editions of Malory's *Le Morte Darthur* were generally available. These were *The History of the Renowned Prince Arthur* (Walker and Edwards, 1816), *La Mort d'Arthur* (R. Wilks, 1816) and *The Byrth, Lyf, and Actes of King Arthur,* ed. Robert Southey (Longmans, 1817). See James D. Merriman, *The Flower of Kings: A Study of the Arthurian Legend in England Between 1485 and 1835* (Lawrence: The University Press of Kansas, 1973), pp. 130–31, for a discussion of the influence and character of these editions. In 1858 Thomas Wright revised and edited the text of the 1634 Stansby edition. His *La Mort d'Arthur,* in somewhat modernized language, enjoyed sufficient popularity to require a second edition in 1866. In 1868 Sir Edward Strachey published a new edition, "for modern use." The simple, contemporary language of Strachey's version of *Le Morte Darthur* proved very popular and from this point forward, Malory's narrative rivals that of Tennyson as a source for visual subjects.

16. See Christine Poulson, "'The True and the False': Tennyson's *Idylls of the King* and the Visual Arts," in *The Arthurian Revival: Essays on Form, Tradition, and Transformation,* ed. Debra N. Mancoff, (New York: Garland, 1992), pp. 97–114, for the popularity of specific women's subjects. See also Mancoff, *The Arthurian Revival in Victorian Art,* pp. 171–78.

17. The other artists, selected on the suggestion of the poet, were William Mulready, Clarkson Stanfield, Thomas Creswick, J.C. Horsely, Edward Landseer, Dante Gabriel Rossetti, John Everett Millais, and William Holman Hunt. Of the fifty-five illustrations, only six were of Arthurian subjects. See Mancoff, *The Arthurian Revival in Victorian Art,* pp. 149–55, for a full discussion of the Arthurian images in the Moxon Tennyson.

18. See Mancoff, "In Praise of the Patriarchy: Paternalism and Chivalry in the Decorations in the House of Lords," *Nineteenth-Century Contexts,* 16 (1992), 47–64, for Maclise's position in the chivalric revival in art.

19. Cf. Edward Burne-Jones's drawing *Sir Galahad* (1858) or George Frederick Watts's oil painting *Sir Galahad* (1862), both found at Fogg Art Museum, Harvard University, Cambridge, Mass.

20. John Ruskin, "Of Queen's Gardens," sec. 68, *Sesame and Lilies,* in *Works,* ed. E.T. Cook and Alexander Wedderburn, 39 vols. (London: George Allen, 1903–12), Vol. 18, p. 22.

21. See Joan Perkin, *Women and Marriage in Nineteenth-Century England* (Chicago: Lyceum, 1989), pp. 4–5, on how royal marriages, good or bad, served to influence society.

22. See Susan P. Casteras, *Images of Victorian Womanhood in English Art* (Rutherford, New Jersey: Fairleigh Dickinson University Press, 1987), p. 50, for a discussion of the woman's role as wife and mother.

23. William Acton, *The Functions and Disorders of the Reproductive Or-*

gans (London: Sutton, 1857), p. 102.

24. There is little mistaking the fact that modern readers *and* scholars are uncomfortable with this subject. Our own capacity for sympathy with Guinevere's situation, and our horror at her humiliation, even cloud our reading of its original reception. For example, in her excellent essay on "Guenevere," Lynne Pearce states, "It is perhaps something to their credit that no Pre-Raphaelite artist ever attempted to illustrate Tennyson's 'Guinevere.' Despite their evident penchant for passivity, sickness, and dementia, the humiliation Guinevere suffers as she grovels at Arthur's feet—though graphic—has elicited no visual response of which I am aware" (*Woman/Image/Text* [Toronto: University of Toronto Press, 1991], p. 124). Yet Archer was a Pre-Raphaelite associate, and a half-century later, the scene was still current, and even selected by women, as in Florence Harrison's illustration of the poem in *Tennyson's "Guenevere" and Other Poems* (London: Blackie, 1912).

25. This line was changed in 1882 to "Scarce other than my knight's ideal knight," diminishing the equation of Albert with Arthur, putting the Prince in service to the King rather than on an equal plane. For a full discussion of Tennyson's "Dedication" and its reception, see Mancoff, "'Albert the Good': Public Image and Private Iconography," *Biography: An Interdisciplinary Quarterly,* 15 (1992), 140–64.

26. Algernon Charles Swinburne, *Under the Microscope* (London: D. White, 1872), p. 35, and Swinburne to William Michael Rossetti, December 28 1869, in *The Swinburne Letters,* ed. Cecil Y. Lang, 6 vols. (New Haven: Yale University Press, 1959), Vol. 2, p. 78.

27. This attitude ranged beyond the critical arena. In Anthony Trollope's *The Eustace Diamond* (1873), the dizzy Lizzy Eustace reads an Arthurian romance to her stodgy cousin Frank Greystock, who voices admiration for King Arthur, who did not go on the Quest "because he had a job of work to do" (*The Eustace Diamonds* [New York: Dodd, Mead, 1919], pp. 226–27). In the story, Frank is the embodiment of all that is dull, grey (note his name), and conservative, and he bores the romantic Lizzy in all he says and does. His association with the mythic King is as much Trollope's comment on the prevailing image of Arthur as his characterization of stolid Frank.

28. John Reed, *Victorian Conventions* (Columbus: Ohio State University Press, 1975), p. 156. See also Garrett Stewart, *Death Sentences: Styles of Dying in Victorian Fiction* (Cambridge, Mass.: Harvard University Press, 1984).

29. Martin Tupper, "Life's End," as quoted in Reed, p. 157.

T.H. White and the Legend of King Arthur

From Animal Fantasy to Political Morality

François Gallix

Posterity has not given Terence Hanbury White (1906–1964) the prestige that the diversity, richness, and originality of a body of work consisting of more than twenty-five volumes and numerous unedited texts should have assured him.[1] One of the reasons for this lack of enthusiasm for a writer whose talent was honored several times[2] and who attained considerable success through adaptations of his Arthurian work for radio, theater, and film[3] is undoubtedly due to the impossibility of including him within the limits of a well defined literary group. Ill at ease in an age whose customs and values he disliked, White always defied any attempt to classify him in any group other than that of the large family of "the British eccentrics."

White was not only a novelist, chronicler, historian, poet, naturalist, letter writer, and moralist, but also a researcher, painter, secondary school teacher, falconer,[4] and great devotee of hunting and fishing.[5] He was always ready to acquire new techniques in order to be able to describe them and use them in his work. His thirst for learning helped him struggle against loneliness and fortify himself against misfortune: "'The best thing for being sad,' replied Merlyn, beginning to puff and blow, 'is to learn something. That is the only thing that never fails.'"[6]

Because White had so much enthusiasm for so many different things, some critics were prompt to classify him as a dilettante even though White desperately attempted to offer his readers an image diametrically opposed to this and at the same time hoped that they would share his extreme curiosity: "I am the most serious, unwhimsical, hard-working, scholarly, learned, serious writer."[7]

The great success of the posthumous publication of the fifth volume[8]

Originally published as "T.H. White et la légende du roi Arthur: de la fantaisie animale au moralisme politique," *Études anglaises*, 34 (1981), 192–203; translated by Edward Donald Kennedy.

that provided a continuation to White's Arthurian tetralogy marks perhaps the beginning of a new and fairer appreciation of this work. Begun as a fable and a story for both children and adults ("It seems impossible to determine whether it is for grown-ups or children"[9]), this Arthurian series is concluded with a satirical pamphlet that attempts to establish the bases for a society without war. This article will investigate White's transformation of what was originally a simple animal fantasy into a treatise on political morality.

The Sword in the Stone

Although in retracing the adventures of the Knights of the Round Table White closely followed his source, Sir Thomas Malory's *Le Morte d'Arthur,* he nevertheless created an original work. His special contribution was to give psychological depth to the numerous characters that appear in this romance, particularly Lancelot, Arthur, and Guenevere. He also created without source authority the account of the youth and education of the future king of Gramarye which takes up most of the first volume. In fact, Malory says nothing about what happens from the moment when the child is entrusted to Sir Ector by Merlyn and the decisive moment when Arthur becomes king by successfully pulling the sword from the stone.

White took advantage of this complete freedom which his source left him to procure for the young Arthur the education of which he had been able to dream for himself. White, as both teacher and student, Merlyn and Arthur, gives himself no limits and offers his student the apprenticeship that only a magician could offer. He has the future king develop in the animal world by transforming him for a time into a fish, a hawk, a grass snake, an owl, and a badger.[10] On January 14, 1938, he wrote to his friend and former professor at Cambridge, L.J. Potts: "It is not a satire. Indeed, I am afraid it is rather warm-hearted—mainly about birds and beasts."[11]

The young Arthur's incursions into the animal world contribute greatly to the success of *The Sword in the Stone.* On September 3, 1938, David Garnett published a favorable review in *The New Statesman and Nation* and discussed the interest and originality of these chapters:

> The best bits of it indeed are the direct descriptions of nature, of country life, of the behaviour and appearance of birds, beast and fish. . . . Thus he enters into the soul of a hawk, of a grass-snake, of a badger, of a fish. . . . These chapters in *The Sword in the Stone* show, in my opinion, real poetic imagination.[12]

White had planned from the start to write a tetralogy on the adventures of King Arthur. On June 28, 1939, he mentioned this in a letter to L.J. Potts concerning the second volume that he had just finished: "*The Witch in the Wood,* which Collins will send you is book 2 of a projected 4 books about the doom of Arthur."[13]

Hitler at King Arthur's Court

On December 6, 1940, White informed Potts of his plan to add a fifth volume the tone of which would be totally different from that of the preceding ones:

> . . . I am going to add a new 5th volume, in which Arthur rejoins Merlyn underground (it turns out to be the badger's set of vol. 1. . . .) I have suddenly discovered that (1) the central theme of *Morte d'Arthur* is to find an antidote to war, (2) that the best way to examine the politics of man is to observe him with Aristotle, as a political animal.[14]

From that time on, his determination would only be strengthened: the culminating point, the outcome, and the very reason for the first four books would have to be found in the fifth:

> The last book, number five, is, I hope, the crown of the whole. The epic theme is War and how to stop it. . . . you see, The Round Table was an anti-Hitler measure.[15]

This modification of White's work, this disruption in its deepest sense, occurred when the world was being torn apart and when White found himself confronted with an unbearable dilemma. It seemed to him, in fact, as utterly absurd to agree to being used as cannon fodder as to remain on the sidelines without participating in the war. Between 1939 and 1942 his hesitations and reversals were continuous until he finally decided to remain in Ireland where he lived, without, however, ever managing to put his conscience at rest.

White then shared with Arthur and Merlyn the scruples and uncertainty that were contending within himself. Hitler paralleled Mordred and Sir Bruce Sans Pitié. *Mein Kampf* found an answer in the pacifist philosophy of the magician turned moralist.

But White was not content with expressing new ideas in this fifth book. He also felt he had to modify the first three books that had already been published.[16] This was the beginning of a long conflict with his publishers.[17] The fifth book was finally abandoned,[18] and he had to wait until 1958 for *The Once and Future King*[19] to be published as a tetralogy. It was a new edition. The second book in particular, originally entitled *The Witch in the Wood,* had to be completely rewritten. White inserted in the first book the two episodes from the fifth book describing the society and customs of the totalitarian ants and those of the peaceful and free wild geese. He also set forth the essential points of his political and pacifist theories in a virulent pamphlet "The Insolence of Man" that he wrote when he realized that the fifth book would not be published and that he later renounced in 1944.

THE PACIFIST PHILOSOPHER

Through his experiences with animal communities and especially through his reading, White was hoping to develop the basis for a new Utopia in which the dilemma in which he was trapped could no longer occur: a world without war. It was a matter of considering man and his institutions by following the proceedings of the biologist. Man is an animal, by far the most ferocious, one who deserves the name *Homo Ferox* instead of *Homo Sapiens.* In the animal world few species know war: "It is only among the most highly organized of political creatures (ants, men, microbes) that genuine war is found."[20]

It was sufficient then to study the warlike species, particularly the ants, and to determine what differentiated them from others in order to find out what led them to war. By then applying to man the results of this research, one could suppress the cause of fratricidal warfare and form a society finally rid of this scourge. In Ireland the villagers in Doolistown sometimes watched with curiosity this strange bearded scholar, armed with a magnifying glass and a bottle of red ink, capturing ants in a sack in order to transport them from one ant colony to another. On June 17, 1942, he noted in his journal:

> I suppose I ought to face it and make some record of personal observations on ants during the past two years. I started them because they were important to the question of war.[21]

White tried to verify and to complete what he had read in Julian Huxley's work *Ants.*[22] In the 1935 Phoenix edition which was found at Alderney at the time of his death, White had underlined and annotated numerous passages and written on the fly leaves a draft of a letter beginning with "Dear Dr.? Professor H.?" in which he informed the biologist of his plans to publish "The Insolence of Man":

I am trying to write a book about the politics of animals, for the Pelican sixpenny's—if they will take it and I am stuck in a chapter on war, for lack of true examples except the Harvester ants. . . .

The seventh chapter (pp. 85–98) of Julian Huxley's work on ants "Warfare and Slavery" most attracted White's attention. According to the biologist, there are three causes that can provoke the warlike activity of certain species of ants: the possession of portable objects, scarcity of food, and the instinct to protect their territory. If the possession of portable objects and scarcity of food are the principal causes of war, war could be attributed to the notion of property itself. Could the capitalist system be the chief reason for all the conflicts that put nations in opposition to one another? Could Marx have been right?

Such is the question that King Arthur asks himself on the day before the battle that is going to bring about the defeat of the chivalry of the Round Table. Trouble could arise chiefly from the fact that one could say *my* realm, *my* wife, *my* property, with war being declared between the haves and have-nots:

> Perhaps the great cause of war was possession, as John Ball the communist had said. "The matters gothe nat well to passe in Englonde," he had stated, "nor shall nat do tyll every thyng be common, and that there be no villayns nor gentylmen."[23]

But this solution surely could not suit the profound individualism of White, whose political opinions reflected a great nostalgia for Toryism and the England of the eighteenth century and who saw in the egalitarianism of what he called the "Farewell State" the cause of all trouble. White then had to do all he could to try to refute an idea that risked leading him to extol a type of society that went against his deepest convictions. The comparative study of the brain of man and that of animals was a determining element.

CEREBRUM AND CEREBELLUM

As early as January 13, 1938, along with photographs of barn owls and sketches of hoods for the falcons that he was training, White drew along side of one another in his journal the brain of a man and that of a bird. He continued to think about this, and on April 26, he noted: "I do wish I knew the size of the cerebrum of the ant. . . ."[24] On December 6, 1940, he tried to gather information from his friend and literary mentor, the writer David Garnett:

Do you happen to know off hand, of a pretty elementary but efficient book about brain anatomy in *animals, fish, insects,* etc.? I want to know what sort of a cerebellum an ant has, also a wild goose.[25]

David Garnett did not give White an answer on this precise point, and he gave me the reasons for this in a letter that he wrote on October 6, 1978:

[White] . . . had made up his mind that man is the only animal to fight its own species except the ant (He left out the honey bee) and he only wanted to scratch together some evidence about brains . . . I did not recommend the name of a book on the brains of insects because I do not know one and was too busy to do his research for him.

The danger was great, in fact, that White would investigate in scientific works only the parts that supported his thesis and not take account of others. White, for example, indeed refrained from paying any attention to the warning that Julian Huxley placed in the introduction to his work:

Innumerable comparisons have been made between human society and the social organization of ant, bee or termite; theories have been advanced and morals pointed. . . . almost without exception the moral has been false, the analogy misleadingly used.[26]

The subject that he took on was difficult and demanded serious research and great rigor mixed with much prudence. White realized, moreover, that he was showing a certain amount of scientific naïveté in adventuring into an area about which he knew little:

Unfortunately we shall have to go delving into the subject of the brain, which is obscure, not fully understood, and perhaps misunderstood by me. It is only fair to say at once that I am not a specialist on brains, but I do my best.[27]

On January 8, 1941, he confided the nature of his projects to L.J. Potts and asked his aid and advice in a long letter containing a drawing of four brains and cerebella of an ant, a goose, an elephant, and a man, followed by a table asking for the comparative weight of each. He summarized then the purpose of his research: "Everything depends upon the difference between cerebrum and cerebellum."[28]

White consulted numerous works on this subject, particularly *The*

Evolution of Man[29] by G. Elliot Smith, *Man's Place in Nature*[30] by T.H. Huxley, and *Vertebrate Zoology*[31] by G.R. de Beer. His reading permitted him to formulate a simple, indeed a rather simplistic conclusion: the volume and weight of man's brain in relation to his cerebellum distinguishes him from other animals. The brain is the seat of individual conduct while the cerebellum controls the instinctive reactions:

> The specialty of man . . . is his neopalium. This is the part of the brain, which, instead of being devoted to instinct, is concerned with memory, deduction and the forms of thought which result in recognition by the individual of his personality.[32]

MAN, THE CAPITALIST ANIMAL

According to the laws of evolution, each species must, in order to survive, develop to the maximum what constitutes his essential characteristic, his own originality. For White, the political conclusion was immediate; by means of somewhat tortuous reasoning, he believed he had found the missing link: "Capitalism is man's specialty just as his cerebrum is."[33] Thus it would be then an error against nature itself for man to attempt to create a system that abolished private property since that and capitalism (which exists only among men) gave man his originality.

On the contrary, man ought to act in conformity with his evolution and with his special place in the animal world by turning his back to collectivism and strengthening capitalism. On August 13, 1940, White noted in his journal that communism was a system that could not function and that led to war. In fact, animals who, like the ants, abolished individual property killed themselves in frequent deadly wars. He ended by expressing a wish for the happiness of man:

> He should increase his capital rather than diminish it. (Man is the most capitalist of all the animals, therefore develop it. This seems a firm objection to Communism.)[34]

But White developed his ideas further. In reality the obstacle to peace is not individual capitalist ownership, but collective ownership, and it is therefore proper to abolish it in order to put an end to wars:

> I would make a world in which every individual was at liberty to have as much property as he liked, but in which no community was allowed to have any property whatever.[35]

Private property is not the cause of the warlike attitude of certain types of ants, but rather the existence of common territory that threatens a system of collective ownership and leads to war. Merlyn states, in fact, that the animal species that have the sense of private ownership are not warriors, but those who attempt to restrain or suppress ownership are always warlike:

> It is the birds, with their private wives, nests and hunting ground . . . who remain at peace. . . . The owners of private property in nature are pacific, while those who have invented public property go to war. This, you will observe is exactly the opposite of the totalist doctrine.[36]

But all species of ants are not warriors, and White would indeed have wanted to be able to prove that those that are not are ignorant, like the wild geese, of the notion of territory. Not being able to demonstrate this, he contented himself with suggesting it in his journal:

> The known warfaring ants all seem to claim territory. The pacific ants (together with the thousands of other gregarious animals, like bees, which do not go to war) seem not to claim territory.[37]

All that White had to do now was provide support for his theories and to include them in his Arthurian work. Merlyn served as a faithful spokesman for him in drawing the king into two diametrically opposed animal societies: the totalitarian nightmare of the warrior ants and the paradise of the free and peaceful wild geese.

King Arthur and the Ants in the Brave New World

In the allegory of his stay among the ants, the king finds himself involved in a society that is both communist and fascist, the two terms being, in White's opinion, very close in meaning. When Merlyn analyzes the ants' political system by affirming "They are the perfect communist state,"[38] the badger, who has some sympathies for the theories of Marx, protests: "I would have thought that ants were more like Mordred's fascists than John Ball's communists." Merlyn then concludes: "The one is a stage of the other. In perfection they are the same!"

Allusions to Hitler's fascism are numerous. The national hymn broadcast by the loudspeakers to incite the people to war is "Antland Over All."[39] The ants know the fascist salute: "A live ant came down the pathway carrying a third. It said: 'Heil Sanguinea!'"[40] And the fact that the Sanguineae consider themselves superior offers them sufficient justification to enter upon fratricidal combats:

> Their beloved country had no slaves at all, a disgraceful state of affairs which would have to be remedied if the master race were not to perish.[41]

Slogans in the form of syllogisms broadcast by the radio recall the notorious doctrine of *Lebensraum* preached by Hitler in *Mein Kampf*:

> A. We are so numerous that we are starving.
> B. Therefore we must not cut down our numbers but encourage large families. . . .
> C. When we are so numerous and starving as all that, obviously we have a right to take other people's syrup.[42]

Other passages recall *Brave New World,* and the work of Aldous Huxley clearly influenced White when he described the depersonalized world of the ant hill. Doesn't one of the ants conduct himself as the worst of the Alphas? "How lucky we are in the 'A' nest, don't yew think, and wouldn't it be hawful to be one of those 'orrid' Bs."[43] There is also a parody of the republican slogan that somewhat resembles that of the Great Ford, "Community, Identity, Stability;"[44] in the society directed by "Ant the Father" this formula becomes "Liberty, Brutality, Obscenity."[45] Finally the haunting rhythms that the loudspeakers repeat without ceasing in the ant hill "mammy—mammy—mammy" clearly recall the hypnopedic couplets murmured to the deltas and epsilons in order to condition them.

White also anticipated George Orwell: his "Ant the Father" is almost a preliminary sketch of "Big Brother," and the extremely condensed vocabulary of the ants ("done, not done") foreshadows the "Newspeak" of the Oceanians. The ants had no words for happiness, freedom, or liking;[46] similarly "Newspeak" suppressed the words "free, honour, justice, morality."[47] Finally, there are in these two totalitarian societies the same rhetorical and logical processes in the slogans posted to the walls and the same perverse attempt, through the deviations from accepted meanings, to manipulate the masses to whom they are addressed: "War is Peace, Freedom is Slavery, Ignorance is Strength,"[48] "Everything not Forbidden is Compulsory."[49]

It is a collectivist system. Individual ownership is never mentioned since the production of syrup and the breeding of herds of beetles who risk being threatened from the other nest are collective. Even the stomachs of certain ants belong in some way to the community, thus permitting the workers to be nourished when they wish. The negation of the person as an individual is here transposed onto the biological plan. King Arthur found this the most shocking aspect of this totalitarian society.

The ants have a sense of collective territory that is pushed to extremes. The two ant hills that Merlyn studied are very clearly set off from one another, and membership in each nest is marked by a specific odor that permits the ants to recognize their friends and to chase off intruders:

> Merlyn had remembered to give him the proper smell for this particular nest; for, if he had smelled of any other nest, they would have killed him at once.[50]

In fact, the recognition of a border is the cause of the war between the two ant colonies and will bring about the mobilization of the Red Army. The two nests, until then separated, are bound by a bridge thanks to Merlyn's intervention:

> . . . the enormous hand came down from the clouds, carrying a straw. It placed the straw between the two nests, which had been separate before, so that now there was a bridge between them.[51]

An ant breaks it and is killed immediately: it is the beginning of the war.

Journey to the Land of the Geese

White contrasts this collectivist and warlike society to the freedom and happiness of the peaceful wild geese who constitute a model for man to follow, an ideal society.

If White had not been able to read the best known work of Konrad Lorenz, *Das sogenannte Böse,* published at Vienna in 1963 shortly before White's death, and translated into English as *On Aggression*[52] in 1966, he was nevertheless familiar with other of his works and cited the name of the Austrian biologist several times.[53] Lorenz often tried to explain human behavior by comparing it to that of animals, particularly the greylag geese.

The society of wild geese is strikingly individualistic, which does not exclude a minimum of organization and a certain hierarchy. Monogamous, the geese group themselves in families and have leaders that are not elected but chosen for valor and merit that are recognized by all. They are often the oldest members of the flock, "venerated old gentlemen whose breasts were deeply mottled."[54] (White had obviously not considered female rulers eligible!) When a father dies, the eldest son can eventually succeed him, but if he is not capable of leading the others, another respectable and wise gander will be chosen in his place. The geese organize themselves in order to keep watch so that they are not surprised by their natural enemies: man, the falcon, the fox, or the ermine. It is not a matter here of a phenomenon of war in which animals of the same species oppose one another, but of the normal struggle between different animals who must fight one another in order to protect themselves and survive.

When Arthur attempts to explain to a female goose the behavior of men and their way of waging war and then asks her if it is the same among geese, she is unable to understand him and is profoundly horrified:

> How ridiculous! You mean a lot of geese all scuffling at the same time . . . an army of geese to kill each other? . . . what a horrible mind you must have . . . what creatures could be so low and treacherous as to murder the people of its own blood?[55]

This is similar to the reaction of the King of Brobdingnag when Gulliver offers to manufacture for him cannons and bullets capable of destroying an entire city:

> The King was struck with Horror at the Description I had given of these terrible Engines, and the Proposal I had made. He was amazed how so impotent and groveling an Insect as I (such were his Expressions) could entertain such inhuman Ideas . . .[56]

In order to make his illustration coherent White had to emphasize that this free and peaceful society permitted its members to own property. On November 14, 1940, he wrote in his journal:

> . . . geese . . . They are pacific, domestic, organized, can talk, imitative, quick to learn, adaptable, clever. I wish they had possessions.[57]

The female goose to whom Arthur is talking is precise on this point: the wild geese allow the existence of private property in the organization of their patriarchal society, but for them the acquisition and accumulation of riches is not the goal of life: "And yes, she said, they did have private property besides their meals . . . The nest was private. . . ."[58]

On the other hand, collective ownership is totally absent from their political and economic system. The female goose finds Arthur's account of the customs of the ants and their collective stomach revolting. The geese, according to her, recognize no limit to their space:

> They had no communal possessions, nor did they make a claim to any part of the world. The lovely globe, they thought, could not belong to anybody except itself, and all their geese had access to its raw materials.[59]

Thus the wild geese are ignorant of war, White concludes, because they recognize no boundaries. The moral that man must draw from these two allegories in order to achieve a world without war is quite clear. The old king Arthur, on the day before his final battle, formulates it perfectly while recalling the lesson that Merlyn had wanted to make him understand when he was a child:

> He remembered the belligerent ants, who claimed their boundaries, and the pacific geese, who did not. . . . preserving their own kinds of civilization without war because they claimed no boundaries.[60]

"WHAT ARE BOUNDARIES PLEASE?"
"IMAGINARY LINES ON THE EARTH, I SUPPOSE."[61]

There are elsewhere, according to White, certain races of men who, while living under a system where private property is recognized, are not warriors. These people are ignorant of the notions of territory and border:

> But the true nomad, but the Lapp, but the Esquimau. . . . all remain pacific because they make no territorial claim, because they do not attempt to monopolise access to raw materials.[62]

The solution thus seemed simple: wars exist only because nations are separated by borders. According to Merlyn, if one could abolish nations and their artificial boundaries, one would eliminate wars:

> You must abolish such things as tariff barriers, passports and immigration laws, converting mankind into a federation of individuals. In fact, you must abolish nations, and not only nations but states also; indeed, you must tolerate no unit larger than the family.[63]

Like Bertrand Russell and the Swiss Auguste Forel, whose *Le Monde social des fourmis du globe comparé à celui de l'homme*[64] he had read, White dreamed of a world federation and an international government:

> The peace treaty, if it really is to be a treaty which ends wars, must demote our present nations to the rank of states—like the United States of America and it must promote a United State of the World.[65]

With borders abolished each state would preserve its own institutions, with the condition that they would permit free passage of men and products. It would not be a question of a world federation of identical states directed by the same political system, but of many states, large and small, preserving their own identity, culture and laws: "there would be no reason why England would not continue to govern herself as a democracy, Russia as a communist [*sic*], Ireland as a theocracy."[66]

But White knew that this world without borders was unrealizable and utopian, and he foresaw the criticism that politicians and economists would bring against him. He envisioned then a more realistic intermediary situation, borrowed from the works of Streit and Curry, that could serve as a step toward a more ambitious project:

> It is in fear of debâcle, that the authors Streit and Curry have suggested a compromise, which is at least a step in the right direction.[67]

On the day after Munich, the American journalist Clarence K. Streit envisioned in *Union Now*[68] the creation of a federation, along the lines of the American model, that would include the United States, the Commonwealth, France, Belgium, Holland, Switzerland, Denmark, Norway, Sweden, and Finland. This federation, which would be able to restrain Germany, Italy, and Japan, also had the attraction of a World Union that could lead to peace. In 1941 because of the German advance and the changes in national boundaries, Streit proposed in *Union Now with Britain*[69] a limited union of seven English-speaking countries: the United States, the United Kingdom of Great Britain and Northern Ireland, Canada, Australia, New Zealand, and South Africa. W.B. Curry returned to Streit's ideas in his work *The Case for Federal Union*,[70] by giving a more British slant to the question.

White, however, had no illusions about the practicality of his ideas. With the outbreak of the conflict that enflamed the world and had shown that man clearly deserved the unenviable title of "Homo Ferox," he knew that these massacres were far from being the last and that the time had not yet come to establish on earth this world without war of which he had dreamed with Merlyn and King Arthur. The temptation was strong then to imitate the old king who in his disappointment and bitterness dreamed sometimes of abandoning his fellow Yahoos in order to find again the wisdom and companionship of the peaceful and free geese: "I will go away with the goose people, where I can die in peace."[71]

White's tetralogy, revised in 1958, ends, however, much more optimistically than the fifth book. In the latter, in fact, the cruelty of man sets in motion the war between Mordred's troops and those of his father King Arthur at the very moment when it seemed that the confrontation could have been avoided.[72] *The Once and Future King,* on the other hand, ends the evening before this same battle. The old King Arthur, who believes that he has actually seen Merlyn, when it was only a dream (a very beautiful ellipsis of *The Book of Merlyn* that White wrote when he decided not to publish the fifth book), took up again the concern to which his whole life had been devoted and made it coincide with the hope that the author had of a world without boundaries:

> There would be a day—there must be a day—when he would come back to Gramarye with a new Round Table which had no corners, just as the world had none—a table without boundaries between the nations who would sit to feast there.[73]

NOTES

1. Works about White include his biography by Sylvia Townsend Warner: *T.H. White: A Biography* (London: Cape with Chatto and Windus, 1967) and editions of his correspondence: *The White-Garnett Letters,* ed. David Garnett (London: Cape, 1968); and *T.H. White: Letters to a Friend: The Correspondence between T.H. White and L.J. Potts,* ed. François Gallix (New York: Putnam, 1982; New York: Berkley, 1984), new ed. (Gloucester: Alan Sutton, 1984). Quotations from the White/Potts letters are from the edition published by Alan Sutton. Also see François Gallix, *T.H. White: An Annotated Bibliography* (New York: Garland, 1986).

2. *The Sword in the Stone* (London: Collins, 1938) and *Mistress Masham's Repose* (London: Cape, 1947) were chosen by The Book of the Month Club.

3. A series of six B.B.C. broadcasts in 1939; *Camelot,* a musical comedy by Lerner and Loewe, Broadway 1960, London 1964; films by Walt Disney in 1963 and Joshua Logan in 1967.

4. See *The Goshawk* (London: Cape, 1951).

5. See *England Have My Bones* (London: Collins, 1936) and *The Godstone and the Blackymor* (London: Cape, 1959).

6. *The Once and Future King* (London: Collins, 1958), Fontana edition, p. 181.

7. Quoted from the B.B.C. television broadcast "Monitor," 1959.

8. *The Book of Merlyn* (Austin and London: University of Texas Press, 1977).

9. Letter to L.J. Potts, January 14, 1938. See *T.H. White: Letters to a Friend,* pp. 86–87.

10. On July 6, 1942, White noted in his journal the surprise that he had ex-

perienced on learning, four years after having written *The Sword in the Stone,* that the transformations of the young Arthur were in conformity with the evolution of the human fetus: "I was astonished to find that *The Sword in the Stone* was a complete allegory of this development, even getting the various steps more or less accurate, i.e. the boy begins as a fish and ends as a mammal. . . ." (This unedited journal is at the University of Texas at Austin.)

11. Warner, p. 98; also *T.H. White: Letters to a Friend,* p. 86.

12. *The New Statesman and Nation,* September 3, 1938, p. 349.

13. *T.H. White: Letters to a Friend,* p. 98.

14. Warner, p. 178.

15. Garnett, p. 86, Letter of June 8, 1941.

16. *The Sword in the Stone* (London: Collins, 1938); *The Witch in the Wood* (New York: Putnam's, 1939; London: Collins, 1940); *The Ill-Made Knight* (New York: Putnam's, 1940; London, 1941).

17. White compiled a thick file of 163 pages made up of copies of his letters, responses of the editors, and his own comments. He probably planned to publish this compilation to which he had given the title "Trouble with Collins" and which is at the University of Texas at Austin.

18. This is the last volume which was published posthumously.

19. *The Once and Future King* (London: Collins, 1958) consists of *The Sword in the Stone, The Queen of Air and Darkness, The Ill-Made Knight,* and *The Candle in the Wind.*

20. Warner, p. 177, "Journal," April 26, 1939.

21. Unedited "Journal," June 17, 1942 (University of Texas at Austin).

22. Julian Huxley, *Ants* (London: Chatto and Windus, 1930).

23. *The Once and Future King,* Fontana edition, p. 630.

24. Unedited "Journal," (University of Texas at Austin).

25. Garnett, p. 76.

26. Julian Huxley, *Ants,* p.3.

27. "The Insolence of Man" (University of Texas at Austin). White had first written, then struck out: "perhaps most grossly misunderstood by me."

28. *T.H. White: Letters to a Friend,* pp. 122–26.

29. G. Elliot Smith, *The Evolution of Man* (London: O.U.P., 1927).

30. T.H Huxley, *Man's Place in Nature* (London: Macmillan, 1906).

31. Gavin Rylands de Beer, *Vertebrate Zoology* (London: Sidgwick and Jackson Ltd., 1928).

32. *The Book of Merlyn,* p. 116. White often uses the term "neopalium," invented by G. Elliot Smith to designate the cortex, seat of the associative memory.

33. *The Book of Merlyn,* p. 28. Also see chapter 4 of "the Insolence of Man": "The 1920 brand of communism seems unlikely to work with man. It seems to me that when nature's stress in one line of ancestry has been on increasing individuality, it is useless to fly in her face by aiming at the opposite."

34. Unedited "Journal," August 13, 1940 (University of Texas at Austin). Also see *The Book of Merlyn,* p. 99: "The owners of private property in nature are pacific, while those who have invented public property go to war. This, you will observe, is exactly the opposite of the totalist doctrine."

35. Unedited "Journal," February 2, 1941 (University of Texas at Austin).

36. *The Book of Merlyn,* pp. 98–99.

37. Unedited "Journal," June 26, 1942 (University of Texas at Austin).

38. *The Book of Merlyn,* p. 64.

39. *The Book of Merlyn,* p. 59; *The Once and Future King,* p. 126.

40. *Ibid.,* p. 50. In the revised text, the word play has disappeared. White no longer found it indispensable in 1958: "It said: 'Hail, Barbarus,'" *The Once and Future King,* p. 121.

41. *The Book of Merlyn,* p. 59. In *The Once and Future King* this allusion to

the hierarchy of the races has been suppressed: "If the dear race were not to perish," p. 126.

42. *The Book of Merlyn*, p. 60; cf. *The Once and Future King*, p. 126.

43. *The Once and Future King*; cf. p. 125. White added the allusion to *Brave New World* while revising the first version (see *The Book of Merlyn*, p. 56).

44. Aldous Huxley, *Brave New World* (London: Chatto and Windus, 1932), Penguin edition, p. 15.

45. *The Book of Merlyn*, p. 67.

46. *The Book of Merlyn*, p. 51.

47. George Orwell, *Nineteen Eighty-Four* (London: Secker and Warburg, 1949), Penguin edition, p. 246. The totalitarian society of the ants under the direction of "Ant the Father" also recalls the dehumanized universe described by the Russian writer Yevgeny Zamyatin in his prophetic political novel *We*, which was first published in its English translation in 1924. Orwell had emphasized its importance.

48. *Nineteen Eighty-Four*, p. 7.

49. *The Book of Merlyn*, p. 49.

50. *Ibid.*, p. 50. See *Ants*, p. 31: "It seems probable that the friendliness or hostility of the workers to the other ants of their own species depends on smell, each nest having some subtle 'nest-smell' which is caused by each of its inmates."

51. *The Book of Merlyn*, p. 58. The intervention of an outside observer risks making the experience seem less realistic; in *The Once and Future King*, p. 120, Arthur himself, transformed into an ant, links the two nests.

52. Konrad Lorenz, *On Aggression* (Fakenham: Wyman Ltd., 1966). Lorenz's first articles appeared in 1927; their first translations into English began appearing in 1934.

53. See *The Book of Beasts* (London: Cape, 1954), p. 141, and *The Master* (London: Cape, 1957), Puffin edition, p. 85.

54. *The Book of Merlyn*, p. 84.

55. *The Book of Merlyn*, p. 82. Also see *The Once and Future King*, pp. 167–68: "But what creatures could be so low as to go about in bands, to murder others of its own blood?"

56. Swift, *Gulliver's Travels* (O.U.P., 1971), p. 129. Swift's work influenced the Arthurian work of White, who wrote a continuation of Gulliver's Travels in *Mistress Masham's Repose*.

57. Unedited "Journal" (University of Texas at Austin).

58. *The Book of Merlyn*, pp. 83–84.

59. *Ibid.*, p. 83.

60. *The Once and Future King*, p. 637.

61. *The Once and Future King*, p. 168.

62. "The Insolence of Man," p. 56. Also see Garnett, p. 118, and *The Elephant and the Kangaroo* (London: Cape, 1948), p. 32. The same idea appears in Aldous Huxley, *Ends and Means* (London: Chatto and Windus, 1937), p. 90.

63. *The Book of Merlyn*, p. 101; also see *The Elephant and the Kangaroo*, p. 32.

64. Auguste Forel, *Le Monde social des fourmis* (Geneva: librairie Kundig, 1922). White had the first edition that was translated into English in 1928 on which he wrote a number of commentaries in the margins and on the fly leaves.

65. "The Insolence of Man," chapter 7, p. 2.

66. "The Insolence of Man," chapter 7, pp. 2, 3 (manuscript text).

67. "The Insolence of Man," chapter 7, p. 71 (typewritten text).

68. Clarence K. Streit, *Union Now* (London: The Right Book Club, Cape, 1939).

69. Clarence K. Streit, *Union Now with Britain* (Harmondsworth, Middlesex: Penguin, Nov. 1939).

70. W.B. Curry, *The Case for Federal Union* (Penguin, Nov. 1939).

71. *The Book of Merlyn*, p. 105.

72. One of Mordred's officers, in drawing his sword to kill an inoffensive grass snake, causes the massacre that will lead to the death of King Arthur: *The Book of Merlyn*, p. 130.

73. *The Once and Future King*, p. 637.

Conceptions of King Arthur in the Twentieth Century

Raymond H. Thompson

Twentieth-century responses to the figure of King Arthur have ranged through every hue of the spectrum. To some authors he is an idealized figure, an inspiration to all who seek a nobler way of life, while to others he is an unscrupulous and brutal tyrant, spreading fear and terror among foes and followers alike; some perceive him as a man of destiny who shapes events through the force of his personality and vision, while others see only a struggling swimmer, soon swept away by the fierce tide of events beyond his control; some exalt his triumphs over rebellious Britons and invading Scots and Saxons alike; some lament the tragedy and pathos of his fate, betrayed by his wife and best friend; some rage against his follies as he squanders the chance to save his people; some laugh at the comical predicaments into which his aspirations lead him. Between these extremes just about every shade and combination of opinion may be found.

Amidst such bewildering variety, the task of discerning the major conceptions of King Arthur is a challenge. Indeed, it is easier in some ways to view the various representations of his figure as a series of points on the slope of a graph between different extremes or, to return to our original metaphor, as subtly differing shades along the entire range of the spectrum. Yet, just as to the human eye the spectrum seems to divide itself into distinct colors, so the representations of Arthur do lend themselves to certain noticeable, if at times overlapping, groupings.

Many of the works written earlier this century share, with those of the closing decades of the nineteenth century, an interest in the love triangle among Arthur-Guenevere-Lancelot. In these works Arthur may attract sympathy or criticism, but he never escapes some loss of status. He is, after all, the deceived husband, a man who has failed to satisfy his wife. However good his reasons or bad hers, he is robbed of dignity by being placed in a situation that has been the butt of ribald jokes from time immemorial. In a patriarchal society, moreover, her defection is a sign of the waning power of an aging monarch, and it is both a cause and a symptom of the conflict of loyalties that breaks the Round Table. Without firm leadership, the unifying Arthurian vision loses its force, to be superseded by other, more personal, priorities.

At best Arthur is portrayed as noble but too trusting and naive, a man out of touch with the reality of what is going on at his court. It is thus that he emerges from Laurence Binyon's play *Arthur: A Tragedy* (1923). He even attains some tragic stature by recognizing that his own blindness and weakness have contributed to the fall of the Round Table. In John Erskine's historical novel *Galahad* (1926) and Georgene Davis's poetic drama *The Round Table* (1930), however, Arthur seems lamentably slow to recognize that his own self-deception has contributed to the downfall. John Steinbeck's novel *The Acts of King Arthur* (1977), like the many short poems celebrating the love between Lancelot and Guenevere, ends before Arthur has time to discover his betrayal. He thus remains ignorant of the passion that dominates the action in the latter part of the book.

Too often, however, it is left to others to enlighten Arthur and to explain to him how he has contributed to his own misfortune. In Edwin Arlington Robinson's poem *Merlin* (1917) Merlin emerges from seclusion to tell the king that he must place responsibilities to his realm above personal anguish over the adultery of Lancelot and Guinevere. The disastrous consequences of Arthur's inability to implement this advice, however, unfold in *Lancelot* (1920), Robinson's next Arthurian poem. In Clemence Housman's novel *The Life of Sir Aglovale de Galis* (1905) it is Aglovale who dramatically confronts the king with his faults. Arthur and his court attain glory through the pursuit of honor rather than truth, of appearance rather than reality, and the king condemns Aglovale as dishonorable because he admits his sins rather than deny them. Yet by refusing Launcelot the right to defend his own and the queen's reputation in trial by combat, Arthur is himself choosing the path of truth rather than honor. It is, however, too late. Many will not support the king "when, by the rule and custom he himself had established, himself would he not abide."[1] Moreover, pursuit of the truth will uncover other sins previously concealed by the splendor of the court's achievements, sins that include Arthur's incest and the murder of the children born on May Day. Trial by combat, on the other hand, would prove a ghastly mockery of justice, as all would recognize.

In Lord Ernest Hamilton's novel *Launcelot* (1926) Arthur fades into an anonymous figure, too easily swayed by Agravain's accusations against the noble Launcelot. In Graham Hill's play *Guinevere* (1906) and Philip Lindsay's novel *The Little Wench* (1935) he again emerges as a weak and suspicious character in his dealings with the lovers, and this alienates any sympathy we might have for him. Nor can he avoid responsibility for the double standard that prevails at his court. Thus in Lindsay's novel we learn that "Mellygraunce had misbehaved, not by the act of rape, but by permitting the act to become known."[2] Yet in some ways this willful blindness and anger against the adulterers is preferable to the helplessness that he sometimes exhibits as he is swept aside by events totally beyond his control. Thus in John Masefield's poem "Midsummer Night" (1928) Arthur is, according to Mordred, no more than an unwary victim of his son's plots.

This focus upon the love triangle inevitably damages Arthur's reputation. Sometimes it is because we are shown too little of his achievements to redress the balance, but too often his response—ranging from naiveté and blindness, through arrogant self-deception, irresponsible jealousy, and vindictive anger, to weakness, both personal and political—is unworthy of so renowned a monarch. Fortunately for Arthur, however, interest in the love triangle waned as the twentieth century progressed. Not only are his failures in love balanced by his achievements elsewhere, but the impact of the love affair is often significantly reduced. Sometimes it may even be omitted entirely, as a later French invention inappropriate in attempts to reconstruct the history behind the legend.[3]

Arthur is accorded the most undiluted admiration in three groups of works: poems that recall his reign as a golden age; juvenile novels where he represents the model of responsibility in serving his kingdom; and adult novels where he is idealized. The poems are mainly very short and they paint a nostalgic picture of the past, as in Marian Boyle's "Artorius Rex Invictus" (1987), which summons Arthur to return and restore a golden age. This nostalgia also permeates the many short lyrical poems that use places such as Tintagel, Camelot, and Avalon to initiate a philosophical meditation. Arthur's reign is recalled in glowing terms primarily to create a stark contrast with a troubled present. Thus John D'Arcy Badger's sonnet sequence *The Arthuriad* (1972) condemns the modern vices of cruelty, fanaticism, and selfishness, and it calls for a return to the values of moderation represented by Arthur. In order to dramatize contemporary problems, these poems refer only briefly to Arthur, using him as an appropriately distant symbol of better times.

The juvenile novels present Arthur as a great ruler in order to provide their young protagonists with the opportunity to serve a worthy figure. The historical novels, such as *Page Boy for King Arthur* (1949) and

Squire for King Arthur (1955) by Eugenia Stone, E.M.R. Ditmas's *Gareth of Orkney* (1956), and Catherine Peare's *Melor, King Arthur's Page* (1963), follow the various adventures and misadventures of the young people as they learn the responsible behavior that will win the noble king's approval. The fantasies, on the other hand, are more likely to place Arthur among, or at the head of, the forces fighting for good against evil, for Light against Dark. The young protagonists prove themselves by choosing to side with him despite the suffering they must undergo as a result. In Jane Curry's *The Sleepers* (1968) they help Myrddin foil a plot by Morgan le Fay and Medraut to destroy Arthur and his knights as they lie sleeping in an underground cavern; in Robert Newman's *The Testing of Tertius* (1973) they help Arthur and Merlin against Urlik, a black wizard and manifestation of the Dark Power; in Susan Cooper's *The Grey King* (1975) and *Silver on the Tree* (1977) they fight for the Light against the Dark that is rising to engulf humanity; in Pamela F. Service's *Winter of Magic's Return* (1985) and *Tomorrow's Magic* (1987) they help Merlin first to bring Arthur back from Avalon to lead Britain out of the new Dark Age of its nuclear winter, then later to fight against Morgan le Fay and her mutant hordes. Although not written exclusively for younger readers, *The Green Knight* (1975) and *The King's Damosel* (1976) by Vera Chapman also fit this pattern. Arthur is portrayed as the noble monarch whom the protagonists serve at the cost of much personal suffering.

These poems and juvenile novels allow but brief glimpses of Arthur, whose function is to represent a way of life made all the better by contrast with a most unattractive alternative, and it is the latter that is given more attention. Thus in *Merlin's Ring* (1957) by Meriol Trevor, Felix chooses to help those loyal to Arthur, recognizing that "the only real defeat is to give in to evil, to ambition and spite and greed."[4] Arthur plays a larger role, however, in a group of science fiction and fantasy novels.

Under the tutelage of Merlin, Arthur tries to build a more civilized way of life for his people in *The Once and Future King* (1958) by T.H. White, in Andre Norton's *Merlin's Mirror* (1975), and in Stephen R. Lawhead's *Arthur* (1989). In White's novel Merlin, as an agent of some divine power only vaguely hinted at, transforms Arthur into a variety of creatures in order to teach him "that Might is only to be used for Right . . . turning a bad thing into a good";[5] Norton's sage acts as an agent of benevolent extraterrestrial beings known as the Sky Lords, helping his protégé as he seeks to establish a kinder and more tolerant world; Lawhead's sage is one of the Fair Folk, descendants of refugees from the advanced civilization of Atlantis, and he assists Arthur's attempts to transform his realm into the Kingdom of Summer, which will embody the Christian virtues of peace, justice, and compassion. In Peter David's *Knight Life* (1987) and in *The Forever King* (1992) by Molly Cochran and Warren Murphy, Arthur returns to the present age and again finds assistance from Merlin: in the former he successfully campaigns to become mayor of New York; in the latter he defeats a wicked sorcerer whose life has been miraculously prolonged by the healing powers of the Grail. In *The Hawk's Gray Feather* (1990) by Patricia Kennealy, which transposes Celtic legend into a space-faring universe, Arthur battles to restore the legitimate royal house, of which he himself is a member, after the throne has been usurped by an evil magician.

Whether in the past, present, or future, Arthur is portrayed as a righteous and benevolent leader. He may not be without faults but they are invariably trivial, the consequence of youthful inexperience and the generous nature that makes him so beloved. By contrast, those who oppose him are marked by a barbaric cruelty and arrogant self-interest that make him all the more attractive. His downfall is accomplished by external forces of evil, rather than his own human frailty. Most works, however, offer a more balanced portrait of Arthur, ranging from the admiring to the critical.

The most impressive among them are three novels that reveal a hero whose own internal struggle mirrors the external war he must wage and who recognizes how his own flaws contribute to the final disaster at Camlann. In *The Pagan King* (1959) by Edison Marshall, Arthur eventually sheds his youthful illusions, discovering: 1) that he fulfilled the auguries of the predestined leader only through the manipulation of events by his great-uncle and mentor Merdin; 2) that Vortigern, his cruel foe, is none other than his own father; 3) that Modred, his half-brother and rival, is a generous antagonist; and 4) that he has been repeatedly and disastrously deceived by Vivain whose friendship masks bitter enmity. Arthur, however, does not brood. Armed with this dearly won lesson about the power of human credulity, he hands over the throne to his successor in a personally stage-managed exit on a barge with three queens, then exuberantly sets off with his true love in the guise of a bard, accompanying her songs that metamorphose harsh reality into glorious legend: "earth will remain uninhabitable, and life intolerable," he proclaims, "without kind lies."[6]

In Rosemary Sutcliff's *Sword at Sunset* (1963) Artos is clear-sighted about his faults from the outset of his career, acknowledging that his lapse of vigilance allows his half-sister to seduce him, that his neglect of his wife leads to her adulterous affair, and that his kindness of heart holds his hand from destroying dangerous enemies when the opportunity is given him. Yet Sutcliff makes it clear that these mistakes are the consequence of virtues rather than vices. Artos's lapse in vigilance is a consequence of the trust of others; his neglect of Guenhumara is the result of his placing duty above personal feelings; his mercy stems from care for others. This care is most poignantly expressed in the grief that he feels for the death of those who follow him into battle, be they his faithful hounds, his courageous young warriors, or his closest friends, including Ambrosius, Aquila, and Gwalchmai. Furthermore, Artos not only accepts responsibility for his mistakes, but understands that he must pay the price. He recognizes his role as the Sacred King whose duty it is to die as a sacrifice for his people. It is a sacrifice that, like Christ, he makes out of love for them.

In Parke Godwin's *Firelord* (1980) Arthur emerges as "one of the most vigorous and attractive characterizations of the king in modern fiction, balancing idealism with pragmatism, romanticism with humor, compassion with heroic self-sacrifice."[7] These qualities create an inspiring leader, but it is the growth of his sense of compassion that provides the structure for the novel. This learning process starts during his stay with Morgana and the Prydn when he recognizes that "we're human because we care,"[8] and it culminates when he hears his weary men singing on the last day of the siege at Badon. He realizes then that he loves all his people, both the "flowers" and the "fruit" (p. 391). Yet he also accepts that this love entails sacrifice:

> To be a king, to wear a crown, is to know how apart and lonely we are and still exist and *dare* to love in the face of that void. To crown your brow with knowledge as sharp as thorns, bright and hard as gold. (p. 91)

The image of the crown of thorns recurs throughout the novel as Arthur absorbs his painful lessons, particularly the loss of his dear friends Geraint and Kay.

Since Arthur is the narrator in these three novels, we follow step by step the inner struggles that he undergoes and establish a bond of sympathy with him. He emerges as an impressive figure, heroic enough to fight against heavy odds, yet compassionate enough to care for others; human enough to make mistakes, yet wise enough to learn from them. Other writers may paint a favorable portrait but because they tell the story from other points of view they allow fewer insights into his soul.

A number focus upon Arthur's military campaigns, and under such circumstances he usually plays a distinguished role. Two plays from 1942, Clemence Dane's *The Saviours* and A. Fleming MacLiesh's *The Destroyers*, both reflect the exigencies of war in their condemnation of its savagery even while they commend Arthur's heroic resistance against his evil foes. This heroic spirit is emphasized in another play, Robert Cedric Sherriff's *The Long Sunset* (1955), in which Arthur rallies Romano-British resistance against the Saxon invaders.

Among the novels, several confine themselves to Arthur's earlier campaigns, culminating in his resounding victory at Badon. In W. Barnard Faraday's historical romance *Pendragon* (1930) Artorius is a valiant and dutiful soldier, but rather naive and slow-witted. Fortunately, his limitations are compensated for by the shrewdness of Gwendaello (Guenevere) who falls in love with him after he rescues her. We are accorded only a fleeting glimpse of Arthur in John Cowper Powys's *Porius* (1951) where we learn:

> That fabulous hero with that historic sword was gone. The courtly emperor bestowing names upon brave steeds, and learning the names of beautiful ladies, was gone too. The man who dominated them now was a man of pure undiluted generalship, realistic, practical, and competent.[9]

The Duke of War (1966) by Walter O'Meara provides an account by a young Romano-British girl of the events surrounding the Battle of Mons Badonis. To her eyes Arthur is a noble and patient leader, determinedly holding together his quarrelsome allies on the one hand, while for the good of Britain he steadfastly ignores the affair between Lancelot and Guenevere on the other. In Keith Taylor's novella "The Brotherhood of Britain" (1992) an Irish bard saves the noble Artorius from a plot on the eve of his stunning triumph at Badon. By contrast Arthur is much less embattled in both Roy Turner's *King of the Lordless Country* (1971) and Douglas Carmichael's *Pendragon* (1977) where he moves remorselessly from victory to victory.

Those novels that deal with the last Battle of Camlann as well as the earlier campaigns reveal the consequences of the betrayals simmering beneath the surface of *The Duke of War,* and as a result they grow more critical of his failure to deal with them. In *The Emperor Arthur* (1967) by Godfrey Turton, *The Crimson Chalice* trilogy (1976–78) by Victor Canning, and *Excalibur!* (1980) by Gil Kane and John Jakes, Arthur is still a great and high-minded ruler who places duty before his own personal interests. In *The Bear of Britain* (1944) by Edward Frankland, however, he is too honorable to capitalize upon his triumph at Badon by enforcing unity on the feuding local tyrants: "A man may take it upon him to do as you counsel me to do," he tells Medraut in response to this advice, "and good may come of it; but for good or ill I am not that man."[10] Because he is unwilling to use "lies and treachery" (p. 177) as a means to an end, he finds that power steadily slips away from him until he is reduced to little more than a figurehead.

This pattern of an honorable leader unable to control the political rivalries that eventually destroy Britain recurs in other novels. In George Finkel's *Twilight Province* (1967, published in the U.S. as *Watchfires to the North,* 1968), Arthur is reduced to a rather remote war leader who is overshadowed by others such as the narrator, Bedwyr, and whose death has less impact upon his followers and allies than is usually the case. Although Arthur is made high king after his victory at Badon, his inability to control the minor kings causes him to fade gradually from the political scene in John Gloag's *Artorius Rex* (1977). In Marvin Borowsky's *The Queen's Knight* (1956) Arthur is presented as a slow-witted country oaf, set up by the powerful Lords of the Council as a puppet king. Although he wins support for his vision of a nobler world, he and it are both eventually brought down by those motivated by pride and ambition, by jealousy and treachery.

The poems that deal with Arthur's entire career are, as we might expect, more interested in developing his symbolic potential. In *Taliessin Through Logres* (1938) and *The Region of the Summer Stars* (1944) Charles Williams examines the failure of Arthur's kingdom to fulfill its spiritual potential. Arthur's sin of egotistic self-love, which finds expression in his act of incest and his war against Lancelot, is both a cause and symptom of its decline from the values of visionary Logres to those of mundane Britain. He becomes, thus, a symbol of the human failure that leads to the loss of the Grail as well as the fall of his kingdom. John Heath-Stubbs's *Artorius* (1973) treats Arthur more favorably, showing him engaged in such traditionally heroic quests as the journey to the underworld to be shown a vision of the future. Here too, however, the focus is upon the symbolic value of such actions. The Arthurian story becomes primarily a vehicle for exploring the nature of literary tradition.

Female authors, by and large, pay closer attention than do their male counterparts to the domestic problems that play so large a part in Arthur's downfall, seeing them as an important symptom of the political divisions that destroy the Britons. Arthur remains a noble figure, particularly in Joy Chant's *The High Kings* (1984), where he displays compassion in the frame narrative, heroic energy in the traditional stories; and in Catherine Christian's *The Sword and the Flame* (1978, published in the U.S. as *The Pendragon,* 1979) where he even forgives Guenevere and Lancelot for their affair. Nonetheless, this focus inevitably shows him to less advantage than on the field of battle, where he can defeat his enemies through personal valor and tactical skill alone. In Jane Viney's *The Bright-Helmed One* (1975) the exploration of the father-son conflict of Arthur with his sons Medraut and Anr on the one hand, and with his father Utha on the other, focuses attention upon his weaknesses in the area of personal relationships. The incest with his sister Morgause and the ceaseless plotting against him by her and various members of their mutual family loom large in a series of trilogies: Mary Stewart's *The Crystal Cave* (1970), *The Hollow Hills* (1973), and *The Last Enchantment* (1979), together with a fourth novel, *The Wicked Day* (1983); Gillian Bradshaw's *Hawk of May* (1980), *Kingdom of Summer* (1981), and *In Winter's Shadow* (1982); Sharan Newman's *Guinevere* (1981), *The Chessboard Queen* (1984), and *Guinevere Evermore* (1985, though here the roles of Morgause and Morgan le Fay are reversed); and Persia Woolley's ongoing trilogy of which *Child of the Northern Spring* (1987) and *Queen of the Summer Stars* (1990) have appeared to date.

In *The Mists of Avalon* (1983) by Marion Zimmer Bradley it is Morgaine, rather than Morgause, who commits incest with Arthur and gives birth to Mordred. There is genuine love between them, but guilt and political differences drive them apart and lead her to conspire against her brother. The focus upon the conspiracies reaches its peak in Fay Sampson's sequence *Daughter of Tintagel* (1989–92) in which all three of Arthur's sisters wield formidable power, both political and magical. In the fifth book, *Herself* (1992), Morgan confesses her love for her brother despite her hostile behavior on numerous occasions, but she places much of the blame upon Arthur for his unwillingness to share power with women.

The attention to Arthur's difficult relationship with his family and the plottings of various factions in the royal court reveal a beleaguered and often error-prone figure. Since his military victories usually take place off stage, they do not compensate for the inadequacies of his domestic conduct. He may be clumsy and tongue-tied in contrast to his sophisticated wife, as in Newman's *Guinevere,* or he may be unduly influenced by her compulsive demands, as in Bradley's *Mists of Avalon;* he may be unwisely reluctant to share love and power with Morgan le Fay, as in Sampson's sequence, or he may fall so deeply in love that he becomes emotionally dependent upon her, as in *The Road to Avalon* (1988) by Joan Wolf; he may be unduly suspicious of Morgause's influence upon Gwalchmai/Gawain in Bradshaw's *Hawk of May,* or not suspicious enough in Stewart's *Wicked Day.* Almost invariably, his judgment is suspect, his insight limited. Thus in both Bradley's *Mists of Avalon* and Sampson's *Herself* Arthur fails to achieve the full insight into the mistakes and character flaws that have contributed to his own downfall, unlike his half-sister. His inability to consider the needs of women inspires a number of short poems also, including Margaret Atwood's sequence

"Avalon Revisited" (1963). When he enters the world of women, thus, Arthur is revealed to be as lacking in understanding and consideration as any man, and the consequences, both for political stability and personal fulfillment, are disastrous.

Arthur's reputation has farther to sink, however. Where the female authors just discussed find him misguided and insensitive rather than malevolent, a group of male authors see him as a brutal oppressor. In *The Island of the Mighty* (1972), a three-part drama by John Arden and Margaretta D'Arcy, Arthur is a tyrant who manipulates people for his own political advantage. In *The Green Man* (1966) Henry Treece portrays him as an aging but basically admirable war leader despite his expedient tolerance of behavior he condemns. In *The Great Captains* (1956), however, the younger Arthur is ambitious and violent, while in *The Eagles Have Flown* (1954) his barbarism contributes to the disillusionment of the young protagonists. Perhaps worst of all, though, is his characterization in Peter Vansittart's *Lancelot* (1978) and *Parsifal* (1988). Here he appears as a suspicious and unprincipled tyrant who disposes of those he perceives as a threat: "The doomed merely vanish."[11] In these works Arthur represents the harsh and oppressive face of authority: his attempts to unite the kingdom are prompted by personal ambition rather than patriotism, and his punishment of dissent is seen as an attack upon individual freedom.

Arthur also figures prominently in two sword and sorcery novels, acting with the sadistic brutality typical of characters in the genre. In *The Bull Chief* (1977) by Chris Carlsen he treacherously slays a loyal follower, and in *The Dragon Lord* (1979) by David Drake he is driven by ambition to become a mighty conqueror, regardless of the cost in suffering to others. Arthur is diminished too by the satire aimed at the Arthurian world in Robert Nye's *Merlin* (1978). The chivalrous exterior of Camelot is, we discover, "built upon a secret cesspool" in which the king gives rein to erotic fantasies, "revelling in incest with his sister."[12]

Ironic treatments are rarely so harsh upon Arthur, however. In the short stories of P.G. Wodehouse and Theodore Goodridge Roberts, for example, he is but lightly touched by the gentle humor at the expense of chivalric pretensions, and in Don Marquis's "King O'Meara and Queen Guinevere" (1930) the kindly monarch worries more about the unhappiness of his best friend Lancelot than about the fact that this unhappiness is caused by love for Guinevere. In Thomas Berger's *Arthur Rex* (1978), on the other hand, the idealism and innocence of Arthur, as well as his knights of the Round Table, yield comedy of the highest order. This innocence provides such protection against evil that Arthur is able to prevail over his foes until the final battle of Camlann. As the king lies mortally wounded by the treacherous Mordred, he despairs at last over "the triumph of perfect evil over imperfect virtue, which is to say, of tragedy over comedy. For have I not been a buffoon?"[13] He is comforted, however, by the ghost of Gawaine who reminds him, "can we not say, without the excessive pride which is sinful, that we lived with a certain gallantry?" (p. 483). This "certain gallantry" is the capacity for self-sacrifice in a noble cause, regardless of the consequences, and it transforms innocence into heroism and folly into wisdom, for only by being willing to embrace idealism, however impractical it may appear, can we hope to create a better world where love and decency can prevail.

One last major conception of Arthur remains to be examined, and that is as a figure whose actions are controlled by destiny. A number of the authors already discussed, notably Stewart and Canning, explore the influence of destiny on Arthur's life, but it has a special impact in a number of works that transpose his story from his own era to another. In Tim Powers's *The Drawing of the Dark* (1979) the spirit of Arthur is resurrected as Brian Duffy, an Irish soldier of fortune during the Turkish siege of Vienna in the sixteenth century. Duffy is reluctant to believe he is anyone other than himself, but he is fated to play a crucial role in repelling the invaders.

The love triangle of Arthur-Guinevere-Lancelot is played out again by modern lovers in a number of works. Frank Davey's verse sequence *The King of Swords* (1972) describes the end of a love affair in terms of the life and death of Arthur; in Dell Floyd's one-act play *King Arthur's Socks* (1916) Gwen chooses to remain in her comfortable marriage with Professor Arthur Robinson rather than run away with Lance Jones, an artist; in Nicole St. John's gothic romance *Guinever's Gift* (1977), by contrast, the characters struggle unavailingly to break the pattern that repeats itself in two generations against the backdrop of archeological excavations at Glastonbury for the coffins of Arthur and Guinever; *The Grail: A Novel* (1963) by Babs H. Deal transposes the tale to the setting of U.S. college football, where the love affair between the quarterback and the coach's wife dooms the team's attempt to complete an unbeaten season. The most impressive of these modern reenactments is *The Lyre of Orpheus* (1988) by Robertson Davies. During the staging of *Arthur of Britain, or The Magnanimous Cuckold,* a fictitious opera by E.T.A. Hoffmann, an affair between the sponsor's wife and the director serves to explore the relationship between art and life, and the importance of assuming the right personal myth in order to flourish as both an artist and a human being. Arthur Cornish, the sponsor, saves his marriage by forgiving his wife, becoming, in other words, a magnanimous cuckold.

Some science fiction transposes the Arthurian legend into the future. In *The Dragon Rises* (1983) by Adrienne Martine-Barnes, King Arthur is an incarnation of an eternal spirit continually reborn as a successful war leader. He leads his space fleet to victory but manages to avoid the fatal love triangle and betrayal by showing greater consideration for his wife. In Michael Greatrex Coney's *Fang, the Gnome* (1988) and *King of the Scepter'd Isle* (1989) Arthur arrives on the scene to find that everyone already knows his story, and their expectations force the amiable young man into an aggressive and ultimately fruitless attempt he might otherwise not have made to impose upon others the principles of chivalry. In C.J. Cherryh's *Port Eternity* (1982) a spaceship with a crew whose psychological conditioning has been loosely modeled upon their Arthurian namesakes is marooned in space. Under the stress of this crisis they find themselves increasingly trapped by their Arthurian personae.

Arthur must also relive his story in three fantasy novels. In *Raven* (1977) by Jeremy Burnham and Trevor Ray he is reborn as a rebellious youth who becomes the reluctant leader of a conservationist movement to save an ancient network of caves linked, appropriately enough, with his own cave legend. In Guy Gavriel Kay's *The Fionavar Tapestry* (1984–86) he is summoned to fight for the forces of Light against those of the Dark in expiation for his sin of slaying the children in his attempt to kill Mordred. For their heroic self-sacrifice and devotion he, Guinevere, and Lancelot are freed from the recurring pattern of love and betrayal they have been forced to relive, and they sail off to their final rest. In Welwyn Wilton Katz's *The Third Magic* (1988) the two young protagonists eventually discover that they are Arthur and Morgan le Fay, doomed to live out their traditional story of love mingled with antagonism.

Whether forced to lead the resistance against external aggression once again, or to reenact the anguish of the love triangle, Arthur's destined role is to suffer. This accounts for his reluctance to undertake his responsibilities in *Raven, The Drawing of the Dark,* and *The Fionavar Tapestry.* Yet this understandable reluctance humanizes him, making all the more heroic his final acceptance of a destiny whose cost he knows only too well. Weighing the need of others against his personal feelings, he dons once again the lonely mantle of greatness or, as Godwin puts it, the crown of thorns.

It is this capacity for unstinting and clear-sighted self-sacrifice that marks the most admiring among the various conceptions of Arthur we have considered: the idealized king, the tragic hero, the inspirational military leader, even the impractical idealist. Although diminished by his failure in marriage, a failure that has attracted increasing attention in recent years as writers reflect the values of feminism, his predicament inspires as much sympathy as criticism. But rarely is he depicted harshly, and even then it is as a man typical of a harsh age.

This reluctance to condemn Arthur is no surprise, because the power of the legend lies in its ability to inspire us with the same vision that inspired his followers so long ago. And that it will do as long as we continue to dream of a better and brighter world. Amidst the new Dark Age that seems forever rising, a darkness born of our own failure and despair, Arthur remains a beacon of hope, not of easy success, but of the ever-renewed determination of the human spirit to strive for a nobler way, regardless of the cost.

NOTES

1. Clemence Housman, *The Life of Sir Aglovale de Galis* (1905; rev. ed. London: Cape, 1954), p. 236.

2. Philip Lindsay, *The Little Wench* (London: Nicholson and Watson, 1935), p. 172.

3. Cf. the Author's Note in Rosemary Sutcliff's *Sword at Sunset* (London: Hodder and Stoughton, 1963).

4. Meriol Trevor, *Merlin's Ring* (London: Collins, 1957), p. 183.

5. T.H. White, *The Once and Future King* (London: Collins, 1958), pp. 254–55.

6. Edison Marshall, *The Pagan King* (Garden City, N.Y.: Doubleday, 1959), p. 373.

7. Raymond H. Thompson, *The Return from Avalon: A Study of the Arthurian Legend in Modern Fiction* (Westport, Conn.: Greenwood, 1985), p. 128.

8. Parke Godwin, *Firelord* (Garden City, N.Y.: Doubleday, 1980), p. 89.

9. John Cowper Powys, *Porius: A Romance of the Dark Ages* (London: Macdonald, 1951), p. 352.

10. Edward Frankland, *The Bear of Britain* (London: Macdonald, 1944), p. 177.

11. Peter Vansittart, *Lancelot: A Novel* (London: Owen, 1978), p. 111.

12. Robert Nye, *Merlin* (London: Hamish Hamilton, 1978), p. 175.

13. Thomas Berger, *Arthur Rex: A Legendary Novel* (New York: Delacorte, 1978), p. 483.